CRIMINAL PROCEDURE II
FROM BAIL TO JAIL

Examples and Explanations

CRIMINAL PROCEDURE II
From Bail to Jail

Examples and Explanations

Richard G. Singer
Distinguished Professor of Law
Rutgers, The State University of
New Jersey School of Law

ASPEN
PUBLISHERS

111 Eighth Avenue, New York, NY 10011
www.aspenpublishers.com

© 2005 Aspen Publishers, Inc.
A Wolters Kluwer Company
www.aspenpublishers.com

Permissions
Aspen Publishers
111 Eighth Avenue
New York, NY 10011

Printed in the United States of America

1 2 3 4 5 6 7 8 9 0

ISBN 0-7355-5063-8

Library of Congress Cataloging-in-Publication Data

Singer, Richard G.
    Criminal procedure II: from bail to jail / Robert G. Singer.
        p. cm. — (Examples & explanations series)
    Includes index.
    ISBN 0-7355-5063-8 (alk. paper)
    1. Criminal procedure — United States.   I. Title.   II. Series.

KF9619.3.S56 2005
345.73'05 — dc22   2004055410

To Daniel and Hana—

Twins definitely different in temperament,
but firmly alike in love, fun, and soccer.

Summary of Contents

Contents

A (Very) Short
Preface and Request

Although students may not believe it, academics rarely write for the purpose of owning Ferraris. I wrote this book in the hope that it may bring to students both clarity of doctrine and some insight of theory in one of the less illuminated corners of criminal practice. The book cannot succeed in that goal unless I actually learn what students have found helpful and unhelpful. I implore all readers, therefore, to take the time to write me at *rsinger@crab.rutgers.edu* and tell what they liked, and didn't, in the work. If we get to a second edition, future readers will reap the benefit of those comments.

Richard Singer

January 2005

Acknowledgments

Every acknowledgment page announces that no book is written by one person, even if the spine bears only one name. I, of all people, certainly know the truth of that view. Many people contributed, in many different ways, to this work. Deans Rayman Solomon and John Beckerman allowed me to teach the course involved here (and only that course during one semester) at just the right times, so that I could benefit from the osmotic effect. My students at Rutgers Law School, particularly in the fall 2003 course on criminal procedure, provided substantial insight into what was right—and wrong—with earlier drafts. Many of their comments on the draft manuscript resulted in significant changes in the final version. Student readers of this book who enjoy it can thank them. My secretary, Ms. Jackie Morfesis, pored over innumerable drafts of unintelligible typing and undecipherable handwritten comments and somehow made the piece legible. Her meticulous work made this entire project much more professional. My thanks, too, to the other members of the "secretariat"—Fran Brigani, Debbie Carr, Kaeko Jackson, Denise Johnson, Louise Waters, and Celia Hazel—who all pitched in, sometimes under extreme time constraints. I must also acknowledge Tom Ryan and Melanie Gordon, who, when the "unthinkable" occurred, and my computer "crashed," were able to find chapters in the cyberashes. Thanks to my editors—Elizabeth Kenny Lori McElroy, and Richard Mixter—who tolerated long silences and too many missed deadlines. Without their indulgence, this book absolutely would not be here. To the unknown reviewers, both of the proposal and of the finished manuscript, whose many cogent comments made me rethink, I owe many thanks, even when I did not agree with everything they said. Finally, of course, my family. Not only did my wife, Karen Garfing, make the "usual" sacrifices of doing more than her fair share of runs to soccer practice; she made incisive, cogent comments on every chapter, often suffering through more than one draft. Her unflagging support and ceaseless good humor (even in some very trying times) made this effort much more pleasant than it should have been. Finally, Daniel and Hana, the twins to whom this book is dedicated, who waited patiently at the Cranium board or snow-covered hill while I finished "just one more sentence" of this work. I promise them that at the next snowfall, we'll be the first people at that hill.

CRIMINAL PROCEDURE II
FROM BAIL TO JAIL

Examples and Explanations

1

Introduction

The police cars come to a screeching halt. Defendant Dan Dastardly emerges from his car, hands in the air. The police conduct a warrantless search authorized by the exigency of the moment, and give Dastardly his Miranda warnings. Dan, in handcuffs, sneers at Steve McGarrett, who utters those infamous words: "Book 'im, Danno."

Now what? What does it mean to "book him"? And what happens after that, during the long interval between arrest and trial? In a short, graphic depiction, the major steps in the process are shown on the next page in Figure 1.1.

This book will explore each of these steps in turn. As we do so, keep in mind that each of the actors in the system are well aware of the powers (and restrictions on the powers) of people in other parts of the system. That is critical to understanding many of the things that lawyers do during this process. Here we go, Danno.

A. Sources

Students who have studied the materials on police investigative techniques, canvassed thoroughly in Bloom and Brodin, Constitutional Criminal Procedure, know that the vast majority of topics in that area are now governed almost exclusively by decisions of the United States Supreme Court relating to constitutional prohibitions. Questions of searches and seizures, police interrogation techniques, lineups, and other such areas, have been subjected to detailed scrutiny by the United States Supreme Court. Even considering the increasing numbers of state courts who are interpreting their own state constitutions to provide greater protection to their citizens than the Supreme Court has said is provided by the U.S. Constitution, constitutional interpretation dominates the landscape.

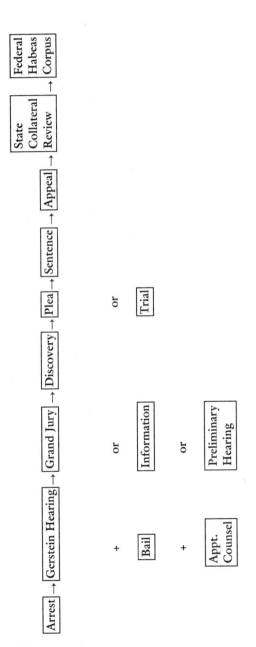

Figure 1.1

It was not always so. Fifty years ago, before the "Warren Revolution" in the Supreme Court, it was the rare decision which held any part of the Bill of Rights applicable to the states at all. Even then, the standards established for assessing the validity of police conduct tended to be fairly flexible and open-ended (for example, the due process clause was said to proscribe only conduct that exceeded the "conscience of the court").

In the activities discussed in this book, the law is much more in the status it was in the pre-Warren days. Although in several key areas — for example, the selection of juries — the United States Supreme Court appears to have established meaningful standards of conduct, in the main the Court has been far less "active" in these areas than in those of police (mis)conduct.

One could ponder why that is so. It may be that in the direct confrontation of police with defendants the Warren Court was as much concerned with perceived racial or class bias by those actors as with institutional failures. Surely, it is true that many of the decisions of that Court were based, either tacitly or expressly, on the fear that the criminal justice system so adversely affected minorities, or poor minorities, that to them criminal justice was an oxymoron. On the other hand, it has been suggested that judges trust fellow lawyers (prosecutors, defense counsel, other judges) to act responsibly and reasonably, and therefore afford them more leeway than they allow non-lawyers. Or it might be that the conduct of lawyers in court (or even in pre-trial proceedings) is more visible, and hence less subject to rewriting than the conduct involved during investigations.

Whatever the reason, however, the result is clear — there is less unequivocal law from the United States Supreme Court on these questions. That means, indubitably, that state governments are left to supervise these arenas more carefully and thoroughly. In this regard, there are two main actors — (1) state courts as case-deciders; (2) state courts as administrative agencies. Two other forces, far less active, are (3) the legislature; (4) executive agencies, such as the prosecutor's office, and the police force. A brief excursus on this situation may be helpful here.

Students are familiar with state courts as deciders — indeed creators — of common law and statutory questions. As cases and controversies come before them, courts must decide an individual's plea for justice. In so doing, the courts may — and often do — set out rules which are to be followed by other parties in later similar cases. As students are well aware, however, the "law of the case" is so restricted to the particular facts of that case. It is always possible in a later case to "distinguish" the case, and therefore narrow the applicability of the rule by reinterpreting the rule set out as applying *only* to instances involving the specific facts of the case (e.g., the rule applies only to red Volkswagens, not to all small cars, much less to all cars).

But courts are more than deciders of individual cases. Supreme Courts are the highest authority in a state (judicial) agency. As such, those courts must establish rules for all manner of questions arising during judicial proceedings. To take an extreme example, courts must decide whether briefs should be limited to a specific number of pages. It would be unlikely that a case would raise that question in a justiciable fashion; yet a court might well wish to create such an administrative rule.

In the past fifty years, courts have established a panoply of regulations that affect areas of the conduct of litigation many (though not all) of which would be unlikely to arise during a specific case. Equally, a specific case may involve an area of conduct which the court, as an administrative agency, considers too complex to be adequately resolved during that specific case. In adopting such rules, usually recommended by committees composed of persons on all sides of the litigation spectrum, the state Supreme Court acts essentially as a legislature for lower courts. These rules, however, are subject to change and reassessment even in the absence of a case or controversy that arises in a judicial setting.

The point here is that, unlike the investigation of crime, the adjudication of criminal charges is subject to regulation by a number of distinct processes and institutions. There is no uniform "criminal procedure law" in this area; the *lack* of uniformity is greater than in many other arenas — torts, contracts, etc. — precisely because crime control has been considered to be a "local" or "state" matter. Even if the United States Supreme Court has not spoken on an issue, or has left the area essentially ungoverned by the Constitution, a lawyer (and hence a student) must look beyond that level to determine whether there is a state court decision governing the question. There may well be a rule of procedure established by the state supreme court in its "legislative" capacity. Indeed, as we shall see, many of the areas discussed in this book *are* so governed. This means that there is less uniformity in the law governing this subject area than there is in many subjects to which students may have been exposed. In civil procedure, states have tended to adopt, almost verbatim, the federal rules enunciated by the Untied States Supreme Court. In the area of criminal procedure, however, states have elected not to follow the federal lead, but to promulgate their own regulations, many of which are in sharp contrast to the federal rules. Here, therefore, there is a wide range of rules on almost every subject.

In the absence of some controlling regulation, such as a constitutional decision, or a state court created rule of court, judges are more apt to look for guidance in other sources. One such group of sources, to which we will refer frequently, are sets of rules proposed by impartial arbiters. While, of course, this would include law professors, more commonly we (and courts) will seek suggestions from such sources as the National Conference of Commissioners on Uniform State Laws' Uniform Rules of Criminal Procedure; the American Law Institute's Model Code of Pre-Arraignment Procedure (hereafter ALI); and the American Bar Association's Standards of Criminal Justice (hereafter ABA).

Finally, because many of the issues covered in this book involve the conduct of *lawyers* — prosecutors and defense counsel — the rules of ethics of a particular state governing lawyers' conduct are likely to apply even if there are no court rules or decisions that cover the question. For example, even if a state does not require disclosure of particular items generally (see chapter 6), the failure to disclose in a specific case might violate the state's rules of ethics. Of course, violation of rules established by the constitution or state decisional law is likely automatically to constitute an ethical infraction. Ethics should guide discretion in ways that the law does not—and perhaps cannot—purport to reach.

Of course, the United States Constitution is supreme here—if it requires specific action, that requirement cannot be ignored by the states. But if, as is often the situation, the Constitution is deemed to be silent, or to be relatively open-ended, then state courts' decisions and the state court rules must be explored as well. During the journey of this book, therefore, we will often refer to, and compare, state court decisions and state rules of criminal procedure.

B. An Overview—The Importance of Discretion

This book deals with most of the events that occur after a defendant is arrested. For this reason, the course is sometimes referred to as "from bail to jail," and is distinguished from the "investigative" part of the process—search and seizure of materials, interrogation—which usually occurs before arrest in so-called "street" crimes. There, the defense attorney must act retrospectively, challenging what the state (police officers, etc.) have already done. In "white collar cases," on the other hand, the defense attorney may well become involved *before* the defendant is arrested, and well before an indictment. There is often much more leeway for lawyering skills in some cases. Although we will use the "street crime" as the paradigm case (as in the Dan Dastardly example above), always remember that the processes involved may occur in slightly different order and, therefore, provide more avenues for lawyering skills.

Perhaps the single most important thing to remember about this arena is that, like all systems, there are a significant number of points at which discretionary decisions either allow the process to continue, or halt the process. Thus: (1) a police officer may decide not to arrest a defendant, even if there is good evidence he has committed a crime; (2) a prosecutor may decide not to prosecute at all, or to prosecute on a lesser charge; (3) the grand jury, or a preliminary hearing, may determine that there is not sufficient cause to continue the prosecution; (4) juries may acquit the defendant, even if he is obviously guilty; and (5) judges, in their sentencing capacity, may impose a sentence substantially above or below the norm imposed in such cases. Moreover, any actor in this vast administrative process may attempt to influence, or even substantially constrain, later actors. A police officer who does not report key details in his report may well have precluded a prosecutor from seeking certain charges from the grand jury. And a jury may substantially reduce a judge's sentencing power by acquitting the defendant of the most serious charges against her.

Many analogize discretion to squeezing an inflated balloon: When one seeks to restrict the discretion in one part of the system, it will emerge at another point (the "hydraulic theory"). For example, if the legislature mandates sentences for all crimes, judicial discretion in sentencing is removed. But someone — the prosecutor, the jury, prison officials — will now have more power (discretion) to affect the ultimate fate of the defendant. Thus, wherever discretion appears, the question will be not whether it can be eliminated, but rather whether it can be regulated in such a way so that others in the system are not more empowered than before.

Justice Brandeis once extolled the states as "laboratories of democracy." By refusing to "constitutionalize" most of these trigger points, and only marginally impinging on the discretion within the system, the United States Supreme Court has enhanced that view. This book will, sometimes directly, but always indirectly, explore the strengths and weaknesses of those laboratories.

2

Early Decisions about the Newly Arrested Defendant

A. The Probable Cause Hearing and the Initial Appearance

McGarret told Danno to "book" Dan. "Booking" is an administrative process, occurring at a police station, at which the police identify the defendant, indicate the charges upon which he is arrested, and fingerprint and photograph him. But wait—maybe we're getting ahead of ourselves. First things first. Should the police even have seized Dan at all? Assume that the police arrested Dan, as they arrest most offenders, without an arrest warrant. While *they* believed they had probable cause for their actions, the Fourth Amendment requires the police to bring Dan to an impartial fact finder, usually a judge-magistrate, who will ascertain, based almost entirely on the evidence of the police, whether they had probable cause to seize Dan and to hold him for the alleged crime. In *Gerstein v. Pugh*, 420 U.S. 103 (1975), the Supreme Court held that such a "probable cause" hearing must be held within a "reasonable time." In a later decision, *County of Riverside v. McLaughlin*, 500 U.S. 44 (1991), the Court appeared to set the outside limit on such a hearing at no more than 48 hours after the arrest, although a careful reading of the decision suggests that the hour limit was only a presumptive guideline. These decisions were based on the *Fourth* rather than the *Fifth* Amendment, and do not directly address the issues of due process involved in such hearings.

This "probable cause" hearing need not be elaborate. After all, if the police had had the time to appear before a magistrate before the arrest, they would have obtained a warrant *ex parte*, on the basis of hearsay, informer's information, etc. That kind of *ex parte* procedure is clearly constitutional. The fact that the police now have Dan in custody does not affect the level of proof needed to "seize" him. Moreover, as students of the "investigation" part of the criminal process know, defining "probable cause" is difficult, but all agree that, because it is simply a means of initiating the process, it is a relatively low standard of proof. See Bloom and Brodin, Constitutional Criminal Procedure, Ch. 4 (3d ed. 2000).

Even if Dan is not constitutionally entitled to a *Gerstein* hearing (for example, if there had been an arrest warrant), all jurisdictions, either as a matter of statute or court rule, require that he be brought before a judicial officer to be apprised of the charges against him, and of his constitutional rights, such as the right to counsel, which will be available for the rest of the criminal proceeding. This is purely an informational event—the defendant need not (and usually is advised not to) speak , much less enter a plea to the charges. These charges are likely to be conveyed by means of a *complaint*—an informal paper that summarizes the facts (as then known and alleged) sworn to before a magistrate. This complaint will quickly be supplanted by more official papers filed by the prosecutor.

P.S. Remember we started with "booking." While, again in theory, the probable cause hearing ought to precede the "booking" (suppose the magistrate says there was not probable cause), in real life, booking almost always occurs first.

As a practical matter, the *Gerstein* probable cause issue is often combined with this proceeding, usually called an "initial appearance." And, again for administrative convenience, a determination of bail, discussed below, may be made at this same proceeding. CAVEAT: Different jurisdictions sometimes refer to this very first hearing as a "preliminary hearing," rather than a "probable cause" hearing. That, however, may cause confusion later when we examine a true "preliminary examination" in contrast to a grand jury proceeding (see Chapter 5). Thus, it is best to refer to *this* proceeding as either a *Gerstein* or "probable cause" hearing. Nor, strictly speaking as well, is this an "initial appearance," discussed immediately below in the text, but because the two proceedings are often merged, the probable cause aspect of the process may become lost in the "initial appearance" aspects. There, are then, three terms which you should not confuse, even if the courts sometimes do:

- *Gerstein or "probable cause" hearing*—must be held within 48 hours of a warrantless arrest; its sole purpose is to determine whether the police had probable cause to arrest the defendant.
- *Initial appearance*—before a magistrate who (a) informs the defendant of the charges in the complaint; (b) sets bail; (c) determsines whether

defendant is entitled to appointed counsel. Held even if the defendant was arrested pursuant to a warrant. Often combined with a *Gerstein* hearing if the arrest was without a warrant.

- *Preliminary hearing or examination*—a term improperly used to describe either or both of the above proceedings.

B. Bail

1. The Mechanics of Bail

Assume that the magistrate finds that there was probable cause to arrest Dan. What should the police do now with him? Should they throw him in jail and hold him there until trial? Let him return to his house for afternoon tea? Race down to the courthouse and try him that afternoon?

a. Bail before the 1960s

Dan, of course, wants to be released *now*. He wants to return to his family, and his job, and to seek evidence rebutting the charges against him. But the problem is that he may skip town. On the other hand, if *all* defendants were detained pending trial, the jails would quickly be overcrowded. English and American law, therefore, established the idea of "bail" as an attempt to assure the defendant's return for trial, but to avoid his incarceration pre-trial. Initially, defendants were required to obtain a surety who, should the defendant abscond, would be tried (and punished) in his place. Over several centuries, this notion changed to simply having the defendant, or the surety, proffer an amount of money, or real property, which would be forfeited if the defendant did not return for trial.

Since most defendants are relatively poor, any amount of money bail set by a judge might well be prohibitive. These defendants go to *bailbondsmen* to whom they give a percentage (usually 10%) of the bail amount. The bailbondsmen then submit to the court the entire bail amount. If the defendant appears for trial, the bondsman gets his money back—but the defendant does not get the 10 percent which he has placed with the bondsman. If the defendant absconds, the bondsman is theoretically liable to forfeit the entire bail amount, though this rarely happens. On the other hand, the bondsman is authorized to hire "bounty hunters" to pursue the defendant and obtain his return, unrestrained by the Constitution[1] (because the bounty hunters

---

1. See, e.g., *United States v. Rose*, 731 F.2d 1337 (8th Cir. 1984). See generally, Andrew Patrick, Running from the Law: Should Bounty Hunters Be Considered State Actors and Thus Subject to Constitutional Restraints?, 52 Vand. L. Rev. 171 (1999).

are merely enforcing a contract between the defendant and the bondsman).[2] While bailbondsmen and bounty hunters obviously perform an important role in enforcing bail conditions and pursuing "bail jumpers," there has always been a tension surrounding their work. Thus, for example, in *Schilb v. Kuebel*, 404 U.S. 357 (1971), Justice Blackmun, speaking for the court, referred to the "professional bail bondsman system with all its abuses . . . in full and odorous bloom . . .".

b. Bail Reform in the 1960s and Later

Beginning in the 1960s, both courts and legislatures began recognizing that requiring money bail from many indigent defendants was tantamount to precluding release on bail. Moreover, many argued, and some studies seemed to support the argument, that persons incarcerated prior to trial were more likely to be convicted, and, when convicted, likely to receive a harsher sentence than those who had secured their release on bail.[3] Initially, on an experimental basis, the VERA Foundation in New York attempted to establish methods by which facts surrounding the defendant's character and his ties to the community could be quickly verified. Personnel were placed in police stations or jails and interviewed the defendant almost immediately after arrest, obtaining facts that might be verified by calls to family members, or employers, even prior to the first setting of bail. Such bail agencies are now a fixed part of the pre-trial firmament in most urban jurisdictions.

The experimental programs proved successful — defendants whose ties to the community and/or character could be quickly established were released on bail, and overwhelmingly returned for later court appearances.[4] Based in part upon these felicitous results, the entire paradigm shifted. In the federal system, for example, Congress enacted the Federal Bail Reform Act of 1966, which established a presumption that all (federal) defendants should be released without any money bail at all — released on their own

---

2. See *Taylor v. Taintor*, 83 U.S. (16 Wall.) 366 (1872).

3. At least one court found that, in the particular circumstances in that case, a white attorney representing a black defendant would have great difficulty in finding witnesses and persuading them to testify for the defendant. This, said the court required release. See *Kinney v. Lenon*, 425 F.2d 209 (9th Cir. 1970). Recent figures indicate that two-thirds of detained defendants were convicted of a felony, compared to 46 percent of released defendants. See Bureau of Justice Statistics, Felony Defendants in Large Urban Counties, 1998, p.24 (NCJ Report # 187232 2001). These data, however, do not reflect whether those detained were already more likely to have committed felonies, and therefore, were more likely to be detained.

4. Although statistics are always somewhat suspect, it appears that 76 percent of released defendants make all scheduled appearances, and 95 percent return for trial. See Bureau of Justice Statistics, *supra*, n.3, p.21. Most of the failures to appear seem to be because of poor notice; only 5 percent remained a fugitive after a year.

recognizance (ROR). (This presumption was later endorsed by the American Bar Association Criminal Justice Standards.) The statute expressly provides, for example, that "the judicial officer may not impose a financial condition that results in the pre-trial detention of the person." For instances where the court was doubtful about pre-trial release, judges were instructed to set increasingly stern conditions for release, culminating, if necessary, in some sort of money bail. States followed the same reform path, either by abolishing money bail, or by providing the same kind of service, at a 10 percent rate, that bondsmen had previously provided. The significant distinction, however, was that if the defendant came to trial he would receive his 10 percent surety amount back (less a small administrative fee).[5] This system, known as "cash bail," has been replicated in many states. The dramatic leap from surety-money bail as the primary means of detaining defendants to these other systems has been swift and full.

Although far less common than pre-1960, money bail may still be required in many states for at least some offenses. Courts have consistently rejected the argument that indigent defendants unable to make bail, even of a small amount, are denied equal protection of the laws. Cf. *Schilb v. Kuebel*, 404 U.S. 357 (1971) (upholding as not unconstitutional Illinois' state bail system, by which defendant was required to forfeit 1 percent of his bail, to cover administrative costs). See, however, Justice Douglas' opinion in *Bandy v. United States*, 81 S. Ct. 197 (1960): "To continue to demand a substantial bond which the defendant is unable to secure raises considerable problems for the equal administration of the law . . . Can an indigent be denied freedom, where a wealthy man would not, because he does not happen to have enough property to pledge for his freedom?" See also *Pugh v. Rainwater*, 557 F.2d 1189 (5th Cir. 1977).

Determining Bail

In theory, the amount of bail—or the conditions attached to pre-trial release—should be a result of the weighing of several factors, of which the most important are:

1. *The seriousness of the crime charged.* All crime is serious; but some crime is more serious than others. The more serious the crime, the higher the penalty, and the less likely, all other things being equal, the defendant will return voluntarily.

2. *The evidence against the defendant.* If the evidence is overwhelming, and the defendant knows that, voluntary return becomes less likely.

---

5. These fees are not unconstitutional. See *Broussard v. Parish of Orleans*, 318 F.3d 644 (5th Cir. 2003).

Remember, however, that this determination can be made only on the evidence that the police or prosecution believe they have at the time the determination is made. Facts uncovered at a later time during the investigation may change the assessment here.

3. *The defendant's ties to the community.* A defendant who has lived in, or has other ties to, the community is assumed less likely to leave than one who is a transient passing through.

4. *The character of the defendant.* The defendant's past criminal record may be considered here: a transient religious leader may be deemed more likely to return for trial than a three-time convicted felon (who may face life in prison) even if he has a family in the community.

Assessing the facts in each case may be extremely difficult. Of the four factors cited above, only the first is both relatively unchangeable and not subject to subjective evaluation: The legislatively set maximum penalty for robbery does not alter with the facts of the specific case. For that reason, among others, courts setting bail are likely to look at the charge as the most important criteria. Thus, many jurisdictions have established a "bail schedule," under which a specific charge generates a specific presumed bail unless there is overwhelming reason to vary from that presumption. It is *possible* that reliance on such a schedule would now be held unconstitutional. In *Stack v. Boyle*, 342 U.S. 1 (1951), the Supreme Court intimated — but did not need to *hold* — that every bail determination must be made on the particular facts of the case, including those related to the defendant.

As to the second factor, police are unlikely to suggest that their evidence is weak, particularly when, as is often the case, the first bail decision is made prior to the defendant obtaining counsel. Until the processes of ROR described above, the third and fourth factors almost always depended, at least at the initial appearance, solely upon the defendant's statements. It would have been unusual, at least at the first setting of bail, that that information could be validated.

2. *The Procedures of Bail*

Because the most important immediate concern of an arrested defendant is obtaining release, initial bail determinations are often made in informal settings, without counsel, and often without any set procedures. This is not surprising; defendants are not anxious to delay the moment of the first determination of bail, hoping that the decision will be such as to allow them to go home. And for persons charged with minor offenses (variously defined by the states), many states allow the setting of bail (or release on a summons or citation) to be done by the police in the police station. Moreover, initial bail decisions are made on the basis of what may be very skimpy evidence — almost always hearsay evidence of some sort. Again, however, waiting for evidence which would be admissible under the rules of evidence, and for the defendant to obtain evidence supporting his desire for no (or low) bail might result in delaying the defendant's release.

Surprisingly, there appears to be no definitive answer as to whether the defendant or the prosecutor has the burden on the flight risk question, or what the standard of proof is. If the standard of proof remains whether there is probable cause to believe this defendant has committed a crime, one might expect that bail would be denied frequently. Obviously, the prosecutor must rely on whatever information she has at the time to carry that burden.

In at least some states the victim may appear and present evidence.[6] This practice seems undesirable, however, since the victim is unlikely to be able to speak to the defendant's flight risk, and is more likely to simply ask for some kind of protection from the defendant.

While states do not preclude attorneys from representing defendants at the first determination, requiring an appointed counsel be present at that first determination would be extremely difficult. Although the bail hearing has been said *not* to be a "critical stage of the (criminal) proceeding," which is the litmus test for deciding whether there is a right to appointed counsel (see Chapter 10), the United States Supreme Court in *Coleman v. Alabama*, 399 U.S. 1 (1970), appeared to lean in the direction of seeing this proceeding as a Sixth Amendment "criminal prosecution," where there would be a right to appointed counsel. In light of his desire for a speedy resolution (and hopefully, release), however, a defendant might well waive that right (if it were so established) at that hearing. Of course, whether at the initial bail hearing or at any later proceeding, if the defendant has counsel, he will be allowed to participate in that proceeding.

Suppose, at his initial appearance, at which bail is being set, the defendant, attempting to avoid liability, says to the magistrate: "I shot him, your honor, but only after he lunged at me with that knife." The defendant does not know (particularly, if he has not been so informed by a lawyer) that his claim of self-defense does not go to undermine the probable cause basis of the prosecution—at least not at this point of the proceedings. If the defendant later wishes to deny that he shot the victim, can the statement made at the bail hearing be used against him? The case law is unclear as to whether a defendant's statements at a bail hearing, usually made without the presence of counsel, are "coerced" within the meaning of the Fifth Amendment, and therefore barred from trial. On the one hand, no one actually compels the defendant to speak; indeed, magistrates often caution the defendant that he need say nothing at the proceeding. On the other, a defendant who does not speak is unlikely to obtain (or at least fears that he will not obtain) a "favorable"

---

6. See, e.g., Mo. Const. art. I, sec. 32.

bail. Is that pressure sufficient to make any statement "involuntary" under the Fifth Amendment? See *State v. Fenner*, 381 Md. 1, 846 A.2d 1020 (2004) (statement is admissible).

This discussion of the initial determination of bail suggests one very important point—the decision on bail is always fluid. Because bail as initially established is based upon fragmentary facts (usually a police recitation of barebone facts relating to the crime, followed either by the defendant's silence, or his unverified assertions of his ties to the community (and sometimes his protestations of innocence)), the amount of bail, or the other conditions of release, imposed upon a defendant is always subject to reassessment. The amount of bail may be revised upward or downward whenever the factors above are perceived to change. Thus, if the leading witness against the defendant recants his statements to the police, the court may perceive that the likelihood of conviction has sufficiently decreased as to warrant a change of the conditions of release. Conversely, if the victim emerges from a coma to identify the defendant as the perpetrator, the amount of bail may be increased, or the conditions of community release made more restrictive. And while most bail is set initially in the absence of counsel, once counsel is obtained (either privately or through appointment), facts may be garnered which will support the defendant's earlier naked assertions, whether relating to the crime, or to his eligibility for bail. Thus, motions for reduction (or removal) of bail are quite common.

3. Preventive Detention — Security of the Community as a Criterion of Bail

a. The "Capital" Exception to Bail

The Eighth Amendment to the Constitution provides that "excessive bail shall not be required . . ." Some writers have argued that this means that all defendants must be constitutionally entitled to some level of bail. After all, if jurisdictions could assure that the bail set was not "excessive" by simply not allowing bail at all, the provision would become relatively meaningless. Notwithstanding this rather straightforward interpretation of the provision, the Supreme Court has never held that bail is constitutionally guaranteed, and has in fact strongly intimated that it is not. The prime explanation for this is historical; both before and after the Revolution, defendants charged with capital offenses were not afforded the opportunity for bail. Thus, the Court has said, there must be "some" exceptions to the otherwise plain meaning of the provision, and the exceptions would be established pragmatically. Today, at least 40 states preclude bail in "capital offenses, where the proof is evident or the presumption great." See, e.g., Vt. Const. chapter II, sec. 40. It has been held that placing the burden on the defendant to show that the proof of his guilt is not "evident" is unconstitutional, *State v. Purcell*, 778 N.E. 2d 695 (Ill. 2002) (applying state constitution) but other courts allow the state to place the burden on the defendant. See *Commonwealth v. Baker*, 343 Mass. 162 (1961); *State v. Arthur*, 390 So. 2d 717 (Fla. 1980), *aff'g, Arthur v. Harper*, 371 So. 2d 96 (Fla. Dist. Ct. App. 1978).

b. Non-Capital Felonies

The "capital" exception was established when many, indeed most, felonies were subject to capital punishment. It seems commonsensical that a defendant facing death, particularly if the evidence is strong, might decide to see his aunt in Rio if allowed out on bail, and never return. But suppose the defendant is charged with offenses that could—or must—result in imprisonment of 150 years? Or life imprisonment without the possibility of parole? Some states extend the "capital exception" to these situations as well, on the ground that the punishment threatened is "the equivalent" of death, and, therefore, just as likely to result in the defendant's absconding.

A majority of states allow preventive detention of non-capital felons in some situations, either explicitly, or by interpretation of clauses not unlike those of the Eighth Amendment. Indeed, recent legislation in a number of states has made bail either unavailable, or difficult to obtain, for defendants charged with, among other crimes, stalking or domestic violence. Such statutes *precluding* bail in cases involving non-capital charges have been viewed warily, and on occasion held unconstitutional. See, e.g., *Hunt v. Roth*, 648 F.2d 1148 (8th Cir.), judgment vacated for mootness, 455 U.S. 478 (1981) (Nebraska statute prohibiting bail in sexual offenses involving penetration by force where the proof is evident or the presumption great violates the excessiveness clause of the Eighth Amendment). But see *State ex rel Romley v. Rayes*, 206 Ariz. 58 (Ariz. App. Div. 1, 2003) (upholding a Constitutional provision, adopted by voters, precluding bail for certain sexual offenses if the case is "evident" and the "presumption of guilt" "great"). Indeed, the European Court of Human Rights has held that a similar practice of automatically denying bail, at least based solely on the fact that defendant had a prior record, violated the European Convention of Human Rights. See *Caballero v. United Kingdom* (Application No. 32819/96, Decided 8 Feb. 2000). On the other hand, at least since the *Salerno* case, discussed below, there is no *a priori* reason to believe that these statutes are *per se* unconstitutional.

c. Preventive Detention—Locking the Barn While the Horse Is Still There

Even if a magistrate concludes that a defendant charged with eight separate incidences of commercial burglaries is not a flight risk, she might be concerned that, if released pending trial, he may continue his life of crime — or that he would intimidate witnesses against him. Until *United States v. Salerno*, 481 U.S. 739 (1987) the magistrate could not overtly consider those fears — the attempt to assure the defendant's return to trial was the only acceptable *articulated* basis for setting the amount of bail. In the real world, however, judges faced with defendants whom they deemed likely to commit further crimes if released pending trial (even if they would return) would simply raise bail to a level they thought impossible for the defendant to reach. The magistrate would argue (if pressed) that, while a single burglary might not warrant a high bail, the cumulative penalty which the defendant faced necessitated what would otherwise be an "excessive" bail because of flight risks. Thus, community safety was an ever-present, if unstated, concern in setting bail.

Salerno removed the need for judicial subterfuge and endorsed, at least in limited circumstances, denial of bail based upon an assessment that the defendant would commit more crimes if released. The case involved the federal 1984 Bail Reform Act, which amended the 1966 Act referred to above. As noted above, under the earlier statute:

- there was a presumption that the defendant was to be released on his own recognizance;
- if the judge found that such release was problematic, she was still to release the defendant on a series of increasingly severe conditions;
- if those conditions were still not sufficient, money bail could be set.

Critics believed that persons so released were committing crimes pending trial, and pointed to data that a sizable percentage of those released pending trial were arrested for another felony.[7] These data, however, were less probative than they would first appear, since they did not include figures on how many of those charges resulted in conviction. (On the other hand, there may well have been released defendants who committed offenses but were not arrested for them. Thus, the data were truly unhelpful in deciding this matter.) Nevertheless, Congress amended the 1966 statute explicitly to provide, for the first time in American history, for "preventive detention" of individuals charged with certain enumerated felonies, if a judge, after a hearing, were persuaded by clear and convincing evidence either that the defendant was a flight risk, *or* that he would be a risk to the community if released pending trial.

Although the challenge in *Salerno* to the statute was facial, and not as applied, the facts of the case are not unimportant. Anthony ("Fat Tony") Salerno, charged with a number of racketeering offenses, including murder,

---

7. In 1998, 84 percent of persons released pending trial were not rearrested, while 10 percent were rearrested for charged felonies. See NCJ report, *supra*, n.3 at p.22.

was alleged to be the "capo" of one of the most important Organized Crime families in the United States. His co-defendant, Vincent ("The Fish") Cafaro was a major figure in that organization. It is difficult to imagine two defendants for whom the statute was enacted, if not these two. Moreover, because the challenge *was* facial, the statute would be upheld if the Court could imagine *any* set of facts which would allow such detention. Suppose, for example, that a defendant were to say unequivocally "*If* I am released, the first thing I will do is kill the 50 people who informed on me." Only if that statement would not warrant preventive detention could the Court invalidate the statute.

The Court ultimately held that the statute was narrow enough, and sufficiently difficult to invoke, that *on its face*, it was not unconstitutional. Initially, the Court decided that the detention did not involve the Eighth Amendment because the detention was "regulatory" and not "punitive."[8] It then pointed out that the statute:

- provided for a full hearing, complete with counsel, cross-examination, and presentation of witnesses in front of an impartial judicial officer, who had to issue written findings of fact before detention could be ordered;
- placed upon the prosecution the burden of proof by clear and convincing evidence that *no* set of conditions can be established that would satisfy the goals of the statute (appearance and non-crime);
- provided that a detained defendant should be tried as promptly as possible, and given priority before others;
- provided that detainees should, as much as possible, be housed in facilities other than those used to house convicted offenders.

Whether the Court would uphold a statute if one or more of these provisions were not in the statute—of if defendant could show consistent violation of the provisions—was not before the Court. But the fact is that most (federal) detainees are housed not in the Ritz Carlton, but in Metropolitan Correctional Centers or in local jails, and *do* find themselves next to convicted felons. Most defendants are not tried within a "short" period of time, or even within the 90 days provided by federal statute. While these extensions may be explained at least in part by pointing to defense requests for continuances, it may be that the delay is inconsistent with the Court's assumption in *Salerno*.

---

8. In a wide variety of instances, the courts have been faced with attempting to decide whether a particular governmental action is punitive, and hence activates the procedural protections of the Bill of Rights, or "regulatory" and is governed, if at all, only by a sense of balance under the due process clause. That dilemma will be ignored here, except to note that the Court relied primarily on legislative intent—if the legislature defined the action as "regulatory," only grossly excessive processes would then allow the Court to override that definition.

Salerno also appears to have settled that:

- the Eighth Amendment does *not* guarantee the possibility of bail to all defendants, even all those charged with non-capital offense;
- the presumption of innocence has no effect upon a pre-trial detainee's status; the presumption is merely a procedural device for allocating the burden of proof at trial. In other words, between arrest and trial the "presumption" has no effect, and the defendant is not "presumed" to be either innocent or guilty.

While it is possible to read *Salerno* extremely narrowly, both because it was a facial challenge, and because the Court emphasized these statutory limitations upon preventive detention, that has not been the case. Nearly twenty states have statutorily authorized such detention based upon *Salerno*. Moreover, subsequent decisions by the lower federal courts (and state courts drawing sustenance from the opinion) have not narrowed *Salerno*.

One aspect of the 1984 Act, not involved in *Salerno*, is the statute's (rebuttable) presumption that there is no set of conditions that will assure the safety of the community from persons charged with (a) capital or life imprisonment offenses; (b) some drug offenses; (c) a "crime of violence"; or (d) any felony, if the defendant has twice before been convicted of any of the offenses mentioned in (a) through (c). Lower courts have upheld this presumption on the ground that it shifts only the burden of production, and not the burden of proof (remember that in the federal statute, the prosecutor's burden is clear and convincing evidence). Equally unclear is what "community safety" entails. Obviously, it includes possible crimes against the person. But suppose the judge concludes that the defendant will, if released, (continue to) sell drugs, or obstruct justice? Aren't *all* criminal acts by definition a danger to the community?

One other aspect of preventive detention may be troubling—it asks the fact finder to make explicit predictions about future (criminal) behavior. Yet scores of studies, conducted with varying methodologies, have concluded that the ability to predict future behavior, much less future *criminal* behavior, much less future criminal *violent* behavior, is very weak. Nonetheless, this inability has not troubled the courts. Assuming proper procedural protections, the courts, including the United States Supreme Court, have upheld judgments based upon such predictions. See, e.g., *Schall v. Martin*, 467 U.S. 253 (1984) (juveniles); *Kansas v. Hendricks*, 521 U.S. 346 (1997) (sexual predators). Moreover, the argument that the emphasis on predicted behavior somehow taints the decision ignores the fact that *every* bail decision involves the judge's prediction about the defendant's potential to flee.

In an odd way, since all defendants charged with "non-bailable" offenses are in one sense being preventively detained, *Salerno* may suggest that such provisions are constitutionally suspect, since the Court relied on the premise that the federal statute involved there expressly required the determination of detention to be made on an individual, case-by-case basis.[9] Essentially, this is the *Stack* requirement applied to non-capital offenders. The contrary argument, of course, is that the capital exemption is historically based, and that it is implicit in the Eighth Amendment itself.

It is not easy to determine whether the approbation given by the *Salerno* decision to preventive detention has resulted in more or less pre-trial detention. Recent statistics indicate that about two-thirds of federal defendants were released pending trial, while about a third were preventively detained under the statute's provisions and procedures. While 33 percent may seem like a high percentage to be preventively detained, particularly given the statute's presumption in favor of release, we cannot know what percentage of federal prisoners were preventively detained prior to 1984 (or 1966) by judges imposing very high bail as a subterfuge for such community protection. As one Department of Justice Department report acknowledged, "pre-trial detention has largely been substituted for bail as a means of detaining defendants." The data from the states seem to indicate that preventive detention is infrequently imposed: Although approximately 36 percent of state defendants were detained until disposition of their case, about 80 percent of those were actually allowed release on money bail, but were detained because they were unable to make the amount. Thus, only 20 percent of that group, or 7 percent of all state defendants, appeared to be held preventively.[10]

On the other hand, while *Salerno* technically was concerned only with whether a defendant could be denied bail based upon possible future criminality, it has also allowed the use of such concerns in setting the amount of bail. To some this may appear undesirable; but if judges were already using these concerns in setting bail, it may be better to have the process transparent and openly discussed.

The concern that gave rise to these preventive detention statutes—that at least some pre-trial releasees would commit more crime—cannot be gainsaid, even if the data are unhelpful. But many states have chosen another (sometimes supplemental) way of confronting this issue by increasing the defendant's sentence for one of those crimes. While this does not prevent the second crime directly, as preventive detention would, the hope is that the threat of increased punishment will deter the second crime, without requiring the government to rely on somewhat shaky inferences about character and future behavior.

---

9. In *Demore v. Kim*, 538 U.S. 510 (2003) the Court decided that such individualized bail decisions were not constitutionally mandated, at least with respect to non-citizen permanent resident aliens, who could be incarcerated while they were awaiting proceedings to deport them.

10. See NCJ report, *supra* n.3 at p.18.

Finally, suppose the defendant is released on bail and then charged with a new crime, or with a violation of a condition of bail — for example, to report to the probation office once a month. If the only issue on bail is possible flight, one might suggest that even these acts do not affect *that* determination. (If Dan refused to turn in his passport, on the other hand, the inference that he intends to flee might be substantial.) On the other hand, if possible danger to the community is a consideration, even an alleged violation might be sufficient to warrant reconsideration of the bail set earlier. Some courts have suggested that this is erroneous — that disregard, even disrespect of, the judiciary or the government generally, is not grounds for denying or revoking bail.

C. Pre-Trial Diversion

Beyond bail, or conditional release, many jurisdictions provide other methods by which a defendant can avoid pre-trial incarceration. The most important of these, because it can often mean the defendant entirely avoids trial, and a criminal record, is pre-trial diversion (often referred to as PTI (Intervention)). Essentially, a defendant is placed in the community, sometimes under intense supervision, rather than tried; if he does not commit another crime for a specific period of time, the record of his arrest and charge may be either sealed or destroyed. Since these programs often involve disputes about prosecutorial discretion, we will postpone that discussion until the next chapter.

EXAMPLES

1. In a small town in rural South Dakota, Karen is arrested (without a warrant) on Friday evening and taken to the police station, where she is told that she is charged with insurance fraud. She is placed in a jail cell. She demands to be brought to a magistrate, but the magistrate is sick, and the local judge is at a conference several hundred miles away. On Monday afternoon, she is finally brought before the magistrate, now recovered, some 69 hours after being arrested. What remedies does she have?

2. Jack, CEO of Outron Corp., was arrested after a grand jury returned a 78 count indictment for fraudulent practices. At the initial appearance before a magistrate, the magistrate relied upon hearsay testimony before the grand jury, testimony which (as we shall see in Chapter 6) is not discoverable by the defendant in many jurisdictions. The magistrate thereupon set bail at $5,000,000, declaring that she believed Jack to be a flight risk. May the magistrate properly consider such testimony?

3. Carol works for a top secret federal agency. They come to suspect her of trading secrets to another country, but indict her, instead, for several felonies dealing with misuse of a government computer. The government then seeks preventive detention under the Federal Bail Act of 1984. Testimony at the detention hearing involves hearsay that the secrets are critical to the defense of the United States. The judge finds, by clear and convincing evidence, that the defendant is a flight risk. She is turned over to the custody of the Department of Justice, which then places her in solitary confinement in a nearby federal prison, asserting that there is a great danger that she may communicate governmental secrets to any visitor. What likelihood is there that Carol will prevail if she appeals her preventive detention?

4. Ramon has been arrested, without a warrant, on a charge of larceny of $240.00. (a) At the initial appearance, the magistrate denied bail entirely, saying that larceny in that county was a non-bailable offense. Is the magistrate's action defensible? (b) At the initial appearance, the presiding magistrate sets bail at $5000, based upon the custom of the county that all larcenies, whatever the amount allegedly stolen, should be bailed at $5,000. The magistrate concedes that he did not have facts about Ramon's ties to the community, nor about his prior criminal record. (Ramon has no such record.) Ramon does not have sufficient funds to make bail. If he argues that bail based *solely* upon the crime is "excessive" under the Eighth Amendment, will he be successful?

5. Rick has been harassing his exwife, Helen, and was charged with burglary, unlawful mischief, and trespass for entering her house. He was released on bail, including a condition that he not associate with nor harass her, nor enter her premises without being accompanied by a police officer. Prior to that date, Helen had allowed Rick to sleep on a sofa on her back porch because he was homeless. When Rick, contrary to the bail conditions, reappeared on the porch and refused to leave, he was arrested and charged with trespass and alcoholic beverage violations. The judge revoked his bail on the old charges, and refused bail on the new charges, based upon Rick's conduct. Is this valid?

6. John Byrd is arrested by federal authorities and charged with receiving child pornography through the mails, a federal offense. James Heffner, the prosecutor, seeks to detain Byrd without bail pursuant to the 1984 Bail Reform Act. Heffner puts on evidence that Byrd has around his house thousands of pictures of naked young people. The government also asserts that when the search warrant for the subject video tape was executed, there were "two young children in the house, both of whom stated that they had been sexually molested by the defendant . . ." "[p]addles and photographs of nude children were also discovered in the house. . . . Furthermore, state charges for molestation of juveniles

were filed. During the time when those charges were pending, the defendant . . . continued to regularly molest two children." Heffner also presents psychiatric testimony that persons who molest persons not in their family are likely to continue to do so. The government concedes that Byrd is not a flight risk (groan) (sorry about that). May Byrd be detained on the theory that he is a danger to the community?

EXPLANATIONS

1. It is often said that there is no right without a remedy. But this may prove the exception to that saying. Karen has clearly been held in excess of the 48-hour standard enunciated in *McLaughlin*. The burden therefore would fall upon the government to demonstrate that its failure to bring her to an initial appearance was unavoidable. The difficulty is that the courts have yet to create a remedy for that violation. Of course, one possible remedy might be to require the police to release her, but one assumes that she would only be rearrested immediately as she left the police station or court house. If Karen had confessed during her incarceration, her statement might be suppressed, under *McNabb v. United States*, 318 U.S. 332 (1943), and *Mallory v. United States*, 354 U.S. 449 (1957). See Bloom and Brodin *supra* p.267. Other than this, Karen might have a civil suit against the police, but if they in fact had probable cause to detain her, it is unlikely that she would succeed, for reasons that are beyond the scope of this book. Moreover, while Karen might seek her "release" as soon as she is brought to the magistrate, it is more likely that this issue would not be litigated until a later date perhaps even after her trial. At that point, of course, the issue is really moot.

2. Yes. There is nothing wrong with the magistrate's use of, or reliance upon, such testimony. The rules of evidence do not apply at bail hearings, and the reasons for grand jury secrecy would outweigh the defendant's need to see the evidence. See, e.g., *State v. Campisi*, 64 N.J. 120 (1973).

3. For several reasons, Carol should win her appeal and be released. She is not charged with a crime of violence, and she is not a likely flight risk. Moreover, flight risk can be minimized by intensive surveillance and control of passport.

   Nevertheless, in a real case involving similar, but not identical facts, the result, at least initially, was different. This problem tracks the case of Dr. Wen Ho Lee, which graphically illustrated the problematic aspects of bail determinations generally, and of preventive detention decisions specifically. Lee, a Chinese American, had worked as a physicist at Los Alamos National Laboratory for over 20 years when, in 1999, he was arrested and charged with a variety of offenses relating to national defense information. The government believed he had stolen, and delivered to the Chinese government, information on how to construct a nuclear weapon, and on deployment of those weapons in the United States. The government, using the Bail Reform Act involved in *Salerno*, sought Lee's preventive detention on the basis that, if Lee had not communicated with the Chinese government, he should be totally precluded from doing so pending trial. At the detention hearing, FBI agents and others testified that the information in question constituted the "crown jewels" of American security. On the basis of that (and other) testimony, the court ordered Lee detained without bail pending trial. The Justice Department, fearful of some leak, then placed Dr. Lee in solitary confinement, often chained to his bed.

Almost immediately thereafter, however, the government's case began to undergo serious questioning. Persons who until then had not been vocal about the charges came forward, and Lee's attorneys received much new information about the charges. The "crown jewels," they learned, were vastly overstated — if not paste, they were certainly not material for the Tower of London. Despite several motions between December and September to reconsider the detention order, Lee was unable to persuade the judge to grant him bail. Only after nine months of solitary confinement was he able to amass sufficient information and expert testimony to persuade the judge that the initial bail determination, made under the strictures imposed by *Salerno,* had not merely been wrong, but the result of misleading evidence and testimony, which could not have been seriously challenged at the first hearing.

As described more in Chapter 6, on discovery, Lee also won a motion to obtain discovery of numerous Justice Department files. Within days, the government agreed to a plea bargain to one count of a minor felony of misusing a computer. At the hearing on his plea, the district court judge excoriated the government, accusing some of the witnesses at the December hearing of lying, and apologizing to the defendant, saying: "I feel I was led astray last December . . . I sincerely apologize to you, Dr. Lee, for the unfair manner you were held in custody."

The *Lee* case shows, again, the difficulties that defendants can face if there is some doubt as to whether they should be allowed release on bail and, if so, what the amount should be. The government had had months to prepare its case against him. Even though Lee was aware that he was being scrutinized over that time, he had not obtained attorneys until just before the indictment. Thus, even his counsel at the hearing was unable to present any persuasive information to counter the government's case. Moreover, the facts as alleged in the December hearing constantly changed, and Lee's view of the case, and of the proofs, (as well as the government's) had constantly altered. Bail is the first decision, but it is certainly not final.

For more on the case, see My Country v. Me, by Wen Ho Lee.

4. (a) In theory, Ramon should win his challenge in each case. In *Stack v. Boyle*, the court declared that "standards relevant to the purpose of assuring the presence of that defendant" must "be applied in each case to each defendant," thus appearing to undermine any reliance on the kind of schedule which this magistrate employed. On the other hand, the Court has never held that bail is *required*, at least in capital cases. This outlandish behavior, however, is likely to become a cropper—it is hard to argue that larceny and capital homicide are equivalents.

    (b) Ramon is on shakier ground here. Courts have not been willing to hold unconstitutional such a bail schedule, perhaps because that could be seen as mandating, for every jurisdiction, the kind of bail agency described in the text, a requirement that might be onerous in small communities. Thus, federalism concerns have played a part in not invalidating bail schedules. Ramon's better avenue is to seek a reconsideration of bail, based upon facts that he, and his counsel, can now generate. Moreover, while courts—and legislatures—have been sensitive to the claim that money bail unfairly penalizes the poor, they have not equally been willing to hold that money bail is by definition "excessive" simply because the (impoverished) defendant does not have sufficient funds.

5. No. This is a real case, in which the court held that only interference with the criminal process would warrant a refusal of bail. Noting that the defendant was never charged with abuse, or with assaulting or threatening his wife, the court declared that there must be a nexus between the defendant's violations and disruption of the prosecution, and that "(F)lagrant disregard of conditions may show disrespect for the judicial system, but . . . do not necessarily threaten the integrity of the judicial system." *State v. Sauve*, 159 Vt. 566, 621 A.2d 1296, (1993). Clearly, the preference for liberty pending trial was a major consideration in this court's determination.

6. No. First, the Federal Bail Reform Act carries a presumption that all defendants should be released on their own recognizance. There is no *prima facie* reason to believe that the presumption is not relevant in this case. On the other hand, the Act establishes a (rebuttable) presumption in favor of detention if a case involves a "crime of violence." While child molestation *is* such a crime, passive possession of pornography is not itself violent. In *United States v. Byrd*, 969 F.2d 106 (5th Cir. 1992), upon which this example is based, the court declared that Byrd could not be held without bail. Said the court: "There can be no doubt that this Act clearly favors non-detention . . . detention can be ordered only after a hearing . . . even after a hearing, detention can be ordered only in certain designated and limited circumstances, irrespective of whether the defendant's release may jeopardize public safety." Thus, the Court declared, a defendant's threat to commit another (non-violent) crime,

standing alone, will not justify pre-trial detention. Note, however, the government did not put on specific evidence relating to Byrd's propensity for child molestation. Had it done so, the court suggested in dictum, the case "might have" involved a crime of violence, even though the specific charge did not. The real problem here was the evidence, not the statute.

Of course, state statutes might vary in both their wording and their legislative history and allow pre-trial detention even without such evidence at the hearing. But given the predilection for liberty noted by the *Byrd* court, pre-trial detention is still not favored.

3

Charging Decisions

"The prosecutor has more control over life, liberty, and reputation than any other person in America."

Robert Jackson, United States Attorney General and Justice of the United States Supreme Court, and Chief United States Prosecutor at the Nuremberg Trials[1]

A. Introduction

Although the bail decision is somewhat discretionary, we are now ready to see discretion in its grandeur. As we move through this chapter, keep in mind the "hydraulic theory" of discretion—that however we restrain discretion in one area, it will reappear in another. Thus, for example, if Hana, the prosecutor, had to prosecute every person arrested, the police, rather than the prosecutor, would have the discretion not merely to arrest, but essentially to resolve charging questions as well. Similarly, as we will see in Chapter 11, many criticize sentencing guideline systems, which limit judicial discretion in sentencing, because they believe the sentencing power has effectively been given to prosecutors.

The first instance where this discretion becomes apparent is in the actual charges which the state, represented by the prosecutor, will bring against Dan. (From this point on, we will talk of the prosecutor "bringing charges." As we will discuss in Chapter 4, however, in many states, only the grand jury can actually "bring charges" (and even in the remaining states, where the

---

1. Robert Jackson, The Federal Prosecutor, 24 Am. Jud. Soc'y J. 18 (1940).

prosecutor can indeed "bring charges" by filing an "information," there may be other procedures for keeping the case moving)). Remember — the "initial appearance" was held quickly after Dan's arrest, and quite possibly relied only upon the police's testimony as to what they were told (and saw) about the basic crime.[2] There may have been no prosecutor (as well as no defense attorney) present. In the next days and weeks, however, lawyers will become involved on both sides.

Thus begins an intricate dance between prosecutor and defense. In this book, we will approach the process as though the prosecutor "controls" the timing. But that may be a fiction — defense attorneys may well bring motions, initiate negotiations, etc., on their own. And certainly a good lawyer — whichever side she represents — will want to "outguess" the other, thereby maneuvering to thwart the other's actions. As we move through these materials, keep asking yourself (if we do not): "What would I do *now* if I were (defender; prosecutor)?" "How would I respond to (the other side's) actions?". Good lawyering is "proactive" — attempting to assess the other side's strengths and weaknesses and probing them early and often.

Remember also that while the scenario we have painted involves the typical process of an arrest without a warrant, and before an indictment, many indictments precede arrest. In these instances, defense counsel who learn of the grand jury inquiry may be even more aggressive, attempting to preclude an indictment entirely (for example, by seeking immunity by helping the state prove its case against other defendants), or to dilute any charges which the prosecutor might be contemplating.

B. The Decision to Prosecute

1. The Public Prosecutor

Although most criminal prosecutions in England had been conducted by the victim in tandem with tort suits against the perpetrator of the harm, American colonies, almost from their establishment, relied upon publicly elected prosecutors to bring most of the criminal prosecutions. Scholars dispute why this occurred, but public prosecution is an essentially American invention. Today, although many states provide for some participation by the victim (and perhaps his counsel) in a prosecution so long as the proceeding is "controlled " by the prosecutor, only a few states allow a victim to

---

2. In some other systems, prosecutors often interview a suspect before proceeding. See, e.g., Castberg, Prosecutorial Independence in Japan, 16 UCLA Pac. Bas. L.J. 38, 52 (1997).

proceed against a defendant if the prosecutor has decided against criminal sanctions, and then only if a court appoints the counsel.

A system of prosecution by public prosecutors rather than by the victim has many strengths. For example, it avoids blackmail by the victim, who in early England could, and often did, threaten criminal prosecution unless the defendant "compromised" (settled) the tort suit. It also prevents the courts from being used as conduits for unreasonable, vengeance-seeking victims (or their survivors) who are incapable of neutrally assessing the defendant's criminal responsibility. It also means that poor victims will have their rights protected even if they could not afford the costs of prosecution. And it encourages fiscal responsibility by assuring that public monies are spent on types of crime, and individual instances of crime, deemed "important" by the public.[3]

But there are also pitfalls. Prosecutors, who are elected in all but a handful of states, and many of whom aspire to higher office,[4] may decline to prosecute defendants who are politically well connected, or favored by the public; similarly, prosecutors may proceed against persons disfavored by the public, or refuse to prosecute where the victim is disfavored (such as occurred in mob lynchings). Finally, where the case is extremely difficult to prove, and requires expenditures that the prosecutor does not have, even a valid criminal prosecution may be foregone. Real victims of real crimes may thus be left without remedy.[5]

Finally, remember that while we talk of "the prosecutor," it is important to distinguish between the chief prosecutor in a particular office, who sets general policy, and the many "line prosecutors" who handle the cases day by day. The extent of supervision of those line prosecutors by their superiors determines how much discretion each has individually, and the degree of discretion generally exercised by the office.

---

3. Again, however, there is a double edge here. Because "street" crimes are said to be easier to prosecute and prove than complex white collar offenses, well-placed offenders are less likely to be targets of prosecution. The prosecution, in 2002–2004, of high-level officials in a number of major corporations ensued only after their exploits resulted in economic and psychological injury to literally millions of employees and investors who demanded action. There are, as well, possibilities of racial or ethnic bias lurking behind indecisions to prosecute street, but not "suite," crime.

4. As examples, consider Earl Warren, who was attorney general and governor of California, and who sought the republican nomination for president or, Dewey, former prosecutor and then governor of New York, who nearly became president running against Harry Truman. Even appointed prosecutors may purposely seek out unpopular defendants and then run for political office. See, e.g., Rudolph Guilliani, who became mayor of New York City after having served as the United States Attorney in that jurisdiction.

5. The victim may often have the option of a civil suit against the defendant, but there will be no criminal proceeding, with punishment (in contrast to compensation).

2. The Basic Decision — Whether to Charge the Defendant at All

a. Factors Involved

It is extremely unlikely that Hana will decide not to prosecute Dan Dastardly, at least if that crime which the police assert Dastardly committed is a relatively important one, such as bank robbery. But suppose the charge were jaywalking? Shoplifting? Or possession of one marijuana cigarette? Police officers may have incentives — personal advancement or institutional loyalty — to arrest defendants whom even they know will not be prosecuted. But prosecutors have different criteria; for them, each case, even if it ends before trial, may consume significant resources.[6] And big cases will consume big resources — the homicide prosecution of O.J. Simpson, for example, is estimated to have cost the Los Angeles prosecutor's office several million dollars. While few would suggest that murders should not be prosecuted, the hard reality is that the resources used on that single prosecution could have been equally used to prosecute hundreds, perhaps even thousands, of other crimes. One might object that it is not the prosecutor's job to weigh such factors, but to bring every legitimate case, allowing others (judges, juries, etc.) to decide the individual defendant's guilt or innocence, and the social harm done by the crime. Indeed, it is often argued that in other systems, in particular those on the European continent, virtually every crime *is* prosecuted, and that prosecutors do not perceive their job to weigh the kinds of factors listed above. While that conclusion is heatedly debated,[7] the fact is that American prosecutors do see these decisions as a major part of their power, and of their job. Moreover, a system of mandatory prosecutorial charging would dramatically shift more power to the police, who already

---

6. Although the bulk of *crime* occurs in major cities, the overwhelming majority of local prosecutors function in rural communities or small towns. While Los Angeles County had over 600 assistant prosecutors in the 1970s, across the country offices are small — 74 percent of the prosecutors were either performing their duties as "one-person" offices or with less than four assistants. The Prosecutor's Charging Decision: A Policy Perspective (Nat'l Inst. of Law Enforcement and Justice 1 (1977). Moreover, the prosecutor may have limited control over the resources available to her office — 60 percent of the offices surveyed in 1972 received 90 percent or more of their funds from county government. Thus, proposals which envision large offices, with many prosecutors and a sizable hierarchical bureaucracy, may strain most prosecutorial offices. This is surely one reason why the courts — particularly the Supreme Court — have been reluctant to impose restrictive constitutional regulations upon such offices.

7. See, e.g., Goldstein and Marcus, The Myth of Judicial Supervision in Three "Inquisitorial" Systems: France, Italy, and Germany, 87 Yale L.J. 240 (1977).

have the power, at least in nonserious offenses, simply to fail to arrest or charge.

Furthermore, it is at least possible that the legislature purposely "overcriminalizes" the law and underfunds the prosecutor, establishing a "bark and bite" system in which the prosecutor is expected intelligently to exercise discretion. Less cynically, observers beginning with Aristotle have noted that legislatures must enact "universal" statutes, that do not, and cannot, consider potentially important facts of a specific case. Even the most carefully drafted statutes are bound to be not fully determinative when a specific case is weighed. Someone, it is argued, must decide whether the legislature, if apprized of the precise act of which Dan stands accused, would have wanted the prosecution to continue. Discretion, therefore, is essential not only to efficient justice, but to effective justice as well. Once again, the public prosecutor is the repository of that discretion — American notions of "individualized justice" are critical. As Dean Roscoe Pound wrote:

> No legislative omniscience can predict and appoint consequences for the infinite variety of detailed facts which human conduct continually presents . . .[8]

While we tend to think of prosecution of alleged crime as the norm, the data will not support that assumption. Federal prosecutors decline as much as 63 percent of the cases brought to them,[9] perhaps because many federal crimes are also state offenses, and can be prosecuted in state court. While state prosecutors are unlikely to decline as frequently — in part because there is no "other" agency which can prosecute if the state (county) refuses to do so — it is still likely that a substantial percentage of all reported (alleged) crimes are not prosecuted at all.[10] Some of this is undoubtedly due to good lawyering by defense counsel, who act quickly and decisively before the prosecutor is committed to prosecuting.

In the past 20 years or so, many prosecutorial offices have established in-house guidelines for the declination decision. Washington, for example,

---

8. Roscoe Pound, Criminal Justice in America 36 (1945). See also: "Prosecutors are mediators between phenomenally broad legislative pronouncements and the equities of individual cases." Frase, The Decision to File Federal Criminal Charges: A Quantitative Study of Prosecutorial Discretion, 47 U. Chi. L. Rev. 246, 246-247 (1980).

9. See Statement of Assistant Attorney General Phillip Heymann before the Committee on the Judiciary of the United States Senate (April 23, 1980).

10. In 1970, it was estimated that Los Angeles county prosecutors declined 50 percent of all felony arrests. See Donald McIntyre and David Lippman, Prosecutors and Early Disposition of Felony Cases, 56 A.B.A.J. 1154 (1970).

has adopted such guidelines by statute. See Rev. C. of Wash., sec. 9.94A.440(1).[11] Among the factors listed there are:

1. whether the statute is antiquated;
2. whether the violation is de minimus;
3. whether the victim's motives are improper;
4. the request of the victim.

b. Deciding WHETHER to Charge

Using the slight amount of information contained in the original complaint, and whatever information she may glean from discussions with the police, other investigators, the victim, and others, Hana has two decisions to make: (a) *Whether* to charge Dan with a crime at all; and (b) *with what crime* to charge him.

What, then, should a prosecutor consider in deciding whether to prosecute at all? Although many prosecutorial offices do not make their policies public, others have revealed their guidelines. The most common factors given for deciding whether to prosecute include:[12]

- The *kind* of crime. Is it "serious"?
- *Punishment goals:* Will prosecution deter others? Is there a need for retribution? Does this defendant appear dangerous?
- The *severity* of this particular crime. Shoplifting may be relatively "innocuous", but shoplifting the Hope Diamond is (or may be) another matter.
- The *evidence.* Even recognizing that this is an early stage of the investigation, is there sufficient evidence, or the likelihood of obtaining sufficient evidence, not merely to bring the case, but to win it?[13]
- The *individual defendant.* Does this defendant have a criminal record? Is she likely to be "rehabilitated" in a probation setting? Is a prosecution necessary to deter her actions in the future?

---

11. See also California Crime Charging Standards (1996), a relatively dense (53 pages) compilation of standards and commentary on how and when to charge, published by the California District Attorneys Association.

12. For another set of proposals, see ABA Standards Relating to the Prosecution and Defense Function 3-3.9 (1993). However vague and fluid these factors may seem, it should be remembered that it is only within recent decades that these factors have been officially acknowledged by prosecutors at all. Prior to the 1980s, virtually no prosecutor would have published, much less adopted, even a list of such factors.

13. If the evidence *now* is insufficient, the prosecutor has to decide whether to allocate further resources to look for more evidence; if the decision is made to terminate investigation, it is likely that the defendant will never be charged.

- *Alternative, civil paths* available either to the government or the individual victim, such as a tort suit, *qui tam* action, collateral proceedings (such as professional disciplinary sanctions).
- *The possibility of defendant's cooperation* in bringing other actors to justice.

There is a debate as to whether the prosecutor is ethically, or practically, required to consider, either at the initial charging stage or later, evidence negating the defendant's guilt, or raising possible defenses. While some argue that the prosecutor is intended to be an advocate for the state, others argue that failure to take such claims into account are both unethical (because even an accusation can harm a defendant) and wasteful (because if the defendant ultimately prevails, resources will have been unsuccessfully, if not needlessly, expended).[14]

C. Attacking the Decision to Prosecute — The Defendant Without an Immediate Remedy

1. Generally

Defendants who seek to have the charge against them dismissed on the grounds that the prosecution is "unfair" are almost certain to lose. The speeder who concedes he was speeding, but complains that others were going faster than he, even while he was being ticketed, is raising a sterile claim. Unless the prosecution has grossly abused its discretion, courts have consistently held these judgments to be within the total power of the executive and, as a matter of separation of powers,[15] they will not interfere. Even if the improperly charged defendant will be (or is likely to be) acquitted, the defendant will suffer extraordinary financial and emotional costs attendant simply upon a charge being laid — loss of reputation, job, marriage, friends, etc., may all follow once a charge has been made, and not even an acquittal is likely to undo all the damage. Still, judicial review of a decision to prosecute is highly proscribed. In *United States v. Armstrong*, 517 U.S. 456 (1996),

---

14. See, e.g., the California Standards, cited, n.11 *supra*, which argue that "whenever the accused makes a statement that . . . negates criminal liability the statement should be investigated, if possible, no matter how implausible it may seem," but that affirmative defenses are different because "the data necessary to establish them is usually unavailable to the prosecutor at the charging stage." *Id.*, at p.7, 15.

15. This refusal is ironic — from early colonial days until the mid-nineteenth century, the prosecutor was thought to be a judicial, rather than an executive officer.

the Court called the charging decision a "core executive constitutional function." And in *Wayte v. United States*, 470 U.S. 598 (1985), it used these words:

> "the decision to prosecute is particularly ill-suited to judicial review. Such factors as the strength of the case, the prosecution's general deterrence value, the Government's enforcement priorities and the case's relationship to the government's overall enforcement plan are not readily susceptible to the kind of analysis the courts are competent to undertake."

2. *"Selective Enforcement"*

Every decision to prosecute is, in some sense, "selective." But if the selection is "improperly" based, it is subject to some judicial scrutiny. In *Yick Wo v. Hopkins*, 118 U.S. 356 (1886), the Court held that a prosecutor who prosecutes *only* members of a specific ethnic or religious group has violated the equal protection clause. In *Hopkins*, the local government prosecuted only Chinese owners of laundries operating without a permit; the Court found such prosecution unconstitutional. But in the intervening century, such claims have rarely been successful, in part because none of the possible remedies for selective prosecution is particularly palatable. If the Court concludes that the prosecutor has singled out the defendant because of the defendant's gender, religion, race, or political unpopularity, it is faced with the dilemma of either (a) allowing the prosecution to proceed, notwithstanding that the prosecutor was improperly motivated, or (b) preventing the prosecution of a possibly guilty defendant.[16] The latter remedy is not unique to this area: The exclusionary rule, imposed to deter unconstitutional police conduct, may well result in the inability of the prosecutor to convict a clearly guilty defendant.[17]

Dismissing the prosecution is a drastic step, particularly at the stage of the proceedings at which a defendant is likely to raise such a challenge—just

---

16. The court might allow the prosecuting office to appoint an "outside" prosecutor to evaluate the cases against the current defendant and the "other" putative defendants. See *Bragan v. Poindexter*, 249 F.3d 476 (6th Cir. 2001).

17. As suggested earlier, many of these violations are ethically improper, and disciplinary action could be taken against the prosecutor. In *United States v. Wilson*, 149 F.3d 1298 (11th Cir. 1998), the court suggested that trial courts should respond to prosecutorial misconduct by "direct sanctions against an offending prosecutor *individually*," including (1) contempt citations; (2) fines; (3) reprimands; (4) suspension from the court's bar; (5) removal or disqualification from office; and (6) recommendations to bar associations to take disciplinary action. 149 F.3d at 1303. Ironically, however, not even the *Wilson* court was willing to print the name of the prosecutor; indeed, in the vast majority of cases, even where a court finds gross misconduct, the prosecutor is not named.

after the prosecutor has made the charges, or the indictment has been returned. At that point, before the defendant has proffered evidence of innocence, the court is likely to rely heavily on the state's prima facie (or stronger) case of guilt. Moreover, the defendant, for purposes of the motion, must concede his guilt at least arguendo. In attempting to negotiate a balance where a defendant alleges such discrimination, courts have therefore, not surprisingly, established an extremely high barrier. Viewing these challenges as sounding in equal protection ("The prosecution chose me out of the hundreds of alleged violators only because of my [race, religion, etc."]), the decisions apply the usual equal protection calculus, requiring the defendant to show *both*

(1) *discriminatory impact* and
(2) *discriminatory intent*.

The standard of proof which the defendant must carry is described in various ways: "a clear preponderance of the proof," a "reasonable inference of impermissible discrimination," and "convincing evidence." So long as the constitutional standard remains so high, effective judicial oversight over prosecutorial discretion seems unlikely. Most of the litigation has involved defendants seeking discovery of the files of the prosecution, in an attempt to garner sufficient data to allow inferences about either impact or intent. Understandably, courts are reluctant to order the prosecutor to turn over many raw files to the defendant. Thus, if files are to be "discovered," the Court may well have to screen these materials *in camera* first. Leaving aside any concerns about judicial intrusion into executive processes, such screening is very time-consuming.

In *Wayte v. United States*, 470 U.S. 598 (1985), defendant alleged that, of several hundred thousand persons who had not registered for the military draft, the United States prosecuted only those who notified the government of their refusal to register on political grounds. The district court required the Justice Department to open its files to the defendants, to allow them access to the information available to the department, but the Supreme Court reversed, imposing a "rigorous standard for discovery in aid of" a selective prosecution claim. Similarly, in *Armstrong v. United States, supra,* the defendants alleged that federal officials in Los Angeles were prosecuting only black sellers of cocaine. The defendants put forward several newspaper clippings, and an affidavit from a paralegal in a public defender's office supporting this claim. The Supreme Court held that the defendants had failed to proffer sufficient evidence to warrant discovery into the files of the federal prosecutor. There must be, said the Court "a credible showing of different treatment of similarly situated persons."

This, of course, is a Catch 22. An allegation that the prosecution knows of, but is failing to prosecute, members of other groups who are violating the law almost always requires some scrutiny of the prosecutor's files. When courts deny discovery of those files, they are virtually assuring that the defendant will be unable to raise even a prima facie case of selective prosecution.[18]

Even where the defendant can produce some such evidence — in one case, for example, the defendant store hired a private detective to show that other stores were also selling banned items on a Sunday, but were not prosecuted[19] — the burden is extremely high, and only rarely will be sufficient to support the inferences required.

a. Discriminatory Impact

Assuming that he has some facts upon which a claim may be predicated, the defendant must first show that he is the object of (unconstitutional) discrimination. It is insufficient for him to show that Mormons are being prosecuted; he must also demonstrate that other persons with other religious affiliations (a) commit the same crime; and (b) are not being prosecuted or (c) are not being prosecuted to the degree that Mormons are being prosecuted. *Ah Sin v. Wittman*, 198 U.S. 500 (1905).

Thus, prosecuting (usually female) prostitutes, but not their (usually male) customers might not be suspect, because the two groups (prostitutes and customers) are not arguably similarly situated. But a showing that there was no prosecution of male prostitutes might meet the first step, because "prostitutes" are similarly situated. Logically, showing that the two groups — the one to which the prosecuted defendant belongs and the nonprosecuted group — commit similar offenses would seem to be part of the proof of impact, but the courts have usually seen it as a separate criterion the defendant must prove. Thus, unless the defendant can show that there are others violating the statute, he will be unable to succeed, even though he convinces the court that the prosecutor is pursuing (or persecuting) him and other defendants because of race, politics, religion, etc. For example, the inability of the defendants in *Armstrong, supra*, to show that there were other (nonminority) offenders who were not prosecuted was fatal to their claim for discovery.

It will be difficult for defendants (or even the prosecution) to show how many more people are committing the offenses than are arrested and charged, since most crimes are notoriously underreported. But even if the defendant somehow leaps that hurdle, defining those who are "similarly situated" is extremely difficult. Assume, for example, that the defendants are

---

18. "*Armstrong* effectively requires proof of an equal protection violation before a court could allow the defendant to engage in discovery of the prosecution's motive. Such discovery would then be used to establish the equal protection violation." Henning, Prosecutorial Misconduct and Constitutional Remedies, 77 Wash. U. L.Q. 713, 750 (1999).

19. *People v. Utica Daw's Drug Co.*, 16 A.D.2d 12, 225 N.Y.S.2d 128 (App. Div. 1962).

charged with "selling cocaine." Are sellers of other drugs (heroin, crack, marijuana) "similarly situated"? What about "manufacturers" of cocaine? What about persons who sell in larger amounts? Smaller amounts? May defendants who sell primarily to children use statistics relating to those who sell only to adults? Recently, the United States Supreme Court underscored how hard it will be to demonstrate that the defendants are "similarly situated" with another group. In a one page per curiam opinion, the Court rejected an attempt to seek discovery of the files of the Department of Justice based upon allegations that the federal death penalty was invoked against blacks at a disproportionate rate. The Court noted tersely that the allegations had not argued that the aggravating factors in the defendant's group and the control group were similar. *United States v. Bass,* 536 U.S. 862 (2003) ("raw statistics regarding overall charges say nothing about charges brought against *similarly situated defendants*"[20]) (emphasis added).

b. Discriminatory Intent[21]

The second step in proving selective enforcement, also a usual criterion in equal protection cases, requires a defendant to show that this discrimination is *purposeful*—that the state has purposely singled out this "protected" group, and intended to prosecute only its members. See *Oyler v. Boles,* 368 U.S. 448 (1962). If the problems of proof and data are difficult for the first step, this second step is virtually impossible to fulfill. After all, prosecutors are unlikely to announce, even in internal memoranda, that their office will only prosecute Mormons, or women, etc. Instead, as in virtually all cases where mental state is relevant, the party carrying the burden (in this case the defendant) must rely on inferences—that there appears to be no bona fide reason for prosecuting only Mormons and, therefore, the explanation "must" be animus toward Mormons.[22] Statistical evidence comparing the percentage of blacks in the population with the percentage of prosecutions for certain kinds of offenses involving black defendants has been held insufficient because it shows nothing about the number of minority and majority

---

20. See, e.g., *United States v. Tuitt,* 68 F. Supp. 2d 4 (D. Mass. 1999); *United States v. Smith,* 207 F.3d 662 (11th Cir. 2000) (defendants, charged with violating absentee voter laws by having written false information or forged names on an absentee applications were not similarly situated with other, noncharged, persons who merely harassed potential voters, or took pictures of persons voting).

21. See generally, Peter Henning, Prosecutorial Misconduct and Constitutional Remedies, 77 Wash. U. L. Q. 713 (1999).

22. But see *Oregon v. Kennedy,* 456 U.S. 667, 675 (1982): "A standard that examines the intent of the prosecutor, though certainly not free from practical difficulties, is a manageable standard to apply. It merely calls for the court to make a finding of fact. Inferring the existence or nonexistence of intent from objective facts and circumstances is a familiar process in our criminal justice system."

group members who in fact have committed the particular crimes. Moreover, even if those data were available, the defendant would have to show that the prosecutor *knew* about those other possible criminals, and had jurisdiction to prosecute them, before any inference of discriminatory intent could be drawn. Finally, courts may be reluctant to dismiss a prosecutor's nondiscriminatory explanation for what appears to be blatantly obvious bigotry: A judicial finding that the prosecutor *did* intend to discriminate against minority group is likely to severely damage the prosecutor's career for years. While such a result may not be unwarranted for a truly bigoted prosecutor, unless the court is convinced that this was not a momentary aberration, the judge may well accept—with whatever inward reservations—the prosecutor's explanation. Indeed, some might argue that constant probing of a prosecutor's mental state would, in the long run, engender even greater harm in the criminal justice system.

Because proving the actual intent of any actor, whether a criminal defendant, a prosecutor, or a legislative body, is always problematic, courts sometimes employ an objective standard to infer intent. Fourth Amendment analysis employs an objective ("reasonableness") standard (though the police's good faith but misplaced reliance on a warrant may save an unreasonable search).[23] As you go through this book, look for instances in which the courts have either demanded proof of bad intent, or used an objective standard, not dependent on intent. Consider, as well, what would happen if the "intent" requirement in these areas were either objectivized or eliminated. This would not resolve the other question in these cases, however; the barrier of demonstrating that other "similarly situated" persons were not prosecuted because of their (race, gender, etc.), would still be very high.

c. An Alternative View—Judicial Integrity

Critics of the Fourth Amendment jurisprudence of the Supreme Court will recall that in several opinions Justice Brennan, in particular, disagreed with the view that deterring police (mis)conduct was the goal of the exclusionary rule. Instead, he suggested, the rule prevented the courts from indirectly tolerating such misconduct. That view, which, if applied to the area of selective enforcement might eliminate the requirement of demonstrating discriminatory intent, has been embraced by some courts. *See People v. Utica Daws Drug Company*, 16 A.D.2d 12, 225 N.Y.S.2d 128 (App. Div. 1962).

---

23. *United States v. Leon*, 468 U.S. 897 (1984). See generally, Bloom and Brodin, 237-238.

d. Prosecutorial "Defenses" to Selective Enforcement

Virtually no cases have survived the first barriers to discovery and, therefore, to proof. But even if a criminal defendant successfully cleared those hurdles, prosecutors would raise a number of plausible explanations for the "proved" discrimination. Even invidious discrimination may be warranted. Thus, for example, if only *young* speeders were being prosecuted, the prosecutor might argue that statistical evidence demonstrates that young speeders are more dangerous, or more common, than older speeders. Or that *white* CEOs of companies with more than $5 billion in assets are more visible than other inside traders, and therefore more likely to be deterred than other such criminals. Or that *female* prostitutes were more likely to engage in street solicitation, while male prostitutes were more likely to be employed by agencies, which would require greater expenditure of funds to ferret out. While some of these arguments may be more plausible than others, given the general deference which courts have given to prosecutors in overviewing their charging practices generally, it might be expected that most of these explanations would be accepted without stringent oversight. (We will reach this same problem several times in this course; see especially Chapter 8, discussing *Batson v. Kentucky* and peremptory challenges.) Indeed, the federal prosecutors in *Armstrong* might argue that they were prosecuting only (or disproportionately) black crack dealers because (a) the state was handing over crack dealers because of the harsher penalties in federal court; (b) while any crack user is obviously hurt, the injury caused to young blacks (the majority of customers of black dealers) was, on the whole, more socially devastating. Indeed, federal prosecutors might have pointed out that the ratio of white to blacks among federal drug prisoners is about 3-2, while the ratio among state and local drug prisoners is closer to 2-3.

This is not to say that the selective prosecution claim has never been successful. In *People v. Walker*, 14 N.Y.2d 901 200 N.E.2d 779 (1964), a landlord who had concededly violated certain housing regulations was allowed to show that, of all such violators, she was singled out for prosecution of housing code violations because she had exposed corrupt practices in the Department of Buildings. In *People v. Utica Daw's Drug Co., supra*, the court allowed the defendant to argue that, of all stores selling certain banned items on Sundays, only it was being prosecuted. And in *United States v. Steele*, 461 F.2d 1148 (9th Cir. 1972), the defendant prevailed when he showed that all four persons prosecuted for refusing to answer questions on the census form were members of the census resistance movement.

3. Vindictive Prosecution

The second exception to the general rule that courts will not monitor charging decisions occurs when the defendant alleges that the prosecutor has selected a specific charge out of a sense of vindictiveness. The initial case on vindictiveness involved a defendant who successfully appealed a conviction and was sentenced, on reconviction, to a harsher term for the same crime. The court there applied a rebuttable presumption that the harsher sentence was imposed because the judge was irked that he had been reversed. That rebuttable presumption was later applied to an instance where the defendant, having been convicted in a lower court, invoked his right to a de novo trial in a higher court, only to be prosecuted for a higher charge.[24] In *United States v. Goodwin*, 457 U.S. 358 (1982), the Court declined to impose a presumption of vindictiveness in pre-trial prosecutorial actions, declaring:

> There is good reason to be cautious before adopting an inflexible presumption of prosecutorial vindictiveness in a pre-trial setting. In the course of preparing a case for trial, the prosecutor may uncover additional information that suggests a basis for further prosecution or he simply may come to realize that information possessed by the State has a broader significance. At this stage of the proceedings, the prosecutor's assessment of the proper extent of prosecution may not have crystallized. In contrast, once a trial begins, and certainly by the time a conviction has been obtained, it is much more likely that the State has discovered and assessed all of the information against an accused and has made a determination, on the basis of that information, of the extent to which he should be prosecuted. Thus, a change in the charging decision made after an initial trial is completed is much more likely to be improperly motivated than is a pre-trial decision . . . the timing of the prosecutor's action in this case suggests that a presumption of vindictiveness is not warranted. A prosecutor should remain free before trial to exercise the broad discretion entrusted to him to determine the extent of the societal interest in prosecution. An initial decision should not freeze future conduct. . . . To presume that every case is complete at the time an initial charge is filed, however, is to presume that every prosecutor is infallible, an assumption that would ignore the practical restraints imposed by often limited prosecutorial resources.

Intriguingly, where a defendant argues that he is being *vindictively* prosecuted, the courts use an objective, rather than a subjective, standard to assess whether the prosecutor's motives were vindictive.

---

24. *Blackledge v. Perry*, 417 U.S. 21 (1974). *Blackledge* seemed to apply a *per se* rule that all such higher charges were absolutely precluded. However, in *Goodwin*, the Court interpreted *Blackledge* as having established only a presumption, and it has been read that way ever since.

D. Deciding *Not* to Prosecute

1. *The Victim without a Remedy*

If Hana decides to prosecute Dan, that decision will be reviewed by many others in the course of the criminal process — the grand jury, the presiding judge, and ultimately the petit jury. But a decision *not* to prosecute is not reviewable, even for an abuse of discretion — as a result of the separation of powers doctrine, courts will not review a decision not to prosecute. Courts believe that prosecutorial judgments as to the weight of the evidence, the need for deterrence, the allocation of executive resource, etc., are virtually beyond the power of the judiciary to assess.

Declining to provide some review against unreasoned declination of prosecution is hard to rationalize. Prosecutors may decide not to prosecute domestic violence or date rape cases not because they are difficult to win, but because they believe this to be a private matter, or because they think the law is wrong. They may not bring murder prosecutions against members of mobs that lynch minority victims because they empathize with the lynching. In such situations, the prosecutor is not "really" using discretion to protect the (entire) public's interest; to preclude any judicial (or other) review seems anomalous. Thirty years ago, the National Advisory Commission on Criminal Justice Standards and Goals recommended judicial review of decisions not to prosecute, but that has not come to fruition.

Again, the problem is discerning the "real" reason for nonprosecution. Many of the cases mentioned above, for example, are extremely difficult to prove. Witnesses (and victims) recant their testimony in domestic abuse cases; the paper trail on stock market transactions may be incredibly slippery; prosecutors may argue that local juries will acquit lynchers, and that public funds should not be expended in futility. Some states provide for the appointment of a special prosecutor when the local prosecutor has declined to proceed. Thus, Pennsylvania allows a disenchanted victim to ask a court to appoint a special prosecutor for that case. Pa. Stat. Title 16, §1409.[25] See, generally, Annot., 84 A.L.R.3d 29 (1978). In the aftermath of Watergate, concern that prosecutors might not pursue defendants within the federal executive branch, or who were politically well situated, led to the creation of an "Independent Counsel" law, by which a specially appointed federal prosecutor would investigate allegations of criminal action on the part of members of the federal executive. By the late 1990s, however,

---

25. See also Rev. Code Wash §10.27.170-190; Mich. Rev. Stat. 767.41; Neb. Rev. Stat. §29-1606.

Congress decided that this system, too, had its flaws, and failed to renew the legislation.[26]

Once the defendant has been indicted, however, the situation is arguably different. A number of jurisdictions provide, either legislatively or by court rule, for judicial review of a prosecutorial motion to *nol pros* (cease a prosecution) but courts are exceptionally deferential to the executive's decision, and will overrule only if it appears that the government is seeking an advantage over the defendant. Rule 48(a) of the Federal Rules of Criminal Procedure, for example, calls for granting of a motion to dismiss unless the motion is clearly contrary to the public interest. See *State ex rel. Unnamed Petitioners v. Connors*, 136 Wis. 2d 118, 401 N.W.2d 782 (1987), holding unconstitutional a statute allowing a judge to permit the filing of a private complaint after the prosecutor declines to prosecute; *People v. Municipal Court*, 27 Cal. App. 3d 193, 103 Cal. Rptr. 645 (App. Cal. 2 Dist. 1972) (same); *Landis v. Farish*, 674 P. 2d 957 (Colo. 1984) (narrowly construing Colo. Rev. Stat. sec. 16-5-209).

Judicial reluctance to allow or provide any oversight of prosecutorial discretion not to charge has led many to argue for a victims' bill of rights, included in which would be the victim's right, in one way or another, to proceed in some way even if the prosecutor declines the case. Moreover, some states have sought to mandate prosecution of certain crimes—among them domestic abuse,[27] drunken driving, possession of firearms—but in virtually all instances prosecutors (often with the help and instigation of defense counsel) have found ways to avoid these mandates. Many continental systems allow persons unhappy about a decision not to charge to obtain internal office review by a prosecutor's superior.[28] See Comment, 65

---

26. In *Young v. United States ex rel. Vuitton et Fils S.A.*, 481 U.S. 787 (1987) the Supreme Court, in a supervisory power opinion, held that district courts have the authority to appoint a private attorney to prosecute a criminal contempt case, but should do so only as a last resort. It is not clear, however, whether *Young* is restricted to contempt cases, in which the appointment serves to protect the judiciary (not a private victim) against a possible overturning of a contempt citation. Moreover, Justice Blackmun, in a lone concurrence, would have held that appointing an interested party's counsel to prosecute for criminal contempt is a violation of due process. Several state courts have so held. See *State v. Harrington*, 534 S.W.2d 44 (Mo. 1976); *Cantrell v. Virginia*, 329 S.E.2d 22 (Va. 1985), and *People v. Benoit*, 575 N.Y.S.2d 750 (N.Y. Crim. Ct. 1991). See also *Biemel v. State*, 37 N.W. 244 (Wis. 1888).

27. E.g., Florida Stat. sec. 741.2901; Wisconsin Stat. sec. 968.075 (both "encouraging" prosecution in such cases).

28. In Japan, an 11 person committee, serving for six months and consisting of lay citizens, reviews all decisions not to prosecute. Eight votes are necessary to override a prosecutor's decision to suspend prosecution. See Castberg, *supra* n.2, at 61. West, Prosecution Review Commissions: Japan's Answer to the Problem of Prosecutorial Discretion, 92 Colum. L. Rev. 684 (1992).

Yale L.J. 209, 233 (1955). In many of these systems, however, prosecutors generally remain on the job for a lifetime, and are expressly trained, even in law school, for such positions.

Where the prosecutor *wants* the assistance of the private party, the courts are likely to be more agreeable to private participation. Indeed, many states provide for private assistance, *so long as* the prosecutor still "controls" the proceedings. See, e.g., Tenn. Code Ann. sec. 8-7-401. See also *State v. Boykin*, 298 N.C. 687, 259 S.E.2d 883 (1979) (private prosecutor in a capital case). On the other hand, in *People v. Eubanks*, 14 Cal. 4th 580, 59 Cal. Rptr. 2d 200, 927 P.2d 310 (1996), a corporation charged that several of its employees had conducted industrial espionage against it. The prosecution claimed that the case would take months to investigate and prepare, and that none of its lawyers were sufficiently proficient in computer crime to successfully try the case. The corporation offered to pay these expenses, and to provide computer experts to train the prosecutorial staff, or even to provide computer-trained lawyers to try the case. The California Supreme Court held that the prosecutor's office was barred from accepting such assistance, because private prosecution, or even possible private influence of the decision to prosecute, violated the state constitution.

Of course, the individual victim may seek damages in a typical civil proceeding, for tort or breach of contract. In some instances, a *qui tam* action will be available, in which the victim sues for himself as well as for the state. But the *qui tam* is a civil action, subject to specific statutory limitations. In some instances, if the state "takes over" the *qui tam* action, the plaintiff is entitled to a specified portion of whatever civil damages the government obtains.

2. *Agreeing Not to Prosecute — Waiver of Civil Claims*

When Dan was arrested, the police "trashed" his car, and then his apartment, causing thousands of dollars of damage. Whereupon Dan filed a civil suit against the police. The prosecutor thereafter agreed not to prosecute Dan's peccadillos, if he would sign a written agreement not to pursue his civil rights claim. If Dan agrees, can he later claim the agreement was coerced and proceed with his civil suit? And can the prosecutor thereafter revivify the criminal charges?

Most courts, recognizing that prosecutors want to discourage civil suits, even if they are otherwise valid, because they require resources to defend, or because they might chill the police in effectuating an arrest or search, have upheld such agreements not to prosecute. In *Town of Newton v. Rumery*, 480 U.S. 386 (1987), the First Circuit had held all such agreements invalid, but the Supreme Court reversed, holding that at least some such agreements would be valid, assuming it could be shown that they were truly voluntary. The balance is a tenuous one: If the police have violated Dan's rights, those rights should be vindicated, even if Dan is a scumbag robber. On the other hand, if Dan wants to waive his rights, both constitutional and civil, there is no *a priori* reason to preclude him from doing so. Moreover, in most instances whether the police violated Dan's rights will be murky at best, and would require a substantial trial. If we trust prosecutors not to abuse their power, there is no obvious reason for denying them this specific application, even if it is somewhat distasteful.

E. The Decision to Prosecute: *WHAT* to Charge

Once a prosecutor has decided to proceed against a defendant, there is still the all-important question as to what crimes should be charged. The prosecutor is not bound by the charge contained in the original police complaint—information gleaned from a number of sources may tell her that the police were either over (or under) aggressive in their assessment of the facts as she now understands them to be. This judgment must be made *de novo*.

In some instances, which we explore in Chapter 9, the Double Jeopardy Clause, or rules as to aggregation and severance might compel, or at least strongly induce, particular charges. Thus, if Eloise is found with 10 bags of heroin, each containing 1 gram, she might be charged with 10 possessions of one gram each, or with one possession of 10 grams. Similarly, she might be charged with possession with intent to distribute (particularly if the amount is aggregated), as well as attempted sale (depending on how the jurisdiction defines attempt). As we will see later, constraints on punishment and on sentencing might make the charging decision relatively straightforward.

But many decisions are more complex. Even a simple robbery of a convenience store might confront the prosecution with various possible charges: (1) robbery; (2) armed robbery; (3) possession of a gun; (4) possession of a gun while committing a felony; (5) possession of a gun by an ex-felon; (6) theft of the getaway car; (7) etc., etc., etc. Again keeping in mind that the facts known about the case are likely to change from day to day and that the initial charge will affect at least the bail decision, if not others, how should the prosecutor select the "initial" charge?

The situation is even more complicated if the defendant has committed a series of acts, each of which might be prosecuted, or some of which might be declined. Finally, prosecutors are often afforded the luxury of choosing between two statutes that punish the same offense but with different penalties. In *State v. Tanya Caskey*, 539 N.W.2d 176 (Iowa 1995), for example, defendant's behavior could have been charged as either an aggravated misdemeanor or a Class C felony. Convicted of the latter crime, she appealed on the ground that she should have been prosecuted for the lesser offense, but to no avail— the level of charge, said the court, was solely in the hands of the prosecutor. There are no federal constitutional prohibitions in such a statutory scheme. See *United States v. Batchelder*, 442 U.S. 114 (1979).

As one might suspect, courts have been loathe to overview charging decisions for much the same reasons they give for not overseeing the prosecution decision itself. If there are any "guides," they tend to be found in statements promulgated by prosecutorial offices themselves. Typical is that of the United States Attorney's Manual, which provides that the attorney should charge "the most serious offense that is consistent with the nature of the defendant's conduct and that is likely to result in a sustainable conviction."

These criteria are perhaps unavoidably vague. After all, if discretion is to remain discretion, particularly since the facts upon which they are based may be altered daily, even other prosecutors must rely on the good judgment of the person actually involved in the decision. But other questions can be raised. For example: Why should the highest, and not the lowest, possible crime be charged? A significant charge will almost certainly affect the amount of bail (or of the severity of conditions of release), possibly leading to the continued confinement of the defendant. On the other hand, if the guideline adopted the lowest possible crime as the criterion, we might release a defendant who is a true flight risk, since he fears the greater charge will occur at some time.

Fifty years ago, any such guidelines would have been tightly held, and there is good reason to believe that not even these guidelines constitute "all" the culture of the prosecutor's office.[29] Moreover, every published set of guidelines expressly declares that it does not create "rights" for defendants, and courts have uniformly upheld such statements. Even with all these caveats, however, the mere fact that such guidelines are now public reflects a major change in prosecutorial perspective.[30]

Just as clear are the court holdings that the decision to prosecute in one jurisdiction, rather than another, based primarily, if not exclusively, on the punishments available is beyond judicial review. *Hutcherson v. United States*, 345 F.2d 964 (D.C. Cir. 1965). A(n) (in)famous example occurred in New York City, where then United States Attorney Rudolph Guilliani proclaimed that on "federal" day, chosen randomly once a week, many drug offenders arrested by state or city police would be prosecuted in the federal system, which had much harsher penalties than the state system. Although this was

---

29. In 1982, the Department of Justice refused to disclose *to Congress* its strategy for prosecuting persons who failed to register for the draft, lest disclosure affect the behavior of potential nonregistrants.

30. Complete skeptics will argue that these guidelines are intended merely to placate public (and defense attorney) clamor, and bear no resemblance to real life.

never challenged in litigation, even assuming that the challenge survived the usual litany about prosecutorial discretion, a general deterrence rationale would clearly support such a policy.

CAVEAT: Remember that a decision *to* prosecute, and the level of the charges, are in theory reviewable by both the grand jury (see Chapter 4) and the trial jury (see Chapter 8). The primary issue here is whether a defendant must bear the difficulties involved in preparing for, and going through, a trial before having the validity of the prosecutorial decision assessed.

F. Pre-Trial Diversion

Probably since the beginning of time, prosecutors who did not wish to prosecute, but were loathe to simply release the defendant, found informal ways of assuring that the defendant provided restitution to the victim, sought rehabilitative help, performed community service, etc. Such "pre-trial diversion" programs have now become institutionalized.[31] Defendants who meet criteria defined by statute or court rule (usually limited to first offenders and excluding at least some kinds of serious felonies) may avoid trial for a "test period" in the community, but on a number of conditions, such as those above. Success may result in sealing, or total erasure, of the charge and Dan's criminal record. Although many critics were concerned that prosecutors would use pre-trial diversion programs to bring into the system defendants they would previously have declined to prosecute there is little evidence of this. In 1998 less than 5 percent of all felony defendants were placed in diversion programs of any kind. Bureau of Justice Statistic Felony Defendants in Large Urban Counties, 1998 p.24 (2001).

Suppose, however, that while Dan meets the basic criteria of the program, Hana either refuses to recommend such placement, or actively argues against it? Consistent with the deference shown prosecutors, courts refuse to overrule prosecutorial refusal to seek or allow such placement. In at least one state, however, where the pre-trial program was established by the judiciary pursuant to its rule-making power, the courts have been far more willing to reverse a prosecutorial decision not to permit such placement. See *State v. Caliguiri,* 158 N.J. 28 726 A.2d 912 (1999).

EXAMPLES

1. Marsha, the prosecuting attorney in Los Angeles County, receives a phone call from the Police Captain in Precinct 9 that Winona, a famous

---

31. For a recommended statutory scheme for diversion, see Model Pre-Arraignment Code §§320.5-320.9.

movie actress, has been arrested on suspicion of shoplifting in a well-known luxury department store. The captain says that the store indicates there is a surveillance tape, but no one has seen it yet. The police report indicates that the manager says she had $5000 worth of merchandise under her coat. State law divides the felony of larceny into two "degrees" (petit and grand), depending on the value of the goods involved: The dividing line is $1,000. Shoplifting is defined by state law as removing any item of sale from a store without paying for it; shoplifting is a misdemeanor. Burglary is defined by state law as entering (without breaking) any building with the intent to commit a felony therein. (a) Should Marsha prosecute Winona at all? (b) If so, on what charge(s) should she seek an indictment? (c) Can Winona successfully challenge this prosecution on selective enforcement grounds?

2. You are the chief prosecutor in Shropshire County. Dennis Rogers, the Dean of Shropshire Law School, has just called to tell you that the school's disciplinary committee has suspended Roscoe Pound, a student at the school, for becoming involved in a physical encounter with another student over ownership of a criminal procedure casebook. Pound broke the other student's hand. Rogers declares that it is the law school's policy to inform the prosecutor's office whenever a student is officially sanctioned for conduct that could be considered criminal. Pound has compensated the injured student, and covered all medical fees, and has agreed to work pro bono in the local small business tax program. Rogers is sure that a criminal conviction would make Pound unable to pass the Character Committee's criterion, and Pound would therefore be unable to take the bar examination. He urges you not to prosecute Pound. What should you do?

3. As the federal prosecutor in the case of Dr. Lee (see example 3, Chapter 2, p.22), you have received a motion to discover the Department of Justice files on a claim of discriminatory prosecution. The defendants bolster their claim by arguing that (1) Dr. Lee is the *only* person ever charged for mishandling government materials that had not been formally classified; (2) Numerous people who have transgressed similar regulations relating to high security documents have been internally sanctioned or not sanctioned at all including: (a) a CIA director who used an unsecured personal computer to access top secret files; (b) an employee who removed "highly sensitive details and gave other sensitive information to the Japanese"; (c) others who mishandled secret documents; (3) A former counterintelligence official who participated in the investigation of Dr. Lee declares, in an affidavit, that Dr. Lee was targeted because he was "ethnic Chinese"; (4) A posting to the Los Alamos Employees Forum by one of its employees charges that he personally observed that the Department of Energy engaged in racial profiling of Asian Americans at Los Alamos during these investigations. How would you respond?

4.   Assume that you have been retained by one of the executives involved in any of the securities and accounting fraud scandals which became public in the early 2000s. One of the charges is insider trading. You note that all of the defendants, like your client, have been white, male, and over 50. What is the likelihood that you could successfully bring a claim of selective discrimination? What evidence would you look for before even making such a claim?

5.   Police arrested Roderigo, who was clearly intoxicated, driving his car at 2:30 A.M., half a mile from the Memorial Hospital. Roderigo was bleeding badly, and told the officers that he had been assaulted in the parking lot of the Nearby Inn, by three men. He had crawled to his car and was on his way to the hospital. You are the prosecutor. Do you charge Roderigo with driving under the influence? What facts might you wish to determine even before charging him?

6.   George Skoler, age 45, was dying from cancer when he robbed the First National Bank, in an attempt to obtain funds to support his children before his death. The penalty for robbery is 5-20 years. As defense counsel, what arguments do you make to the prosecutor about the possible charges?

EXPLANATIONS

1.   (a) Marsha might well not prosecute Winona, allowing the store to settle the matter civilly. But there are other considerations:

(1) The fact that the press may know of the story might lead Marsha to fear that, if she did not bring charges, there would be allegations that her office "coddled" celebrities. Marsha *could* see that as undermining respect both for her office and for criminal law generally.

(2) While the fact that this case could generate a great deal of publicity and thereby enhance Marsha's career is obviously unacceptable as a basis for decision, it is certainly permissible for Marsha to consider that publicity might be seen as a deterrent to anyone thinking about committing this kind of crime. See, e.g., *Moog Industries, Inc. v. FTC*, 355 U.S. 411 (1958). Indeed, in a very similar, real case, critics argued that if the defendant had been poor, she would not have been prosecuted, and therefore argued selective enforcement. But that misses the major point here — prosecutors often selectively enforce cases that are likely to give a "big bang" for the resources used: "singling out" a notorious defendant might well be justified precisely on the grounds of that defendant's notoriety.

(3) The possibility of a tape suggests that this case could be easily won — otherwise, it might be difficult to prove intent, a critical factor in the larceny charges. Marsha hasn't seen the tape yet, but she should get her hands on it posthaste.

(b) Marsha is considering a larceny charge (grand or petit), two possible shoplifting charges, or a burglary charge. The shoplifting seems obvious, whether or not there is a surveillance tape. Winona's (likely) claim that she intended to pay for the items before she left the store, but simply forgot, would be more plausible if the items were in a shopping bag. On the other hand, attempting to prove that Winona entered the store with the intent to take the items may be very difficult, unless she has a past record for such acts. It will be easy for her to assert that she simply "got carried away." At this point, Marsha could follow the advice in the federal prosecutor's manual, and charge the burglary, or she could now bring the lesser crimes, hoping that further investigation (remember that charging doesn't end the game) would allow her to prove the pre-existing intent. Bringing the higher charge now, if it later turned out that there was no such proof so that the charge would have to be dropped, might be more embarrassing. On the other hand, as we will see in the double jeopardy chapter, Marsha may want to consider that if Winona quickly offers to plead to the shoplifting, and Marsha agrees, Marsha may later be barred from charging burglary, even if there is strong proof of intent. One more point — the hypo leaves purposely unstated what the item was. Consider the difference between a small diamond earring and a substantial-size belt. Even if the values were the same, would the ease of hiding the item be relevant to the likelihood of conviction?

(c) Winona will surely not win this. Aside from the fact that "celebrities" are not a suspect class, the prosecutor, if forced to explain the decision to charge, could use Winona's very celebrity against her, as indicated above.

2.   Dean Rogers has really put it to you. The evidence is fairly convincing that Pound committed an assault; there is certainly "probable cause" to believe this, and a conviction is likely. But the conviction will have severe consequences for Pound. Those aren't criminal consequences, and it's not punishment (see Singer and Lafond, Criminal Law Examples and Explanations, Chapter 2, for a discussion of why not all suffering is punishment). But did the legislature really expect such assaults to be prosecuted, when the results would be so enduring? On the other hand, would you hesitate to prosecute a nonlawyer (to-be) under the same circumstances? Can you really consider the "collateral consequences" of Pound's conviction? Should the law tolerate such consideration? And why should your weighing of those factors be any more important than other persons — such as the victim, or the jury? Does Pound's willingness to make restitution persuade you? Or is it simply an attempt to avoid prosecution? Did any of your legal training give you greater ability to make these kinds of moral and ethical decisions? Should you even be making them? Why didn't you go to medical school, as your parents wanted?

In short, there is no "law" here. And even if this prosecutor's office has issued guidelines, they are unlikely to help answer the question in the specific factual setting which this, or any other individual case, presents. A guideline which cautions against "unnecessarily harsh" results, for example, must be interpreted to determine whether that caution includes noncriminal results, such as Pound's possible loss of a livelihood as a lawyer.

3. Things don't look so good, do they? The government doesn't really want to counter with affidavits rebutting the inferences and conclusions drawn by Lee's supporters that would raise an issue of fact and implicitly concede the need for discovery. The best approach is not to attack the veracity of these statements, but to suggest that Dr. Lee is unique — that while the statutory (and administrative) charges against him may use the same words as used in dealing with other employees, no one else has allegedly stolen "the crown jewels" (see the example in Chapter 2). Even if the terms used by defendant ("secret documents," "top secret files," etc.) were accurate — the materials stolen (and possibly given to the Chinese) were much more critical to national security. Thus, while admitting the surface similarity of the charges, you would want to provide the court with distinguishing underlying facts. In the actual case, the trial judge found that Lee had established a *prima facie* case, and ordered discovery. Two weeks later, the government reached a plea agreement with Dr. Lee, dismissing all but one count, and agreeing to time served (in solitary confinement).

4. Don't even try. The only possible arguments here would deal with equal protection and "suspect" or "quasi suspect" classes — gender and race. In order to make even a prima facie case of discrimination, you must show that there are "similarly situated" persons of the other (race, gender) committing the same offenses but who are not being prosecuted. That, of course will be hard to do; most executives of these firms were, in fact, white males. You might be able to point to Martha Stewart, but she *was* prosecuted, (but not for insider trading). Perhaps you could make the case that she was guilty of insider trading, but how would you get the facts to show that? Perhaps from the SEC proceedings, which were not criminal. It is highly unlikely that you could even meet the first hurdle. But assuming that you did, you would still have to show that the prosecutor did not pursue Stewart, but did pursue your client (and others like him) *because* they were male. Finally, if you succeeded in both those ventures, the prosecutor would argue that since most CEOs are white males, prosecuting your client and others like him is more likely to deter those CEOs than if blacks or females were prosecuted. Indeed, a prescient prosecutor might even suggest that to prosecute too many black or female CEOs, might lull the white males into thinking they were less likely to be prosecuted.

5. The New Jersey prosecutor in this case did. *State v. Romano*, 355 N.J. Super. 21, 809 A.2d 158 (App. Div. 2002). The real issue here is whether a prosecutor should ever consider not prosecuting a defendant who is clearly guilty, and on what basis that decision might be predicated. If you believe, as American prosecutors and courts clearly do, that prosecutors have discretion not to charge even clearly guilty defendants, you might want to know whether Roderigo could have gone back into the bar (and if he could have, why he did not—e.g., whether he was afraid of the customers there). You might also check whether Roderigo has a history of drunk driving. In the real case, the facts were actually more extreme: The defendant was arrested only two-three hundred feet outside the parking lot. His conviction was reversed on appeal, because the trial court did not consider the possibility of the defense of necessity.

6. Obviously, for George this prison sentence—indeed any prison sentence—will mean that he will never live with his family again. You could state it more dramatically—"the five-year sentence is a death sentence"—and the legislature didn't establish death as the penalty. On the other hand (a) he committed a serious crime; (b) any prisoner might die in prison. Should terminally ill people be given a "pass" on such factors? You know that a failure to prosecute will not be judicially reviewable; but the prosecutor would like to be a judge someday. Perhaps you should suggest that she charge George with a crime which does not carry a mandatory minimum, and hope that the judge would take that avenue. Indeed you might even urge the prosecutor to press that approach sentence upon the court. We will revisit these issues in Chapter 11 on sentencing.

4

The Grand Jury: Gathering Information and Overseeing the Prosecutor's Charging

"Historically, (the grand jury) has been regarded as a primary security to the innocent against hasty, malicious and oppressive persecution . . . standing between the accuser and the accused . . . to determine whether a charge is founded upon reason or was dictated by an intimidating power or by malice and personal ill will."

Wood v. Georgia, 370 U.S. 375 (1962)

"The grand jury would indict a sandwich."

Courthouse lore

A. Introduction

The grand jury has an estimable history. The early Norman conquerors of England, who had no local law enforcement agencies, simply asked the local citizenry (1) what crimes had occurred and (2) who had committed them. This body, known as the presentment jury, provided the King's agents with facts about local crime and criminals. Thus began our grand jury.

The framers of the Constitution perceived the grand jury not only as an investigative institution, but as protecting a citizen against an overzealous king. In a famous incident involving John Peter Zenger, a newspaper editor whose prosecution generated much of the heat for rebellion, three separate colonial grand juries refused to indict Zenger.[1] The framers believed that the grand jury, consisting of ordinary citizens, would protect the freedom of citizens from an overreaching (and arguably politically motivated) prosecutor. Thus, the Fifth Amendment of the Constitution guarantees that:

> No person shall be held to answer for a . . . crime, unless on a presentment or indictment of a grand jury.

The Supreme Court has held that this part of the amendment does not apply to the states. *Hurtado v. California*, 110 U.S. 516 (1884).[2] Nevertheless, at least eighteen state constitutions[3] and the federal system, require Hana to bring the case to a grand jury. If that body finds probable cause to believe Dan committed a crime, it will charge him with that crime in an *indictment* (sometime referred to as a true bill).

Although the grand jury is convened by a judge at the request of a prosecutor, once it begins to sit, it is, in theory, totally independent of each. The prosecutor is deemed to be only a "legal advisor" to the grand jury, not entitled to be present at its deliberations, and no judge is present at any time.

---

1. The king then proceeded by information (see Chapter 5), but the petit jury refused to convict. See Chapter 8.

2. During the nineteenth century, few western states were able to establish sitting grand juries, in part because of the distances they would have to cover. The Court's decision in *Hurtado* might be seen as recognizing that reality. Moreover, although California actually provided a preliminary examination, the *Hurtado* court did not focus on that point in determining that the failure to provide a grand jury did not violate the Fifth Amendment. Although both *Lem Woon v. Oregon*, 229 U.S. 586 (1913), and *Hurtado* were decided long before the current interpretations of due process and selective incorporation were established, the Supreme Court has shown no desire to revisit those issues. Thus, as a federal constitutional matter, no state *must* provide the defendant with any hearing, before any private or public tribunal, before trial. Most states have chosen to provide one or the other kind of proceeding.

3. Nineteen states appear to require grand juries in every felony; in a few additional states, a grand jury indictment is required in capital cases only.

Most grand juries are today selected in the same manner as jury wheels. There is no constitutionally required method of selecting those who will serve on the grand jury; the only requirement is that the process not discriminate against a specific "cognizable" or "protected" group. As of 1990, thirty-one states provided for some form of "random selection," while nineteen states adhered to a much older process known as the "key man" system, in which judges, or jury commissioners, personally selected members of the grand jury. Despite much outside criticism, the key man system has been consistently referred to (in dictum) as constitutionally adequate. See, e.g., *Turner v. Fouche*, 396 U.S. 346 (1970). The process remains to this day. In *State v. Dilosa*, 848 So. 2d 546 (La. 2003), the Louisiana Supreme Court overturned the key man system in Orleans Parish (in which New Orleans is located)—the one parish in which it remained—but on state, not federal, constitutional grounds. Although it may vary, the usual number of grand jurors is twenty-three—of which a majority is 12—a number that continues to have its magical powers. See Chapter 8. Because the Sixth Amendment applies to "criminal proceedings," which begin with an indictment, it does not govern the grand jury. Challenges to the composition of the grand jury, therefore, are based on equal protection grounds, and hence are effectively limited to racial, ethnic, and gender discrimination.

B. The Grand Jury as an Investigative Body

In most "street" crimes, arrest precedes investigation, and the investigation is primarily conducted by police. In contrast, however, are complicated criminal offenses in which it may be very difficult to determine whether a crime has been committed at all, much less who committed it. (Can you say "Enron"?) It is easy to determine that a bank robbery has occurred, but how can Hana ascertain whether a bank customer who claims to have lost $3,000 over five years has been the victim of a computer mistake, or an embezzling bank teller? Here, investigation, sometimes taking years, must precede arrest and charge. Usually that investigation will be managed by the grand jury.

1. Subpoena Power

Originally, grand jurors were selected because they knew everything that went on in their small vicinage. In a metropolis, however, that is no longer possible. Today, grand jurors rely almost exclusively on prosecutors, who themselves rely on police, possible victims, and a few others, to bring to them at least the hints of a crime. To further explore this evidence, however, grand juries are now armed with incredibly broad subpoena power, allowing them to investigate virtually anyone, anywhere, to determine whether a crime has been committed. The common phrase is that the grand jury is entitled "to every man's evidence." Although these subpoenas are signed by a judge, the judge's signature is pro forma: The grand jury is an independent body whose investigation may be impeded by no official, including a judge. In *R. Enterprises, Inc. v. United States*, 498 U.S. 292 (1991), the Supreme Court essentially held that a grand jury's investigative powers were unlimited:

> (T)he grand jury . . . can investigate merely on suspicion that the law is being violated, or even just because it wants assurance that it is not. . . . The function of the grand jury is to inquire into all information that might possibly bear on its investigation until it has identified an offense or has satisfied itself that none has occurred. . . . A grand jury investigation is not fully carried out until every available clue has been run down and all witnesses examined in every proper way to find if a crime has been committed.

Given this breadth, said the Court, a subpoena will stand "unless the district court determines that there is no reasonable possibility that the category of materials the Government seeks will produce information relevant to the general subject of the grand jury's investigation."[4]

Because a subpoena is issued by a grand jury through a court, it is much more powerful than other investigatory techniques. Dan must answer or plead a relevant privilege. If he pleads a relevant privilege then, as discussed below, he may receive immunity; if he has no privilege, he must either provide the information requested or be found in contempt of court (which he may then appeal).

2. Secrecy of Grand Jury Proceedings

The grand jury's sweeping subpoena power is permissible in large part because the proceedings in the grand jury are entitled to absolute confidentiality. Any person divulging any information given to the grand jury is subject to contempt of court — except that a witness appearing before the grand jury may disclose what questions the grand jury asked her. Readers may remember the swell of accusations that the office of the prosecutor guiding the grand jury that was investigating President Clinton "leaked" aspects of grand jury testimony.

The bounds of secrecy are rigorously observed. In *United States v. Sells Engineering, Inc.*, 463 U.S. 418 (1983), the United States Supreme Court held

---

4. We will not discuss here the Fifth Amendment questions raised when a subpoena is used to obtain individual or corporate files; suffice to say that there is much law — and some confusion — as to the limits of the subpoena power here, but that resistance to a subpoena is unlikely to be successful.

that, under the Federal Rules of Criminal Procedure, a United States Attorney involved in a criminal investigation could not provide grand jury evidence to another U.S. Attorney, involved in a civil proceeding against the same defendant, unless a court approved. This requires the construction, within the prosecutor's office, of a "firewall" around the grand jury's testimony.[5]

The secrecy of grand jury records does not cease once the criminal case has ended. Even then, any person seeking those records must show a "particularized need" that outweighs the interest in continued grand jury secrecy. *Douglas Oil Co. of California v. Petrol Stops Northwest*, 441 U.S. 211 (1979).

Nor may the grand jurors disclose, even after the term has ended, what occurred during those proceedings. *In re Special Grand Jury 89-2*, 2004 U.S. Dist. LEXIS 3942 (D. Colo.), former members of a grand jury sought permission to release information and freedom to speak publicly about what they had learned about the (mis)operation of a facility which manufactured plutonium and nuclear bombs. The Court dismissed the petition, holding that the "adjudicat(ion) and balanc(ing) the competing interests of grand jury secrecy and the interests of the petitioners in public disclosure" was a political question, and that any decision would be advisory only.

a. Conferring Immunity

One of the hotly debated powers of the grand jury, exercised through a judicial order to a witness which requires him to testify, grants that witness immunity from (some) criminal prosecution. This immunity overrides the witness's Fifth Amendment rights against self-incrimination, and the witness must testify or be held in contempt of court. Generally, immunity is either "*use*" or "*transactional*." The former prevents any prosecutor, in any jurisdiction, from using the testimony of the immunized witness, or anything derived from that testimony, against the witness in a later proceeding. Transactional immunity, however, forbids any later prosecution based upon any information, whether related to the testimony or not.

Use immunity is subject to the "independent discovery" exception. If the prosecutor can demonstrate that a later prosecution is not tainted by any evidence given, or even influenced, by the evidence obtained as a result of the immunity grant, the prosecution may proceed. However, courts have been extremely rigorous in restraining this exception, establishing a "heavy

---

5. A "firewall" seeks to assure that no one working on (a) a civil complaint against Smith (for example, a civil tax claim); (b) another criminal case involving Smith learns of what has transpired at a grand jury proceeding. More recently, a federal appeals court held that disclosure to another federal district pursuing a criminal prosecution against the same defendant was not covered by *Sells*. Impounded, 277 F.3d 407 (3d Cir. 2002).

burden" which the prosecutor must carry by "clear and convincing evidence" that the evidence has not been tainted by the immunized testimony. In one of the most notorious of these instances, Congress had granted immunity to Oliver North, a marine major who worked for the National Security Council, who then testified before Congress concerning criminal events involving NSC shipments of weapons to "freedom fighters." Prior to North's testimony, prosecutors sealed the evidence they intended to use against him in a later criminal proceeding, but his conviction was reversed because the prosecution could not show that witnesses against him at the trial had not heard, or been influenced by, his Congressional testimony. *North v. United States*, 910 F.2d 843 (D.C. Cir. 1990).

Transactional immunity is much broader. Even if the government *has* independent evidence against the witness, it is still barred from prosecuting him. In the typical classroom example, even if the government, prior to John's testimony, had a video tape of John committing the crime, if John has been given transactional immunity, he is free from prosecution.

Of course, whether any immunity shall be granted and if so, what kind, is usually the subject of heated debate between the prosecutor and the witness's counsel. Until *Kastigar v. United States*, 406 U.S. 472 (1972), it was believed that the Fifth Amendment required all immunity to be "transactional," but *Kastigar* held that only "use" immunity was constitutionally required.

b. "Pocket" Immunity

Immunity conferred pursuant to statute by a court subsequent to a grand jury request should be distinguished from so-called "pocket immunity." In the former instance, the Court is ordering the defendant to waive her Fifth Amendment rights; such an order is binding everywhere in the United States, and no other prosecutor, state or federal, may use any information obtained pursuant to such a grant. "Pocket immunity," on the other hand, occurs when the prosecutor, on her own, agrees not to prosecute the witness for any crimes to which he may admit during his testimony. This form of immunity, not sanctioned by a court, is really only a variation of prosecutorial discretion not to prosecute, and binds no one other than the individual prosecutor's office.

c. "Runaway" Investigative Grand Juries

As a practical matter, members of the grand jury are unlikely to know whom to investigate, and rely heavily upon the prosecutor to decide whom, and what papers, to subpoena. Thus, while the prosecutor is theoretically merely a "legal adviser" to the grand jury, in fact she provides the evidence, as well as the names of targets, subjects, and witnesses, to whom subpoenas should be directed. On occasion, however, sparked by information obtained from these sources, grand jurors may seek to go beyond the parameters which the prosecutor has set. When this occurs, the pejorative term "runaway" grand jury is employed, although in fact and theory, the grand jury is merely carrying out its basic task — to ferret out crime and bring the criminals to justice.

A famous example of a "runaway" grand jury involved President Richard Nixon. When the grand jury hearing evidence about the Watergate break-in sought to indict Mr. Nixon as a co-conspirator, Special Counsel Leon Jaworski had to persuade them against this, apparently arguing that to do so would unleash years of litigation over whether a sitting president could be indicted. Ultimately the grand jury was persuaded, and named Mr. Nixon as an unindicted co-conspirator.

Another example occurred in the Rocky Flats Nuclear Weapons Plant in Colorado. In 1989, after the facility had been operating for nearly 40 years, FBI and EPA investigators conducted several raids on the facility. A grand jury was convened, which returned indictments against several individuals, and also prepared a report excoriating those who managed the place, but the prosecutor refused to sign the indictments, and the court would not release the report. Much litigation ensued to disclose the reports and other information, but in 2004, a district court refused to allow the former grand jury members to disclose any such information.[6]

d. Evidence in the Grand Jury

Because the investigative power, particularly the subpoena, is so broad, grand juries obtain much information that would be inadmissible at a trial — hearsay, improperly seized evidence, possibly even coerced confessions. The Supreme Court has held that, as a constitutional matter, grand juries may rely on such information. *Costello v. United States*, 350 U.S. 359 (1956); *United States v. Calandra*, 414 U.S. 338 (1974).[7] Moreover, since it is controlled by the prosecutor, the grand jury is likely to hear only evidence that demonstrates that a crime has occurred and that the soon-to-be defendant ("target") committed it. There is no constitutional requirement that

---

6. *In Re Special Grand Jury 89-2*, 2004 U.S. Dist. Lexis 3942 (D. Colo.). See L. Ackland, Making a Real Killing: Rocky Flats and the Nuclear West (2d ed. 2002).

7. *Calandra* was explained by pointing out that the purpose of the exclusionary rule (deterrence of police conduct) would not be enhanced by precluding the use of evidence at the grand jury stage. This explanation is, at best, problematic, since police know that few cases actually get to trial. To the extent, therefore, that the evidence can be used to obtain an indictment to which the defendant might plead, police might be encouraged to obtain "illegal" evidence.

the prosecutor provide the grand jury with any information favorable to the defendant. *Williams v. United States*, 504 U.S. 36 (1992). The American Bar Association Rule 3-3.6 (b) provides that "No prosecutor should knowingly fail to disclose to the grand jury evidence which tends to negate guilt or mitigate the offense." Some states follow the *Williams* rule; others apply a narrower version of the ABA approach.[8]

Thus, in *State v. Gaughran*, 260 N.J. Super. 283 (Law Div. 1992), the alleged victim in a sexual assault case testified before the grand jury that the assault had lasted 90 minutes. The assistant prosecutor did not present to the grand jury, medical examination results that demonstrated no evidence of any physical or sexual assault. Applying a test that requires disclosure only if the evidence both is "clearly exculpatory" and "directly negates guilt," the *Gaughran* court dismissed the indictment. Only a few states have a rule that is more broadly articulated, such as requiring the presentation of all evidence which is "favorable" to the defendant. Although prosecutors may chafe at the concern that failure to provide the grand jury with "exculpatory" information may generate litigation at some later point, the fact is that the standard which the courts have set, however articulated,[9] has generally been so high that few decisions have actually invalidated an indictment because the prosecutor failed to disclose information to the grand jury.

e. Inapplicability of the Sixth Amendment

The Sixth Amendment, by its terms, only applies to "criminal proceedings." Thus, none of the protections guaranteed by that amendment apply to grand jury proceedings, because the criminal process does not begin until after the grand jury has completed its work. *United States v. Mandujano*, 425 U.S. 564 (1976). Thus, the defendant is not entitled to be present to confront witnesses against him, nor to present evidence to the grand jury,

---

8. See Annot., Duty of Prosecutor to Present Exculpatory Evidence to State Grand Jury, 49 A.L.R. 5th 639 (1997).

9. For example, New Mexico requires that prosecutors must present evidence that "directly negates the guilt of the accused" (N.M. Stat. Ann. Sec. 31-6-11(B)). Similarly worded tests require presentation of evidence "substantially favorable to the accused" (*Lipscomb v. States*, 700 P.2d 1298 (Alaska App. 1985)); or which is "clearly exculpatory" (*State v. Coconino County Superior Court*, 139 Ariz. 422, 678 P.2d 1386 (1984)); or which " might reasonably be expected to lead the grand jury not to indict" (*Miles v. United States*, 483 A.2d 649 (D.C. 1984)) or "would materially affect grand jury proceedings" (*State v. Moore*, 438 N.W.2d 101 (Minn. 1989)); or which "implicates a complete legal defense or could eliminate needless or unfounded prosecution" or which "directly negates guilt and is clearly exculpatory" (*New Jersey v. Hogan*, 144 N.J. 216, 676 A.2d 533 (1996)).

nor to have counsel present at the grand jury proceedings. Indeed, when a witness is interrogated by the grand jury, his counsel must wait outside the grand jury door, and the witness must request permission to consult with counsel (often after every question) before he may leave the room. Only those protections afforded by the "due process" clause of the Fifth Amendment apply; as seen below, they are minimal indeed.

C. The Grand Jury as a Screening Device

Once it has obtained the information it (or the prosecutor) thinks important, the grand jury has three options: (1) it may issue a "presentment"; (2) it may indict persons it believes have committed crimes; (3) it may refuse to indict any person. Whichever of these steps it takes, the grand jury, in this view, is essentially screening the prosecutor's decision to charge specific defendants with specific crimes.

1. Presentments

A **presentment** is essentially a report, and while it may name persons the grand jury thinks have committed crimes, it does not officially "charge" them with the crime, and leaves that to other institutions. At common law, the "presentment function was at least as important as the indictment; and its inclusion in the Constitution shows its significance to the framers." Lettow, Reviving Federal Grand Jury Presentments, 103 Yale L.J. 1333 (1994). Indeed, colonial grand juries "had become multipurpose administrative bodies in a frontier culture. They were monitoring public officials, administering public affairs themselves, and even initiating legislative policy." Wright, Why Not Administrative Grand Juries?, 44 Admin. L. Rev. 465, 468 (1992). Today, however, grand juries issue few presentments, in part because naming persons as having committed crimes, without actually charging them so that they may respond in court, is extraordinarily harmful.

2. Indictments

In most instances, the grand jury does charge someone with a crime; this charging document is known as an *indictment*. It is, for most practical purposes, a presentment which has been signed by the prosecutor and filed in court.

Although "(b)y the time of the United States Constitution, the grand jury had evolved to its purest form: A citizen's tribunal set resolutely between the state and the individual,"[10] the grand jury is now portrayed by many as a "rubber stamp" of the prosecutor. In 1984, federal grand juries indicted defendants in 99.6 percent of the cases brought to them by the prosecutor.[11] Of course, prosecutors may be screening the cases before they are brought to the grand jury, but most observers attribute this high indictment rate to several factors: (1) the secrecy of grand jury proceedings; (2) the evidence they obtain and the absence of any countervailing voice;[12] (3) the low level of proof needed for an indictment; (4) the refusal of many courts to oversee the actions of prosecutors in grand jury proceedings.

The grand jury should indict a defendant if it finds that there is *probable cause* to believe that a crime has been committed by the named defendant. This standard, which uses the same words but is slightly different from the one used in assessing police searches and seizures,[13] is seen as very low, and as requiring only a bare minimum of evidence of a crime connected to the defendant. This is not necessarily surprising. From the prosecutor's viewpoint, the point of the indictment is to (1) obtain custody over the defendant and possibly deny him bail; (2) begin the process which will

---

10. Justice Mosk, in *Johnson v. Superior Court of San Joaquin County*, 15 Cal. 3d 248, 539 P.2d 792 (1975).

11. Beall, Note, What Do You Do with a Runaway Grand Jury? A Discussion of the Problems and Possibilities Opened Up by the Rocky Flats Grand Jury Investigation, 71 S. Cal. L. Rev. 617, 631 (1998).

12. As noted above, prosecutors are the "legal advisers" to the grand jury. They thereby dominate the grand jury, usually "suggesting" whom to subpoena, whom to indict, and for what. They also provide instructions to the grand jury on the law. One of the most (in)famous instances in which prosecutorial instructions were challenged was the case of the subway shooter, Bernhard Goetz, *People v. Goetz*, 68 N.Y.2d 96, 497 N.E.2d 41 (N.Y. 1986). Goetz argued that the prosecutor's instructions on self-defense were unduly restrictive. That argument went all the way to the New York Court of Appeals, which delivered a very important opinion on self-defense, although Goetz was ultimately acquitted by the petit jury of all those counts. Hawaii, in an attempt to overcome the dominance of the prosecutor, has actually provided in section 11 of Article I of its Constitution for a nonprosecutorial counsel to the grand jury to give it legal advice.

13. Many argue that the "probable cause" needed to indict (or file an information, see the next chapter) should be "greater" than that needed to authorize an arrest. This is particularly so, when the arrest is made on the spot, without any opportunity for police to coolly to assess facts. The common hypothetical is that the police may have "probable cause" to arrest two defendants, only one of whom committed the crime, rather than having to choose to release one on the street. When the issue, however, is whether the prosecution should proceed, and the state has been unable to obtain further proof against either, the balance might then swing against the state. Contrarily, however, few would contend that "probable cause" means "preponderance of the evidence." As we have said frequently already, the process of investigation of crime is a continuing one; the possibility of finding new evidence should not be forgotten. Perhaps a test of "*prima facie* cases," where possible defenses are not considered, could fill the gap, and a few, but only a few courts have adopted this approach.

culminate in trial, where the defendant will have counsel and the rules of evidence (as well as other protections) to challenge the charge. From the defendant's perspective, however, the standard is far too low—as one court put it, a wrongful presentment (or indictment):

> ". . . is no laughing matter. Often it works a grievous irreparable injury to the person indicted. The stigma cannot be easily erased. In the public mind, the blot on a man's escutcheon, resulting from such a public accusation of wrong doing is seldom wiped out by a subsequent judgment of not guilty. Frequently the public remembers the accusation, and still suspects guilt, even after an acquittal."

> *In re Freid*, 161 F. 2d 453 , 458-9 (2d Cir. 1947)
> (Frank, J., concurring)

Courts are reluctant to review grand jury processes. In part, this reticence is institutional in nature. Because the grand jury is neither a court, nor a prosecutor, courts view their power to supervise either the grand jury or the prosecutor as exceptionally limited. Thus, in *Williams v. United States*, 504 U.S. 36 (1992), the trial court dismissed an indictment because the prosecutor had failed to present exculpatory evidence to the grand jury. The Tenth Circuit Court of Appeals affirmed, but the Supreme Court reversed, declaring that the grand jury "belongs to no branch of the institutional government," and finding that the trial court had no authority to create a rule requiring presentation of such evidence.[14] In so holding, the Court disavowed any supervisory power over grand jury proceedings, at least in the absence of a previously established rule of criminal procedure, or constitutionally prohibited conduct by the prosecutor. Since there are few such rules, *Williams* has been seen as granting the prosecutor virtually carte blanche in her conduct before the grand jury.

Courts also hesitate to oversee grand jury processes because they fear (1) that creating too many rules would turn the process into a "mini-trial," and (2) that allowing challenges to grand jury processes will delay the adjudicatory process.

In *United States v. Mechanik*, 475 U.S. 66 (1986), the Court held that a petit jury conviction rendered harmless virtually any error committed by the prosecutor in grand jury proceedings (in *Mechanik*, it was allowing two witnesses to testify in tandem, in violation of the Federal Rules of Criminal Procedure[15]). A year later, in *Bank of Nova Scotia v. United States*, 487 U.S. 250 (1988) it held that even a pre-trial challenge to errors in the grand jury

---

14. Remember that a number of state courts *have* established such a requirement, although the standard is an exceptionally high one.

15. Other "errors" might include leaks of materials before the grand jury, (unknowingly) presenting false evidence, operating under a conflict of interest and misinforming witnesses that they could not reveal to others the substance of their own testimony.

was insufficient to warrant dismissal of the indictment, absent clear evidence that the error "substantially influenced" the grand jury. *Mechanik* may actually induce trial courts to delay acting on motions involving alleged misconduct in the grand jury room, because either a conviction or acquittal will effectively render the motion moot. The combined holdings of *Mechanik* and *Nova Scotia* essentially insulate from judicial oversight most prosecutorial misconduct in the grand jury. The only likely successful path to invalidating an indictment now lies in an attack on the composition of the grand jury itself under the equal protection clause. All other challengers need not apply.[16]

Disciplinary action against the prosecutor for ethical violations, of course, would still be available, but since defendants would not obtain the benefit of a finding of prosecutorial abuse, only the rare defendant would pursue the matter. In two recent statutes, Congress has sought to provide some "noncriminal" oversight of overzealous prosecutors. The Hyde Amendment to 18 U.S.C. §3006A provides that a "prevailing party" in a criminal prosecution may seek recovery of expenses, including attorneys' fees, if the indictment was "vexatious, frivolous, or in bad faith." The McDade Act, 28 U.S.C. §530B, requires federal prosecutors to comply with the ethics rules of the state bar in which the federal district is located. The emphasis here is on rules governing *ex parte* interviews of witnesses and possible targets. Both provisions seek to control "improper" prosecutorial conduct without directly interfering with the grand jury or other investigative functions. See Henning, Prosecutorial Misconduct in Grand Jury Investigations, 51 S. Car. L. Rev. 1 (1999).

The reluctance to encourage challenges to an indictment is understandable. Overturning a conviction and requiring a new trial seems an excessive remedy, even if the grand jury's reaction was taken in response to intentional prosecutorial error. *United States v. Hasting*, 461 U.S. 499 (1983). Overturning the conviction and disallowing a new trial would seem even more excessive. Even pre-trial relief may seem both futile and disproportionate, since in most instances the prosecutor will simply reindict the defendant (assuming the statute of limitations has not run). But this "realistic" view means that there is essentially nothing to deter overzealous prosecutors from abusing the grand jury process.

In several jurisdictions, courts parse both grand jury instructions and prosecutorial behavior. In *State v. Sivo*, 341 N.J. Super 302, 775 A.2d 227 (2000), for example, the grand jurors several times requested that the prosecutor bring

---

16. Prior to *Mechanik*, many federal courts had expressly invoked their supervisory power to regulate grand jury investigations. See, e.g., *United States v. Serubo*, 604 F.2d 807 (3d Cir. 1979) declaring that "the federal courts have an institutional interest, independent of their concern for the rights of the particular defendant, in preserving and protecting the appearance and the reality of fair practice before the grand jury."

in evidence relating to "higher up" defendants. When the prosecutor assured them he would do so later, but then failed to carry out that promise, the trial court invalidated the indictments (against "low-level" personnel) that the grand jury did issue. While that judgment was overturned on appeal even the appellate court recognized the power of courts to discipline prosecutorial misbehavior by throwing out indictments.

The real dilemma in reviewing grand jury proceedings is that grand juries perform two different functions: (1) investigation; (2) accusation. The need for secrecy, which then engenders the exclusion of defendant and defense counsel, as well as other limitations, really ends when the investigation ends. If, at that point, the grand jury process became public, many of the problems discussed in this chapter might be alleviated. That view is explored in the next chapter.

England, the birthplace of the grand jury, abolished it in 1933. And in 1973, the National Advisory Commission on Criminal Justice Standards and Goals recommended that states do the same thing. Because the provision is part of our Constitution, however, abolition is unlikely at the federal level. Instead, critics of the current grand jury have sought to alter its perceived shortcomings. Thus, some states now provide that defendants may testify before the grand jury. While a sympathetic defendant might persuade the grand jury not to indict, most defense counsel advise against appearing before the grand jury (particularly since defense counsel still may not have a right to be in the room) because the testimony is sworn and could later be used to impeach the defendant, should there be a trial, and should he testify. Similarly, a strong minority now permits defense counsel to be present at her client's testimony (but not to object to questions, nor to present evidence). Essentially, this provides a form of discovery; where the state's discovery rules are relatively narrow (see Chapter 6), this discovery may be helpful.

EXAMPLES

1. Your client, Belinda, has just received a subpoena requiring her to appear before the grand jury in one week. What do you do?

2. Billy Ray and Jimmy Bob were arrested in Billy Ray's car. The police found 500 grams of cocaine under the front seat. Billy Ray has sent the prosecutor, from jail, a notarized letter stating that the cocaine was his and only his, and that Jimmy Bob was unaware of the drugs. Must she disclose this letter to the grand jury? Should she?

3. During the grand jury proceedings, Sam, the prosecutor, called three separate witnesses to the alleged crime, each of whom testified that the defendant (1) warned witnesses not to say anything to the police until the defendant's lawyer arrived; (2) refused to speak to the police before his lawyer arrived, even though he was not under arrest. Moreover, the prosecutor referred to this silence during his legal advice to the grand

jury. He further told them that they could draw an inference about the defendant's guilt from his silence. Can the defendant successfully challenge the indictment on the basis of such conduct ?

4. Kim, a prosecutor, has presented photo arrays to six witnesses, three of whom identified the defendant, two of whom were unable to identify any of the persons, and one of whom expressly declared that the defendant was not the person he saw. She also has (a) the rap sheet of a witness who identifies the defendant as the perpetrator; (b) a police report that there was extremely poor visibility that evening. Which, if any of these pieces of information, must Kim present to the grand jury?

5. Called as a witness before the grand jury, and appearing without counsel, George, Nick's best buddy, responds, in an answer to a question from the grand jury foreman, "I gave Nick the gun, but I told him it wasn't really the best weapon to use in a bank robbery." The prosecutor thereupon indicts George as a co-conspirator and facilitator. If George attacks the indictment because he was not given Miranda warnings before his answer, what result?

6. You represent Reynaldo, who has been indicted for mail fraud. You learn that his former secretary, Frank, has been subpoenaed by the grand jury. You are concerned that Frank will provide more information, under oath, against Reynaldo. He may also provide subpoenaed papers which the prosecutor would be able to obtain under the state discovery rules. What can you do, and will you be successful?

EXPLANATION

1. Pick up the phone and call the prosecutor. You need to know whether the prosecutor merely wants to talk to Belinda as a witness, or whether Belinda is a "target" (possible defendant) of the investigation. If so, you will want to schedule a "pre-appearance" conference with the prosecutor. If Belinda has any information at all which is relevant to the investigation, you will negotiate for immunity. Transactional is better, but use immunity is a good start. Note that the granting of immunity usually benefits persons of relatively low status within an organization (criminal or otherwise), because organizational crimes require substantial investigation before charges can be brought against anyone.

2. This example is based upon *United States v. Short*, 777 F. Supp. 40 (D.D.C. 1991). In many jurisdictions, this would not even pose a problem, since they refuse to impose any duty on the prosecutor to disclose any information to the grand jury. But even in those jurisdictions that do require some disclosure, the issue is complicated. In *Short* itself, the court dismissed the indictment because the co-defendant's letter, which it characterized as "substantial exculpatory evidence" had

not been presented to the grand jury. The opposite result was reached in *State v. Evans*, 3527, N.J. Super 178, 799 A.2d 708 (N.J. Super. Law Div. 2001). Although the New Jersey Supreme Court had held in an earlier decision, that "clearly exculpatory" materials must be presented to the grand jury, the trial court in *Evans* determined that the letter did not meet that standard. Thus, there are two questions — one legal and the other ethical — which the prosecutor must face. As a legal matter, and assuming that there is no controlling authority in your jurisdiction, the fact that two courts, employing tests using virtually the same words, have reached different results, would seem to protect a decision not to disclose the letter to the grand jury. Moreover, as we will see in Chapter 6, whether the letter would be discoverable after indictment might be a relevant consideration. The *Evans* court was also concerned that deciding credibility factors would "require the grand jurors to engage in . . . extensive weighing of factors . . . that . . . would . . . transform it from an accusative to an adjudicative body." Furthermore, the grand jury might disbelieve the letter, and it was therefore not "clearly" exculpatory. But if the grand jury might — even most likely will — reach that conclusion, what is the harm to the prosecutor's case of presenting the letter? The ethical question, however, is harder.

3. This is (possibly) a trick question. The first issue is whether the prosecutor has violated any rule, constitutional or otherwise. While such a comment would clearly violate constitutional limits if done at trial, the Court has indicated doubts whether those rules apply at the grand jury level. See *United States v. Hasting*, 461 U.S. 499 (1983), where the Court assumed that this would be constitutionally impermissible, but concluded that the misconduct would be subject to the harmless error rule (see Chapter 12). Moreover, even if a prosecutor cannot comment at trial on defendant's silence, courts that allow grand juries to consider evidence which cannot be admitted at trial would almost certainly find no "prejudicial" error in the prosecutor's actions here.

The second question is whether, even assuming a violation of rule or constitution, there is any remedy for any possible violation. Here, the answer might depend on whether the challenge occurs before or after conviction. As the text indicates, the *Mechanik* court held that a conviction essentially negates any error that occurred in the grand jury, at least unless the defendant can demonstrate "prejudice." *Bank of Nova Scotia* seems to carry this stance to a pre-trial challenge as well. The only "prejudice" which might have occurred here is the indictment itself. For example, no witness was "locked into" testimony which might be used at trial (since that evidence could not be admitted at trial).

4. The general rule is that the prosecutor need not present any potentially exculpatory evidence to the grand jury. However, in a number of states,

various standards are used to require such disclosure. In cases involving at least some of these issues, a New Jersey court, using a standard that required disclosure only if the evidence "negated guilt" and was also "clearly exculpatory," held that failure to disclose contrary identifications did not violate that standard. *State v. Cook*, 330 N.J. Super. 395, 750 A.2d 91 (2000). While much of the evidence in question might go to impeaching the witnesses (and hence might be discoverable before trial — see Chapter 6), it is unlikely that even states requiring presentation to the grand jury of favorable evidence would find any (reversible) error if Kim keeps all this information in her file during the grand jury procedures.

5. Surprise. This is a frequently litigated question, and the answer is mixed. As a matter of constitutional law, George is (probably) not entitled to Miranda (or similar) warnings, because he is not in custody (and he could have refused to answer on Fifth Amendment grounds). See e.g., *Mandujano v. United States*, 425 U.S. 564 (1976); *United States v. Wong*, 431 U.S. 174 (1977). Many states, however, require such a warning at least as to "targets" of an investigation, but as a matter of judicial decision or statute. On the facts given here, it is not clear whether George was a "target" before the grand juror asked the question; if not, fewer states would require a warning.

6. If this were post-trial, *Mechanik* would probably preclude any complaint at all. Even so, you are unlikely to be successful in preventing Frank's appearance, or his production of the records. The "black letter" is that once Reynaldo has been indicted, the prosecutor cannot use the grand jury as an investigative body. But courts have generally looked to the prosecutor's intent in determining whether the prosecutor is abusing the grand jury's powers. If the investigation is ongoing, the fact that Frank may provide some further information against Reynaldo will probably be insufficient to stop the process. If, however, the court concludes that the prosecutor's only reason for calling Frank is to obtain information which Frank could otherwise now refuse to provide, the Court may be sympathetic. See *United States v. Dardi*, 330 F.2d 316 (2d Cir. 1964). Some courts require that the defendant also show prejudice. See *United States v. Sellaro*, 514 F.2d 114 (8th Cir. 1973).

5

Alternatives to the Grand Jury: Informations and Preliminary Hearings

Once Hana has decided to prosecute Dan, and on what charges, that decision must become formalized, and Dan must be notified, so that he (and his attorney) can begin to prepare for trial. Grand juries are required in 19 states. But in the others, Hana can proceed:

1. by *information* and/ or
2. through a *preliminary hearing* which will result in a "*binding over*."

A. "Information"

In a small minority of jurisdictions, Hana need only file with the appropriate court an "*information*" — a piece of paper which simply recites (some of) the evidence (information) against Dan, and the charges. The information will be forwarded to Dan, and criminal proceedings will begin. This procedure, allowing the state to proceed against Dan without any intervening review of the prosecutor's charging decision, has been upheld against a constitutional challenge.[1] When the prosecution files an information, many states require a more formal procedure — the *preliminary hearing.*

B. Preliminary Hearing

In slightly more than 20 states, Hana must ask for a *preliminary hearing,* before a judicial officer, to determine whether there is *probable cause* to believe, based upon the evidence provided by Hana, that Dan has committed a crime (usually, but not always, the precise crime Hana has sought to charge). *CAVEAT*: This is *not* the same question posed at the *Gerstein v. Pugh* hearing (see Chapter 2) — there, the question was whether, under the Fourth Amendment seizure clause, the police at the time of arrest had sufficient evidence to seize him. Here, the question is whether, in light of the accumulated evidence, there is reason to proceed with the criminal prosecution. To the extent that it goes beyond setting bail and apprizing the defendant of the charges the police have raised, the initial hearing looks backward to the arrest; in contrast, the preliminary hearing looks forward to the possible trial.

Preliminary hearings are conducted by an impartial judicial officer (usually a magistrate, although some magistrates need not be lawyers). Most critically, this is an adversary proceeding. Defendant is present. Although the Supreme Court has held that the confrontation clause of the Sixth Amendment does not apply at a preliminary hearing, *Goldsby v. United States,* 160 U.S. 70 (1895), the Court has also held that, as a matter of due process, if counsel is present, she should be able to perform lawyerlike acts, such as: (a) cross-examining state's witnesses; (b) presenting evidence on behalf of the defendant; and (c) "marshaling" the evidence in an attempt to persuade the magistrate not to allow an information to be filed. *Coleman v. Alabama,* 399 U.S. 1 (1970). The degree to which any of these roles is allowed, however, varies among jurisdictions, and the extent of cross-examination is limited to substantive matters. When the magistrate believes the questions are primarily for discovery, she may stop the questioning. Some states appear to apply the rules of evidence, but in the vast majority, nonadmissible evidence may be introduced by the prosecution, while a few states require a "residuum" of probative (admissible) evidence upon which the fact finder may rely.

---

1. *Lem Woon v. Oregon,* 229 U.S. 586 (1913) (murder charge could be instituted by prosecutor filing a complaint). See *Gerstein v. Pugh,* 420 U.S. 1203 (1975) (affirming, in dictum, the rule of *Lem Woon*).

Defense counsel rarely expects to "win" a preliminary hearing[2] — the standard of probable cause is seen as too low, and defense counsel is often unwilling to disclose any defenses he may have, thus making it difficult for the magistrate to determine the validity, for example, of a possible alibi. Defense counsel, however, may try to use the preliminary hearing as a discovery tool.[3] In using this tool, however, defense counsel must be careful. On the one hand, examining a witness for the prosecution may provide information or ammunition for impeachment, should that witness testify at trial. The United States Supreme Court has held, on several occasions, that a witness's testimony may be admitted at the trial, if the witness thereafter becomes unavailable, so long as defense counsel has a meaningful opportunity to cross-examine a witness, whether or not cross-examination occurred. *California v. Green*, 399 U.S. 149(1970); *Ohio v. Roberts*, 448 U.S. 56 (1980). On the other hand, attorneys on both sides are aware that a witness who repeats a story, particularly under cross-examination, may become more entrenched with that view than if there had been no such examination. Thus, heatedly challenging an eye witness's testimony at the preliminary hearing may "lock in" that witness to what otherwise might have been a weak identification. While defense counsel must consider these concerns, he must also remember that over 90 percent of all cases do not get to trial (see Chapter 7).

Since the purpose of a preliminary hearing is to determine whether there is probable cause to proceed against the defendant, if a grand jury has indicted the defendant, a preliminary hearing is deemed unnecessary. Thus, where the grand jury has conducted the investigation and issued an indictment (and arrest warrant) before the defendant was arrested, there will be no preliminary hearing.[4] Prosecutors who wish to avoid a preliminary hearing may move to a grand jury before a preliminary hearing may be held, thereby mooting the preliminary hearing. *State v. Edmonson*, 743 P.2d 459, 113 Idaho 230 (1987). In some instances, the prosecutor's purpose may be to protect the victim (for example, in a sexual assault case, to avoid requiring frequent public testimony) or other legitimate purposes (to reduce the number of hearings necessary to proceed against several linked defendants). But often the prosecutor may simply wish to preclude even the minimal amount of discovery the defense might glean. Because a prosecutor

---

2. Percentage of dismissals range from 2 to 30 percent, but many of the dismissals at the high end probably occur in jurisdictions where prosecutors do little screening before bringing cases to such a hearing.

3. Readers may remember the prosecutions of both Kobe Bryant and Scott Peterson, in which each defendant obtained a lengthy preliminary hearing, and defense counsel ostensibly learned much information about the prosecution's case.

4. A few states require an adversary preliminary hearing even after a grand jury. See, e.g., *People v. Duncan*, 388 Mich. 489, 201 N.W.2d 629 (1972); *State v. Freeland*, 295 Or. 367, 667 P.2d 509 (Ore. 1983).

can always convene a grand jury, the decision whether to have a public or private hearing at which the defendant's rights are so dramatically different is purely within the prosecutor's discretion.

Although the following chart does not consider specific states or jurisdictions, it does outline the pertinent differences between grand jury and preliminary hearing processes as a general matter.

Table 5.1

	Grand jury	*Preliminary Hearing*
Evidence	Can be only hearsay	Similar, but often requires residuum of admissible evidence
Does D have right to be present?	No	Yes
Does D have right to present witnesses?	No	Yes
Does D have right to testify?	No	Yes
Right to counsel in room?	No	Yes
Right to appointed counsel?	No	Yes
Right to cross-examination?	No	Yes
Right to transcript?	No[5]	Yes
Presiding officer	Prosecutor; foreman	Magistrate; judicial officer of some sort
Standard of proof	Probable cause	Probable cause

Given these benefits, defendants would prefer a preliminary hearing, if only as a method of discovery. Prosecutors would prefer a grand jury. This often results in a "race to the courthouse," which is usually won by the prosecutor. Moreover, defendants frequently waive a preliminary hearing either because (a) they may be able to obtain the information through discovery processes; (b) they do not wish to provide any hint as to their "defense"; or (c) the expense, both financial and tactical (prosecutors may reward defendants who waive preliminary hearings by offering more attractive plea bargains). (See Chapter 7.)

EXAMPLES

1.   You are the public defender in Claritin County. Your client, Bill, was arrested yesterday (Wednesday) for bank robbery. You are about to appear at his *Gerstein v. Pugh* hearing. You know that the grand jury

---

5. An increasing number of states provide transcripts of grand jury testimony, including prosecutorial instructions to the grand jury and to an indicted defendant. None of these, or other changes, has been held to be constitutionally required, however, and the federal system continues to provide for no pre-trial disclosure, nor defendant participation, as a right, even as a matter of criminal rule. (See Chapter 6.)

meets only on Tuesdays. Besides seeking Bill's release (on his own recognizance or bail), what other motions will you make?

2. You represent Esmerelda, whom Eager Beaver, the prosecutor, charged with conspiring to sell amphetamines. After a preliminary hearing, at which the defendant testified, the magistrate dismissed the complaint. Thereafter, Beaver presented the same facts to the grand jury, but did not inform them of either (1) Esmerelda's testimony at the hearing; or (2) the results of the hearing. You learned of these events three days before trial. What will you do, and what are your chances of success?

3. Eduardo is charged with the second degree murder of Ramon. At a preliminary hearing, defense counsel asks an eyewitness to the shooting in question whether she heard Ramon threaten Eduardo with death. The prosecution objects. How should the magistrate rule?

EXPLANATIONS

1. You should certainly move for an immediate preliminary hearing to be held no later than next Monday. If the prosecutor seeks a continuance (as she is likely to do), be prepared with arguments — both practical and legal — against it. You may wish to suggest that the prosecutor is seeking to deprive the defendant of his right to a public hearing. But be careful. As we will keep reminding ourselves throughout this book, your relationship with the prosecutor is a continuing one, even in this case, and you don't want to antagonize someone with whom you will be dealing for the next few months. And — just in case your motion is denied — you should move (at least verbally and preferably with papers) for whatever discovery the jurisdiction allows. (See Chapter 6.)

2. *In Johnson v. Superior Court of San Joaquin County*, 15 Cal. 3d 248, 539 P.2d 792 (1975), the case upon which this example is based, the defense counsel sought a *writ of prohibition* restraining the *court* from proceeding to trial. (It's often helpful to know those antiquated writs.) But even if that kind of proceeding is available, remember that most jurisdictions have no requirements about what the prosecutor must present to the grand jury, and that even where there are such requirements, they speak in terms of evidence which is "clearly exculpatory" and "directly negativing guilt." While the defendant's testimony would almost surely negate guilt, it might not be clearly exculpatory. Fortunately for Mr. Johnson, the test in California at the time required the prosecutor to present evidence "reasonably tending" to negate guilt, a much lower standard, and Mr. Johnson obtained his writ of prohibition. If you're lucky, you and Esmerelda live in California. And remember, if you had learned of Eager's conduct after the trial,

Mechanik, and its state progeny, would probably mean you were out of luck. Timing really is everything.

3.   Since the only question at the preliminary hearing is whether there is probable cause that Eduardo intentionally killed Ramon, this question, which apparently attempts to raise a self-defense issue, is irrelevant. (Even though all jurisdictions, save one, require the prosecution to disprove self-defense, once properly raised by the defendant (see LaFond and Singer, Criminal Law: Examples and Explanations, Chapter 16), this is not part of the *prima facie* case.) Thus, the magistrate should sustain the objection. On the other hand, if the witness were to become unavailable at trial, the failure to allow this question might mean that the entire testimony would be precluded as substantive evidence, because the defense was precluded from effective cross-examination. Thus, the magistrate will have to weigh these two factors before she makes her decision.

6

Evidence Disclosure (Discovery)

Under our criminal procedure, the accused has every advantage. While the prosecutor is held rigidly to the charge, he need not disclose the barest outline of his defense. He is immune from question or comment on his silence; he cannot be convicted when there is the least fair doubt in the minds of any one of the twelve. Why, in addition, he should in advance have the whole evidence against him to pick over at his leisure, and make his defense, fairly or foully, I have never been able to see.

Judge Learned Hand, in *United States v. Garsson*,
291 F. 646, 649 (S.D.N.Y. 1923)

The anachronistic apprehension that liberal discovery, if extended to criminal causes, will "inevitably" bring the serious and sinister dangers of perjury in its wake will seem strange to many when coming from this court which has been generally commended for its aggressive sponsorship of liberal discovery. . . . (W)e ought not in criminal causes, where even life itself may be at stake, forswear in the absence of clearly established danger, a tool useful in guarding against the chance that a trial will be a lottery or mere game of wits and the result at the mercy of the mischiefs of surprise. We must remember that society's interest is equally that the innocent shall not suffer and not alone that the guilty shall not escape. Discovery, basically a tool for truth, is the most effective device yet devised for the reduction of the aspect of adversary element to a minimum.

State Supreme Court Justice William Brennan, *State v. Tune*,
13 N.J. 203, 228, 98 A.2d 881 (1953) (Dissenting)

Overview

Back in the good old days, lawyers practiced "trial by ambush" — each side had to guess what evidence the other side would present, and hope there would be no surprises, such as a secret witness. Civil discovery, whatever its weakness, has mitigated at least that vice of litigation.[1] Discovery in the criminal arena has not moved so far; while trial by ambush is no longer quite the order of the day, neither does criminal discovery, at least in most jurisdictions, emulate the "open file" approach common to civil litigation. Until the middle of this century, many common law judges believed they had no power to order discovery (or disclosure). Thus, there was little mandated discovery until legislatures began to order it.

While the United States Supreme Court, both in its administrative capacity and its constitutional authority, has edged slightly in the direction of requiring discovery, the states have adopted varying positions between total nondisclosure, and (virtually) total disclosure.

The most salient explanation for this reticence is that criminal defendants are not civil defendants. Persons facing severe punishments may take drastic steps to prevent conviction, including destruction of evidence and intimidation (or even extermination) of witnesses. While one should not cavalierly discount these possibilities, few defendants actually act in this way. Where such information is generally available, the prosecution may always ask the court for a protective order, either totally hiding the information from the defense counsel, or explicitly charging the defense counsel not to reveal this information. This latter process puts an impartial arbiter, rather than a party to the litigation, in charge of the decision. Still, in "narrow discovery" jurisdictions, government officials often declare that "our" criminals are worse than those of other jurisdictions.[2]

Of substantial, if not equal, importance is the concern that prosecutorial files might contain significant information, such as the names of confidential informants, jeopardizing ongoing investigations. This fear, however, may be addressed by providing that the information should be provided to defense *counsel*, but not directly (or indirectly) to the defendant.

Similarly, Judge Learned Hand argued, defendants may shape their own evidence to fit within gaps in the prosecutor's case, a concern which Justice

---

1. W. Glannon, Civil Procedure: Examples and Explanations, Chapters 19, 20.

2. This claim is frequently made, for example, by those dealing with "organized crime." Indeed, even though those defendants could also be prosecuted in state courts, where discovery may be more readily obtainable, state prosecutors on occasion will "turn over" state-indicted defendants for federal prosecution for the obvious purpose of precluding discovery. A study of threats generally (not limited to organized crime figures) indicated 26 percent of witnesses said they had been threatened by the defendant, or his family, or friends. Michael H. Graham, Witness Intimidation 4 (1985).

Brennan labeled "a hobgoblin" and a "complete fallacy." [3] Of less weight is the fear that redacting voluminous prosecutorial data to avoid disclosure of such information will spend scarce governmental resources.

A. "Brady" Materials — The Constitutional Minimum

The United States Supreme Court has held that the state *must* disclose to a defendant evidence that is *material* and *favorable* to the accused. *Brady v. Maryland* 373 U.S. 83 (1963). In *Brady* itself, the court appeared to use the word "material" in the normal sense of evidentiary rules. In more recent decisions, however, it became clear that evidence is material *only if there is a "reasonable probability" that the verdict would have been different had defense counsel received the evidence. Kyles v. Whitley*, 514 U.S. 419 (1995).[4] The result is that the nature of the prosecutor's constitutional duty to disclose has shifted from: (a) an evidentiary test of materiality that can be applied rather easily to any item of evidence (Would this evidence have some tendency to undermine proof of guilt?) to (b) a result-affecting test that obliges a prosecutor or an appellate court to make a counterfactual, retrospective prediction.

Moreover, *Brady* "does not require the prosecution to disclose all exculpatory and impeachment materials; it need only disclose material that, if suppressed, would deprive the defendant of a fair trial." *United States v. Coppa*, 267 F.3d 132 (2d Cir. 2001). Finally, since the rule applies only to "material" information, favorable "nonmaterial" information apparently may remain undisclosed, as may all nonfavorable material information.

Several things should be noted about this approach. First, it focuses on the evidence's impact at defendant's *trial*; yet 90 percent or more of all cases never reach trial. Second, the rule focuses not on the prosecutor's motives in failing to disclose, but on the potential impact of the evidence. Questions of the prosecutor's ethics appear to be irrelevant in determining whether the failure to disclose has violated the Constitution. As one writer has put it, "The Court is indifferent to the *moral culpability* of the prosecutor as long as the defendant receives a *fair trial*."[5] Third, the burden is on the

---

3. Brennan, The Criminal Prosecution: Sporting Event or Quest for Truth, 1963 Wash. U. L. Q. 279, 291.

4. And, the Court emphasized, "the adjective is important." *Kyles v. Whitley*, 514 U.S. 419 (1995). Some have criticized the *Brady-Kyles* test on the ground that it tolerates even intentional discovery violations if the defendant's guilt is "overwhelming."

5. Leslie Griffin, The Prudent Prosecutor, 14 Geo. J. Legal Ethics 259, 263 (2001).

defendant to show prejudice, not on the state to show the lack of prejudice.[6] Fourth, the test is highly subjective. In determining whether there is a "reasonable probability" that the result would have been different, judges must attempt to guess at how a lawyer (the best? average? experienced?) would have acted had the evidence been disclosed. This counterfactual approach is extraordinarily complex. In *Kyles*, for example, the majority and dissenters spent pages attempting to guess at how a good attorney would have used the nondisclosed evidence.

The *Brady* duty is a continuing one—whenever[7] the prosecutor uncovers *Brady* material, he must disclose it. Moreover, disclosure is automatically required—it does not depend on whether the defendant had made a generalized, or even a specific, request for exculpatory material.[8]

Brady thus requires the following analysis:

- Is the information "material" as that word has been defined, i.e., is it favorable to the accused?
- Did the prosecution suppress it?
- Was this discovery the only, or the most reasonable, way defendant could have found this information?

We will discuss each of these (and more) in this chapter.

1. Defining "Materiality"

The *Brady* rule is easy to articulate, but difficult to implement. First, there is the matter of definition—what evidence is "material"? Since the

---

6. Two commentators have noted that, if the evidence *had* been disclosed, an appellate court on review of the conviction would view all the evidence as well as any inference that could be drawn therefrom, in a light favorable to the government. By requiring the defendant to show prejudice where the evidence is *not* disclosed, the appellate courts effectively view even undisclosed evidence in a light favorable to the government. "Where, then," asks the authors, "is the incentive to disclose it?" Seer and Osler, Criminal Procedure, 34 Tex. Tech. L. Rev. 649, 690 (2003). Compare the "harmless error" test discussed in Chapter 12.

7. The duty would seem to apply even after conviction, although there is little case law either way on this point. See Note, 15 St. Thomas L. Rev. 245 (2002).

8. Initially, the U.S. Supreme Court appeared to differentiate between instances where the defendant had made a request for specific (or at least general) information, and those in which there had been no request. The theory was that a defense counsel who had made a specific request, but who had been told that there was no evidence meeting that request, would be lulled into a sense of false confidence. The Court, however, has now moved away from that position. Some state courts, however, appear to differentiate, requiring the prosecutor to carry the burden of showing, if the defendant has made a specific request, that undisclosed evidence "would not have affected the verdict," while placing on the defendant, who has not made a request, the burden of showing prejudice. *State v. Laurie*, 39 N.H. 325, 653 A.2d 549 (1995); *Comm. v. Gallarelli*, 399 Mass. 17, 502 N.E.2d 516 (1987).

definition is retrospective, information that could be material in one case need not be in another. Moreover, the concern is with the effect at trial. Suppose Xavier, charged with robbing the First National, adamantly denies he committed that crime, but has confessed to robbing the Second National, with a similar modus operandi, for which Augustine is being prosecuted; is that confession sufficiently "favorable and material" to Augustine, such that the prosecutor must disclose it? Suppose that Xavier is going to be a witness for the prosecution in Augustine's trial? In *Giglio v. United States*, 405 U.S. 150 (1972) the Court held that evidence which could be used to impeach a witness was sufficiently "favorable" as to fall within the *Brady* disclosure requirement. But under such a rule, if Xavier is not going to be a witness, his confession may not be "material" within the meaning of *Brady*. What if one (or more) eyewitnesses, whose reports to the police are *not* discoverable, recant their identification? What if the police have learned that an eyewitness has "some difficulty" in discerning items at a distance? Are these "material"? "favorable"?

A second problem with *Brady*'s approach is that the person initially determining whether the evidence is "*Brady* material" is hardly impartial. Even the most even-handed prosecutor is likely to want to avoid disclosure, particularly if the evidence weighs strongly in the defendant's interest. If the prosecutor can persuade herself that the evidence does not meet the *Brady* test, her decision not to disclose, even if determined at a later date to be wrong, is not subject to ethical criticism. In *Agurs v. United States*, 427 U.S. 97 (1976), the Court refused to *mandate* disclosure except in extreme circumstances, but urged disclosure by indicating that the "prudent prosecutor" would always disclose where the evidence was ambiguous. The Court's standard, however, pulls against this salutary admonition—a standard encouraging (though not mandating) disclosure would put the burden on the prosecution to demonstrate (perhaps by a very high standard such as clear and convincing evidence or beyond a reasonable doubt) that the absence of the evidence did not affect the verdict, rather than putting the burden on the defendant.

2. *Aggregating the Nondisclosed Evidence*

It is now clear that, in determining whether evidence should have been disclosed, the court should count *all* evidence which can meet the *Brady* test and use it *cumulatively*. In *Kyles v. Whitley*, 514 U.S. 419 (1995), Kyles was charged with a homicide in a convenience store theft, and escaping in the victim's car. The police had taken the license numbers of all cars in the parking lot shortly after the robbery. Moreover, the police received much of their information about Kyles (including the possible hiding spot of the robbery loot) from "Beanie," who had been linked to other similar crimes. Among the items which the police did not disclose to the defendant were:

1. Kyles's license plate was not among the license plates in the parking lot;
2. Beanie's initial call to the police;
3. A tape recording of Beanie's later conversations with the police in which he increasingly pointed to Kyles;
4. Evidence linking Beanie with other robberies of a similar nature;
5. Evidence linking Beanie to another homicide;
6. Conflicts in the eyewitness testimony, such as, some described someone similar to the defendant, others did not, and suggested someone like Beanie;
7. An internal police memorandum regarding a search of Kyles' trash.

The Court held that even if none of these items, individually, would meet the *Brady* test and require disclosure, if considered cumulatively and all of them could fit within that rubric, then disclosure of all the items was required. The dissenting Justices argued that each piece of evidence must be assessed separately, rather than cumulatively. The majority approach would seem to be sensible, lest the prosecutor seek to "pick and choose" which items to disclose based upon its individual impact. See, e.g., *Monroe v. Angelone*, 323 F.3d 286 (4th Cir. 2003).

But *Kyles* revealed another problem: Each opinion sought to assess (1) how the defense counsel might have used the evidence to frame the case; and (2) what the jury might have thought of these pieces of evidence, assuming not only their admission, but that defense counsel would maximize their importance to the jury. Attempting to assess one counterfactual is hard enough — trying to determine the impact of a number of undisclosed items becomes extraordinarily difficult, particularly where the issue is how the jury might react to the evidence. That problem was sharply demonstrated by the various opinions in *Kyles* itself, as well as in a subsequent case, *Strickler v. Green*, 527 U.S. 263 (1999), in which the Court appeared much more deferential to the trial outcome, and about which a commentator has observed: "If the words (of *Kyles* and *Strickler*) are the same, the music seems different."

These difficulties merely reflect the problems of any retrospective rule. (See, for example, the discussion of the "harmless error" rule in Chapter 12.)[9] Courts are reluctant to overturn a conviction even if, given the same nondisclosure prior to trial, they would be willing to grant some kind of relief. See *United States v. Sudikoff*, 36 F. Supp. 2d 1196 (C.D. Calif. 1999), where the court, explicitly relying on the premise that the pre-trial standard for discovery should be broader and less restrictive than the post-trial standards of

---

9. Some courts state that *Brady* errors are not subject to a harmless error analysis — but that is because the *Brady* test itself requires a showing that the nondisclosure was not "harmless."

Brady, employed a standard of whether the evidence "might reasonably be held to be favorable" to the defense.

B. Nonconstitutional Rules of Discovery

Much evidence, even cumulatively, will not meet the *Brady* requirements. Most obviously, for example, a defendant's confession is unlikely to be "favorable" to him. Virtually all states, and the federal system, have gone beyond *Brady*, and require the government to disclose certain kinds of information. We will discuss below each of the major kinds of information which are the target of discovery motions. As you read through these, keep in mind that many attorneys are still infused with the notion of "trial by ambush," and are extremely reluctant to part with any information. Just as a prosecutor may persuade himself that information is not material within *Brady*, both sides' reluctance to disclose will increase exponentially with the adverse implications to be drawn from the information. Each attorney will narrowly interpret the wording of each discovery provision, attempting to avoid including the information in that interpretation. As one example, consider a court rule allowing defendants to discover statements which witnesses have given to the police. If the statement must be signed in order to be the witness's statement, the attorney[10] can avoid discovery by not having the witness sign it, or by simply taking "notes" of the conversation. The point is not that the rules are manipulable, nor that meretricious attorneys will manipulate them; the point is that to change the "culture," it may require much more than a mere change in the written rules.

A second problem permeating many court rules turns on the precise wording of the rule. Some rules require that the attorney disclose any evidence which he "possesses"; other rules require disclosure only of items he "intends to offer" at trial. Two contrary issues arise here. If an attorney "possesses" a statement which would be harmful to his case, he will certainly not "intend to offer" it at trial. Yet in a search for truth, this is precisely the type of evidence we want the parties to disclose (subject to other limitations considered below). On the other hand, asking an attorney to determine — sometimes months in advance — what evidence she will use at trial is inherently problematic. More importantly, such provisions could lead to litigation, either before or after conviction. Even though the impetus for such a

---

10. Most of the questions of discovery involve what the defendant may require the prosecutor to disclose. But a number of jurisdictions allow the prosecutor to discover at least some documents which defense counsel controls. We use the term "attorney," although most of the time the issue really relates to "prosecutor."

limitation is to avoid requiring an attorney to turn over masses of information to the opponent, the potential bases for litigation would argue for broader disclosure. In 1991 an amendment to Federal Rule 16 discarded the "intended use" requirement as to a written record containing the substance of defendant's oral statements, but retained the "intended use" limitation for disclosing oral statements where there is no such writing.

Many of the more important types of information to which discovery rules in the United States may apply are discussed below. But two general observations may be in order. First, there is a broad range among the rules. Some, such as Arizona (R./ Crim P. 15.1/15.2); Florida (Rule 3.220); Hawaii (R. Penal P. 16), and Illinois (Sup. Ct. R. 411-14) provide for very broad discovery. These are often referred to as *open file* states. At the other extreme, the federal rules, followed by a number of states, severely limit discovery beyond that which is mandated by *Brady*. Most jurisdictions fall in the middle. Second, even where the rule is essentially the same between jurisdictions, the rationale for the rule may differ widely, thus leading to possibly different outcomes in those jurisdictions, depending on the facts of the instant challenge. Third, these rules *supplement, rather than supplant, Brady*. In every instance, but particularly in those jurisdictions with narrowly written rules, defense counsel will attempt to assert that the information is "*Brady* material," thus avoiding any possible restrictive interpretation of the rules.

Since many casebooks discuss Federal Rule 16, and since many states emulate it, we reproduce it here in its entirety. Remember, however, that the majority of states are much more generous in one or more of the categories covered by the rule, even if they otherwise follow it.

(a) Government's Disclosure.

(1) Information Subject to Disclosure.

(A) *Defendant's Oral Statement.* Upon a defendant's request, the government must disclose to the defendant the substance of any relevant oral statement made by the defendant, before or after arrest, in response to interrogation by a person the defendant knew was a government agent if the government intends to use the statement at trial.

(B) *Defendant's Written or Recorded Statement.* Upon a defendant's request, the government must disclose to the defendant, and make available for inspection (copying or photographing) all of the following:

(i) any relevant written or recorded statement by the defendant if:

- the statement is within the government's possession, custody, or control; and
- the attorney for the government knows — or through due diligence could know — that the statement exists;

(ii) the portion of any written record containing the substance of any relevant oral statement made before or after arrest if the defendant made the statement in response to interrogation by a person the defendant knew was a government agent; and

(iii) the defendant's recorded testimony before a grand jury relating to the charged offense. . . .

(D) *Defendant's Prior Record.* Upon a defendant's request, the government must furnish the defendant with a copy of the defendant's prior criminal record that is within the government's possession, custody, or control if the attorney for the government knows — or through due diligence could know — that the record exists.

(E) *Documents and Objects.* Upon a defendant's request, the government must permit the defendant to inspect and to copy or photograph books, papers, documents, data, photographs, tangible objects, buildings or places, or copies or portions of any of these items, if the item is within the government's possession, custody, or control, and:

(i) the item is material to preparing the defense;

(ii) the government intends to use the item in its case-in-chief at trial; or

(iii) the item was obtained from or belongs to the defendant.

(F) *Reports of Examinations and Tests.* Upon a defendant's request, the government must permit a defendant to inspect and to copy or photograph the results or reports of any physical or mental examination and of any scientific test or experiment if:

(i) the item is within the government's possession, custody, or control;

(ii) the attorney for the government knows — or through due diligence could know — that the item exists; and

(iii) the item is material to preparing the defense or the government intends to use the item in its case-in-chief at trial.

(G) *Expert witnesses.* At the defendant's request, the government must give to the defendant a written summary of any testimony that the government intends to use under Rules 702, 703, or 705 of the Federal Rules of Evidence during its case-in-chief at trial. If the government requests discovery under subdivision (b)(1)(C)(ii) and the defendant complies, the government must, at the defendant's request, give to the defendant a written summary of testimony that the government intends to use under Rules 702, 703, or 705 of the Federal Rules of Evidence as evidence at trial on the issue of the defendant's mental condition. The summary provided under this subparagraph must describe the witness's opinions, the bases and reasons for those opinions, and the witness's qualifications.

(2) *Information Not Subject to Disclosure.* Except as Rule 16(a)(1) provides otherwise, this rule does not authorize the discovery or inspection of reports, memoranda, or other internal government documents made by an attorney for the government or other government agent in

connection with investigating or prosecuting the case. Nor does this rule authorize the discovery or inspection of statements made by prospective government witnesses except as provided in 18 U.S.C. §3500.

(3) *Grand Jury Transcripts*. This rule does not apply to the discovery or inspection of a grand jury's recorded proceedings, except as provided in Rules 6, 12(h), 16(a)(1), and 26.2.

1. *Defendant's Statements*

Suppose that the police give Dan his Miranda warnings but (not having read Bloom and Brodin) he nevertheless gives them a statement. Incredible as it seems, less than fifty years ago, courts refused to require the state to give Dan a copy of his own statement, or confession. Although the apparent policy here was to prevent Dan from molding his testimony to gibe with the statement, the explanations for nondisclosure were sometimes incredible. Thus, one court indicated that the police need not give Dan "his" statement because, while the words were "his," the paper on which the words were written belonged to the state. Today, virtually all jurisdictions require disclosure of these statements. Even then, however, there are problems of interpretation.

For example, Federal Rule 16 (and the state rules following this language) provides that the government must disclose:

(1) "any

    (a)[11]   relevant written or recorded statements made by the defendant. . .

    (b)   the portion of any written record containing the substance of any relevant oral statement made by the defendant whether before or after arrest in response to interrogation by any person then known to the defendant to be a government agent . . . (and)

    (c)   the substance of any other relevant oral statement made by the defendant . . . in response to interrogation by any person then known by the defendant to be a government agent if the government intends to use that statement at trial."

The first clause is straightforward—assuming we know what a "statement" is, and what is "relevant." The second clause restricts discoverable oral statements made by a defendant and recorded in a "written record" to those made to a known government agent; the obvious point is to protect the identity of undercover agents to whom the defendant makes incriminating statements. The third clause concerns such statements which are *not* put by the agent into a written report; at that point, only those which are intended to be used at trial are discoverable.

---

11. Alphabetical headings are by author; they do not appear in the rule.

Most state rules are not so restrictive. New Jersey, for example, provides that records of statements of any person whom the prosecutor knows to have relevant evidence is to be disclosed to the defendant. N.J. R 3:13-2(6,7). California makes all defendant's statements discoverable, whether or not written or recorded. See Cal. Pen. Code §1054.1(b). North Carolina provides that the defendant is entitled to inspect and copy any of her relevant written or recorded statements, and that the prosecutor must divulge the "substance" of any oral statement relevant to the case, regardless of whom the statement was made to, unless the informant is a prosecution agent who will not testify at trial.

2. Information about Witnesses

a. Names and Addresses

It happens in every courtroom movie; the prosecution or defense calls a "surprise witness" whose testimony clinches the case one way or the other. Unhappily, as the twenty-first century begins, that image is still real in many states. While over half of the states provide for discovery of the names and addresses of all persons known to have relevant information, a substantial number of jurisdictions, following the federal lead, do not make such information available. Others require disclosure only of persons "intended" to be called at trial, thereby permitting the prosecutor to hide from the defendant a potentially favorable witness (assuming *Brady* is not activated). Again, the primary explanation is fear of witness intimidation. Federal courts put a heavy burden on defendants to show a need for witness list disclosure. See *United States. v. Alex*, 791 F. Supp. 723 (N.D. Ill. 1991). Those courts have considered, among other factors: (1) the type of crime charged; (2) defendant's history of violence or witness intimidation; (3) whether the evidence could be easily altered; (4) defendant's resources.

In 1975, the Conference Committee of the Senate and House, rejecting a proposal to allow such disclosure, declared that "A majority of the Conferees believe it is not in the interest of the effective administration of criminal justice to require that the government or the defendant be forced to reveal the names and addresses of its witnesses before trial. Discouragement of witnesses and improper contact directed at influencing their testimony were deemed paramount concerns in the formulation of this policy."

b. Statements

Suppose that Joe tells the police that Dan has admitted to him that he has committed a bank robbery, and that the police then make a written record of Joe's tale. Under the federal rules (and states which emulate them), the police report of Joe's declaration is not discoverable, even if the prosecution intends to use Joe's statement (or Joe) at trial[12] — only statements made *by a defendant* to governmental agents are discoverable under the last two clauses of the first provision. If Dan is to learn of Joe's full statement, or even Joe's evidence about Dan's alleged statement, it must be through a provision allowing discovery of witness statements generally.

A substantial number of states either totally preclude defense pre-trial access to statements made by interviewed witnesses,[13] or leave it to the discretion of the judge.[14] At least 14 follow the *Jencks Act* of the federal system, which does not require pre-trial disclosure of witness statements, requiring disclosure only after the witness has actually testified at trial.[15] As with disclosure of names and addresses, the policy supporting nondisclosure is clear: We wish to assure that the witness will not be harassed (or worse) before trial.[16]

c. Impeachment Evidence

Some evidence is useful primarily as impeachment of witnesses and others. Most commonly, if the prosecution has agreed with a witness either not to prosecute him at all, or to reduce the charges against him in exchange for testimony against the defendant, the explicit details of that arrangement, even if not yet set in writing, must be disclosed to the defendant to allow impeachment. Most of this information will be covered by the *Brady-Giglio* rule that impeachment evidence is "favorable" to the defendant and must be disclosed. See *Monroe v. Angelone*, 323 F.3d 286 (4th Cir. 2003). Even if the witness has not yet reached a deal, that discussions of possible "leniency" have occurred should be disclosed. *Comm. v. Strong*, 563 Pa. 455, 761 A.2d 1167 (2000). Similarly, failure to disclose the prior criminal record of a witness, even if not dealt with by Federal Rule 16, is clearly covered by *Brady* and *Giglio*.[17] Other information, however, such as statements by co-defendants, are sometimes open to discovery (about one-third of the states), but

reaching a deal
w/ witness
is discoverable

---

12. There may be an issue of admissibility here, but assume for now that Joe's declaration would be admissible.

13. Approximately 20 states make pre-trial access to the statements of witnesses who have been interviewed a matter of right.

14. E.g., Mississippi and Alabama require further showings that the statements are "material" and "relevant" or "essential" for cross-examination.

15. For a summary of all states' rules, with an appendix comparing them, see Note, Defendant Access to Prosecution Witness Statements in Federal and State Cases, 61 Wash. U. L. Q. 471 (1983).

16. Podgor, Criminal Discovery of Jencks Witness Statements: Timing Makes a Difference, 15 Ga. St. U. L. Rev. 651 (1999).

17. *State v. Nelson*, 330 N.J. Super. 206, 749 A.2d 380 (App. Div. 2000); *People v. Martinez*, 127 Cal. Rptr. 2d 305 (Cal. App. 4 Dist. 2002).

these issues are sometimes expressly left to court rule or decision. North Carolina, for example, requires disclosure of co-defendant statements *if* "the State intends to offer (the statement) in evidence at their joint trial." Otherwise, the statements are dealt with as any other statements (not discoverable in that state, for example, until after the witness has testified). In the most recent decision, *Banks v. Dretke*, 124 S. Ct. 456 (2004), the prosecution allowed two witnesses to testify to statements the state knew to be untrue, *and* did not disclose the impeaching evidence to the defendant. Not surprisingly, the Court found this to be a *Brady-Giglio* violation cognizable on habeas corpus (see Chapter 12).

3. Police Reports

Some states explicitly provide for disclosure of every police report "in the possession, custody, or control of the prosecutor,"[18] but a large number do not directly address the issue, leaving discovery of only parts of the report which would fall under other provisions. (For example, in a prosecution based upon an automobile accident, police observation of road conditions *might* be exculpatory, but not material within *Brady*.) Under Federal Rule 16, the defendant is not entitled to the prosecutor's investigative file, at least if the "302" report accurately captures the contents of interview notes. *United States v. Brown*, 303 F.3d 582 (5th Cir. 2002); *United States v. Davidson*, 2004 WL 595039 (S.D.N.Y.). And in some states, any potentially exculpatory material in police reports, including information about alternate suspects are *Brady* material. See *Harrington v. State*, 659 N.W.2d 509 (Iowa 2003).

4. Expert Reports and Witnesses

Many systems require early disgorgement of the names of experts and their reports, by both prosecutors and defense. The reasons seem fairly clear —these reports may require rebuttal by other experts, who will require time to analyze both the general questions in the trial as well as the experts' reports. Federal Rule 16 requires disclosure of reports that the prosecutor intends to use in its "case-in-chief" (i.e., not in impeachment or rebuttal), or reports that are "material to the preparing the defense." If the report of an expert employed by the prosecutor *disfavors* the prosecution's view, but does not directly favor that of the defendant, it is not clear that it is discoverable, since it may not be material to preparation of a defense. This rule does not differentiate expert witnesses and their reports from other witnesses, even though once the expert report is in, recantation by the expert is likely to seem suspect, so they are arguably less subject to intimidation. On the

18. E.g., N.J. R 3:13-3(c)(8).

other hand, many jurisdictions hold that the prosecution must disclose information which casts doubt upon an expert witness's accuracy. Discovery relating to expert reports may also entail a right to discovery of the expert or laboratory's standard operating procedures, including its quality assurance manual. *Cole v. State*, 378 Md. 42, 835 A.2d 600 (2003).

5. *Information About the Police*

Sometimes defendants want to challenge the veracity of the police officers who arrested or interrogated them. Yet police personnel records may be protected by other statutes. As a general rule, therefore, these records are nondiscoverable. Some states, such as California, have established specific procedures for *in camera* judicial examination of police officer records. *Pitchess v. Superior Court*, 11 Cal. 3d 531, 522 P.2d 305 (1974). Others require disclosure if the records are "likely to contain information relevant to the officer's credibility."[19]

6. *The Work Product Exception*

Students familiar with the civil system of discovery know the difficulties caused by the concept of "work product"—the idea that material prepared for trial, by the attorney or persons working directly under her direction, is not discoverable. That rule applies in the criminal sphere as well *United States v. Nobles*, 422 U.S. 225 (1975). And it is no more transparent in criminal than in civil matters. But, as *Nobles* makes clear, the move toward restricting what qualifies as work product continues in the criminal area. There, the Court held that the prosecutor could discover a report relating to possible witnesses written by an investigator hired by the defense counsel. The Court declared: "(defendant) did not prepare the report, and there is no suggestion that the portions subject to the disclosure order reflect any

---

19. *State v. Harris*, 316 N.J. Super. 384, 720 A.2d 425 (App. Div. 1998). Canada allows discovery of the following information about police officers:

- statements of any individuals who have brought complaints against the arresting officer;
- the phone numbers and address of those individuals;
- statements made by the arresting officer in relation to any complaints;
- the disposition of any complaints and the criminal record of the arresting officer, including any discharges granted under the Criminal Code;
- police service records describing the nature of any misconduct found to have been committed by any of the officers and the penalty imposed;
- any outstanding formal allegations of misconduct before the police disciplinary tribunal.

R. v. Tomlinson (1998) 16 C.R. (5th) 333 (Ont. Prov. Div.); *R. v. Thiebeault* (1997) B.C.J. No. 3080 (B.C. Prov. Ct.).

information that he conveyed to the investigator." Thus, the Court held, these were not defendant's "statements," and hence mandated disclosure was not a violation of the Fifth Amendment self-incrimination clause.

C. Timing of Discovery

Timing is everything. Neither *Brady* nor its progeny directly addressed a critical issue of discovery — *when* must the information be disclosed? The normal standard is that the disclosure must be made "in time for its efficient use at trial." In *United States v. Gil*, 297 F.3d 933 (2d Cir. 2002), one or two business days before trial, the prosecutor turned over to the defendant, two boxes of documents accompanied by a 41 page index designating over 600 exhibits. Defense counsel did not find until after trail among these documents, a memorandum which unquestionably supported his contention that defendant's conduct had been authorized by the government. The court noted that "a conscientious defense lawyer would be preoccupied working on an opening statement and witness cross-examinations and all else," and that "(t)he defense (at that time) may be unable to divert resources from other initiatives and obligations that are or may seem more pressing." The court then noted "the government runs a certain risk when it turns over so late documents sought by the defense for so long," and held that the documents, even though disclosed, were "suppressed" within the meaning of *Brady*.

In federal cases, the problem is even made even more intricate by the so-called *Jencks Act*, copied by Federal Rule 26.2 and many states, which provides that:

> After a witness called by the United States has testified on direct examination, the court shall . . . order the United States to produce any statement . . . of the witness . . . which relates to the subject matter as to which the witness has testified.

The federal courts are divided over whether the *Brady* general rule — "in time for effective use" — is trumped by the more specific Jencks Act language.[20] Some require disclosure befrore trial, while others take a "balancing" approach, attempting to distinguish those statements are

---

20. At least five circuits hold that the Jencks Act controls the timing of disclosure. See, e.g., *United States v. Scott*, 424 F.2d 465 (5th Cir. 1975); *United States v. Jones*, 612 F. 2d 453 (9th Cir. 1980) (Jencks Act dominates). Others require pre-trial disclosure, at least in the discretion of the judge. See, e.g., *United States v. Starusko*, 729 F.2d 256 (3d Cir. 1984). At least one court allowed the prosecution to obtain a mandamus overturning a discovery order which permitted discovery of materials prior to trial. See *In re United States*, 834 F.2d 283 (2d Cir. 1987).

merely for impeachment from those which contain some *Brady* material. See *United States v. Beckford*, 962 F. Supp. 780, 790-792 (E.D. Va. 1997) (collecting cases). In those remaining jurisdictions that follow the Jencks Act language, because disclosure occurs during trial, the typical defense response is to ask for a continuance. But the time given is almost bound to be shorter than that necessary to read the statements (particularly if they are lengthy) and investigate not merely their substance, but any possible leads they might provide.[21] And if the statement is lengthy (imagine a declaration by an Enron executive which attaches multiple documents relating to discussions with the company's accountants), the defense side may find itself wallowing in reams of arcane material. Even with a continuance (often unlikely in a jury trial), the defense will be put at a serious disadvantage.

Moreover, since most cases never get to trial, many defendants are unlikely ever to know that there were favorable, undisclosed materials.[22] The United States Supreme Court recently appeared to endorse this result. In *United States v. Ruiz*, 536 U.S. 622 (2002), the Court held that a defendant considering pleading guilty was not entitled to discovery, prior to deciding whether to enter that plea, of *Giglio-type impeachment material*.[23] The Court indicated, but did not hold, that there might be a right to pre-plea disclosure of *Brady exculpatory material going to actual guilt*. Although the lower court had contended that a plea could not be "knowing" unless made with complete knowledge of the government's *Brady* material (see Chapter 7 on plea bargaining for a more complete discussion of the knowledge requirement), the Supreme Court emphasized that *Brady* was intended to assist a defendant *at* trial, and not necessarily before.

---

21. In *Boss v. Pierce*, 263 F.3d 734 (7th Cir. 2001), *cert. denied*, *Pierce v. Buss*, 535 U.S. 1078 (2002), the prosecutor gave to the defense an investigative report summarizing an interview conducted four days before the trial began. Defense counsel was unable to conduct an investigation at that point. Only after the conviction did a new defense attorney obtain information, using the summary as a lead, that garnered information which eventually led to a reversal of the conviction. See also *Leka v. Portuondo*, 257 F.3d 89 (2d Cir. 2001).

22. Many courts will be unsympathetic to a defendant who seeks to have a guilty plea, otherwise voluntarily entered, overturned because he has now learned that the prosecutor failed to disclose some evidence which, if disclosed, (1) would have persuaded him to go to trial; (2) might have resulted in an acquittal. The harmless error rule, discussed in Chapter 12, will frequently insulate such nondisclosure, even if it were purposeful.

23. The actual issue in *Ruiz* was the validity of a government demand that, to obtain a more lenient sentence in exchange for a plea, the defendant waive her right to disclose any *Brady* material. The Ninth Circuit had held such a condition *per se* invalid. Thus, the case could be construed as holding that a defendant has a right to impeachment evidence before trial, but can waive that right. Obviously, the government has an incentive to include such a waiver clause in every plea agreement.

The American Bar Association provides that disclosure should be made at a "specified and reasonable time prior to trial." (Rule 11/2.1 Standards for Criminal Justice: Discovery (3d ed. 1994). And many court rules actually specify a particular time period (15, 30, or 60 days) after a specific event (request by the defense; unsealing of an indictment, etc.). But others are vague on this matter, holding that *Brady* itself does not specifically address timing of discovery, and that so long as the defendant receives the material in time for its "effective" use at trial, *Brady* is met. See *United States v. Higgs*, 713 F.2d (3d Cir. 1983). Where there is no statutory conflict, courts continue to allow the prosecutor to delay disclosure, so long as the defendant has some opportunity to use the material during trial, should there be one.

Some decisions have distinguished between impeachment materials and materials which go directly to exculpation, arguing that the latter, unlike the former, "may require significant pre-trial investigation in order to be useful to the defendant at trial." See *Beckford, supra.*

D. Non-Brady Discovery: A Recap

Table 6.1 summarizes the basic approach taken by "open file" jurisdictions (exemplified by the ABA proposals), by "narrow" jurisdictions (such as the federal rules) and by "intermediate" states. These summaries, however, cannot capture the nuances and possible differences among the various state rules; only a close parsing of a particular state's rules (as interpreted by its judiciary) can perform that function. Note carefully — *these summaries relate only to non-Brady/Giglio evidence — there is much that might be discoverable under those cases.*

E. The Defense Duty of "Reasonable Diligence"

Some courts hold that a prosecutor's failure to comply with *Brady* or discovery rules is not reversible error if defense counsel did not exercise "due diligence" in seeking to obtain that information. The view is that such a requirement serves "to weed out incredible claims of ignorance, to prevent sandbagging, and is consistent with a focus on actual knowledge. . . ." *United States v. Zagaari*, 11 F.3d 307 (2d Cir. 1997). These courts explain that such evidence is not "suppressed" by the prosecutor. *Coleman v. Mitchell*, 286 F.3d 417 (6th Cir. 2001) (information "would have been discoverable with minimal investigation by petitioner's counsel"). Other courts are less tolerant of prosecutor nondisclosure. In *Pierce v. Boss, supra*, defense counsel had interviewed a witness once, who had thereafter disclosed

Table 6.1

Type of Information	*Federal Rule*	*Intermediate*	*ABA Proposals*
Defendant's statements	Any relevant (not merely "material") written or recorded statements and the "substance" of any oral statement if the defendant knew he was talking to a government agent	Discoverable	Discoverable, if they relate to the "subject matter of the offense"
Defendant's prior criminal record	Discoverable	Discoverable	Discoverable
Witness statements	Not discoverable until witness testifies	Usually discoverable	All statements of all persons having information that *relates* to the subject matter of the offense
Police reports	Not discoverable unless specific matter is covered by other rules	Similar to Fed. Rule	Essentially the same as Fed. Rule; some "open file" states require full disclosure
Witness names and addresses	Not discoverable	Discoverable	All persons known to have information
Witness past criminal history	Not discoverable	Usually discoverable	Disclosure required of any witness "to be called by either party"
Expert report	If intended to be used in as if chief or material to preparing defense case	Almost always discoverable	All reports are to be disclosed; if prosecution intends to call expert, must disclose qualifications and give a description of the proposed testimony
Grand jury transcripts	Not discoverable	Not discoverable	Full disclosure required
"Deals" for testimony	Not discoverable	Discoverable	Discoverable: Must disclose the relationship including the nature and circumstances of any agreement, understanding, or representation . . . that constitutes an inducement for the cooperation of testimony of the witness
Tangible objects	Books, papers, photos, etc., if intended to be used in case-in-chief or material to use in preparing defense	Anything relevant	Anything which "pertains to" the case or were obtained from or belong to defendant

(continues)

Table 6.1 (continued)

Timing	There is no specific time set by Federal Rule for discovery. Generally, "in time before trial to be useful". However, witness statements are discoverable only under the Jencks Act, and Rule 26.2, after the witness has testified	Times vary, but usually stated within 30-60 days of (a) a request; or (b) the date of indictment or information	"as early as practicable in the process"

to the prosecutor exculpatory information which the prosecution had not disclosed to the defendant. The court declared that even an astute defense counsel would not have thought to ask that witness questions about the matter she disclosed to the prosecutor only days before trial:

> We regard as untenable, a broad rule that any information possessed by a defense witness must be considered available to the defense for *Brady* purposes . . . a defense witness may be uncooperative or reluctant. Or . . . may have forgotten or inadvertently omitted some important piece of evidence . . . Or . . . the defense witness (may have learned) of certain evidence in time between when she spoke with defense counsel and the prosecution. . . .

F. Who Is "the Government" for Purposes of Discovery?

Some court rules require the "prosecuting attorney" to comply with discovery; others (such as the federal rules) speak of disclosure by "the government." But who is "the prosecutor" or "the government"? Suppose that, unknown to Hana, the police have information which would be discoverable — has *she* violated the discovery rules? Most rules require disclosure of information which the prosecutor knows "or by the exercise of due diligence" should know is available. . . .[24] Commonly, courts hold that the "prosecution team" has the following component parts:[25]

- all persons within the prosecutor's office
- the investigating agency or agencies (most obviously the police)

---

24. Cal. Pen. Code 1054.1 requires disclosure "if it is in the possession of the prosecuting attorney or if the prosecuting attorney *knows it to be* in the possession of the investigating agencies."

25. The United States Marshall's Service is a part of the prosecutorial team, and any information which that office has, is in the "possession" of the prosecutor. *United States v. Wilson*, 237 F.3d 827 (7th Cir. 2001).

- assisting agencies
- agencies closely tied to the prosecutor

The *Kyles* case rejected the state's contention that a more lenient standard should apply where only the police, and not the prosecutor, knew about evidence. More difficult questions arise when the information is controlled by another jurisdiction — either a different county within a state, or by the federal government (in the case of a state prosecution), or the state government (in the case of a federal prosecution). Courts have generally held that prosecutors in one jurisdiction do not have "control" of prosecutors in other jurisdictions. See, e.g., *United States v. Marshall*, 132 F.3d 63 (D.C. Cir. 1998); *State v. Fukusaku*, 85 Haw. 462, 946 P.2d 32 (1997). Items possessed by a corporation or the victim of the crime are *not* in the prosecutor's possession.

G. Alternative Means of Discovery

Thus far, we have spoken of how a defendant may obtain discovery under either court rules or the Constitution. Even when this discovery occurs, defendants are often required to pay for it (discovery rules frequently simply require the prosecutor to "make available" documents for copying). But there are other methods which may be more fruitful or less costly. First, of course, there is the preliminary hearing (see Chapter 5). Second, in many states, a defendant, acting in her capacity as a citizen, not a defendant, may seek information under the jurisdiction's Freedom of Information Act, or Sunshine Law. Other statutes dealing with specific information, such as reports of family violence for which the defendant has been arrested, may also be available. Finally, a defendant who could afford it might seek to depose a witness, but most court rules do not provide for depositions,[26] and they have been frowned upon as a means of discovery, although they are allowed if it appears that the witness would not be present at trial. In all other situations, ordering a deposition lies fully within the trial court's discretion, and a writ of mandamus requiring trial court to reverse a deposition order will not issue. *United States v. Carrigan*, 804 F.2d 599 (10th Cir. 1986).

H. "Open File" Discovery — With a Caveat

None of the objections to allowing defendants to discover materials in the prosecutor's files are palpably ludicrous. *Some* defendants will destroy or

---

26. A striking exception is Florida. Florida R. Crim Pro. 3. 220.

alter evidence, intimidate or kill witnesses, create fantasies of defense, etc. Even without such venality, defendants are not entitled to know the names of confidential informants, etc., at least so far as those informants' information has not affected the trial. Thus, requiring, either as a constitutional matter or as a matter of court rule, that prosecutors simply open their files to defendants would be unnecessarily beneficent. Still, a number of states, the ABA, and Uniform Rules opt for the "open file" approach. Those jurisdictions which have such a system (or are close to it) do not appear to have had most of the troubles contemplated by opponents of discovery. All provide for a protective order process. Similarly, again subject to Sixth and Fifth Amendment concerns, discovery of the defendant's case, which is often discussed "off the record" in plea sessions, would also appear to expedite the process. Expediency, of course, is not the goal of the criminal process, and the result of such discussions, plea bargains, may themselves be suspect.

I. The Practice of Discovery — "Real Life" versus "Rules"

In many corners of the law, law "on the books" may differ radically from law "in practice." The area of discovery is no different. Consider, for example, methods by which advocates may seek to avoid discovery. If the rule requires that the party turn over "statements" of a witness, the party may avoid discovery by simply not asking the witness to "adopt" or sign the written summary. If, as in California, the rule requires that notes of witness statements be disclosed, the party may instruct the interviewer not to take notes, and rely instead on memory. Since, as one court has put it, the law "does not impose an obligation on government agents to record witness interviews or to take notes during such interviews," there is no document which meets the "letter" of the discovery rules, and hence no violation has occurred. *United States v. Houlihan*, 92 F.3d 1271 (1st Cir. 1996). While "emphatically" condemning an FBI agent who candidly admitted that he took no notes of early interviews with witnesses for the precise purpose of avoiding Jencks Act discovery of possibly conflicting statements among interviews, the Ninth Circuit could find no statutory basis for requiring prosecutors, or their agents, to "create" Jencks Act material. *United States v. Comstock*, 625 F. 2d 854 (9th Cir. 1980).[27]

---

27. The court cited, as "accord," *United States v. Short*, 493 F.2d 1170 (9th Cir. 1974); *Jackson v. United States*, 448 F.2d 963 (9th Cir. 1971). Also, *United States v. Lieberman*, 608 F.2d 889 (1st Cir. 1979).

On the other hand, even prosecutors in the most restrictive of jurisdictions often, indeed one might say usually, disclose much more of their case than the rules require, for one very simple reason — it makes obtaining plea agreements much easier. Defendants often refuse to concede that the government "has the evidence," and they appear willing to roll the dice at trial. Confronted with a mass of evidence, however, only the most intrepid defendant will plow ahead.[28]

J. Discovery from the Defense

Courts and legislatures were slow to require discovery from the prosecution in criminal cases, in part, because they believed that both the Fifth and Sixth Amendments protected defendants from "reciprocal" discovery. That view is now untenable. Beginning by upholding requirements that defendants notify the state if they planned to use an alibi or insanity plea, courts have now upheld rules requiring reciprocal discovery between the two parties. Except for *Brady*-required constitutional discovery, many states now make some, or all, prosecutorial disclosure conditional on reciprocal discovery by the prosecutor from the defense.

The Fifth Amendment wall cracked in *Williams v. Florida*, 399 U.S. 78 (1970), where the Court decided that the defense could be required to disclose alibis. Two years later, the Court made clear that prosecutors could obtain discovery only if the state provided equal discovery by the defendant (although the defendant did not have to avail herself of the right in order to activate the prosecutorial right). *Wardius v. Oregon*, 412 U.S. 470 (1972). See also *United States v. Nobles*, 422 U.S. 225 (1975). Since that time there has been revolutionary expansion in criminal discovery by prosecutors.

The Court has relied upon several theories to support prosecutorial discovery. The most obvious reason for requiring disclosure of alibi or mental incompetence claims is simply practicality — a prosecutor suddenly confronted in the middle of a trial with such a claim would need a fairly lengthy continuance to garner evidence to rebut the claim. Rather than prolong an already commenced trial, courts were willing to tolerate requirements of pre-trial disclosure of those claims.

---

28. This truth is enhanced by the fact that sentencing practices, either tacitly or openly, permit judges to decrease sentences when there are plea bargains. This practice, whatever one thinks of it, has been consistently upheld against challenges that it penalizes a defendant who goes to trial.

Second, courts agreed with Judge Hand that the state is already burdened at trial and that to allow the defendant to obtain information, while precluding the state from doing so, would simply add to that burden. Reciprocity, particularly where non-*Brady* material was concerned, seemed a partial attempt at equilibrium. But, as Justice Douglas noted in *Nobles*, this ignores the fact that the government does most of its discovery in the grand jury. Thorough prosecutors use the grand jury (and its subpoena power) to obtain substantial evidence, to anticipate defenses, to "lock in" witnesses who (otherwise) might prove favorable to the defense, and to gather impeachment material for use in cross-examining defense witnesses at trial. Moreover, the prosecutor can make deals with other potential defendants, which is usually beyond the power of any defendant.

A third argument for allowing prosecutorial discovery, put forward in *Williams v. Florida,* is the notion of *acceleration.* Since the defendant will be forced to produce the evidence at trial, there is no ultimate harm to him — the question is one not of overcoming a Fifth Amendment (or other) right, but merely the timing of disclosure. The acceleration theory, however, ignores (1) the possibility a defendant may decide, after prosecutorial discovery, not to use a particular claim or witness and (2) most cases never get to trial. Moreover, the acceleration theory could be used to require disclosure, immediately after indictment, by both sides, thereby overcoming the Jencks Act (see *supra*, p. 89) or other timing limitations on discovery by either side.

These critiques, however, do not necessarily undermine the general case for reciprocal, and early, discovery in criminal cases. More information is always better than less; early knowledge always trumps late discovery. If a trial, or even a plea negotiation, is to be a search for "the truth," both sides should be as informed as possible.

State rules requiring defense to disclose information to the prosecutor are based on a theory of "reciprocity" — if the defendant does not request discovery under those rules, the prosecutor has no right to obtain discovery from the defense. *CAVEAT:* the prosecutor *still* must disclose any *Brady* information — which makes defining that term critical to defense counsel who do not wish to disclose any part of their case to the prosecution. The broader the *Brady* rule, the less eager will defense counsel be to pursue discovery under state discovery rules.

Defendants argue that limited discovery rights from the prosecutor, or allowing prosecutorial access to evidence obtained by the defense, interferes with the relationship between defendant and his lawyer and thus violates the Sixth Amendment. These challenges have not fared well. Courts sustaining a Sixth Amendment challenge have argued that confidentiality is a crucial element of representation, while courts on the other side have responded that if defendant has put into issue the scientific claim, he should make all of his experts available.

K. Preservation of Evidence

We all lose things, even the best of us. But what happens if the police, or another agency of the state, loses evidence which could be discoverable under *Brady*, or even under discovery rules? In *Arizona v. Youngblood*, 488 U.S. 51 (1988), police threw out semen samples which had been obtained from the victim of a sexual assault. It thereupon proved impossible for the defendant to perform blood group testing to see whether the sample matched his. Reversing a lower court finding that the impact upon the defendant's case violated his due process rights, the Supreme Court held that only a bad faith failure to preserve this material would violate due process.[29] Moreover, the defendant carries the burden of showing that there was bad faith; although the apparent exculpatory nature of the material may assist him in this, there is no presumption, rebuttable or otherwise, that the destruction was in bad faith.

The *Youngblood* "bad faith" rule is also followed by a majority of states, although a few, consistent with the general discovery doctrines, are concerned with the impact upon the defendant's case, rather than the prosecutor's state of mind. As with discovery, however, the prosecutor is responsible for evidence which is, or could be, under his control or under the control of (relevant) other governmental entities.

In *Illinois v. Fisher*, 540 U.S. 544 (2004), the Supreme Court concluded that the *Youngblood* "bad faith" test applies only to material which is not exculpatory in itself, but which might *lead* to exculpatory evidence. Destruction of *Brady* material, which is itself exculpatory, or clearly beneficial to the defendant, would be analyzed only in terms of the prejudice it had caused the defendant, without regard to the good or bad faith of the government. In *Fisher*, the police, after subjecting the white powder to four separate tests which defendant allegedly possessed, nonnegligently destroyed it. The *Fisher* Court held that the police's lack of bad faith was relevant, because there was no assurance that had they allowed the defendant to test it a fifth time, it would have exonerated him. In contrast, perhaps, is the case where the police destroy the (*Brady* exculpatory) report that concludes, after four tests, that the powder was not cocaine.

L. Sanctions

The most common sanctions for a violation of the disclosure rules discovered before a conviction include:

---

29. The *Youngblood* case had a particularly poignant ending. After serving more than 10 years, Youngblood was released from prison, but was soon rearrested for another crime. As the prosecutor prepared for the new trial, he discovered a cotton swab from the initial charge which had been misplaced. DNA testing proved that Youngblood had not committed the first offense.

- a continuance of the trial, allowing the affected party to read the material and perhaps to act upon it (by pursuing leads, etc.);
- exclusion of the nondisclosed evidence, or witness;
- a "curative instruction" that the jury assume certain facts that might have been established through the nondisclosed material;
- mistrial;
- contempt;
- dismissal of the entire prosecution or of specific charges;
- disciplinary action against the violator, or his office.

The usual remedy, when the failure is discovered during trial (as it frequently is) is the granting of a continuance. But clearly that is insufficient in many instances — a trial judge, at least during a jury trial, is unlikely to readily grant a continuance of more than a day or two to allow the injured side to reassess its case in light of the newly discovered evidence.

In *Taylor v. Illinois*, 484 U.S. 400 (1988), the Supreme Court upheld the preclusion of evidence when the defendant did not disclose the availability of a witness whom he intended to use. In *Taylor*, however, the trial court found, and the Supreme Court stressed in its opinion, that there was a strong suspicion that defendant's counsel acted intentionally or in bad faith. More recently, the Court overturned a state-court-established *per se* rule that the defendant could never be precluded from presenting evidence, however improper his counsel's actions. *Michigan v. Lucas*, 500 U.S. 145 (1991). And see *United States v. Davis*, 244 F.3d 666 (8th Cir. 2001), where government failed to produce DNA tests promptly for defendant's examination, trial court's suppression of the evidence was not improper. Readers may recall the Jayson Williams trial, in which the prosecution, despite the fact that the state required an "open file" policy, neglected to provide certain evidence regarding the state's key expert witness. Although the defendant asked either for a mistrial, or that the expert's testimony be thrown out, the trial court instead chose the less drastic path of allowing the defense to reopen its case and requestion prosecution and defense weapons experts.

As a general rule, dismissal of counts is not a sanction readily endorsed by courts. See *Comm. v. Burke*, 566 Pa. 402, 781 A.2d 1136, (2001). A dramatic instance of such a sanction occurred in *United States v. Moussaoui*, 282 F. Supp. 2d 480 (E.D. Va. 2003). Moussaoui, the alleged "missing terrorist" in the 9/11 conspiracy, was representing himself, and had sought the right to interview several other persons being detained by the government, alleging that they could disprove the government's contention that he was part of that conspiracy. When the government refused to allow this discovery, the trial court precluded the government from seeking the death penalty in the case, since those charges were the only ones carrying that penalty. The Fourth Circuit, however, reversed this sanction, ordering the trial court to attempt to find compromise procedures that would both protect Moussaoui and allow the government to pursue the death penalty. *United States v. Moussaoui*, 365 F.3d 292 (4th Cir. 2004).

The general judicial aversion to severe sanctions for discovery violation may have faint traces of "trial by ambush" and antipathy to discovery generally. But there are other concerns as well. Whatever the possible remedy for the impact upon the adverse party's case, lawyer neglect (and worse, lawyer intransigence), should be viewed as an issue separate from the trial. Just as the argument can well be made that defendants should not suffer because of the inadequacy of their counsel [30] (see Chapter 10) neither should the state necessarily lose its opportunity for a fair and accurate conviction simply because the prosecutor has blundered. Courts have looked to remedies going to the trial without considering, at least in most written opinions, disciplinary action against the offending attorney. Whatever one thinks of the exclusionary rule,[31] ethical violations should be handled by hearings on ethics, not (only) by bandaging the violation at trial. Findings that the attorney had violated a rule could be handled by fines, suspension, or further infringements on the practice of law, without necessarily affecting the outcome of the criminal trial. It is likely that prosecutors are unqualifiedly immune from tort suits for *Brady* violation. See *Imbler v. Pachtman*, 424 U.S. 409 (1976).

EXAMPLES

1. Luke, charged with manslaughter, contends that he was at home the night of the murder. He is convicted. He later learns that Laura, the prosecutor, had obtained through a search conducted pursuant to warrant, e-mails that had been sent from his home computer at the time the homicide was committed, but she had never disclosed these materials to him. He argues that the e-mails would have verified his alibi, and that the nondisclosure violated *Brady* and requires a new trial. Does Luke have a case?

2. Peter Prosecutor interviews Wanda Witness in Witness's office. (1) He takes two pages of written notes of Wanda's statements call. Two days later, in his office, he dictates (2) a memorandum based upon the notes and his memory; the memorandum runs six pages. A week later, Wanda

---

30. The argument may have even more weight here, because it is unlikely that the defendant personally will even understand the rules of discovery. While it is possible that defense counsel may consult with the client about avoiding discovery responsibilities, this seems less plausible than discussions about trial strategy generally, which is the major thorn in the side of adequate counsel decisions.

31. Under the exclusionary rule, materials which are seized in violation of the Fourth Amendment or confessions obtained in violation of the Fifth Amendment are excluded from trial, even though they are exceptionally relevant. The purpose of the rule is to curtail undesirable police behavior. See Bloom and Brodin, Chapter 46.

calls Peter and adds several facts which she had forgotten during the interview. Peter (3) notes these, in writing, on the memorandum he had dictated. Which of the above items is discoverable under the Jencks Act (Fed. Crim. Rule 26.2)?

3. (a) Ben and Jerry are charged with robbing a bank and with homicide of a bank teller. Patsy, the prosecutor, hired Edward Expert to determine which gun generated the fatal shot. Expert concludes that it is not possible to determine which gun fired the shot. Patsy decides not to use the report against either defendant. Must Patsy disclose this report to Ben? To Jerry?

    (b) Suppose the state statute provides that while each defendant may be sentenced to life imprisonment, only the actual shooter may be subject to the death penalty?

4. Escobar, a federal prosecutor, interviews Guiliano, a potential witness. Guiliano declares that his friend, Doug, saw the drug deal in question, and that Doug said the defendant was not involved, or even present. Escobar does not call Guiliano at trial. Six months later, the defendant learns of the interview and the statement, and seeks relief on the basis of *Brady*. The defendant also learns that Doug died two months after the trial ended. What result?

5. (a) Raymond has been arrested by the police and charged with assault, based on the complaint of the victim. Priscilla Prosecutor, three days before the preliminary hearing, discovers in the file a letter from the victim addressed to "the prosecutor" in which the victim recants her earlier statements to the police, and maintains that the injury was merely accidental. Priscilla attempts to contact the witness but cannot. At the preliminary hearing, Priscilla calls the police officer who took the original statement from the victim. The magistrate "binds over" Raymond for trial. Has Priscilla violated *Brady*?

    (b) Suppose that, instead of the letter, Priscilla had learned just before the preliminary examination that the victim had died. Would she have to disclose that?

6. Julio, the prosecutor, knows that the affidavit which formed the basis of the search warrant which found the cocaine for which LeRoy is being prosecuted was false. He fears that at a suppression hearing, the cocaine will be suppressed. (a) If he uses the cocaine before the grand jury, must he also inform the grand jury of the legal dubiety of the affidavit; (b) If the grand jury indicts, when must Julio disclose the affidavit's tenuousness?

7. Frankie, operating undercover, had a discussion with Johnny in which Johnny acknowledged possessing cocaine. Frankie tells the district attorney of this conversation, and puts it in writing. Under what circumstances is this discussion discoverable?

8. Phillip Le Carre has been convicted in state court with being one of four persons who robbed the Forty-Seventh National Bank. This is also a federal offense, because the bank is federally insured. After the conviction, Le Carre's lawyer, George Smiley, learns that the FBI had conducted an investigation of the robbery. It had interviewed several witnesses, each of whom had given descriptions which in no way resembled Le Carre. Is Smiley likely to win on appeal if he claims that Moira, the state district attorney, who knew of these interviews, had a duty to turn over these potentially exculpatory interviews?

9. Lincoln is charged with (a) assaulting Meriam, his estranged wife, and with (b) violating an abuse prevention order. Immediately after the alleged assault, Meriam was interviewed by Adrian, an employee of the County Victim-Witness Advocacy organization, a private group which explains the process to victims, notifies them of court dates and the final disposition of the case, and provides information about the availability of social services. The legislature has supported these services with financial support, and by including them within the meaning of the term "prosecutor" in the state's Victims' Bill of Rights. Can Lincoln receive discovery of Adrian's notes of the meeting?

10. Claude Coke has been charged with homicide. He tells his attorney, Gene Hacker, that the killing was in self-defense, and gives Hacker (a) the names of five people who were present at the killing; (b) the name of two people who heard the victim threaten to kill Coke the next time they met; and c) the names of two people who can assert that the victim had a reputation for violence. Under what conditions must Hacker disclose any or all of this information to the prosecutor?

11. Regis is charged with possession of cocaine. The prosecutor, Kelly, learns that the police officer who found the drugs and arrested Regis was, at the time, under investigation for illegal drug activity, and was later indicted. She does not disclose this information to Regis, who pleads guilty to the charge. Can Regis later have the plea overturned?

12. (a) Police, searching an abandoned house, discover a sofa with a bullet hole in it. They take pictures of the sofa, examine the bullet hole, and then take the sofa into their control. Several months later, the sofa has begun to deteriorate, and they have not yet tied it with any crime. As a health matter, they destroy the sofa. Thereafter, a body is discovered elsewhere and it is linked to the sofa. Your client, Cal, is ultimately tried for the murder. He argues self-defense, but the prosecution expert will testify that the angle of the bullet, as examined prior to the destruction of the sofa, would suggest that is unlikely. If you move to exclude the testimony, what is the likely result?

(b) If the trial judge denies your motion to exclude the evidence, what can you do?

EXPLANATIONS

1. No. For several reasons. First, the mere fact that e-mails were sent from his home computer does not demonstrate that Luke sent them. He could have arranged for someone else to do that or, in today's technology, he might have prepared his computer to send them at that time. Thus, the e-mails are not exculpatory. And under *Brady*'s retrospective test, it is hard to say that there is a "reasonable probability" their revelation would have led to a different verdict. Second, even assuming that the e-mails could have bolstered Luke's defense, and were *Brady* material, he had access to those e-mails himself. Courts, generally, hold that "Evidence is not suppressed if the defendant either knew, or should have known, of the essential facts permitting him to take advantage of any exculpatory evidence." *United States v. LeRoy*, 687 F.2d 610 (2d Cir. 1982). While Laura should be chastised, and possibly even disciplined, Luke's conviction stands.

2. Probably none of them. Under the Jencks Act, only statements of a witness are discoverable. Statements are defined as (1) "a written statement that the witness makes or signs, or otherwise adopts or approves; or (2) a substantially verbatim, contemporaneously recorded recital of the witness's oral statement. . . ." Peter's notes do not qualify; had they been very long, they might have met the second clause. Peter's memorandum, while much longer, might be argued to be "substantially verbatim," but it is not "contemporaneously recorded." Peter's notes are not discoverable; they might even qualify as work product. However, if Wanda had written a letter with the same information, or if the telephone call had been tape recorded, the material might be discoverable, the first as a statement "adopted or approved" by Wanda, the latter as a "substantially verbatim contemporaneous record" of her declarations. Note that if this were exculpatory material, it would be discoverable under *Brady*, but the timing issue, discussed in the text, would still apply.

3. (a) No. This is not *Brady* material, since it is not "helpful," much less exculpatory, to either defendant; each would be responsible for the other's actions. Under many state statutes or criminal procedure rules, expert reports are discoverable, but many also require that the prosecutor disclose only reports she "intends to use." One might question this limitation, since defendants would be delighted to learn that an expert hired by the prosecutor has either failed to find inculpatory material or, even better, has found exculpatory material. The latter would be discoverable under *Brady*, but not under the rule.

    (b) Now the answer may be different. The material in *Brady* itself went not to whether the defendant was guilty but to the degree of his punishment. In *that* sense, the report is "exculpatory." But what is the burden of proof at capital sentencing? If the defendant carried the burden of demonstrating that he did not actually kill the victim, the report would be unhelpful. But, since the prosecutor carries the burden of proof, unless Patsy has some other information, this report may make it difficult, perhaps impossible, for her to persuade the jury to send either of these defendants to the gurney. And that would make the report discoverable by each. Again, however, timing would be an issue. Since the report only goes to eligibility for the death penalty, Patsy could keep it concealed until after the two were convicted.

4. This is a difficult legal case, even if it's an easy one ethically. The first question is whether Guliano's statement is discoverable at all. Although it appears to be favorable, it is not admissible, since it is hearsay. Therefore, if Guiliano had been called, it is not obvious that, under the Jencks Act, the prosecutor would have had to disclose this particular piece of the interview, because neither the prosecutor nor the defendant could have asked Guiliano about the statement. In *Wood v. Bartholomew*, 516 U.S. 1 (1995), the prosecutor failed to disclose that a polygraph showed that a witness had lied about whether he had assisted the defendant in the crime. Polygraph results were not admissible. The Supreme Court held that these were not material.

The Court went on to say that defense counsel's argument that he could have used the results to persuade the witness to change his statement was "not reasonably likely." There is a possible implication that had the result been "more likely," disclosure of the inadmissible evidence would have been required. The federal circuits are split, although the majority hold that failure to disclose inadmissible evidence which might lead to admissible evidence violates *Brady*. *Ellsworth v. Warden*, 333 F.3d 1 (1st Cir. 2003). But see *Hoke v. Netherland*, 92 F.3d 1350, 1356 (4th Cir. 1996). Beyond this, suppose the defense had learned about Doug during the trial. Would the trial judge have allowed a continuance while they searched for Doug? If not, then the failure to comply with *Brady* (even assuming there was a *Brady* violation) did not prejudice the defendant. Finally, under the facts as given, the defense did not learn about Doug until well after the trial. Unless the defense can argue that (1) it could have interviewed Doug immediately after the trial; (2) Doug would have spoken to them; or (3) he would have said what Guiliano said he said, it will be difficult to obtain a new trial, based either on a *Brady* violation, or on the more general question of newly discovered evidence.

5. (a) The letter is certainly "material" as defined in *Brady*, and does have to be disclosed. The question is "when?" *Brady* does not specify the timing, and courts have divided on the question. In the disciplinary decision upon which this example is based, the prosecution argued that *Brady* only required disclosure before *trial*, not before the preliminary hearing. The state also argued that the standard of proof at a

preliminary hearing was so low (probable cause) that the defendant suffered no harm by the failure to provide the recanting letter until after the preliminary hearing. As seen in Chapter 4, in many states the prosecutor need not disclose adverse information to the grand jury, which could arguably be seen as the equivalent of the preliminary hearing, even if the evidence is "clearly exculpatory" and "directly negates" guilt.

The court in the case pointed to the ABA Standards for Criminal Justice: Prosecution Function and Defense Function 3-3.11(a) (3d ed. 1993), which requires disclosure "at the earliest feasible opportunity," and concluded that the prosecutor had acted improperly both under that standard, and under the state rule, which required "timely" disclosure. The court therefore rejected the prosecution's argument. The court also found that the preliminary hearing (in contrast to the grand jury proceeding) was a "critical stage" and that "when a prosecutor is aware of exculpatory evidence before *any* critical stage of the proceeding" she must disclose the evidence before the proceeding occurs. However, since the failure to disclose was not "intentional" and since the ABA had expressly added the word "intentionally" into the third edition, the court declined to discipline the prosecutor, whose conduct had not intended to injure the defendant. *In re Attorney C*, 47 P.3d 1167 (Colo. 2002). However, the decision was rendered prior to *Ruiz*, in which the Supreme Court held that a prosecutor need not disclose *Brady* information to a defendant prior to entering into a plea bargain. It is therefore possible that a prosecutor does not have a duty to disclose prior to trial, or at least prior to the time that the plea negotiations stall. That argument was not (directly) open to the prosecutor in the *Attorney C* case.

(b) Unlikely. Although this *information* is likely to mean that Raymond won't be prosecuted successfully, it is not *"evidence"* in the case, nor is it "material" as that term is normally used in evidence law. Moreover, the information does not "directly negate" Raymond's guilt, nor is it "clearly exculpatory." Finally, it is possible this is not information which only Priscilla has—the defense counsel could be keeping an ear out for this information as well. We might want to explore whether this was public information, or whether Priscilla obtained it because of her position. See Aaron, Note: Ethics, Law Enforcement and Fair Dealing: A Prosecutor's Duty to Disclose Nonevidentiary Information, 47 Ford. L. Rev. 3005 (1999).

6.   (a) Julio may present the cocaine to the grand jury without ever mentioning the affidavit. See Chapter 4—the grand jury may rely on suppressible evidence. And even in those jurisdictions requiring the prosecutor to inform the grand jury of evidence which "clearly exculpates" or "directly negates" the defendant's guilt, the weakness of the affidavit does not fit into either of those categories; the cocaine *was* there.

(b) After *Ruiz*, Julio can certainly discuss a plea with LeRoy's counsel without even mentioning the affidavit. And if there is no motion to suppress, there is no need *ever* to inform defense counsel — this is not even *Brady* material (exculpatory evidence).

7. As a general matter, this will not be discoverable. First, under *Brady*, the information is not exculpatory, and therefore not material. Second, under most state rules, and the federal rules, discussions with undercover officers, even if later recorded, are not discoverable because of the possibility of disclosing the officer's identity. Even in an open file jurisdiction, the prosecutor might seek a protective order, at least keeping Frankie's name, and possibly the entire conversation, confidential.

8. No. Although these are potentially *Brady* materials, since they might impeach other witnesses, or allow the defense to call these eyewitnesses, Smiley would have great difficulty meeting the *Brady* standard that there is a "reasonable probability" that the verdict would have been different. More importantly, the FBI is not under Moira's control, and *Brady* only requires disclosure of materials within the state's control. See *Taus v. Senkowski*, 293 F. Supp. 2d 238 (E.D.N.Y. 2003). This may suggest a weakness in the *Brady* test. While it might not be reasonable to ask Moira in most cases to scour the countryside to determine if other law enforcement agencies have information on a crime, in this instance, the crime is clearly also federal, and such a requirement would not be onerous in this situation. If Moira were aware of the FBI's interest, but not of the interview report, or aware of the interview report and had failed to request the FBI to provide her a copy, the answer might be different.

9. The first question is whether the information is within the "possession" of the "prosecutor" or the "government." The office here has no direct ties to the prosecution of the case; its function is primarily informational and protective of the victim. On the other hand, the legislature has endorsed the organization. While the mere inclusion of the organization in the term "prosecutor" may not be conclusive as to how to interpret the discovery rules, the fact that there is often strong cooperation between the office and the prosecutor may be determinative.

But that's not enough. To the extent that the notes are "reports," they may be discoverable pre-trial. But if Meriam has provided Adrian with any "statements," whether exculpatory of Lincoln, or raising possible impeachment of Meriam, they would be discoverable as any other "statements" within the statute, which might mean only after Meriam testifies, if the state uses a "Jencks-Act type" approach. Some federal courts applied the same standard to an agent's notes in determining whether rough notes of a witness's statements have to be disclosed at trial pursuant to the Jencks Act. That standard is always fact-specific, considering such factors as whether the agent intended to track the actual language used by the witness, the length of the notes in comparison to the length of the statement, and how much time intervened between the interview and the memorialization.

10. If Coke intends to deny the killing entirely, and has requested only discovery of *Brady* information, there is no requirement of disclosure at all. On the other hand, if he has moved for discovery of evidence obtainable only under state procedural rules, then he must comply with those rules if they require reciprocal disclosure. Unless he intends to raise a claim of self-defense, in most states Coke need not disclose to the prosecutor that he killed the victim. Some jurisdictions, however, treat a claim of self-defense the same way they treat an alibi or mental incapacity claim, and require at least notice of the defense. Depending on the precise wording of the statute or court rule, Coke will have to disclose some or all of the witness's names.

11. Perhaps. As a normal matter (see Chapter 7 on pleas and plea bargaining), a plea of guilty must contain a "factual basis" for the plea. Thus, Kelly (or even defense counsel) may have conceded the presence and amount of drugs. But it turns out that there was sufficient doubt about the factual basis of the plea to allow Regis to overturn it. But what if, at the allocution, Regis actually admitted possessing the drugs? Shouldn't that be a sufficient "factual basis"? Perhaps. But the (newly discovered) information that the police officer may have planted the drugs will probably work to undermine the plea. See *State v. Parsons*, 341 N.J. Super. 448, 775 A.2d 576, (N.J. App. Div. 2001).

12. (a) This is a real case — *State v. Osakalumi*, 194 W. Va. 758, 461 S.E.2d 504 (1995). The court held, consistent with *Youngblood*, that there was no sign of bad faith on the part of the prosecution, and therefore there was no violation of due process. You might suggest that the fact that prosecution took pictures and examined the sofa before destroying it indicates that they expected to prosecute a criminal act at some point. But the health aspect of the issue is probably sufficient to undermine any argument about bad faith. Of course, since this is a state prosecution, you can argue that the court should take a position more protective of defendants' rights. About a dozen states have declared that bad faith is not a necessary part of the defendant's showing because the destruction of evidence reflects governmental negligence.

(b) This is a good example of how you can lose the battle, but still win the war. A good defense attorney would ask for an instruction to the jury that put upon the prosecution some onus for having destroyed the sofa. From the defense viewpoint, the "best" instruction would establish an "irrebuttable presumption" that the evidence would have favored the defendant. A lesser burden would be that the destruction would establish a "presumption" (rebuttable) or even an "inference" to that effect. In *Osakalumi* itself, the trial judge had instructed the jury that:

> you should scrutinize it with great care and caution. This destruction of evidence occurred before the defendant could examine it. This destruction of the couch may very well have deprived the defendant of evidence crucial to his defense and which may in fact have exculpated him.

But the appellate court said that even that instruction was insufficient. Indeed, the court quoted Justice Steven, concurring in *Youngblood*, who suggested an instruction that would instruct the jury that: " 'you may infer that the true fact is against the State's interest.' As a result, the uncertainty as to what the evidence might have proved was turned to the defendant's advantage." 488 U.S. 59-60. Nevertheless, said the West Virginia court, "in the present case, even if such an instruction were given, it would not have sufficiently protected appellant's due process rights."

The moral: Just because the defense lost the battle, doesn't mean it had to lose the war. And consider, as well, what kind of instruction the prosecutor should have sought, and should seek in the next lost evidence case.

7

Pleas of Guilt and Bargained Pleas

Once Dan has learned whatever he can about the prosecutor's case, he must determine whether to proceed to trial. However, very few defendants actually go to trial; well over 90 percent of all verdicts are accomplished by pleas of guilty—and virtually all of those are the result of plea bargains. We will discuss plea *bargains* in the second section. But it is important to discuss the general concept of guilty pleas before we get to bargaining as such.

A. The Concept of "Pleading Guilty"

If a person is innocent until *proven* guilty beyond a reasonable doubt, why allow a person who is unfamiliar with what "proof" the law requires, to "admit" guilt? Several centuries ago, when the death penalty was the usual sanction, defendants could *not* plead guilty—the government was put to its burden (although out-of-court confessions were commonly obtained and admitted). Some reasons suggested as to why we would allow a defendant to waive a trial include: (1) to save the defendant's soul,[1] because confession is good for the soul. If the defendant actually committed the crime, and wants to atone, there is no obvious reason to preclude him from doing so and put him through what the Supreme Court has referred to as the "cruel impact . . . upon those defendants who would greatly prefer not to contest their guilt" (*Jackson v. United States*, 390 U.S. 570, 583 (1968)); (2) to "spare

---

1. Parents sometimes require their children to admit their culpability, on the theory that learning to take responsibility, and to admit it, builds character. Whether the law should be interested in building the character of adults may be problematic.

themselves and their families the spectacle and expense of a protracted courtroom proceeding" (ibid); (3) to save state resources; (4) to avoid acquitting the truly guilty defendant, because of the serendipity of trial.

None of these reasons is particularly compelling. To save his soul, the defendant could confess elsewhere (in a religious institution, or to a philosophy professor), rather than waive a jury trial. Indeed, some jurisdictions would not permit a defendant to plead "guilty" to a murder charge (although allowing a plea of *nolo contendere* ("I do not contest the charge"); apparently the confession of "guilt" would simply not be allowed.[2] We could reduce the resources entailed in trials by other methods, such as those attempted in Philadelphia, in which "summary" trials replace many straight guilty pleas. Concerns that a jury might be deceived suggest mistrust of jury (or even judge) trials generally. And if a case is *not* airtight, then it means that the prosecution cannot meet the standard of proof which the constitution requires.

B. The Prerequisites of a Valid Guilty Plea

A guilty plea waives most nonjurisdictional constitutional rights, most obviously the rights which are obtained at trial: (1) a jury, (2) cross-examination and confrontation, and (3) the requirement that the government meet the burden of proving guilt, a reasonable doubt standard of proof. (The "big three.") In addition, many "pre-trial" rights, discussed in more detail below, are also lost by a valid guilty plea. See *Tollett v. Henderson*, 411 U.S. 258 (1973) (a guilty plea "breaks the chain of events" which have occurred prior to trial). Before a court will allow a defendant to waive these rights, it must be convinced that the waiver is:

- voluntary; and
- knowing and intelligent

Because the guilty plea is made in public and with the assistance of counsel, the standard for guilty pleas is much easier for the state to meet than that for confessions under the Fifth Amendment.[3] While the Supreme Court has not fully defined "voluntariness" in the guilty plea context, it is clear that a threat which might, in the absence of counsel or in a police station, render a defendant's confession involuntary, would not automatically be deemed coercive of a guilty plea.

---

2. See, e.g, N.S. Stat. Ann. 2A133-1 in *Corbitt v. New Jersey*, 439 U.S. 212 (1978). That provision has since been replaced.

3. See Bloom and Brodin, 257-269 (4th ed. 2004).

Both state and federal court rules make clear that the *judge* must ascertain that the plea meets these criteria — Federal Rule 11, for example, explicitly states that the judge must "personally" question the defendant (and not merely his counsel) about his knowledge and the voluntariness of his plea. *McCarthy v. United States*, 394 U.S. 459 (1969). It is unclear whether this is a constitutional requirement; however, since all courts now do this, the issue may be moot.

1. *Voluntary*

> "(A) plea of guilty entered by one fully aware of the direct consequences, including the actual value of any commitments made to him by the Court, prosecutor or his own counsel must stand unless inducted by threats (or promises to discontinue improper harassment), misrepresentation (including unfulfilled or unfulfillable promises) or perhaps by promises that are by their nature improper as having no proper relationship to the prosecutor's business."
>
> *Brady v. United States*, 397 U.S. 742 (1970)
> (quoting *Shelton v. United States*) 246 F. 2d 571, 572,
> n.2 (5th Cir. 1957).

No one (anymore) puts a gun to the defendant's head to obtain a plea. But suppose the government does the equivalent — threatens the defendant with death if he does not plead guilty, but assures him that the worst punishment he would receive upon such a plea would be life imprisonment? In *United States v. Jackson*, 390 U.S. 570 (1968), the Court declared unconstitutional a statute which did essentially that. But if the defendant pleads guilty under the same statute, the plea is not involuntary. See *Brady* and *Corbitt v. New Jersey*, 439 U.S. 212 (1978).

Beyond the obvious coercion implicit in a threat of physical harm, courts are willing to tolerate many situations as not coercive. In *Bordenkircher v. Hayes*, 434 U.S. 357 (1978), the prosecutor offered defendant, charged with uttering a forged check in the amount of $88, punishable by a sentence of 5-10 years, a recommendation of a five-year sentence if defendant pleaded; if he did not, the prosecutor warned, he would charge defendant as an habitual offender, which subjected him to a mandatory life sentence. Defendant rejected the offer; after a jury conviction, he attacked the life sentence as vindictive. The Supreme Court did not have to decide directly whether a guilty plea under such circumstances would be constitutional, but *in dictum* strongly indicated that it would be valid. The Court found the defendant's refusal to plead noncoerced, and indicated that, had he pled and then attacked the plea, the result would have been the same. The same result ensues if the plea has been induced by threats of additonal charges, or a threat to indict a relative (a "wired" or "packaged" plea), see *United States v. Pollard*, 959 F.2d 1011 (D.C. Cir. 1992); or coerced by a nongovernmental source (such as an employer), *Sanchez v. United States*, 50 F.3d 1448 (9th Cir. 1995). In effect, the courts focus on the defendant's state of mind, not the inducement the state offers; if he actually knows the risks, then the plea is voluntary in virtually all situations.

These results are plausible; hard choices are, nevertheless, choices. And the defendant has placed himself in the situation. Moreover, the defendant receives the advice of counsel, both as to the likelihood of conviction, and the possibilities of punishment.[4] But how far can this view of voluntariness be taken? In *North Carolina v. Alford*, 400 U.S. 25 (1970), the Court held that a defendant who believes he is innocent, either actually or legally, may still enter a valid guilty plea, fearful that a conviction would result in a longer sentence than would a plea (Alford faced the death penalty if he were convicted of the greater charge). The decision essentially elevates the "knowing" leg of the doctrine over the "voluntary" prong; so long as the defendants *know* the chances of conviction, and their consequences, the choice will be deemed valid. Of course, in such instances, someone other than the defendant (usually the prosecutor) will provide the factual basis for the plea at the plea colloquy (see below). Since the defendant is waiving the highest standard of proof (beyond a reasonable doubt), the factual basis need not reach that level of proof. States are divided on whether to allow *Alford* pleas. See *Ross v. State*, 456 N.E.2d 420 (Ind. 1983). The *Alford* plea disturbingly (realistically?) recognizes that innocent defendants may be erroneously convicted at trial, and that a decision by a defendant to plead guilty (usually to a lesser charge) is not irrational or coerced.

2. Intelligent

So long as the defendant is mentally competent, and able to understand his lawyer's advice, courts are reluctant to probe into the defendant's understanding. In *Godinez v. Moran*, 508 U.S. 389 (1993), the Court adopted as the measure of intelligence the standard of competence to stand trial—whether the defendant understood the proceedings and could assist his counsel. This relatively low standard is almost always met; if it is dubious, the Court should delay the plea and inquire as to the defendant's mental ability. Much more important is the information upon which he places that intelligence—whether he "knows" enough to plead guilty.

---

4. "(I)t may be appropriate to presume that in most cases defense counsel routinely explained the nature of the offense in sufficient detail to give the accused notice of what he is being asked to admit." *Henderson v. Morgan*, 426 U.S. 637, 647 (1976).

3. *Knowing*

a. Knowing the Charge—Factual Basis

Federal Rule 11(b)(3) requires that there be a *factual basis* for the plea. Thus, at a "plea colloquy" someone (not necessarily the defendant) must proffer evidence that all the elements of the crime were present. If the defendant acknowledges those facts to be true, there is a factual basis for plea.[5] Indeed, even if the defendant is not aware of all the elements that must be proved, the plea is knowing if the element of which he is ignorant is not crucial.[6] See *Henderson v. Morgan*, 426 U.S. 637 (1976). Twenty years ago, one writer said of this requirement: "Nothing could be less clear from the decided cases than the appropriate scope of judicial inquiry into the factual basis of the plea where any inquiry at all is required. The ambiguity is between the view that the record must show the defendant committed the offenses and the view that all the record need show is that the defendant . . . was rational." J. Bond, Plea Bargaining, sec. 3.55 (1982).

The primary source for determining whether the defendant knows—or has been informed about—these and other rights, is the transcript from the colloquy, but in determining whether defendant (or his counsel) knew these facts, the court may look to other circumstances. The court has never spoken to the burden of proof involved in these proceedings; Rule 11(b)(3) requires merely that the court must be "satisf(ied) that a factual basis exists."

b. Knowing the Impact—"Direct" and "Collateral" Consequences

Beyond demonstrating knowledge of the elements of the crime, the defendant is entitled to know the effects of his plea. After *McCarthy v. United States*, 394 U.S. 459 (1969) and *Boykin v. Alabama*, 395 U.S. 238

---

5. There is no firm indication that even this is a constitutional requirement. *McCarthy v. United States*, 394 U.S. 459 (1969), was clearly a construal of Rule 11, not a constitutionally based opinion. *Alford* hinted that a "factual basis" might be a constitutional prerequisite, but it did not so hold.

6. The Court must advise the defendant that the government has to prove every element of the offense including the quantity of drugs involved, before a plea can be knowing. *United States v. Villalobos*, 333 F.3d 1070 (9th Cir. 2003). See also *United States v. Reyes*, 2002 WL 1290864 (5th Cir.) (court must inform defendant about the sentencing range). Accord: *State v. McDermond*, 2002 WL 1264135 (Wash. App. Div). But he need not be informed that he would be unable to appeal any refusal by the court to depart downward at sentencing. *United States v. Rada*, 319 F.3d 1288 (11th Cir. 2003).

(1969), it is clear that the Constitution requires the court to inform the defendant that he is waiving "the Big Three" constitutional rights:[7]

- the right against self-incrimination
- the right to jury trial
- the right to confrontation

Beyond this, however, the decisions are unclear. The standard language is that defendants are entitled to know the "direct," but not the "collateral" effects of their guilty plea. Under the *federal* rules (but not necessarily as a constitutional matter), the judge must inform the defendant of:

- the maximum aggregate sentence which could be imposed;
- any mandatory minimum penalty;
- any applicable forfeiture, order of restitution, or special assessment;
- the court's obligation to apply the federal Sentencing Guidelines;
- the terms of any provision in the plea agreement waiving the defendant's rights;
- the right to appeal or collaterally attack the sentence.

In some states, additional "direct" consequences include: any mandatory loss of some benefits, and a mandatory listing as a sexually violent predator, which may require life-long registration, and lifetime supervision.[8]

In the majority of jurisdictions, the following have been held to be "collateral"; neither the court nor the prosecutor[9] is required to tell the defendant about the effects the conviction might have upon:[10]

- probation revocation;
- discretionary judicial authority to impose a consecutive or concurrent sentence;
- good-time credits;
- civil service employment;
- federal benefits whose loss turns on facts not known at time of plea;
- right to vote;

---

7. It could also be added that the defendant is waiving his right to issue compulsory process to obtain witnesses at trial, to testify in his own defense (or to remain silent), and present evidence.

8. See, e.g., *State v. Bellamy*, 178 N.J. 127, 835 A.2d 1231 (2003); *Palmer v. State*, 59 P.3d 1192 (Nev. 2002).

9. For a suggestion that *defense counsel* should be *constitutionally* obligated to advise clients of the possible collateral consequences, see Chin and Holmes, Jr., Effective Assistance of Counsel and the Consequences of Guilty Pleas, 87 Cornell. L. Rev. 697 (2002).

10. Of course, individual jurisdictions may vary. See, e.g., *State v. Howard*, 110 N.J. 113 (1988), requiring the trial court to inform the defendant of the possibility of parole consequences of a sentence to adult diagnostic and treatment center.

- unencumbered foreign travel;
- possible appearance before a psychiatric panel before parole;
- possibility of deportation;
- unlikelihood of review of refusal to depart downward in sentence;
- potential immigration consequences;
- future sentencing implications (three-time-loser laws);
- loss of professional licenses (debarment, etc.);
- an order of restitution;
- registration (even life-long) as a sex offender.[11]

The line appears to be between those events which are "sure" to happen, and those which "may," but need not, happen because they are discretionary; as one court put it, "direct" consequences are "definite, immediate and largely automatic," *State v. Ross*, 916 P.2d 405 (Wash. 1996). This explanation, however, does not fit the requirement that the court, at the plea colloquy, inform the defendant of the maximum sentence, since in most systems the actual sentence imposed is discretionary. Moreover, if the reason supporting that requirement is that the defendant's main concern is with the amount of time he will actually serve, one might think that, at least some of the items above would also be required. Except for the possibility that a judge would forget to mention all of these, there appears to be no reason not to assure that the defendant really "knows" all the consequences of a plea. There is, perhaps, a concern that the "possible" consequences are limitless, and that requiring a judge to inform the defendant of every possible consequence would be fruitless, and produce litigation. A checklist—which is already used by judges to comply with Rule 11—could be employed in every case. ABA Standard Pleas of Guilty 14-1.4(c) essentially provides such a list. The apparent reasons for not providing a longer list of such information are (1) the assumption that defense counsel will tell the defendant of these possibilities (see *Comm. v. Begin*, 394 Mass. 192 (1985), (but see *Lacy v. People*, 775 P.2d 1 (Colo. 1989)); (2) preservation of the court's time;[12] (3) concerns that the list would become "endless."

Extraordinarily, one thing the defendant need not "know" before pleading guilty is the strength of the state's case. In *United States v. Ruiz*, 536 U.S. 622 (2002), already mentioned in Chapter 6, and which will be more fully discussed in the section on plea bargaining, the Court held that a guilty

---

11. *State v. Moore*, 2004 WL 601718 (N.M. App.) See also, *Mitschke v. State*, 129 S.W.3d 130, (Tex. Crim. App. 2004), holding that such a registration requirement *is* a direct consequence but is nonpunitive and, therefore, failure to admonish the defendant does not render the plea involuntary.

12. One study found that the average court time per felony plea was 9.9 minutes while misdemeanors were timed at 5.2 minutes. William McDonald, Judicial Supervision of the Guilty Plea Process: A Study of Six Jurisdictions, 70 Judicature 203 (1987).

plea made before the prosecutor had turned over *Giglio* discovery material could be valid at least if the prosecutor had agreed to provide "any information establishing the factual innocence of the defendant." Thus, the defendant need not know even the constitutionally minimal discoverable case against her before validly pleading guilty.

While the defendant must be informed about special parole terms, he need not be informed of his parole eligibility generally. Thus, in *Hill v. Lockhart*, 474 U.S. 52 (1985), the defendant's attorney misinformed him of the effect that his previous felony conviction would have on his parole eligibility. This was insufficient to allow him to withdraw his plea (and, as we will see in Chapter 10, would almost certainly not amount to inadequate assistance of counsel).

As in the insanity doctrine (see Singer and Lafond, Chapter 17) there may be a great deal of difference between "knowing" and "understanding." The defendant is asked at the plea colloquy whether he "knows" these items. But "knowing" the potential maximum sentence, for example, and appreciating the likelihood of receiving that sentence may be significantly different things. Furthermore, the actual conditions under which the plea is taken are not necessarily conducive to deep reflection by the defendant on the precise "elements" of the crime, much less upon the various rights involved.

4. The "Conditional" Plea

Defendants may sometimes wish to plead guilty, but retain the right to challenge, on appeal, a prior judicial decision, such as one refusing to suppress evidence which the defendant claims was illegally obtained. Today, courts allow such a "conditional" plea — if the appellate court agrees with the defendant, the plea is vacated and the case moves forward without that evidence. If the appeal is unsuccessful, the plea (and the sentence) stand.

C. Withdrawing a Guilty Plea

A defendant may become disenchanted with her plea, particularly before she has been sentenced. In most states, a defendant has no absolute right to withdraw the plea once entered. Federal rules provide three different standards for withdrawal, depending on the time of the withdrawal. A defendant who has entered a plea which has not yet been accepted may withdraw it for "any reason or no reason." If she moves to withdraw the plea *after* the court has accepted it, but *before* sentence, she must show a "fair and just reason" for withdrawal. *United States v. Hyde*, 520 U.S. 670 (1997). If the defendant seeks to withdraw the plea *after* sentence, however, most jurisdictions, including the federal courts, virtually preclude relief; a defendant will meet a "near presumption" against granting such motions, and must show that a "manifest injustice" will occur if the plea is not withdrawn. See ABA Standards, Pleas of Guilty 14-2.1(b) Cf. *Pennington v. State*, 286 Ark. 503 (1985). As a practical matter, these defendants must use either a direct appeal or a habeas corpus petition. As discussed in Chapter 12, the "harmless error" rule, and the "miscarriage of justice" standard will make success in such proceedings extremely unlikely. In *United States v. Benitez*, 124 S. Ct. 2333 (2004), where defendant sought to have his guilty plea vacated for a non-constitutional error of Rule 11, the Court applied the *Bagley-Brady* prejudice test (see Chapter 6), requiring the defendant to show a "reasonable probability that, but for the error, he would not have entered the plea." The Court distinguished the case where a *constitutional* error had occurred during the plea colloquy.

If a defendant is allowed to withdraw a plea, most courts declare that whatever concessions a prosecutor might have made to induce the plea are no longer applicable; the parties are returned to square one, and trial (or a new series of pleas and negotiations) must occur. Thus, if Harry, charged with first degree murder, pleads to second degree and then successfully withdraws that plea, the prosecution may proceed with the first degree charge,[13] assuming no vindictiveness. *Blackledge v. Perry*, 417 U.S. 21 (1974).

EXAMPLES

1. Dwayne is charged with mail fraud, an essential element of which is, that there was use of the mails in furtherance of the fraud. Dwayne's letter may not fit that legal definition. If Dwayne acknowledges at the plea colloquy that he sent a letter in the mail, and that it was part of the fraudulent scheme, is his guilty plea "intelligent"? "knowing"?

2. Your client, Toby, unable to make bail, has been incarcerated for six months. He has always maintained his innocence, but now he tells you he wants to plead guilty. His explanation is that the conditions in the jail are horrible; he is particularly distressed by the strip searches which all prisoners must undergo both randomly and before and after every visit. He knows that this does not occur in the state minimum custody facility, to which he is likely to be sent after conviction. Is this plea "voluntary"?

---

13. It is generally agreed that this does not violate double jeopardy, because the prosecutor's voluntary agreement not to proceed with the higher charge never put the defendant in jeopardy of that charge. See *Alabama v. Smith*, 490 U.S. 794 (1989). If, on the other hand, the prosecutor brings *greater* charges than originally brought, problems of vindictiveness and double jeopardy might arise.

3.   (a) Helen is charged with carrying a weapon while selling drugs, a crime which carries a mandatory term of imprisonment of 10 years. The statute also provides for a "special parole term" of five years, which is to be added to the sentence. At the plea colloquy, the trial judge informs her of the maximum possible sentence, and indicates that special parole, in contrast to "normal" parole, occurs *after* service of the sentence. He does not inform her that if she violates special parole she will be returned to prison for the full length of the special parole term the plea is accepted. At her sentencing, the judge informs her of this possibility. At that point, Helen seeks to withdraw her plea. What result?

       (b) Suppose Helen learns only after sentencing about the terms of special parole, and *then* seeks to withdraw (or vacate) her plea. What result?

4.   Jacques is charged with distributing cocaine. Two relevant statutes provide as follows:

       1. Any individual . . . convicted of (such an offense) shall

       (A) at the discretion of the court, upon the first conviction for such an offense be ineligible for any or all (governmental) benefits for up to 5 years after such conviction;

       (B) at the discretion of the court, upon a second conviction for such an offense be ineligible for any or all (governmental) benefits for up to 10 years . . .; and

       (C) upon a third or subsequent conviction . . . be permanently ineligible for all Federal benefits.

       2. Any individual convicted (of drug distribution) . . . shall not be eligible for

       (A) assistance under any governmental program funded under (another statute);

       (B) benefits under the food stamp program. . . .

       You are the judge accepting Jacques's plea. Of which of these provisions, if either, must you inform Jacques for the plea to be valid?

EXPLANATIONS

1.   Probably. In *Henderson v. Morgan*, 426 U.S. 637, n.18 (1976), the Court suggested that there was no constitutional requirement that the defendant be aware of, or be informed about, "every element of the offense." It is difficult, if not impossible, to deduce which elements meet that definition, however, since without all the elements, the state has not proved the crime. In this particular crime, both the fraudulent intent and an *actus reus* would seem to be "critical" elements; whether the mailing had in fact been part of the scheme might be thought of as "noncritical" in the sense that the defendant's moral (if not legal) culpability

has been established. The courts have grappled with attempting to determine which elements are "noncritical." Thus, it is likely that Dwayne's plea will be deemed "knowing," particularly since he was represented by counsel. While counsel can't "replace" the judge, courts frequently indulge a presumption that counsel have (attempted to) inform defendants of the elements of the crime. *Henderson* was, as the Court itself said, "unique" because the trial court there explicitly found that the defendant did not know the critical element of *mens rea*.

2.   Under *Alford* even innocent defendants can plead guilty, if their pleas are "knowing," "intelligent," and "voluntary." Toby's desire to avoid harsh conditions, while hardly irrational, could be seen as rendering his decision "involuntary," if the conditions of confinement were illegal. But the strip searches of the kind mentioned have been upheld as constitutional, particularly in pre-trial detention centers, see *Bell v. Wolfish*, 441 U.S. 520 (1979), so the state's use of them does not constitute unconstitutional pressure. The other conditions, however, might be illegal, and hence render the plea involuntary. Whether Toby's decision is "knowing" and "intelligent," however, may be open to more dispute. If there are litigational, or administrative, methods of dealing with these other conditions, and Toby is not aware of those avenues of relief, his plea might not be "intelligent" or "knowing." Moreover, there is no assurance that he will be imprisoned under easier conditions. If Toby assumes that conditions will be less severe in prison than in jail, he might be acting unknowingly. But since these conditions are not assured, not automatic, the court has no duty to point that out to Toby. *You* have the obligation to point that out to him. This example is based upon an actual case; the trial judge refused to accept the guilty plea. See *New York Times*, Oct. 25, 2000.

3.   (a) Very unclear. The general standard of withdrawal prior to sentencing allows withdrawal for any "fair and just reason." The first question is whether the court had an obligation, at the plea colloquy, to inform Helen of the specific terms of special parole. That, in turn, requires a determination of whether the revocation policy is "direct" or "collateral." Clearly, the *imposition* of special parole *is* direct. But the *revocation*, and the duration of revocation, is discretionary. Nevertheless, most courts would say that the court must inform her of *all* the attributes of special parole, lest she assume that it is like "normal" parole. Still, the failure to inform Helen of these terms would not necessarily make the plea "unknowing." Here, the court must guess whether Helen would have continued to plead guilty had she known of the parole revocation policies. Helen, of course, is claiming that the knowledge of the possibility of a five-year extra sentence, *if* she violated parole, would have affected her decision to plead guilty to a crime already carrying a 10-year

automatic sentence. While this is not implausible, it is at least suspect. A court could go either way here, and not be reversed on appeal.

(b) It is highly unlikely that she'll be allowed to do this. The standard becomes much more difficult: Did the failure to inform Helen of these terms constitute a "manifest injustice"? If the court denies the motion to vacate the plea, it will surely be upheld. Helen will have to seek vacation of the plea on collateral attack, or appeal. That, too, is highly unlikely. See Chapter 12.

4. Although each of these provisions declares that the individual "shall" be ineligible, Section (1) nevertheless makes ineligibility dependent on the discretion of the judge. Thus, the loss of these benefits is not automatic, and becomes collateral. The loss of benefits under Section (2), however, is automatic and is therefore "direct." You must tell Jacques that he'll lose food stamp eligibility. Of course, Jacques might care more about the first kind of government benefits, but his concerns are not relevant here. See *United States v. Littlejohn*, 224 F.3d 960 (9th Cir. 2000).

D. Plea Bargaining — Bane or Salvation?

"There is no glory in plea bargaining. In place of a noble clash for truth, plea bargaining gives us a skulking truce. Opposing lawyers shrink from battle, and the jury's empty box signals the system's disappointment. But though its victory merits no fanfare, plea bargaining has triumphed. Bloodlessly and clandestinely, it has swept across the penal landscape and driven our vanquished jury into small pockets of resistance. Plea bargaining may be, as some chroniclers claim, the invading barbarian. But it has won all the same."

George Fisher, Plea Bargaining's Triumph,
109 Yale L. J. 857,859 (2000).

"Whatever might be the situation in an ideal world, the fact is that the guilty plea and the often concomitant plea bargain are important components of this country's criminal justice system. Properly administered, they can benefit all concerned. The defendant avoids extended pre-trial incarceration and the anxieties and uncertainties of a trial; he gains a speedy disposition of his case, the chance to acknowledge his guilt, and a prompt start in realizing whatever potential there may be for rehabilitation. Judges and prosecutors conserve vital and scarce resources. The public is protected from the risks posed by those charged with criminal offense who are at large on bail while awaiting completion of criminal proceedings."

Blackledge v. Allison, 431 U.S. 63 (1977).

1. An Overview

There is little neutral opinion on the question of the desirability of plea bargaining — you either hate it, or you tolerate it (few people actually love it). On its face, plea bargaining is in tension with the general test of voluntariness of confessions — that the confession "must not be extracted by any sort of threat or violence, or obtained by any direct or implied promises, however slight, nor by the exertion of any improper influence." *Bram v. United States*, 168 U.S. 532 (1897). Applied literally, this standard would invalidate every plea bargain, for there is always a promise or inducement to the defendant to plead. Indeed, several years ago a three-judge panel of the Tenth Circuit startled the legal world by holding that any promise of leniency in exchange for a plea of guilty violated the federal bribery statute, 18 U.S.C. §201(C)(2), which makes it a crime "to directly or indirectly give, offer, or promise anything of value to any person for or because of the testimony . . . to be given by such person. . . ." *Singleton v. United States*, 144 F.3d 1343 (10th Cir. 1998). (After the furor died down, the entire court, *en banc*, reversed the panel, 165 F.3d 1297 (10th Cir. 1999).)

A century ago, plea bargaining was excoriated; attorneys who participated in discussions were threatened with disbarment, if not worse.[14] By the 1960s, however, there was grudging acceptance of the process. In the so-called "*Brady* trilogy," the lead opinion of which was *Brady v. United States*, 397 U.S. 742 (1970), the Court, in dictum, seemed to support the practice.[15] A year later, in *Santobello v. New York*, 404 U.S. 257 (1971), the Court gave *de jure*, and not merely *de facto*, approbation to the process.

Santobello did not stop the debate. Shortly thereafter, the National Advisory Commission on Criminal Justice Standard and Goals, called for an abolition to plea bargaining by 1978.[16] Obviously, the call was unheeded: The practice has not merely survived; it has thrived and grown since that time. Today, plea bargaining is not merely acknowledged — it is seen as the glue which holds the criminal justice system together.

Nearly 90 percent of all cases settle by guilty pleas, and virtually all pleas result from bargaining. The basis of the process is mutuality, the defendant

---

14. "We are aware that the custom has obtained to a considerable extent, for the attorney-general to compromise or settle this class of cases . . . upon payment of a certain sum of money to the State by the defendant . . . but the practice is a vicious one, and meets with our entire disapproval. There is no law authorizing a sentence or any legal substitute, therefore, by consent of the parties, without the imposition thereof by the court." *State v. Conway*, 20 R.I. 270, 273 (1897).

15. As noted above, *Brady* involved a statute which the Court had determined to be unconstitutionally coercive, but to which the defendant had pled guilty prior to the Court's decision. The Court upheld the plea as knowing and intelligent.

16. Courts, Standard 3.1 (1973).

receives (the possibility of) a lower sentence than she otherwise would have received, and the state avoids both the burden, and the risk, of a trial.[17] If every case went to trial, the contention is, courts would immediately become clogged.[18] Critics disagree, pointing to the continent, and even England, where plea bargaining is, essentially, forbidden. Others endorse alternatives to pleas and negotiation, such as the experiment tried in Philadelphia in the 1970s and 1980s, in which "summary trials," lasting an average of two hours, replaced bargaining.[19] Critics also argue that those criminals with the most to offer the prosecutor, information on other criminals, can obtain the greatest concessions: precisely the wrong utilitarian message to deliver to those involved in crime. Conversely, those who cannot offer much, or who decide to go to trial, will receive harsher sentences for the "same" crime, based upon individual characteristics unrelated to culpability. An even more Machiavellian view might argue that it is only plea bargaining which has allowed legislatures to increase statutory sentences, knowing that prosecutors and defense counsel will find methods to evade the harshness in "deserving" cases.

Various studies, and students, of the criminal justice system have found that of two similarly situated defendants (perhaps co-defendants in the same offense), one will often receive a harsher sentence because he went to trial. They argue that this chills the Sixth Amendment right to trial. While some of that increase may be because more details about the crime — and the defendant's culpability — may be revealed at trial, at least some of the differential is explained by the threat (sometimes actually made by trial court judges) — "You took some of my time, now I'll take some of yours."

2. *Types of Bargains*

Prosecutors have enormous power. As we saw in Chapter 3, they can simply refuse to charge the defendant at all, *or* they can charge (1) every possible offense, in a series of counts; (2) very serious offenses carrying

---

17. Another societal gain is that more defendants can be punished, since there is more judicial time available to try cases (or take pleas).

18. See Alschuler, The Prosecutor's Role in Plea Bargaining, 36 U.Chi. L. Rev. 50, 54 (1968), quoting a prosecutor: "Our office keeps eight courtrooms extremely busy trying 5 percent of the cases. If even 10 percent of the cases ended in a trial, the system would break down."

19. See Schulhofer, Is Plea Bargaining Inevitable?, 97 Harv. L. Rev. 1037 (1984). It is alleged that when Philadelphia went to summary trials, the parties debated over whether defendants would waive their right to a jury trial and elect a brief bench trial instead, a process that was facilitated by the fact that the judges who ran bench trials were considered "soft" sentencers. See C. Silberman, Criminal Violence, Criminal Justice 284 (1978).

substantial penalties. Particularly since these decisions are made, as we saw, when not even the prosecutor has all the facts, the tendency is to charge the most severe possible charge, lest the initial indictment need to be superseded with higher charges. This truth, however, means that prosecutors have at least two promises by which they can induce defense agreement:

- *charge bargaining*, by which charges are either removed entirely from the indictment, or "downgraded" to lesser included offenses;
- *sentence bargaining*, in which the prosecutor agrees either to support a specific sentence (lower than the maximum sentence provided by statute) or not to oppose a sentence recommendation by the defense.

Some argue that charge bargaining leads to prosecutorial overcharging, in the expectation that the negotiations will then result in the defendant pleading to the "right" charge. Sentence bargaining, on the other hand, is often criticized as a direct impingement on judicial sentencing discretion. While judges retain the authority to ignore the specific sentence included in a plea agreement, or a specific recommendation by the prosecutor, the reality is that few judges will do that, in part because it would undermine future plea bargaining, which both judges and prosecutors see as crucial to keeping the system moving.

Fact bargaining is a relatively new phenomenon. Until 1980 or so, sentencing discretion was fully in the hands of the individual judge, who could focus on *any* fact in determining the exact sentence within very wide ranges (e.g., 5-20 years). (See Chapter 11.) In the past two decades, many states and the federal government have moved to "structured sentencing" systems, in which sentences are set much more narrowly, and "enhanced" only if specific statutorily circumstances are present (e.g., whether the defendant carried a gun). Because the enunciated duration will depend on these facts, the lawyers on both sides now negotiate about these facts as well; if they agree *not* to mention the gun in the indictment, the judge may never learn of it, and therefore, may never use that fact to increase the sentence. The plea agreement rarely indicates that there was negotiation about these facts — it simply states the facts to be "stipulated" as true.

3. Inducements — Or Threats?

One person's "inducement" is another's "threat." A promise to delete a charge in exchange for a plea is equally, at least, an implied threat not to delete that charge if there is no plea. But no "threat," not even that of the death penalty, will necessarily invalidate a guilty plea, so long as that plea is knowingly and intelligently made. Since (by hypothesis), the penalty threatened by the legislature is constitutionally permissible, it is not the individual prosecutor, but the state government itself, which is positing the possibility of the penalty. Any offer by the prosecutor, then, may be seen as an offer to mitigate a permissible penalty—a merciful, ameliorative act.[20] As the Supreme Court declared in *Brady*, the plea may have been "caused" by the heavier penalty, but it was not "coerced' by that penalty.

Again, because the courts have focused on the defendant's mental state (voluntarism and knowledge), the following inducements by prosecutors if the defendant agrees to a negotiated plea have been held not to be "coercion":

- not to prosecute another person (usually a loved one);
- not to bring greater substantive charges (so long as it is not vindictive);
- not to bring a charge, particularly recidivist charges, which would result in significantly higher penalty (usually life imprisonment);[21]
- not to inform the court of a defendant's cooperation in finding and prosecuting others.

The most potent explanation for not disallowing these (and other) threats is that the defendant who bargains is represented by counsel—a counseled plea is presumptively valid, because the defendant is fully informed by counsel of the real risks involved.[22]

4. *Judicial Participation*

Judicial "inducements" might seem even more coercive, more certain, than those from a prosecutor—while the prosecutor can merely "recommend" a sentence, if the judge participates in the process and " suggests" that a particular sentence "would likely" be accepted, the defendant is likely to believe he can take that to the bank. For this reason, the federal system (Rule 11) and many states (e.g., Pa. R. Crim P. 319 B(1); Ga. Unif. Super. Ct. R. 33.5(a); Mass. R. Crim. P. 12 (b)) prohibit any participation by the court in negotiations. But other states allow such participation. See N.C. Gen. Stat. Sec. 15A-1021(a). The Supreme Court has not addressed the issue. The tension created by judicial participation is between the two prongs of the guilty plea liturgy: Judicial participation makes the plea much more knowing (because the judge essentially guarantees what the sentence will be if there is a plea) but arguably much less voluntary (because the defendant now fears a longer sentence if he rejects the judge's "offer").

---

20. This may explain the different results in *Jackson* (*supra*, pp. 109–110), and an instance where the prosecutor offers to "take the death penalty off the table" in exchange for a plea. In *Jackson*, the statute did not individualize among defendants charged with capital offenses, whereas in the second instance, the prosecutor makes an individualized judgment about who should be given the benefit if constitutional rights are waived.

21. *Bordenkircher v. Hayes, supra*, p.111.

22. If counsel does not adequately inform or advise the defendant, there may be a claim of inadequate representation. See Chapter 10.

Because of these tensions, the American Bar Association has vacillated on whether to endorse such participation. In 1968, the Association encouraged judicial participation, Function of the Trial Judge sec.4.1 (1968), but by 1999 had restricted judicial participation to indicating (dis) approval of an agreement tentatively reached by the parties. Pleas of Guilty 14-3.3 (1999). A late 1970s study found that approximately one-third of criminal trial judges attended plea discussions, a percentage that seems not to have changed in the intervening quarter-century. See Ryan and Alfini, Trial Judges' Participation in Plea Bargaining: An Empirical Perspective, 13 Law and Soc. Rev. 479 9 (1979), and Anderson, Judicial Participation in the Plea Negotiation Process: Some Frequencies and Disposing Factors, 10 Hamline J. Pub. L. & Policy 39 (1990).

An intriguing variation of this process was tried in Detroit, where a special "plea judge" would offer the defendant a maximum ceiling on his sentence in exchange for a guilty plea. If the defendant accepted, the plea would occur; if not, the defendant would be tried by a different judge. See Comment, Pretrial Sentence Bargaining: A Cure for Crowded Court Dockets?, 30 Emory L.J. 853 (1981).

5. *Waiving Rights*

Any guilty plea, even without negotiation, involves waiving some rights — constitutional, statutory, or court created. But prosecutors, particularly since *Santobello*'s endorsement of plea bargaining, have required defendants to waive a significant number of other rights before a plea bargain will be accepted. The law is unsettled here; in the words of one commentator, "The Supreme Court has lurched from one decision to the next without providing meaningful guidance . . . or maintaining any consistent theoretical approach regarding criminal waiver."[23] Thus, in *United States v. Mezzanatto*, 513 U.S. 196 (1995), the Court held that the defendant may waive the right not to have statements made during plea negotiations used against him if he later goes to trial. *Mezzanatto*, however, was a fairly narrow decision — the defenant had agreed to permit the government to use plea negotiation statements *only* to rebut any contradictory testimony by the defendant himself. In *United States v. Velez*, 354 F.3d 190 (2d Cir. 2004), the Second Circuit substantially broadened the point, upholding a waiver of all privileges under Fed. Rule Evid. 401, which would, absent waiver, prohibit the government from using, for any purpose, statements made during a plea negotiation. See also *United States v. Krilich*, 159 F.3d 1020 (7th Cir. 1998). If *Velez* remains law, it is likely that prosecutors will make this waiver as well, a boilerplate part of any negotiation.

---

23. Blank, Plea Bargain Waivers Reconsidered: A Legal Pragmatist's Guide to Loss, Abandonment and Alienation, 68 Ford. L. Rev. 2011 (2000).

The Court held in *United States v Ruiz*, 536 U.S. 622 (2002) that the defendant could waive his *Giglio* rights to discovery of materials which could be "useful" at trial (see Chapter 6). Although the prosecutor in *Ruiz* promised to produce any information which proved defendant's innocence, the proffered agreement would require the defendant to forego discovery of materials useful for impeachment of prosecution witness. *Ruiz* undermines an earlier case, in which the Court had indicated that if any rights are nonwaivable, those that were "fundamental to the reliability of the fact-finding process" might be so deemed.[24] The distinction that the *Ruiz* court drew between directly exculpatory evidence and impeachment evidence, which also goes to reliability, may seem thin but the issues here are more complex than may first appear. Although the *Ruiz* decision may initially seem implausible, it may be helpful to separate two issues in the case. First, could the defendant, *without a plea bargain*, plead guilty before obtaining *Brady* disclosure? Surely the answer to this question, assuming the plea would be voluntary and knowing, would be yes. A defendant who knows he is guilty,[25] and simply wishes to atone for that act, without any bargain, surely should not be forced to wait until the prosecutor has obtained and disclosed all *Brady* information. If a plea would be valid if unilaterally entered by the defendant, the second question then arises: Does the prosecutor's threat to withdraw a bargained-for leniency, unless the defendant waives those same rights, unfairly alter the balance, or affect the *voluntariness* of the plea? In significant part, this may relate back to the timing of disclosure (see Chapter 6). Since, under *Brady* itself, the defendant has no "right" to disclosure until just before trial (or, in the case of a witness's statement, until after the witness testifies) whatever pressure the defendant feels from the prosecutor's withholding that information prior to trial appears not to be unconstitutional coercion. Where, under statute or court rule, disclosure must be much earlier, it is more plausible to argue that prosecutorial refusal to disclose is illegal coercion, and renders null any resulting plea agreement.

Finally, it may be hard to conceive of a defendant "knowingly waiving" a right to information he does not know about. But that may simply be a

---

24. See Kupers and Phillipsborn, Mephistophelian Deals: The Newest in Standard Plea Agreements, 23-Aug. Champion 18 (1999) ("The *Brady* waiver is really an appalling attempt by the government to set us back to another age in criminal procedure").

25. Herein lies a possible flaw — the distinction between "factual" guilt and "legal" guilt. While a defendant may know his conduct, he may not know the legal ramifications of his conduct, or possible defenses to liability. But assuming that he is competently represented, he may be sufficiently apprised of these matters. And if he is not, he may attack his guilty plea on grounds of inadequate representation. See Chapter 10.

semantic problem—if the *Ruiz* case is recast in terms of forfeiture, rather than waiver, it may be more understandable.

A rule forbidding the defendant to plead guilty until *Brady* material had been disclosed might protect him from prosecutorial coercion, but it also denies him a potential bargaining chip in his plea negotiations. If, as we have suggested here, the key issue is knowledge, the defendant who waives this right with regard to the state's evidence-in-chief will also nevertheless be held to have entered a valid plea agreement.[26]

On the other hand, it appears that certain constitutional and statutory claims are not yet waivable, even as part of a plea agreement:

- the right to effective assistance of counsel;[27]
- the right to be tried in a court with proper jurisdiction;
- the right to conflict-free representation (see Chapter 10);
- the right to nonracially discriminatory sentencing;[28]
- the right not to be subject to a statutorily excessive sentence;[29]
- the right against double jeopardy.

6. *Accepting and Enforcing the Bargain*

In contrast to the practice half a century ago, when plea bargaining was done secretly and never mentioned, plea agreements are now contained in written, open documents between the parties which are distributed to the court before the entering of the plea. The agreement recites both the defendant's willingness to plead, and the *quid pro quo* which the prosecutor cedes as consideration for the plea. The agreement must recognize that as to sentencing, the judge can reject any sentence understanding. But while judges may reject the bargain, they are loathe to do so: (1) if the agreement reflects a *charge* bargain, some courts will be reluctant to review what the they deem prosecutorial discretion; (2) courts may believe the system needs such negotiation; (3) they have ongoing relationships with the attorneys.

Deciding whether a defendant has failed to perform her agreement to cooperate may be difficult. In *Ricketts v. Adamson*, 483 U.S. 1 (1987), defendant agreed to testify against his co-defendants, in exchange for being allowed to plead to a charge which did not carry the death penalty. At the co-defendants' trial, he testified as the key witness on direct, but on

---

26. Defendants may also be required to waive their right to file a civil claim against the officers who arrested them (or the governmental unit for which they work). *Town of Newton v. Rumery*, 480 U.S. 386 (1987).

27. *United States v. Attar*, 38 F.3d 727 (4th Cir. 1994).

28. *United States v. Jacobson*, 15 F.3d 19 (2d Cir. 1994).

29. *United States v. Marin*, 961 F.2d 493 (4th Cir. 1992). See generally *Blank, supra*, n.23.

cross-examination he invoked the Fifth Amendment; which gave his co-defendants a clear Confrontation Clause claim guaranteeing that their convictions would be reversed (as they were). Thereafter, defendant was sentenced as agreed to under the plea arrangement. The government wished to retry the co-defendants, and to have Adamson testify once more, but Adamson, arguing that he had complied with the wording of the agreement to testify once, sought more benefits (including release immediately after the co-defendants' retrial, although the original agreement had called for a sentence of more than 20 years). The government then moved to have the plea agreement rescinded, and to have Adamson tried for the capital offense. On the question of whether defendant would have to "retestify" against his co-defendants, the agreement was ambiguous, and one might have expected the Court to construe that ambiguity against the government. But Adamson was clearly manipulating the process (and had done so by invoking the Fifth Amendment) and the Court allowed the state to rescind the plea agreement. The real problem here is that the usual remedies available for a breach of an agreement seem either excessive or impotent. To require Adamson to testify (truthfully) at the second trial would visit upon him no adverse consequences for an apparent breach. On the other hand, to impose the death penalty for his less than forthright testimony seems disproportionate to his offense (he did, after all, testify).[30] This might argue for allowing a Court to impose an "equitable" remedy for defendant breach, such as increasing the length of the sentence, but not totally rescinding the agreement. As a result of these concerns, a wily prosecutor will seek to postpone the defendant's sentencing until all opportunity to cooperate has occurred.

On the other hand, if the prosecutor[31] fails to perform, or the defendant has detrimentally relied, courts have seen several possible remedies. The most frequently used are: (1) requiring specific performance of the agreement; (2) allowing the defendant to withdraw and renegotiate. Defendants, of course, would choose specific performance rather than recission of their guilty plea. After all, who wants to start re-negotiating with the prosecutor whose actions have just been judicially questioned at your instigation? Nevertheless, the consensus is that the choice of remedy lies in the hands of the judge, not the defendant. See *State v. Munoz*, 23 P.3d 922 (Mont. 2001). Washington, and a few other states, sometimes place the control in the hands of the injured party. *State v. Miller*, 110 Wash. 2d 528, 756 P.2d 122 (Wash. 1988).

---

30. Indeed, the Ninth Circuit so held in a later opinion. *Adamson v. Ricketts*, 865 F.2d 1011, 1022 (9th Cir. 1988).

31. The defense counsel, or defendant, may also fail to perform, but the only sanctions then are (1) personal and professional steps against counsel; (2) rescinding the plea and remanding the defendant for trial.

When either side alleges a breach of the plea agreement, courts may hold a hearing, at which the understanding of the parties will be assessed, and their subsequent actions measured. These hearings may be complex, and involve subtle issues. For example, the agreement may be breached by other state agents. In *State v. Matson,* 268 Wis. 2d 725, 674 N.W.2d 51 (Wis. App. 2003), the chief investigating officer wrote a detailed five-page letter to the judge with approval of the police department, recommending a maximum sentence. This was in direct conflict with the plea agreement, and the court allowed the defendant to withdraw the plea. In *Santobello,* the trial court held an inquiry into the extent of the defendant's cooperation. However, in federal court such an inquiry is precluded, because section 5K1 of the Federal Sentencing Guidelines provide that a reduction for cooperation is allowed only "upon motion of the government." Thus, a defendant who believes he has cooperated fully, but who is denied a 5K1 recommendation, has no remedy but to withdraw his plea, if that is allowed. State courts, however, are more aggressive, as in *Santobello.*

In assessing whether there has been performance, it is irrelevant that the prosecutor's nonperformance was purely inadvertent; the defendant may still be entitled to either enforce the bargain or withdraw from it.

If the defendant has detrimentally relied, but the promise is "unfulfillable," a court may create a remedy of whole cloth. Thus, suppose that Leona, relying on a bargain by a state prosecutor which includes a promise that there will be no federal prosecution, thereafter testifies against a co-conspirator, only to learn that the state prosecutor cannot bind the United States. What remedy should the defendant receive? Judges often appear to think themselves restricted, but the equity of the chancellor, which is surely what is being invoked here, is essentially boundless. Substantial reduction of the sentence, for example, might appear to be a more balanced approach in some instances; in others, perhaps, the court could simply order the prosecutor, as an officer of the court, to rescind all charges against a defendant.

Unmentioned in almost all of the cases is the possibility of ethical sanctions against the attorney, either prosecutor or defense counsel, who fails to perform a bargain. While this is not a remedy against the breaching party (the state or the defendant), personal sanctions might have more effect than institutional ones in making sure that *pacta sunt servanda.*

7. *The Contract Analogy*

As suggested by the language used above, many courts, and commentators, have used contract doctrines in determining not only the meaning, but the enforceability of plea agreements. Some argue that the analog is inapt, on the grounds that the parties have unequal bargaining power. Nevertheless, if the prosecutor breaches the agreement, courts may order the government to "specifically perform" the contract. On the other hand, in obvious contrast to usual contract doctrine that an executory contract is enforceable from the time the parties exchange promises, in plea bargains, until the court has accepted the agreement, it is "in embryo," and either side may withdraw from the agreement without apparent sanction. See *Mabry v. Johnson*, 467 U.S. 504 (1984), unless there has been "detrimental reliance. (See Blum, Contracts: Examples and Explanations). Partial nonperformance might require some sanction short of abrogating the entire plea bargain, but many courts employ an "all or nothing" approach. Commentators have suggested drawing even further from contact law, including providing for "cooling off" periods. Indeed, some have argued that the inequality of bargaining power may make plausible an argument that, notwithstanding *Ruiz*, courts should require more disclosure before allowing a defendant to bargain at all. Professors Scott and Stuntz for example, argue that "the contract principles of adhesion, duress, mistake, unconscionabilty, and public policy all suggest that . . . waivers of the right to disclosure of *Brady* material cannot (pass constitutional muster)." Scott and Stuntz, Plea Bargaining as Contract, 101 Yale L.J. 1909, 2074 (1992). In any event, both sides should attempt to make the agreement as clear and unambiguous as possible, so that there is no question whether there has been a breach and, perhaps, what each side contemplates as a sanction for any such breach.

8. *Assessing Plea Bargaining*

As the quotations at the beginning of this subsection indicate, plea bargaining may be the single-most controversial aspect of criminal justice as it is actually practiced. Opponents, such as Professor Fisher, argue that plea bargaining is immoral "justice for sale." Moreover, from a utilitarian viewpoint, bargaining, as immunity generally, appears to benefit those most deeply enmeshed in crime, whereas the "small fish" have insufficient information by which to obtain prosecutorial largesse. They further argue that the process undermines jury trials, and makes both defense and prosecution less exacting in their preparation, because they know that most cases will not get to trial. Finally, they argue that some crimes are so dangerous, or heinous, that any reduction in the threatened sentence is unwarranted.

It would be hard to call the opposing camp "advocates" of bargaining. Instead, they argue that bargaining is a necessary evil, mandated by the burgeoning number of arrests. Since 90 percent of convictions occur as a result of pleas, a decrease to 80 percent would double the number of trials, causing impossible log jams and unconscionable delays. A relapse to 0 percent pleas would be unthinkable. Moreover, while bargaining with the "middle fish" is not palatable, it is said to be the only way to obtain sufficient information to prosecute the true managers and leaders of organized criminal activity. Finally, a bargain avoids the possibility that some weakness in the proofs, or some bizarre jury machination, could let a guilty defendant go.

Many jurisdictions have attempted to eliminate plea bargaining, at least with regard to some crimes, by explicitly mandating arrest, and declaring that plea negotiations shall not be allowed with such charges and establishing mandatory sentences. Conspicuous among such legislation have been sexual offenses, gun offenses, some drug charges, drunk driving, and domestic abuse. Critics have argued that these statutes have been unsuccessful, merely driving bargaining "underground." Thus, prosecutors will bargain with defense counsel before the indictment or information is filed, agreeing to "remove" that part of the facts that make the crime eligible for a plea bargaining ban.

Some commentators think that these are only half measures, and that all bargaining should be banned. In Alaska, during the 1970s, such a statewide ban was imposed on all prosecutors by the Attorney General. The data from this experiment are uncertain; some believe that most bargaining did in fact disappear, while others argue that defendants were simply charged with the crimes to which they "would have" pled, so that the prosecutor simply anticipated the result of hypothetical bargaining.

Surely the strongest argument for retaining bargaining is the fear that the courts would be inundated with trials. In Alaska's experience, however, this did not seem to be the case. Opponents point to other jurisdictions, particularly the European continent, where bargaining is said not to occur, at least to the degree it occurs here, but adherents of bargaining respond that those countries have inquisitorial, rather than adversarial, proceedings. Finally, opponents of bargaining point to some systems, such as Philadelphia's, where many crimes are tried in "summary" trials, in which most facts are stipulated, but a judge, or jury, hears "encapsulated" testimony from witnesses concerning disputed facts and legal arguments. Critics argue that this is simply "slow bargaining."

Plea bargaining is clearly part of the legal landscape as the twenty-first century begins, and is not likely to disappear within the lifetimes of either the author or the readers of this book. The debate will continue.

EXAMPLES

1. Kim enters into a plea agreement which states, in part: "Defendant is aware that 18 U.S.C. §3742(a) affords her the right to appeal the sentence imposed. Knowing that, in exchange for the Government's concessions made herein, the defendant hereby waives to the full extent of the law, all right to appeal her conviction or sentence." At the sentencing, the trial judge declares: "Now, I am finding, as required by the guidelines, that you stole more than $5,000, which requires me to

impose at least a four-year sentence. And that is what I will do. Of course, you have the right to appeal that sentence." Kim, in fact, wishes to appeal. The prosecution argues that she has waived that right. Who wins?

2. (a) Kirk and Jean Luc are charged with armed robbery of the corner grocery store together. The maximum sentence is 10 years. Kirk enters into a plea bargain to a charge of possession of a weapon, and receives a three-year sentence. He also testifies against Jean Luc, describing in detail how the robbery occurred. The jury acquits Jean Luc. Kirk now moves to vacate his plea. May he?

   (b) Assume that the police captured the two long before the robbery, and that the charge against each was conspiracy to rob. Again, Kirk pleads guilty. At Jean Luc's trial, a videotape shows Kirk and Jean Luc discussing some robbery. Kirk testifies that the target was the grocery store. Jean Luc is acquitted. May Kirk vacate his plea now?

3. Bert and the prosecutor of Marin County reached an agreement in which the prosecutor agreed to recommend a 10-month sentence for a street mugging. At the sentencing hearing, the victim, the probation officer of Marin County, an investigating officer for Marin County, two probation officers from Marylu county (who had supervised Bert on his probation for earlier offenses), each testify, and each recommend the maximum (five years). The court imposes a three-year sentence. Is there breach of the plea agreement such that Bert may vacate the sentence?

4. Laurel reaches a plea agreement with the prosecutor that declares that the "government has agreed not to take any action with respect to (her) pilot's license." After the plea is entered, the state licensing board revokes her license. Laurel seeks to vacate the judgment and her plea. What result?

5. Your client, Henrietta, has been charged with aggravated assault, but she has a putative self-defense claim, and you suspect that the only eyewitness is shaky at best. The state has a statute which provides that there can be no plea bargaining in any serious felony "unless there is insufficient evidence to prove the people's case, or testimony of a material witness cannot be obtained, or a reduction or dismissal would not result in a substantial change in sentence." Your phone rings; it is the prosecutor, suggesting a plea bargain. How do you respond?

6. (a) On May 30, defendant Barbara and the prosecutor, after intense negotiations, agree that if Barbara "cooperates with the prosecutor's office in pursuing John Jorge, a known drug dealer," the prosecutor will ask the court to drop three of the four pending charges against Barbara and will recommend a probationary sentence. The plea collo-quy is set for June 25. On June 18, the prosecutor informs you, as

Barbara's counsel, by letter, that he is withdrawing from the agreement, because it appears that Barbara is not a "mule," but a significant participant in the drug trade. What do you do?

(b) Same facts as (a) except that on June 6, the prosecutor had asked Barbara to wear a "wire" in a buy from Jorge and she had done so.

(c) Same facts as (b) except that the prosecution learns of the changed facts only after the plea colloquy. It seeks to vacate the plea, and to try Barbara on all four charges.

(d) Same facts as (b) except that the prosecution, rather than moving to vacate the plea and conviction, now calls you and asks Barbara to testify against Jorge. Barbara — and you — believe that this will put her life in jeopardy.

7. (a) Reynaldo was charged with six counts of bank fraud, each of which carried a possible five-year maximum sentence. He agreed to plead to one of those counts, if the prosecutor dropped the other five; he saw this as avoiding the risk of 25 more years in prison. The judge sentenced him to the maximum five years. State statutes provide that a prisoner is eligible for parole after serving one-third of his term, less good time. In this case, Reynaldo is eligible for parole after 14 months. Soon after his arrival in prison, Reynaldo is told by his fellow inmates that the practice throughout the state is for judges to impose concurrent sentences in all but exceptional cases. Reynaldo feels he's been bamboozled. Can he successfully move — now — to vacate his guilty plea?

(b) Suppose that the sentencing practice mentioned in (a) is mandated by state statute, which allows concurrent sentences *only* where the judge makes written findings explaining why concurrent sentences are inappropriate.

(c) At his first parole hearing, one of the members of the Board tells Reynaldo: "You got your leniency when you got those other charges dropped. We never parole someone who has gone through charge bargaining. You'll be our guest for five years."

8. (a) Ken Lie, CEO of a major corporation, has heard that a number of his employees have been subpoenaed before a grand jury. Lie knows that there is great consternation over a missing $30 million. Lie has received no subpoena, nor has he been informed that he is a target of the grand jury. He comes to you for advice. The state precludes plea bargaining of any crime involving fraud. What do you do?

(b) Suppose Lie has indeed received a letter that he is a target of the grand jury investigation. What do you do now?

9. Enrique helped his friend Rocco to move his furniture from Pennsylvania to West Virginia. The truck crashed only several miles after it crossed the Pennsylvania-West Virginia border. Boxes inside the van

contained over 200 pounds of marijuana. Helen, the United States Attorney for the District of Pennsylvania, which is in the Third Circuit, initially charged Enrique with interstate transportation of a controlled substance, in exchange for a guilty plea to lesser federal offenses, apparently because Helen believed Enrique's claim that he did not know the boxes contained marijuana. The plea agreement provided that "the government" agreed that the transporting charges would be dropped. After Enrique's guilty plea, the U.S. Attorney for West Virginia, which is in the Fourth Circuit, filed an indictment charging interstate transportation of the marijuana into West Virginia. Enrique now moves to preclude the second prosecution, claiming that "the government" includes the Fourth Circuit as well as the Third. What result?

EXPLANATIONS

1. The prosecutor. Although a few courts have held that a blanket judicial assurance of the right to appeal cancels a preexisting waiver of appellate rights, most courts disagree. See *United States v. Michelson*, 141 F.3d 867 (8th Cir. 1998). While such assurances as that given by the trial judge "muddy the waters," they do not effect a *per se* nullification of plea agreement waiver of appellate rights. Because this conclusion is fact-specific, if there is any information which would make this particular assurance unduly powerful, Kim might have a chance. Otherwise, she'll miss one entire leap year cycle.

2. (a) No. Kirk gave a factual basis for his plea both at the plea colloquy and at Jean Luc's trial. His plea was knowing and intelligent, and there is no ground for vacating his plea now. The fact that the jury acquitted Jean Luc is a risk Kirk took. When you roll the dice. . . .

    (b) No. But the argument here is different. Kirk will argue that (1) if the jury acquitted Jean Luc, it must be because there was no conspiracy; (2) if there was no conspiracy, Kirk could not have been a co-conspirator. But that's insufficient. First, the jury's acquittal does not mean they didn't find an agreement; the jury may simply have "nullified." Second, at least under some modern statutes, including the Model Penal Code, the jury may find a defendant guilty of a "unilateral conspiracy." (See Singer and Lafond, Criminal Law, Examples and Explanations, Chapter 13.) Finally, even if the jury found that there was no conspiracy (because the discussion hadn't gone far enough, or there was no overt act, etc.), and therefore Kirk could not "logically" have been a co-conspirator, Kirk's plea was voluntary, and he knew the risks he was taking. The issue is not whether, as a matter of logic, Kirk could not have been a co-conspirator; the issue is whether the plea was knowing and voluntary. It was. As Holmes said, the life of the law has been not logic, but experience.

3. It is not likely that the prosecutor could control the victims' testimony. Moreover, just as he knows that he takes a risk that the judge will not follow a sentencing recommendation, it is not unreasonable to conclude that the defendant knows the victim is likely to be unhappy, and may well urge a more severe penalty. As to the other governmental witnesses, however, the risk analysis is less clear. Probably, the "answer" depends. (Does that sound (too) familiar?) If Bert is in Florida, there has probably been a breach. Florida holds that a prosecutor's plea bargain binds all state agents. *Lee v. State*, 501 So. 2d 591 (Fla. 1987). Most courts, however, are not persuaded. A good example is *State v. Sanchez*, 46 P.2d 774 (Wash. 2002). Two defendants, in consolidated sexual assault cases, had entered plea agreements which bound their respective prosecutors either to make no sentence recommendation, or to recommend a specific sentence. In each case, the prosecutor individually kept that bargain. But in each case, another governmental agent—Sanchez's investigating officer (a local, and not a "state" employee) and Harris's community corrections officer—urged higher sentences. The court held that these last two government agents were not bound by the plea agreement, and that the prosecutor had no statutory authority over either, "explaining" that the agreement was between the prosecutor and the defense attorney (which would mean, one would suppose, that the attorney, and not the defendant, should move for specific performance). The court noted that while, statutorily, the prosecutor was required to notify the *victim* of a proposed plea agreement,[32] there was no duty to discuss the plea agreement with an investigating officer. A concurring opinion distinguished between the IO (a law enforcement officer) and the CCO (an employee of the court). The dissent also looked at the statutory duties of each officer, and concluded that each was an agent of the prosecutor.

The federal courts appear to agree with the Florida position. See, e.g., *Margali-Olvera v. I.N.S.*, 43 F.3d 345 (8th Cir. 1994); see also *Giglio v. United States*, 405 U.S. 150, 154 (1972), probably because there is a "unitary" governmental structure in the federal system. Does it make sense to look at the precise statutory structure? Should one look to the defendant's reasonable expectation? Is there any analog here with the discovery cases as to whether the prosecutor must disclose evidence "in the control of" another governmental agency? (See Chapter 6). Even assuming that there was no collusion between the prosecutor(s) and the

---

32. The vast majority of states have enacted "victims rights" laws, some of which mandate such notification; most statutes, however, simply admonish the prosecutor to do her best to keep the victim informed. Prosecutors who are too much influenced by the victim's views may find their actions monitored by a court. See *State v. McDonnell*, 313 Or. 478, 837 P.2d 941 (Or. 1992).

witnesses in *Sanchez*, and even agreeing that the prosecutor could not control them, why is there not a duty on the part of the prosecutor to inform the defendant of the (probable) views of these witnesses? In *Sanchez* itself, it appears that the prosecutor affirmatively sought out the investigating officer, and discussed the plea agreement. Does it take much to infer that, at least tacitly, the prosecutor (as Sanchez alleged) *knew* that the IO would testify, and would recommend a harsher term? After *Sanchez*, would you expect the defendant to attempt to have the bargain include either a bona fide effort by the prosecutor to control such testimony, or at least impose a duty upon her to notify the defendant that another state employee will take a different view? If you were the defense counsel, and the prosecutor refused to agree to such a clause, what inferences would you draw? What new clauses would you include in any future plea agreements?

4.   Interpreting plea agreements can be incredibly difficult. As indicated in the text, these agreements are usually construed against the prosecutor, who usually drafts them, although there is often discussion of the precise wording. In the case upon which this example is based, the court did not do that — it construed the term "government" narrowly to mean only the prosecutor, and not other government agencies. Since the *prosecutor* had not taken action with regard to Laurel's license, there had been no breach. See *United States v. Rourke*, 74 F.3d 802 (7th Cir. 1996). Does that make sense? Even conceding that the defendant could have sought a definition of "government" or to clarify the term by adding "any government entity of any kind," isn't Laurel's license obviously a sufficient consideration that she would have sought to protect it against *all* governmental action?

5.   This provision, Cal. Penal Code §1192.7, was adopted by vote initiative. If literally enforced, it would seem to preclude any defense attorney from accepting a plea offer, since the conditions for an offer effectively mean the state's case is extremely weak. If that were the case, you'd ask the prosecutor to call back next Feb. 29. But, as you might imagine, prosecutors and defense counsel often reach accommodation in California anyhow.

6.   (a) Wince. A plea agreement is not enforceable until the court has accepted it. Thus, the prosecutor would be able to walk away from this agreement. A motion to compel specific performance would be unavailing.

     (b) Now the facts have changed. Barbara has acted in reliance on the agreement; it is unlikely that she would have put herself at risk by wearing the wire had she not anticipated that the prosecutor would conform with the agreement. In such a situation, the courts are much more willing to enforce her expectations and require specific performance.

But don't wait until the judicial hearing to raise your concerns. Immediately call the prosecutor and remind him of the law on the matter. If you have an ongoing relationship with the prosecutor, and represent many clients, you will probably stop there. If, however, this is a one-time appearance, you might in passing mention the prosecutor's superior, or the disciplinary review board. But prepare your papers to compel specific performance on June 25.

(c) Although prosecutors may seek to vacate agreements on the basis of nonperformance, there is no reason to allow them to overturn the agreement because of a misapprehension of the underlying facts. Barbara has performed the contract, and it has now been accepted by the court. Finality requires no further inquiry.

(d) This is really tricky. It's not a legal issue, but a practical one. If Barbara refuses to testify, the prosecution will argue that she did not "cooperate" as the agreement required, that she is, therefore, in breach, and the sentence should be vacated. This will require the court to decide what the word "cooperate" meant, and the extent to which the obligation extended past the judgment. As a general position, courts in earlier times construed plea agreements against the state, who generally drafted them, and often proffered them on a "take it or leave it" basis. In recent times, however, when both sides negotiate not only about the shape of the undertakings, but the specific wordings, this may be less likely. You may lose this argument — unless you could persuade the court that the prosecutor's new request is merely a gambit intended to manipulate you to refuse to cooperate, so that it could move to vacate.

7. (a) Reynaldo may be right, but there is no relief for him. Nothing in current law requires the court, or anyone else, to tell Reynaldo of the sentencing policies in the state. While the court did inform Reynaldo of the maximum he faced on the one count, there is no legal duty to inform Reynaldo of the sentence he "might have" obtained had he not entered the charge bargain. The courts depend on defense counsel to be aware of these policies, and to tell clients of those policies. Unless counsel's failure to know about these policies — and to tell Reynaldo about them — is ineffective assistance of counsel (see Chapter 10), Reynaldo has learned a good lesson, but he'll still be in prison. Ironically, this is one instance where defendants with public defenders may be in a better situation than those with retained counsel — the latter, unless doing exclusively criminal practice, are likely to be less informed than the former about practices, just as they may be less informed about the sentencing proclivities of individual judges.

This problem is not limited to concurrency. In many sentencing systems, particularly those not using "guidelines" (see Chapter 11), many crimes have sentences that overlap. For example, robbery may be punished by 5-20 years, and larceny by 3-10 years. If the practice within the jurisdiction is to sentence "robbers" to 6 years, a defendant who obtains a charge bargain from a robbery to a larceny charge may still receive the same six-year sentence that he would have received without the reduced charge, and hence without the plea. Again, nothing in legal decisions about plea bargains requires the prosecutor or the court to familiarize defendants, or their counsel, with these vagaries. (The problem can be even more exacerbated; in "individualized" sentencing schemes, individual judges may vary widely in their sentencing philosophies: Judge A may impose prison terms of 5 years for crimes for which Judge B typically imposes probation. See Chapter 11). Again, there is no constitutional rule for disclosing these practices in order for a plea to be "knowing and intelligent."

(b) This strengthens the argument that counsel was ineffective; even if an attorney is not required to be aware of "practices," he might be required to know statutory law. But it is still unlikely that there is relief for Reynaldo for two reasons: (1) the statute does not *mandate* concurrent sentences, so Reynaldo *did* get some benefit — the elimination of the risk (however slight) of consecutive sentences; (2) even if the statute did mandate concurrency, this one failure of counsel, however important to Reynaldo, is unlikely to mean that the entire representation was inadequate. Again, see Chapter 10.

(c) Although the federal rule, and many state rules, require the court to inform the defendant about "special parole" policies, which generally attach *after* full service of a prison term, most courts do not require information about parole *practices*, whether informal or statutory. Thus, for example, many states in the 1990s statutorily precluded parole eligibility for "violent offenders" until they had served more than 80 percent of their sentence. Defendants, or their attorneys, who were unaware of these changes, or who had served time under more lenient standards, were sometimes stunned to discover the new ineligibility rules. But that didn't make their pleas invalid, and rarely resulted in a finding of inadequacy of counsel.

8. (a) This question *really* belongs back in Chapter 3, but it is tied in to plea bargaining, as subsection (b) indicates. At this point, defense counsel is in a quandary. It is *possible* that the prosecutor is not targeting Lie, but that an inquiry, however discreet, might alert the state to such an idea. On the other hand, particularly in light of the ban against plea bargaining, you want to cut the indictment off at the pass, or at least minimize the harm it might do. You could call the prosecutor and offer your client's testimony — if he is a target, the prosecutor should tell you that. And Ken's willingness to present his side of the case may be appreciated. It is probably too early to begin asking for immunity, but you

should be sensitive to that possibility as your discussion with the prosecution progresses.

(b) Here's the bargaining issue. You know that once Lie is indicted, it will be extremely difficult to bargain with the prosecutor, whether over charge or sentence. Your job as counsel now is to bargain over the possible facts — and hence the likely charge — *before* the indictment is issued. You might, for example, seek to persuade the prosecutor that Lie was only negligent, or reckless, rather than purposeful with regard to the $30 million. This might avoid a charge of "fraud," and result in another charge, which could *then* be bargained, because it is not "fraud." Indeed, you might (with Lie's permission, of course) indicate a willingness to plea directly to such a charge, were that the limit of the indictment. There is often room for good lawyering, even in the most rigid of systems.

9. The law here is, to say the least, murky. Clearly, successor prosecutors in the same office are "bound" by their predecessor's bargains. Some courts, following a strict contract analogy, hold that this is the full extent of any contract. *United States v. Russo*, 801 F.3d 624 (2d Cir. 1986). Moreover, if the defense wants to clarify the term "government," it may do so; ambiguity here should not bind a nonparty to the agreement. The Third and Fourth Circuits utilize the law of contract and the law of agency in finding that such plea agreements bind across jurisdictions. *United States v. Harvey*, 791 F.2d 294 (4th Cir. 1986); *United States v. Gebbie*, 294 F.3d 540 (3d Cir. 2002). Is "pocket immunity" (see Chapter 4) analogous?

8

The Jury

"(The jury is) at best . . . the apotheosis of the amateur. Why should anyone think that twelve persons brought in from the street, selected in various ways, for their lack of general ability, should have any special capacity for deciding controversies between persons?"

(Harvard Law School Dean) Irwin Griswold,
Harvard Law School Dean's Report 5-6 (1962-1963)

"(It) is a terrible business to mark a man out . . . But it is a thing to which a man can grow accustomed, as he can to other things . . . And the horrible thing about all legal officials, even the best, about all judges, magistrates, barristers, detectives and policemen, is not that they are wicked . . . not that they are stupid . . . it is simply that they have got used to it.

Our civilization has decided . . . that determining the guilt or innocence of men is a thing too important to be trusted to trained men. It wishes for light upon that awful matter, it asks men who know more law than I know . . . When it wants a library catalogued, or the solar system discovered, or any trifle of that kind, it uses up its specialists. But when it wishes anything done which is really serious, it collects twelve of the most ordinary men standing round."

G. K. Chesterton, The Twelve Men, in Tremendous Trifles 80 (1922)

A. Overview

The common American image of a criminal proceeding is that of a jury trial—prosecuted by Jack McCoy and defended by Perry Mason. But, as Chapter 7 demonstrated, most criminal cases are settled by plea bargains;[1] only the rare case goes to trial, and even among those, nearly half are tried "to the bench" rather than by a jury. In England, where the jury originated, jury trials now comprise only 1 percent of all criminal proceedings. Juries are even rarer in the rest of the (non-Commonwealth) world—many European countries employ "mixed panels" consisting of professional judges and one or two laymen, and most countries use only judges entirely. Still, many argue that the most important contribution made by Anglo-American law to jurisprudential thought and practice is the jury, particularly the criminal jury.

The English "created" the jury trial by accident. Of earlier civilizations, only Greece (and to a lesser extent Rome) relied upon a jury system.[2] Pre-conquest England relied primarily on blood feuds to settle scores. As seen in Chapter 4, the Norman conquerors employed "presentment" juries to inform them of suspected crimes and criminals. But the defendant was usually "tried" by "ordeal," such as being submerged in water,[3] being required to carry an extremely hot piece of iron for a certain distance, etc. The ordeal depended on the participation of a priest (for example, to bless the water). When, in 1215, the Pope forbade priests to participate in the process, the country scampered to find a substitute method of assessing guilt. By default, the presentment jury was given that job. And after several centuries, the presentment jury (now known as the grand jury) was separated from the petit (trial) jury.

The right to jury trial appeared in all 12 of the written state constitutions predating the Declaration of Independence.[4] It is the only "right" protected in the Constitution itself, as well as in the Bill of Rights. Today, every state constitution except one contains the guarantee. Although at least 10 states

---

1. These general figures can be misleading. Larger percentages of "serious" offenses appear to be tried to juries. Moreover, even if only 5 percent of all criminal cases are tried to juries, this would still be approximately 45,000 trials per year, state and federal.

2. The change from blood feud to jury is dramatized in Aeschylus, the Orestia, when Athena herself establishes the jury to thwart vengeance by the Furies against Orestes.

3. In English jurisprudence, the water was blessed by a priest; and the defendant was thrown into the water, while tied. If the defendant sank, it indicated that the blessed water was willing to receive him, and that he was innocent. If the water rejected him, he was guilty. Of course, a declaration of innocence might not mean much to a defendant who sank to the bottom of a pond; he might drown before being rescued. Other cultures used water ordeals as well, but (perhaps because the water was not blessed) took the view that sinking meant guilt, while floating meant innocence. See H. Lea, The Ordeal (1866).

4. See Alschuler and Deiss, A Brief History of the Criminal Jury in the United States, 61 U.Chi. L. Rev. 867(1994).

guarantee jury trial for all offenses,[5] the Sixth Amendment[6] does not require juries if the potential sentence is less than six months. *Baldwin v. New York*, 399 U.S. 66 (1969). Even if the defendant is charged with several minor offenses, whose punishment cumulatively could reach more than six months, the jury right is still not activated. *Lewis v. United States*, 518 U.S. 322 (1996).[7] Originally, juries were required whenever the offense was considered "non petty," which carried a connotation of immorality as well as illegality. In *District of Columbia v. Colts*, 282 U.S. 63 (1930), for example, the court held that a defendant charged with automobile speeding was entitled to a jury trial, because the offense would be seen by the community as "reckless" and an act "of such obvious depravity that to characterize it as a petty offense would be to shock the general moral sense."

Today, however, "seriousness" is equated with the term of punishment. *Blanton v. City of North Las Vegas*, 489 U.S. 538 (1989); *Muniz v. Hoffman*, 422 U.S. 454 (1975). (Fine of $10,000 is still "petty.") As discussed in Chapter 10, this is in stark contrast to the right to counsel, which applies when even one day of incarceration is possible. *Argersinger v. Hamlin*, 407 U.S. 25 (1972).

Moreover, while we often think of a jury as composed of 12 people, that number is not constitutionally required, although there may be no fewer than six people on a jury.[8] Nor, as a Constitutional matter, must the vote be unanimous. *Johnson v. Louisiana*, 406 U.S. 356 (1972).

Jury trial is now almost exclusively an American institution; as suggested by Dean Griswold, many see the jury as an anachronism, composed of persons who cannot understand the testimony or the instructions, and whose verdicts are often incomprehensible. In the last 30 years, however, state and federal legislatures, and the Supreme Court in a series of decisions, has enriched the jury and continued to support its growth. In *Blakely v. Washington*, 124 S. Ct. 253 (2004), discussed in Chapter 11, a majority of

---

5. For example, W. Va. Const. Art. 3, §14; Wyo. Const. Art. 1 sec. 9. The ABA agrees. See ABA Trial by Jury sec. 15-1.1 (3d ed. 1996).

6. It was only in 1968 that the Supreme Court held that the Sixth Amendment applied to the states. *Duncan v. Louisiana*, 391 U.S. 145 (1968).

7. Even if a defendant is not entitled to a jury trial under the Sixth Amendment, a trial judge has discretion to provide for a jury. *United States v. Greenpeace*, 314 F. Supp. 2d 1252 (S.D. Fla. 2004).

8. In *Williams v. Florida*, 399 U.S. 78 (1970), the Supreme Court held that a criminal jury could be smaller than 12, calling that number a "historical accident," but most states still require that number in criminal trials. In *Ballew v. Georgia*, 435 U.S. 223 (1977) it drew the line at six, relying on later studies showing that smaller juries (1) are less able to achieve accurate results; (2) will not be a cross-section; (3) are less likely to foster effective group deliberation; and (4) produce fewer hung juries. ABA Standards, 15-1.1(a) and (b) (1996) recommend 12-person juries, unless the penalty is six months or less.

the Court re-embraced the jury's function of standing between the government and the individual defendant, declaring "Just as suffrage ensures the people's ultimate control in the legislative and executive branches, jury trial is meant to ensure their control in the judiciary . . . (the jury is the) circuit-breaker in the state's machinery of justice. . . ." (SCALIA, J.)

B. Selecting a Jury

In a nonurban, agricultural society, finding impartial jurors would often be left to an official who relied upon his personal contacts around the area—a system known as the "key man" approach to selecting juries. That system, which was used by some federal courts until 1968,[9] persists today in a number of states and localities, and has never been declared unconstitutional. In most jurisdictions today, however, the process of jury selection is highly routinized and automated.

1. Determining the "District"

Obtaining 12 people from a population of (hundreds of) thousands is a daunting task. First, the relevant area must be determined: Is it a "city area" (e.g., the "Village" in New York City), a "city," a "county," a "metropolitan area," or some other area? The Sixth Amendment requires that the jury be selected from the "district" in which the crime occurred, but does not define that term.[10] Lines drawn for other (usually political) purposes are used as a default. But suppose a "district" consists of well-defined, different areas, in which different racial or class groups live, and the crime involves a white defendant accused of injuring a black victim, in a "white" area of the "district." Should the jury be drawn from the "white" area, or from the entire "district"? This question often arises in cases where a defendant seeks a change of venue, arguing that the "local" jury would be impassioned against

9. Note, 57 B. U.L. Rev. 198, 216 (1977) citing Sen. Rep. No. 891, 90th Cong., 1st Sess. (1968).

10. The language of the Sixth Amendment "in the district" was a reaction to the Port Bill of 1773, which empowered Massachusetts judges to transfer trials to another colony or back to England. See Comment, The Constitutional Right to a Trial by a Jury of the Vicinage, 57 U. Pa. L. Rev. 197 (1909); Kershen, Vicinage, 30 Okla L. Rev. 1 (1977). See *People v. Jones*, 510 P.2d 705, 9 Cal. 3d 546 (1973): "A jury drawn either from an entire county . . . or from that portion of a county wherein the crime was committed will satisfy the constitutional requirement" concerning vicinage, but "a jury drawn from only a proportion of a county, exclusive of the place of the commission of the crime, will not satisfy the requirement." But *Jones* was later overruled in *Hernandez v. Municipal Court*, 49 Cal. 3d 713, 781 P.2d 547, (1989), where the court held that "the boundaries of the vicinage are coterminous with the boundaries of the county."

him. Indeed, in a highly controversial case where several white Los Angeles police officers were charged with assault on a black driver, the change of venue from Los Angeles (where the jury would have been significantly racially diverse) to another locale (where the jury was virtually all white) was highly controversial, particularly after the officers were acquitted.[11]

2. Determining the "Pool"

Once the "district" has been determined, jurisdictions may rely on many "source lists" to locate persons living there to create a jury "pool" (also referred to as an "array," "master list," or "jury list"). Most states now employ voting registration lists, often supplemented by motor vehicle registration lists. Challenges arguing that these lists are too narrow, either separately or combined, because many persons either do not register to vote or are not eligible to vote, and many do not own cars, particularly in inner-city areas, have been unsuccessful. See King, Racial Jurymandering, Cancer or Cure, 68 N.Y.U. L. Rev. 707 (1993).[12]

3. Constructing the Wheel

Once a pool is established, officials select the number of persons who will be needed within the next (month; year) to serve on juries in the vicinage, and contact them — "summoning" them to jury duty. This creates the "wheel" (or "venire").

People in the wheel may avoid jury duty if they are (1) exempt; or (2) excused. *Exemptions* usually reflect legislative judgments that as a matter of public policy, whole classes of individuals — law enforcement officers, firefighters, teachers, doctors (military personnel are exempted by federal statute from serving in state juries) — perform sufficiently important public service that outweighs jury duty. Others (such as lawyers) are so likely to be challenged for cause or peremptorily (see below), it is sometimes thought it would waste everyone's time to summons them.[13] As a general matter, statutory exemptions have not been attacked as unduly political and hence nonpolicy based, although some of these (game wardens, for example) might

---

11. A subsequent federal trial, which employed a jury from a (more or less) wider Los Angeles area resulted in a conviction. Whether that was due to the jury composition, of course, was hotly debated.

12. Many countries use voting lists, including Russia, Ireland, Scotland, and Spain. Thaman, Europe's New Jury Systems, The Cases of Spain and Russia, 62 L. & Contemp. Probs. 233, 239 (1999).

13. Many states have now rejected this view, but it is not obviously so irrational as to invalidate a legislative decision to that effect.

be problematic.[14] In *Taylor v. Louisiana*, 419 U.S. 522 (1975), the Supreme Court invalidated a state process by which women who sought to serve on juries had to write expressly to the jury commissioners to be placed on the jury wheel, while men were automatically kept on the jury wheel. In effect, the statute exempted women, while requiring men to serve.

In contrast to exemptions, *excuses* are usually temporary, and are individually based. If service would create hardship, either physical or economic, an individual may be excused from jury duty until the hardship ceases. Thus, if Darryl is currently tending an infant, and cannot afford a sitter, he may be excused until the infant reaches school age (or some similar point in time).[15] But he will not be forever excused, as would be a police officer.

4. *Composing the Wheel*

a. The Cross-Section Requirement

Although the words of the Sixth Amendment require only that the jury be "impartial," the *Taylor* Court held that the term required a *"cross section of the community"* to be present on the wheel. Any procedure which results in the exclusion of any "cognizable" (sometimes referred to as "distinctive") group such as women[16] violated that right. This requirement sought to assure that different perspectives, values, and norms, constitutive of the community, would be reflected in the jury's moral determination that the defendant should be criminally sanctioned and stigmatized for his act.

b. What Is the "Community"?

The term "community" is not used in the Sixth Amendment, and the issue of what constitutes "the community" has seldom been litigated. It has been said that it usually means a previously defined geographical area, as in the "district" specifically referred to in the text of the Sixth Amendment. *United States v. Grisham*, 63 F.3d 1074 (11th Cir. 1995). But, of course, that area may have been defined for other reasons, having nothing to do with a "community" as that term is usual in casual conversation. See *Davis v.*

---

14. In Indiana, licensed veterinarians and dentists are exempt, but doctors are not. See *Burns*, Ind. Code Ann. §33-4-5-7(7), (9) (2000). An early case upheld, as against a general due process claim, the exemption of lawyers, doctors, preachers, and firemen, among others. *Rawlins v. Georgia*, 201 U.S. 638 (1906).

15. In Iowa, a person "solely responsible for daily care of a permanently disabled person in their home" is exempt; in New Jersey, a person who has " obligations to care for a sick, aged, or infirm dependent or a minor child."

16. Prior to 1957, federal jurors were required to meet state juror qualifications. This had frequently resulted in the exclusion of women from federal juries. That was altered by the Civil Rights Act of 1957.

Warden, 867 F.2d 1003 (7th Cir. 1989) "county lines or federal district lines do not magically determine the parameters of a community."

c. Defining "Cognizable Groups"

Defining "cognizable groups" has consumed much judicial energy. In *Lockhart v. McCree*, 476 U.S. 162, 174 (1986) the Court expressly declared that it had "never attempted to precisely define the term 'distinctive group' and we do not undertake to do so today." In *Taylor*, the Court declared that the diluted participation of women meant that "a flavor, a distinct quality" is lost from deliberations. Since there is no reason to think that men and women would disagree on finding facts (whether the light was red or green), the difference is experiential—what is the meaning, the normative impact, of the determination that the light was (red/green) when the defendant ran it? Such normative assessments vary with life experiences, and it is assumed that members of cognizable groups, because of their homogeneity, have life experiences different than those not of that group.[17] Other courts have used different words, but aim at the same idea: e.g., *Barber v. Ponte*, 772 F.2d 982 (1st Cir. 1985) ("a common thread or basic similarity in attitude, ideas, or experience run through the group"). Clearly, women, men, racial groups, ethnic groups—all those referred to in equal protection cases as "suspect" classifications—readily fit within the notion of cognizable group. But courts are deeply divided beyond that unanimity.[18] One commentator has used this definition:

> "They share (1) an attribute that defines and limits the group; (2) a common attitude, idea, or experience that distinguishes the group from other segments of society; (3) a "community of interests" that the jury pool would not adequately reflect if it excluded members of the group."
>
> *Zuklie, Rethinking the Fair Cross Section Requirement,*
> 84 Cal. L. Rev. 101, 102 (1996)

---

17. The concept of a "cross-section" underlines the entire notion of a jury—that all citizens, from whatever background, can properly sit in judgment of a specific defendant, even if (perhaps especially if) they are not familiar with his culture. This is in stark contrast to the early English practice, where there were "mixed juries" in which certain groups, including merchants, aliens, and Jews, were guaranteed to have peers on the jury. See M. Constable, The Law of the Other (1994). Such a "mixed jury" did seek to provide the entire jury with at least some persons who might provide all jurors information about the defendant's culture, an affirmative obligation which current doctrine does not require. The Code of Military Justice allows an enlisted soldier to demand at least one enlisted person to serve on his jury for a court martial.

18. What about the handicapped—blind, deaf, mute, etc.? See *State v. Spivey*, 700 S.W.2d 812 (Mo. 1985) (upholding a state statute excluding the deaf from service).

Finding groups whose members' outlook and experiences are so unique that only they can represent those experiences is extraordinarily difficult. If different perspectives is the key to "cognizability," are card-carrying members of the ACLU sufficiently different from other civil rights organizations as to constitute a "unique" perspective? What about members of the N.R.A.? Arguably, their perspectives can be replicated by many others who do not belong to those organizations; hence they do not bring a "unique" set of values or experiences to the jury. Indeed, if pressed, this test seems unworkable. Assuming, for example, that one reason for defining groups as cognizable is that they have suffered discrimination, can one presume that blacks have suffered a "different" discrimination than "women," who have been discriminated against differently than Jews, or Baptists, or homosexuals?

In *Lockhart,* the Court suggested (but did not hold) that the key was whether there was an "immutable characteristic" that was not "within the individual's control." This dictum, however, seems inconsistent with the Court's earlier emphasis on the different perspectives that a group might bring to the jury's determinative process.[19] In *Thiel v. Southern Pacific Co.,* 328 U.S. 217 (1946), the Court, in its supervisory power, invalidated a process by which persons who earned daily wages, rather than fixed salaries, were excluded from the jury. Some courts hold that a trait which is (either inevitably or as a matter of choice) alterable, such as youth[20] is not "cognizable." In the First Circuit, neither Italian Americans, *United States v. Bucci,* 839 F.2d 825 (1st Cir. 1988); nor Irish Americans, *Murchu (aka Murphy) v. United States,* 916 F.2d 50 (1st Cir.) (1991) constitute a cognizable group.

There are some clear limits to *Taylor.* The Court declared there, and has reaffirmed since,[21] that the cross-section requirement reaches only the jury wheel, and not the specific petit jury that tries the defendant.[22] Thus, there

---

19. Recent decisions have held that "the poor" do not constitute a "cognizable group." See *Anaya v. Hansen,* 781 F.2d 1 (1st Cir. 1986) (opining that the blue-collar workers of *Thiel* would not qualify as a "cognizable group" envisioned in *Taylor, Duren,* and *Lockhart*). See Note, Underrepresentation of Economic Groups on Federal Juries, 57 B.U. L. Rev. 198 (1977). See also Duff, The Scottish Criminal Jury: A Very Peculiar Institution, 62 L & Contemp. Probs 173, 179 (1999) suggesting that Scottish attorneys are concerned that middle and upper socio-economic jurors are being disqualified or excused from jury service.

20. *Barber v. Ponte,* 772 F.2d 996 (1st Cir. 1985).

21. See *Lockhart; Buchanan v. Kentucky,* 483 U.S. 402 (1987); *Holland v. Illinois,* 493 U.S. 474 (1990).

22. The Court in *Lockhart,* at 183 said, although in a different context, that to apply *Taylor* to petit juries would involve what it called "the Sisyphean task of . . . making sure that each (petit jury) contains the proper number of Democrats and Republicans, young persons and old persons, white-collar executives and blue-collar laborers, and so on."

is no constitutional duty that the state affirmatively provide methods to ensure a cross-section, on either the venire or the petit jury.[23]

The Court's reliance on the Sixth Amendment in *Taylor* is critical to understanding later decisions not only in this area, but in the area of peremptory challenges, discussed below. Under Sixth Amendment doctrine, the only question is whether a specific group was adversely affected by the state's selection process; *there is no requirement that the defendant demonstrate a discriminatory intent.* In *Taylor*, no state official prevented women from volunteering for jury service, and there was no evidence that the legislature intended to exclude women from such service. In *Duren v. Missouri*, 439 U.S. 357 (1979), in which women were placed on the jury wheel, but could "opt out," the system was even less likely to deter female participation in the jury system. Nevertheless, the *Duren* Court declared: "in Sixth Amendment fair cross-section cases, systematic disproportion itself demonstrates an infringement on the defendant's interest in a jury chosen from a fair cross-section." Under equal protection doctrine, in contrast, the challenger must show that the process was established for the purpose of discrimination. While grossly disproportionate statistical underrepresentation may establish a discriminatory purpose, *Castaneda v. Partida*, 430 U.S. 482 (1977), the challenger still must persuade the court that the difference is "gross."

A second distinction between equal protection and Sixth Amendment doctrine is that the notion of a "cognizable group" is (at least in theory) much broader than that in other legal areas, most importantly in equal protection law, where only "suspect classifications" are given special protection. Thus, a group may be "cognizable" and protected against exclusion under the Sixth Amendment, but not "suspect" and protected against intentional discrimination under the equal protection clause. One important area where this might make a difference is religion. Various religious sects, particularly cults, might well be "cognizable" and their preclusion from the jury wheel violative of the Sixth Amendment. But that same group might not be "suspect" under equal protection doctrine. In recent years, however, the courts seem to have merged the two definitions, such that only groups who are "suspect" under the equal protection clause will be considered "cognizable" under the Sixth Amendment.

---

23. Some jurisdictions, however, have sought to establish such processes. Thus, DeKalb County, Georgia, divided its entire population into thirty-six categories (e.g., "white male 35-44" "black female, 18-24"). The computer fills the quotas by a random draw from the list of registered voters in the various categories.

d. Measuring Disproportionate Representation

Determining that a "cognizable group" is involved is only the beginning of the issue. The defendant must still demonstrate that the process used by the state resulted in a *disproportionate* underrepresentation of that group in the jury venire. There are two main methods to measure (dis)proportionality: absolutely and comparatively.[24] Assume that women are 50 percent of the population, but only constitute 10 percent of the venire. There is an *absolute disproportion* of 40 percent (50 percent - 10 percent). But compared to the percentage they should constitute (50 percent), they are only 20 percent (10/50) represented. The *comparative disproportion* is thus 80 percent. The difference is critical in groups that form only small percentages of the relevant population. Suppose, for example, that dwarfs were considered a "cognizable group," but only constituted .5 percent of the population. Even a total exclusion would result in only .5 percent underrepresentation under the first method, but a 100 percent underrepresentation using the second approach. For this reason, some courts have suggested that a group must be "reasonably large" to be cognizable.

e. State Response to a Prima Facie Case of Discrimination

To defeat a *prima facie* case, the state has to show a "significant state interest that is manifestly and primarily advanced" by the jury selection scheme. *Duren v. Missouri*, 439 U.S. at 367-368 (dictum). On the other hand, even if the exclusion is done for a beneficent purpose, the impact, and not the intent, is the key. In *Thiel*, for example, the Court deemed it irrelevant that the jury commissioner was well-intentioned in allowing persons who would lose daily wages if chosen as jurors to avoid jury duty.

5. *The Venire — From Potential Service to Juror*

Once the wheel is chosen, the number of persons necessary to serve in the next relevant period of time will be summoned to court. Two further and highly controversial steps are involved: *(1) challenges for cause; (2) peremptory challenges.* Both these mechanisms, based upon perceived characteristics of individual jurors, depend on information which the

---

24. Some courts have used, or suggested, a third method—a "standard deviation" test. See *Ramseur v. United States*, 983 F.2d 1215 at 1232 n.17 (1996); *Hubbard v. State*, 552 N.W.2d 493, 217 Mich. App. 459 (Mich. App. 1996).

attorneys glean from two sources: (1) voir dire; (2) pre-trial questionnaires or similar items. Most cases do not involve questionnaires, but all entail voir dire.

a. Voir Dire — Establishing Information for Challenges

Voir dire[25] is the process by which jurors are asked questions about themselves to assist the court and the attorneys, in intelligently exercising both kinds of challenges. Voir dire was initially conducted by attorneys, but in many jurisdictions it is now conducted primarily by judges, because both sides used the process not only to ferret out information about the members of the jury panel, but also to "indoctrinate" them about their view of the case.[26] Attorneys now argue that judges, who are unfamiliar with the facts of the case, and who are interested in moving the case along, are too cursory in voir dire.[27] (This may be a paradigm example of a self-inflicted wound.)

There is virtually no law on the kind of questions which judges "must" or "may" ask; in the run-of-the-mill case, this is left virtually to the discretion of the judge. The sole exception to this rule occurs where there is a possibility of racial bias, usually in a case involving interracial violence, in which case the court's discretion is somewhat more limited. See, e.g., *Aldridge v. United States*, 283 U.S. 308 (1931); *Rosales-Lopez v. United*

---

25. In England, Ireland, and several other countries, voir dire, and the concomitant challenge for cause, have been abolished; the first 12 people seated are the jury. This extreme animosity to "cause" strikes is exemplified by *M. v. H.M. Advocate*, 1974 S.L.T. (Notes) 25 (H.C.J), as discussed in Duff, *supra* n.19 at 182-183. The defendants were alleged terrorists. The trial judge, responding to a request by defense counsel, asked whether any juror had lost any near relatives in the religious and political disturbances in Northern Ireland. The Appeal Court chastised the judge, declaring "(There) should be no general questioning of persons cited for possible jury service to ascertain whether any of them could or should be excused from jury service in a particular trial . . . The essence of the system of trial by jury is that it consists of 15 individuals chosen at random from amongst those who are cited for possible service . . . It is not a sufficient excuse for a juror to be excused that he . . . might or might not feel prejudice one way or the other towards the crime itself or the background against which the crime has been committed." But if the juror has a personal connection with one of the parties, or has personal knowledge of the facts, he will be excused by the court clerk, usually *before* he is called to the jury box.

26. One of the leading studies of the jury, H. Zeisel, H. Kalven and B. Buchhol, Delay in Court, 103 n.9 (2d ed. 1978), concluded that half the time of voir dire was used to prepare the jury for the case.

27. Voir dire is not the only method by which the parties may obtain information on the potential jurors. If the names and addresses are given to the parties beforehand, each side may attempt to investigate the jurors' background. Rule 421 of the Uniform Rules of Criminal Procedure requires the prosecutor to share information on prospective jurors, subject to the work product rule. For those who have read John Grisham's, Runaway Jury, or seen the movie, be assured that it is fiction, not reality, not even in the most intense trial.

States, 451 U.S. 182 (1981).[28] In a capital case involving a charge of murder of a white victim by a black defendant, a trial judge must explore the possible racism of jurors. *Turner v. Murray*, 476 U.S. 28 (1986).

In death penalty cases, the judge will ask a potential juror about his opposition to the penalty. In *Witherspoon v. Illinois*, 391 U.S. 510 (1968), the Court seemed to say that a juror could be removed only if his opposition was "unmistakably clear," but *Wainwright v. Witt*, 469 U.S. 412 (1985), adopted a less demanding standard — whether the juror's views would "prevent or substantially impair the performance of his duties as a juror." Of course, the standard works both ways — the defendant may inquire whether the juror would automatically impose the death penalty upon a defendant found guilty of capitally-eligible murder. *Morgan v. Illinois*, 504 U.S. 719 (1992). These decisions seem to assume that a person's position on the death penalty would carry over to her decision on the guilt-innocence question; indeed, many commentators believe that a "death qualified" jury is more prone to find a defendant guilty, but the Court has held that even a conclusive showing that this were true would not be relevant. *Lockhart v. McCree*, 476 U.S. 162 (1986).

b. Voir Dire and Juror Privacy

Jurors are citizens, who have been summarily required to disrupt their lives and appear in public. Answering any question may be severely difficult and embarrassing in the unfamiliar surroundings of a courtroom. Surveys of jurors find that even relatively typical questions — what kind of newspapers they read, what bumper stickers they have — may strike them as invasive of their privacy. Suppose the question is even more intimate. A gambling addict will be loathe to admit in open court, or even *in camera*, that he has such an addiction; but if the case involves a defendant charged with embezzling funds to feed his gambling habit, may the defendant's "right to know" outweigh the juror's right to privacy? Some courts have answered that jurors have such a privacy right to resist such questions. *United States v. McDade*, 929 F. Supp. 815 (E.D. Pa. 1996) but in most jurisdictions this is an unresolved issue.[29] See Weinstein, Protecting a Juror's Right to Privacy: Constitutional Constraints and Policy Options, 70 Temp. L. Rev. 1 (1997).[30]

---

28. Requiring, under supervisory power, questions regarding racial bias which might not be required by the Constitution, citing *Ristaino v. Ross*, 424 U.S. 589 (1976) and *Ham v. South Carolina*, 409 U.S. 524 (1973).

29. Georgia Code Ann. §59-125(b) (1996) expressly provides: "In the questionnaire and during voir dire, judges should ensure that the privacy of prospective jurors is reasonably protected."

30. See also, Note, 48 U. Cin. L. Rev. 985 (1979).

c. Challenges for Cause

Challenges for cause, as the term suggests, allow either side to remove a potential juror whose background, familiarity with either the defendant, the witnesses, the attorneys involved, or for some other reason, might suggest they might be less than impartial. Because the Sixth Amendment guarantees an "impartial" jury, there is no limit to the number of challenges for cause either side may seek, and the judge may grant. It is often said that the are two "kinds" of bias upon which a challenge for cause may be based — *implied bias and actual bias.* Whether to allow a challenge for cause is within the discretion of the trial judge, and will be overturned only for an abuse of that discretion. *Mu'Min v. Virginia*, 500 U.S. 415 (1991). Moreover, even when a potential juror appears to be subject to a cause challenge, trial judges will often "rehabilitate" him by asking whether, notwithstanding the problematic situation, the juror could try the case fairly, and on the evidence. Thus, suppose that Eric, a potential juror, opines that he is inclined to disbelieve drug addicts (of whom the defendant or a witness is one). The judge may ask him, "But you could overcome that concern and give this defendant, in front of you, a fair trial, couldn't you?" When Eric, either genuinely, or because he fears judicial wrath if he responds negatively, acquiesces, he has been rehabilitated, and a subsequent appeal on the basis that he should have been removed for cause is very likely to be unsuccessful.

The presence of peremptory challenges, discussed below, has undermined any attempt to fully explicate the law regarding challenges for cause; if the "injured party" feels strongly enough about a dubious juror, the courts appear to reason, he can always use a peremptory challenge to remove him. Moreover, while some courts hold that the loss of one peremptory in order to strike a juror who should have been removed for cause is itself automatic grounds for reversal, others subject the loss to a harmless error analysis.[31]

What *should* be grounds for challenge? Grounds for cause are often listed by statute,[32] which often include a "catch all' provision allowing a challenge if there is "reasonable ground to believe that a juror cannot render a fair and

---

31. Pizzi and Hoffman, Jury Selection Errors on Appeal, 38 Amer. Crim. L. Rev. 1391 (2001).

32. Florida Stat. §§913.02 lists 12 grounds for cause. A challenge for cause to an individual juror may be made only on the following grounds:

    (1) The juror does not have the qualifications required by law;

    (2) The juror is of unsound mind or has a bodily defect that renders him or her incapable of performing the duties of a juror, except that, in a civil action, deafness or hearing impairment shall not be the sole basis of a challenge for cause of an individual juror;

    (3) The juror has conscientious beliefs that would preclude him or her from finding the defendant guilty;

impartial verdict," Ariz. R. Crim. P. 18.4. It is under this last rubric that most issues about cause arise.

The most common sources of (nonstatutory) potential bias are: (1) relationship with one of the parties (or their attorneys); (2) prior experiences (such as being a victim of crime, particularly if the crime was similar to the one at issue); (3) prior knowledge of the case. While none of these is a *per se* disqualifier, it is likely that a court will probe more deeply here than elsewhere — although even here courts attempt to rehabilitate the juror.

The case law on what might constitute cause is very fact-specific and hopelessly confused, for several reasons. Most importantly, whether the trial judge has upheld or denied a challenge, her decision will be reversible only if there was an "abuse of discretion" and harm to the defendant. Thus, one judge may deny a challenge based upon a potential juror's prior law enforcement background, while a second would uphold the same challenge, and both decisions would be upheld (not overturned) on appeal.

Appellate judges are reluctant to overturn a verdict and require a new trial; even the presence of a juror who has mislead the court in answering a voir dire question will not result in a new trial unless the misleading was intentional. Simple juror oversight may not be sufficient. Ark. Stat. Ann. Sec. 16-31-107. For example, a juror in a sexual assault case did not mention that she had been "almost" assaulted by an uncle when she was young. The trial court's refusal to remove her when this was disclosed was upheld on appeal

---

(4)   The juror served on the grand jury that found the indictment or on a coroner's jury that inquired into the death of a person whose death is the subject of the indictment or information;

(5)   The juror served on a jury formerly sworn to try the defendant for the same offense;

(6)   The juror served on a jury that tried another person for the offense charged in the indictment, information, or affidavit;

(7)   The juror served as a juror in a civil action brought against the defendant for the act charged as an offense;

(8)   The juror is an adverse party to the defendant in a civil action, or has complained against or been accused by the defendant in a criminal prosecution;

(9)   The juror is related by blood or marriage within the third degree to the defendant, the attorneys of either party, the person alleged to be injured by the offense charged, or the person on whose complaint the prosecution was instituted;

(10) The juror has a state of mind regarding the defendant, the case, the person alleged to have been injured by the offense charged, or the person on whose complaint the prosecution was instituted that will prevent the juror from acting with impartiality, but the formation of an opinion or impression regarding the guilt or innocence of the defendant shall not be a sufficient ground for challenge to a juror if he or she declares and the court determines that he or she can render an impartial verdict according to the evidence;

(11) The juror was a witness for the state or the defendant at the preliminary hearing or before the grand jury or is to be a witness for either party at the trial;

(12) The juror is a surety on defendant's bail bond in the case.

on the grounds that: (1) her nondisclosure was not intentional; (2) her past experience was not similar to the crime in question; (3) she conscientiously made this known; (4) other jurors were not influenced by that event. *People v. Kelly*, 185 Cal. App. 3d 118, 220 Cal. Rtpr. 584 (1986).

The fact that a juror is employed by the government is not automatic grounds for a cause challenge. *Dennis v. United States*, 339 U.S. 162 (1950). Nor is a juror who is seeking a job with the prosecutor's office barred solely for that reason. *Smith v. Phillips*, 455 U.S. 209 (1982). Similarly, appellate courts have upheld the decision of trial courts not to remove for cause (1) in a rape trial, a psychiatric social worker who counseled rape victims;[33] or (2) an acquaintance of the victim of the crime.[34] On the other hand, a Minnesota court has held that potential jurors who believe that police officers are more truthful than others should be removed for cause. *State v. Logan*, 535 N.W.2d 320 (Minn. 1995).[35]

i. Nullification As a Ground for Cause. Since *Bushell's* case, Vaughn 135, 6 Howell's State Trials 999 (1670), criminal juries have had the ability to "nullify" the law, and acquit a defendant despite overwhelming evidence.[36] Nevertheless, reflecting the judiciary's unease with this jury

---

33. *Tinsley v. Borg*, 895 F.2d 520 (9th Cir. 1990).

34. *Fleming v. State*, 269 Ga. 245, 497 S.E.2d 41 (1998); *Sander v. Comm.*, 801 S.W.2d 665 (Ky. 1990).

35. *United States v. Scott*, 854 F.2d 697 (5th Cir. 1988) (presuming bias on the part of a juror who failed to disclose that his brother was a deputy sheriff in the sheriff's office that had performed some of the investigation in the case). Far more numerous are those cases in which courts have refused to find no bias. See, e.g., *Jones v. Cooper*, 311 F.3d 306 (4th Cir. 2002) (finding no implied bias where a juror stated that several of her relatives had been subjected to arrests or jury trials; that she had gone to the store at which the crime occurred the day after the murder and robbery; that she had strong, religiously-motived views in favor of the death penalty; and that she knew that the defendant had previously received a death sentence); *United States v. Greer*, 285 F.3d 158 (2d Cir. 2002) (rejecting a claim of implied bias because a juror was asked by an acquaintance of the defendant to lend a "sympathetic ear" to the defense and was the brother of a person to whom the defendant had distributed drugs); *United States v. Tucker*, 243 F.3d 499 (8th Cir.2001) (rejecting the defendant's allegations that a juror was presumptively biased against him because the defendant, who had previously been governor of Arkansas, had denied clemency to the juror's husband, a prison inmate); *United States v. Powell*, 226 F.3d 1181 (10th Cir. 2000) (rejecting an implied bias claim where a juror, in a kidnapping and sexual assault case, had a daughter who had been raped 10 years before).

36. This is a broad statement. There are several different kinds of "nullifications"; *Bushell's* only goes to one kind. For example, the jury may (1) dislike or disagree with the law itself—as in *Bushell's* case; (2) like the law, but not as applied to this *kind* of criminal defendant (euthanasia cases); (3) like the law, but not as applied to this particular defendant; (4) like the law but want to send a message to "the authorities" (as some argue occurred in the O.J.Simpson case); (5) like the law, but think the punishment is too great.

power, the decisions are clear that a juror who concedes, upon voir dire, that he will not follow the law, may be excused for cause. *United States v. Samet*, 207 F. Supp. 269 (S.D.N.Y. 2002).[37] This is one basis for the death-penalty voir dire mentioned above.

ii. Pre-Trial Publicity As a Ground for Cause.

In "high profile" cases, defendants will often seek a change of venue on the basis that the publicity has severely compromised the jurors' ability to decide impartially. If they lose that motion, they will nevertheless seek to challenge jurors individually. Initially, persons subjected to widespread news about a case, or a defendant's prior record, were *presumed* to be prejudiced. Cf. *Marshal v. United States*, 360 U.S. 310 (1959). That, however, has changed, at least where the defendant raises the issue as a constitutional (rather than a supervisory power) issue. See *Murphy v. Florida*, 421 U.S. 794 (1975) (distinguishing between a supervisory case, such as *Marshall*, and constitutional cases, such as *Murphy*).

In *Mu'Min v. Virginia*, 500 U.S. 415 (1991), eight of 12 jurors had learned about the case from media reports or other outside sources. All jurors said on voir dire that they could be impartial. The trial judge denied the defendant's motion to question the jurors *in camera*, and refused to ask about the content of the publicity. The Supreme Court upheld this determination, stressing that these issues were generally left to the discretion of the trial judge. Of course, it is true, as the Supreme Court declared in *Irwin v. Dowd*, 366 U.S. 717 (1961) that "(E)ven a juror who has a 'preconceived notion as to the guilt or innocence of an accused' as a result of pre-trial publicity need not necessarily be excluded from the jury panel . . . if the juror can lay aside his impression or opinion and render a verdict based on the evidence presented in court." But if there is any doubt about the ability of a juror to serve on a particular case, why not remove him? Assuming that he could serve on other cases without difficulty, shouldn't the presumption be in favor of removal, assuming that there are alternate jurors who could replace him?

Empirical research has suggested that voir dire usually cannot identify all of the potential jurors who have been prejudiced by pre-trial publicity; indeed, those jurors may not recognize their own bias. And *Mu'Min* does not require the trial court to question a juror individually about the extent of publicity he may have heard. In *Patton v. Young*, 467 U.S. 1025 (1984), where there was a four-year passage between the publicity and the trial, the Court, in determining that there was no clear evidence of bias, found three factors relevant: (1) the strength of the voir dire responses; (2) the nature of the pre-trial publicity; (3) time elapsed.

---

37. Indeed, a juror who refuses to deliberate because he objects to the law may be removed during deliberations. *People v. Williams*, 25 Cal. 4th 441, 21 P.3d 1209 (2001).

d. Peremptory Challenges

Once the jury venire has been winnowed down by cause challenges, there remains the final link in selecting a jury — *peremptory challenges* — which allow either side to strike potential jurors without assigning any reason. At common law, every felony defendant had 35 peremptory challenges, but today that number is far fewer in most cases, primarily because most felonies do not carry the death penalty. The number of peremptory challenges, in contrast to those for cause, is limited, and determined by statute in every jurisdiction.

When the judge has denied a challenge for cause to a juror, a party is likely to use a peremptory challenge to thar juror. The parties indulge "hunches" about jurors, theoretically formed on the basis of the information gained during voir dire or through questionnaires. In high-profile cases, each side may hire "jury consultants" who use opinion polls, psychological profiles, body language, and other such information to assist counsel in using these strikes.

Peremptory challenges were originally premised on the belief that intuition and first impressions, which are hard to articulate and certainly do not constitute "cause," are nevertheless valid human reactions. But in the context of a trial, they are perfidious, allowing each party to act upon stereotypes to remove potential jurors based upon their race, gender, religion, apparent political beliefs, etc. Clarence Darrow, among many other prominent attorneys, painstakingly delineated which jurors the defense should strike:

> "You would be guilty of malpractice if you got rid of an Irishman . . . An Englishman is not so good as an Irishman, but still, he has come through a long tradition of individual rights, and is not afraid to stand alone . . . Baptists are more hopeless than the Presbyterians. The Methodists are worth considering; they are nearer the soil. Beware of the Lutherans, especially the Scandinavians; they are almost always sure to convict. As to Unitarians, Universalists, Congregationalists, Jews, and other agnostics, don't ask them too many questions; keep them anyhow, especially Jews and agnostics. Never take a wealthy man on a jury."

Darrow, Attorney for the Defense, Esquire Magazine,
May 1936, p. 36-37.[38]

---

38. Bailey and Rothblatt, Successful Techniques for Criminal Trials, secs. 6:41-6:45 (1985): "It has often been said that persons of Italian, Irish, Jewish, Latin American, and Southern European extraction are more desirable as jurors than people of British, Scandinavian, or German extraction. The latter are presumably more law-abiding, conservative, and strict, with more rigid standards of conduct. Blind adherence to these over-generalized stereotypes can prove dangerous . . . Generally, retired police officers, military men, and their wives are undesirable . . . Salesmen, actors, artists,

In 1986, the Supreme Court reined in the use of peremptories which appeared to be based solely upon the race of the potential juror.[39] In *Batson v. Kentucky*, 476 U.S. 79 (1986), the Court held that a prosecutor who employed peremptories in such a manner violated the equal protection clause. Later cases have made clear that *Batson* is based on the Fourteenth Amendment and protects the right of the potential juror not to be discriminated against, rather than protecting the Sixth Amendment right of the defendant. *Batson*, therefore, makes no judgment in the way that *Taylor* does,[40] that persons of one race will systematically have different perspectives or even different approaches than those of another race.

Batson's goal is unquestionably salutary — to remove discrimination in jury selection, in at least one corner of the criminal justice system.[41] Implementation of this goal, however, has created administrative difficulties, and perhaps worse. Had the Court in *Batson* relied upon the Sixth Amendment, only the *result* would have been relevant: If a disproportionate number of a protected group were removed by one side, that would be sufficient to require a remedy. Since the Court relied upon the equal protection clause, however, standard doctrine requires the complaining party (since this is usually the defendant, we will use that reference here, but defense counsel, too, are accused of using the race, or gender, card) to prove that the strikes were *intended* to be discriminatory. In *Purkett v. Elem*, 514 U.S. 765, 768

---

and writers are highly desirable." See, as well: "Experienced trial lawyers can often recognize deep seated prejudices that remain unspoken and are illegible to others . . . The eyes of a trial lawyer skim over the faces of jurors the way a blind person's fingers glide over the Braille letters of some unfamiliar book, in search of sights that will help him or her make the right choice." Fahringer, The Peremptory Challenge: An Endangered Species? 31 Crim. L. Bull. 400, 404 (1995). But see White, The Nonverbal Behaviors in Jury Selection, 31 Crim L. Bull. 414 (1995): "(S)tudies suggest that the average lawyer does a poor job of discriminating among jurors."

39. Consider the sense of outrage and desperation of at least one black juror, pre-*Batson*: "Why bother to call us down to these courts . . . we could be on our jobs or in schools trying to help ourselves instead of in courthouse Halls being Made Fools of." Anonymous Letter from excluded juror, quoted in Amicus Brief by Elizabeth Holtzman 18, *Batson v. Kentucky*, 476 U.S. 79 (1986), as cited in Babcock, A Place In the Palladium: Women's Rights and Jury Service, 61 U. Cin. L. Rev. 1139, 1148, n.23 (1993).

40. Because the premise of *Batson* is equal protection of the *juror*, even the defendant who removed him might have standing to object to the strike. See *United States v. Huey*, 76 F.3d 638 (5th Cir. 1996). But see *United States v. Boyd*, 86 F.3d 719 (7th Cir. 1996). (Only claim is inadequate counsel.)

41. To achieve this goal, the Court has extended *Batson* to cover challenges by the defense, *Georgia v. McColum*, 505 U.S. 42 (1992), and to all civil matters. *Edmonton v. Louisville Concrete Co.*, 500 U.S. 614 (1991). The case also reaches gender discrimination. *JEB v. Alabama ex rel. T. B.*, 511 U.S. 127 (1994).

(1995), the Court endorsed a "three-step" procedure by which this proof is to be made:

1. The defendant shows a prima facie case of discrimination. Usually this is statistical: a showing that the prosecutor used a large percentage of his peremptories to strike, e.g., women, or a showing that a large percentage of the women on the venire were challenged.[42]
2. The prosecutor provides an explanation for the strikes.
3. The Court decides whether the prosecutor's explanation is race (or gender, or ethnic) neutral.[43]

The hurdles here are manifold. First, and perhaps not so obviously, how do we know that a given juror (stricken or not) is a member of a suspect class? Is Lucille (Ball) Arnaz, (a redheaded white woman of Irish parents) "Hispanic" because of her last name? [44] This question is often raised in other contexts, such as employment discrimination cases, but there we often have actual data, or are interested in statistical groups rather than a specific individual. Second, what percentage constitutes a "high enough" level to establish a *prima facie* case? Third, what constitutes a "neutral" explanation? Finally, assuming that the explanation is a "neutral" one, on what basis can the trial judge nevertheless disbelieve the attorney, and conclude that the strikes *were* gender-based—and how would that decision be reviewable on appeal?

Unsurprisingly, trial judges are reluctant to conclude that attorneys who proffer neutral explanations are both liars and bigots. In *Elem*, "facial hair" was deemed a sufficient neutral reason. One study found the following to be "neutral" explanations: age, occupation, employment, religious beliefs, demeanor, relationship to trial participants, intelligence, socio-economic status, residence, marital status, previous involvement with the criminal justice system, prior justice experience.[45] In one case, the trial judge, rather than say that he believed the prosecutor was lying, "psychoanalyzed" the lawyer, and

---

42. Courts, of course, differ on what percentage of strikes would create a *prima facie* case. *In ex Parte Branch,* 526 So. 2d 609, 522-623 (Ala. 1987), the court listed factors which would help decide when a defendant had made a sufficient *prima facie* case.

43. See Anderson, Catch Me If You Can! Resolving the Ethical Tragedy in the Brave New World of Jury Selection, 32 New Eng. L. Rev. 343, 376 (1998).

44. How does one show that a potential juror is (or is not) in the protected class? Under Jim Crow laws, "negro" was statutorily defined as a person with 1/32 negroid blood. Should each juror have to show blood type and history? Are all African Americans "black"? Are all persons from South America "Hispanic"? "Latino"? "Spanish"? See *State v. Allen,* 616 So. 2d 452 (Fla. 1993).

45. But see *People v. Allen,* 2004 WL 179472 (Cal. App. 1 Dist.), where the prosecutor's explanations that the challenge was based upon "demeanor," "dress," "how she took her seat" and "her very response to your answers" were insufficient.

concluded that "while the attorney 'honestly believed'" his challenge was based upon body language, it was a subconscious pretext for racism. *People v. Sprague*, 280 A.D.2d 954, 721 N.Y.S.2d 205 (App. Div. 2001). On the other hand, in *Wilson v. Beard*, 314 F. Supp. 2d 434 (E.D.Pa. 2004), the defense showed a videotaped lecture by the prosecutor to new prosecutors, describing in detail, his strategy of systematically excluding certain types of black jurors. The court easily concluded that *Batson* had been violated.

In assessing the truth of the proffered explanation, both trial and appellate courts have compared the struck jurors with jurors who were not struck. Thus, if Hana claims that she removed Juancinto, a Hispanic, because he reads the *New York Times* (hardly a vicious offense, but a sufficient "hunch" that would have been allowed pre-*Batson* as a recognizable basis for employing a challenge), the court will attempt to determine whether Hana also removed non-Hispanic jurors who read the *New York Times*. This is not an illogical methodology, but it ignores the psychology of peremptory strikes: that a lawyer may use his peremptories more liberally at the beginning of the process than at the end, thus allowing someone to stay whom she would have stricken earlier, if given the chance.

Because it is based upon the equal protection clause, *Batson* reaches only "suspect" ("protected") classes under that doctrine's traditional decisions. Sixth Amendment doctrine, however, protects any "cognizable" group from being precluded from the jury wheel. The difference between *Batson* and *Taylor*, between the parameters of the Fourteenth and the Sixth Amendment challenges, is seen in the so-called "dual motivation" cases. In *Hernandez v. New York*, 500 U.S. 352 (1991), the Court held that peremptory challenges to Spanish-speaking jurors who expressed some hesitancy about relying on an in-court English translator, were sustainable even though the persons removed would be disproportionately Hispanic. If defendant had only to show disparate impact, the claim might be successful; but since it is an equal protection claim, disparate impact is not enough—defendant must show intent to discriminate.

When a *Batson* violation occurs, the question then becomes remedy. If the trial judge agrees with the challenge, she may (a) order the jurors (re) seated *People v. Stiff*, 206 A.D.2d 235, 620 N.Y.S.2d 87 (App. Div. 1994); (b) order a new venire; (c) preclude the offending party from using more peremptories; (d) hold the offending attorney in contempt; (e) discipline the attorney for an ethical violation. None of these remedies is without cost. A (reseated) juror who knows that he was removed because of his race, or gender, may find it difficult thereafter to be unbiased in assessing the case of the side who removed him. Striking the entire panel, and beginning again, seems excessively time-consuming and wasteful, not to mention injurious to the other jurors. If, as suggested above, *Batson* is based primarily on the rights of prospective jurors, and not of the defendant, then restarting the jury selection process is consistent with protecting the defendant; reseating the juror (if that is possible) is more consistent with protecting the juror. Of course, if a defense counsel misuses peremptories, and the jury acquits, the only remedy is a sanction against the lawyer.

These difficulties, however, pale beside those presented when the trial judge accepts the neutral explanation, but an appellate court disagrees. At that point, the most obvious remedy is to overturn the conviction, and to find *Batson* errors harmful *per se*. But courts have refused to take that path, as they have in dealing with most trial errors (see Chapter 12). After all, the rudimentary question is whether the defendant received a fair trial by an unbiased jury; unless there is some showing that the juror who replaced the stricken one was biased, it seems difficult for the defendant to succeed on that claim. On the other hand, the equal protection basis seems to lend itself to a *per se* rule. Yet *per se* rules often influence appellate judges in finding no error at all where they would find such error were a more lenient remedy available. A more fitting remedy for discriminatory use of peremptories, perhaps, is disciplinary action against the offending attorney, but again courts are uneasy in taking such action unless the violation is flagrant and constant.[46]

These questions lead to the critical one: Should peremptories be abolished? The Supreme Court has consistently said they are not constitutionally required. States, and even Congress, are free to eliminate them entirely. But only law professors, and an occasional outside observer, seem to think they should do so.[47] Why? Perhaps because there is an intuitive "sense" that there *are* differences among these groups;[48] indeed, one might argue that the

---

46. In *People v. Muhammad*, 108 Cal. App. 4th 313, 133 Cal. Rtpr. 2d 308 (2003), the trial judge fined the prosecutor $1,500 for discriminatory use of peremptories. The appellate court upheld the *power* of the court to take such action, but because no order had been issued prohibiting such action beforehand, the actual sanction was reversed.

47. Abramson, Abolishing the Peremptory But Enlarging the Challenge for Cause, 96 Amer. Phil. Assn. Newsletter 59 (Fall 1996); Hoffman, Peremptory Challenges Should be Abolished: A Trial Judge's Perspective, 64 U.Chi. L. Rev. 809 (1997). Mr. Justice Marshall, concurring in *Batson*, declared that "only by banning peremptories entirely can such discrimination be ended." 476 U.S. at 108. The court in *Minetos v. City University of New York*, 925 F. Supp. 177 (S.D.N.Y. 1996), reviewing the "ten frustrating years" since *Batson,* declared that "All peremptory challenges should now be banned as an unnecessary waste of time and an obvious corruption of the judicial process." Peremptories have been abolished in a number of other countries, including England and Ireland.

48. Thus, in fn. 11 in *J. E .B. v. Alabama ex rel. T. B.*, 511 U.S. 127 (1994), the Court declared that even if there were some statistical evidence that women decide differently, "gender classifications that rests on impermissible stereotypes violate the Equal Protection Clause . . . a shred of truth may be contained in some stereotypes, but (that) requires that state actors look beyond the surface before making judgments about people that are likely to stigmatize as well as to perpetuate historical patterns of discrimination." And Justice O'Connor, also in *J.E.B.*, observed: "the import of our holding is that any correlation between a juror's gender and attitudes is irrelevant as a matter of constitutional law. But to say that gender makes no difference as a matter of law is not to say that gender makes no difference as a matter of fact."

entire cross-section requirement is premised on that view, and that *Taylor* and *Batson* are therefore irreconcilably at odds. But another view is possible:[49] "Although they derive from separate constitutional sources, the 'fair cross-section' and equal protection requirements combine to serve a single goal—insuring that juries reflect the diversity of the American people." Or perhaps it is because there is "a tremendous psychological pressure for lawyers on both sides to exercise some peremptory challenges . . . if they do not (use all their challenges) in most jurisdictions they lose any appellate argument regarding erroneous rulings on challenges for cause."[50]

One (pen)ultimate point: peremptories show that, while we generally speak of "selecting a jury," that is a misnomer. Instead, we "disselect" a jury, removing what each side thinks is the "worst" jurors for its case. One (impish) law professor suggested that, instead, we should allow each side to have affirmative selection, in which each side may prevent the other from removing, on a peremptory basis, any juror who has not been found challengeable for cause.[51]

In the end, unless courts are more vigorous in assessing grounds for cause, peremptories may be an inevitable evil.[52] And, circularly, so long as Courts know that attorneys have peremptories, judges are likely to deny a motion to remove a juror for cause, rather than invite appealable (and reversible) error, expecting that the attorney will use a peremptory to remove that juror.

6. *A Quick Summary*

Some have argued that the recent spate of cases, noted above, which seem to deny "cognizable status" to all groups *except* those already in "suspect" classes makes the overlap between the Sixth and Fourteenth Amendments confusing and unnecessary.[53] On the other hand, to the extent

---

49. See Allen, Stuntz, Hoffmann, Livingston, Comprehensive Criminal Procedure, 1200.

50. Hoffman, *supra*, n.45. at fn. 199.

51. Singer, Peremptory Holds—A Suggestion (Only Half Specious) of A Solution to the Discriminatory Use of Peremptory Challenges, 62 U. Det. L. Rev. 301 (1986). For a case of simultaneous invention, see Altman, Affirmative Selection: A New Response to Peremptory Challenge Abuse, 38 Stan. L. Rev. 781 (1986). But see Zeisel, Affirmative Peremptory Juror Selection, 39 Stan. L. Rev. 1165 (1987).

52. C. Whitebread and C. Slobogin, Criminal Procedure 746 (2000): "The Court's reluctance to allow individualized questions during voir dire, combined with its unwillingness to imply bias from circumstances, means that . . . peremptory challenge . . . may be the only way a defendant can remove from the venire, individuals strongly suspected of bias. Unless the ground for challenges for cause . . . are relaxed considerably, some entitlement to peremptories may be necessary."

53. Maguid, Challenges to Jury Composition: Purging the Sixth Amendment Analysis of Equal Protection Concepts, 24 San. Diego L. Rev. 1081 (1987). See also Beale, et. al., Grand Jury Practice 3:13 (1997). In *Batson* itself, the appellant had

that they do *not* overlap, they seem to contradict each other: *Batson* proposes that racial and gender differences are irrelevant, while *Taylor* claims that they are definitive. A doctrinal explanation is possible: the equal protection cases aim at protecting the *juror*, while the Sixth Amendment cases aim at protecting the *defendant*. The doctrinal confusion between the rules enunciated by the Sixth Amendment and Equal Protection claims is summarized below.

Table 8.1

	Equal Protection	*Sixth Amendment*
Areas Covered	Grand Jury Composition; Peremptory Challenges	Construction of the Wheel
Items to Be Proved	Impact and Discriminatory Intent	Impact Only
Persons Covered	Suspect or Semisuspect Classes	Cognizable, "Distinct" Group
Person Protected	Potential Juror	Defendant

EXAMPLES

1. Horace, who killed his wife after catching her in flagrante delicto, wants the judge to ask each of the jurors whether they have ever had an affair, or discovered that their spouse was having an affair. (a) Should the judge ask the question? (b) If the judge asks the question, may the jurors refuse to answer?

2. Jeremiah Jefferson is prosecuting Courtney Bellows for "illegal possession of a gun by an ex-felon." In response to a questionnaire asking jurors their views on guns, and whether they owned a gun, Juror # 8, James Bogus, has indicated that he belongs to the National Rifle Association. Should Jeremiah ask the other potential jurors how they feel about guns? Should he challenge Bogus for cause, or wait until peremptories, and then remove him from the venire?

3. (a) Suppose that statistics show that, either nationally or in a specific district, the poor, the (very) young, and the elderly fail to register to vote at least 20 percent below the norm for other age and population groups. The jurisdiction relies only upon voter registration lists. Would a challenge to the jury wheel be successful on one or all of these bases?

    (b) Suppose the jurisdiction relied exclusively on drivers' registration lists?

4. Martha, a 58-year-old chief executive, is being tried for stock fraud. She notes that the state statute provides that "persons over 55" need not serve on juries, and are allowed to serve only if they sought to serve.

---

relied solely on the Sixth Amendment argument, but the Court reached out to the equal protection clause, rather than take the Sixth Amendment route.

What are her chances if she challenges that statute, and the composition of the wheel?

5. Sabrina, a white Anglo-Saxon woman, urges Kunstler, her defense counsel, to use a peremptory challenge to strike Jerome, the only African American on the jury venire. "I can't do that," he replies. "He's the only minority member available." After Sabrina is convicted, what are the chances of a successful appeal based upon a *Batson* violation (see Chapter 10 for whether this would be ineffective assistance of counsel)?

6. During jury selection, prospective juror Edith revealed that a cousin to whom she had been close, had been murdered but, through the grace of her church, she had learned to forgive the slayer. Another juror, Martin, acknowledged that he spent 20-30 hours per week at his church or reading religious works. He declared his belief that all people were in a state of grace with God. The prosecutor struck both with peremptory challenges. Defense counsel objected. What should the trial court do?

EXPLANATIONS

1. (a) As indicated in the text, there is little case law on this subject. In *Brandborg v. Lucas*, 891 F. Supp. 352 (E.D. Tex. 1995) a prospective juror refused to answer questions about her income, religious preference, TV and reading habits, memberships in organizations, political affiliation, or income. She was held in contempt by the state court, but the conviction was overturned on federal habeas corpus. The answer to the question might depend on whether the asserted purpose is to establish a cause challenge, rather than peremptory one. Harold's best argument for asking the question, after all, is that it may be relevant in ascertaining a challenge for cause: whether the juror could follow the law — a juror who has forgiven a philandering spouse might find it difficult to follow the law of "heat of passion," reducing a killing to manslaughter. And the prosecutor might wish to exclude peremptorily such jurors, lest they be sympathetic to the defendant. Can it be said that each side has an "interest" in the answer to the question, or merely that each side is "interested" in the answer? And even if there is an "interest" does that outweigh the juror's right to privacy? Or does the juror waive any such right when he submits himself to jury duty?

    An empirical study of jurors' reactions to such questions shows that questions far less invasive than the one suggested here are felt by jurors to be unnecessary. Thus, questions about whether a juror owns a gun, or relating to hobbies, were felt to violate a sense of privacy, even though most jurors answered them. See Rose, Expectations of Privacy, 85 Judicature 10 (July-August 2001). And in *United States v. McDade*, 929 F. Supp. 815 (E.D. Penn. 1996), the trial court, *sua sponte*, restricted inquiries into the jurors' state of health, deeming some questions too intrusive, and totally struck questions regarding television shows watched, newspapers read, or organizational memberships.

(b) Again, judicial discretion generally controls. But if the question is sensitive, the Court should offer (at least) the option of discussing this issue in camera. See *Press-Enterprise Co. v. Superior Court*, 464 U.S. 501, 512 (1984); *Brandborg v. Lucas*, 891 F. Supp. 352 (E.D. Tex. 1995).

2. Hold your fire, Jeremiah. Membership in the NRA is not grounds for cause removal, even where the crime relates to firearms. *United States v. Salamone*, 800 F.2d 1216 (3d Cir. 1986). The question is one of strategy, not law. If the judge allows jurors to be questioned about guns, will other gun-owning (or gun-favoring) jurors feel pressured, and hence react negatively toward Jeremiah and the government, *particularly* since they did not provide any information on this issue on the questionnaire? On the other hand, will they feel that way regardless, so that such a question is relatively harmless? If Jeremiah waits until peremptories, he can surely remove Bogus.

3. (a) The first question here is whether these groups are "cognizable" groups. That usually requires some showing that they are coherent enough, either through experiential facts, or otherwise, to have some "perspective" that other groups can't replicate. Courts have disagreed over whether blue-collar workers, *Anaya v. Hansen*, 781 F.2d 1 (1st Cir. 1986) college students, *United States v. Fletcher*, 965 F.2d 781 (9th Cir. 1992); young persons 18-34, *Barber v. Ponte*, 772 F.2d 982 (1st Cir. 1985) persons under 25, *Johnson v. McCaughtry* 92 F.3d 585 (7th Cir. 1996); those over 65, *Brewer v. Nix*, 963 F.2d 1111 (8th Cir. 1992); or over 70, *People v. McCoy*, 40 Cal. App. 4th 778 (1995) 47 Cal. R. 2d 599; and the "politically alienated," *United States v. Dellinger*, 472 F.2d 340 (7th Cir. 1973) are distinct groups, with distinct perspectives.

As noted in the text, one factor is whether these potential jurors will "change" their characteristics over time. Gender and race are not likely to alter; youth is. But once there is a "cognizable group," the defense has shown a *prima facie* case; it need not show that the process was established to discriminate against these groups — impact is enough. The burden now shifts to the state to show that there are good reasons to use (exclusively) the voter registration lists. Administrative ease would be one such reason; indeed, all challenges to the exclusive use of the list have thus far failed. The state may also argue that not the state, but persons (or groups) unwilling to register to vote, are self-selecting themselves out of the jury process. Moreover, the state can argue that (exclusive use of) many other lists — property tax rolls, drivers' licenses, telephone listings, etc. — will discriminate against some of these groups (certainly "the poor") and perhaps others (urban dwellers who do not need to own cars—except in Los Angeles). Unless the state is charged with an affirmative duty to "force" the wheel to be representative, the challenge will fail.

(b) Same result. In *State v. Mann*, 959 S.W.2d 503 (Tenn. 1997) (appendix) the court declared that using driver's registration was not unconstitutional, even though the defendants argued that voter registration lists should be used. The court declared: "We note that the statistics provided by the Dyer County circuit court clerk reveal that licensed drivers in Dyer County constitute 73.68 percent of the entire population of the county. Thus, it is readily apparent that the list of licensed drivers provide[s] a large and easily accessible source of names, to which all potential jurors have equal access and which disqualifies jurors solely on the basis of objective criteria." See also *Inabinett v. State*, 668 So. 2d 170, 173 (Ala. Cr. App. 1995) (selecting jurors from a list of licensed drivers does not violate the fair cross-section requirement of the Sixth Amendment).

4. Very poor. One might argue that most "old" people have a unique perspective on social questions, and are therefore a "cognizable group." As noted in the text, however, courts are unanimous that "the young" (however defined) are not a cognizable group. And other courts have held that people "over 65" are not a cognizable group either. *State v. Johnson*, 2003 WL 22999449 (Tenn. Crim. App.). Thus, the state could remove them at will. On the other hand, old age is an immutable characteristic; while you can cease being "young," you can't cease being "old," at least not if you can still do jury duty. Thus, there is an argument under *that* approach to "cognizability" that at some point the "old" become a cognizable group. Of course, there still might be a "significant state interest" under *Duren* for allowing the state to exclude this group—fear of senility.

5. Surprise. Although *Batson* appears to preclude consideration of race in employing peremptories, and although defense counsel did exactly that, the court in *United States v. Angel*, 355 F.3d 462 (6th Cir. 2004) held that a "failure to act" (strike) could not be equated with *Batson's* prohibition of an "act." Moreover, the defendant's argument that his counsel struck an "otherwise qualified white juror to make room for the minority juror" was treated as describing a "hypothetical" rather than an actual event reflected in the record. Said the court: "We find no support for the proposition that a defense attorney's *failure to challenge* a juror, even if motivated by race, implicates the equal protection rights of either the juror or the defendant . . . Lawyers do not select jurors, after all; they only remove prospective jurors." A dissenting judge pointed out that the juror was not only kept because of race, but had also expressed, in a drug crime case, a desire to see drug crimes

punished more strictly. In fact, the dissent suggested that, in light of the juror's statement, the district court had an obligation to remove her for cause even if the defense counsel didn't. The dissent also cited *United States v. Nelson*, 277 F.3d 164 (2d Cir. 2002), where the district court had affirmatively sought to empanel a jury that represented the community, denying a *Batson* challenge where the government used 55 percent of its peremptories to strike blacks, and denied a for-cause challenge of a Jewish juror who had "expressed grave doubts about his ability to be objective about the case" (involving a hate crime by a black against a Jew). See also *State v. Reiners*, 664 N.W.2d 826 (Minn. 2003) (trial judge improperly retained black in apparent attempt to provide racial diversity).

6. Start the trial. Do not strike the jury, or provide any other remedy to the defense. At the moment, whether *Batson* precludes strikes based upon religion has not been resolved by the United States Supreme Court, although most courts prohibit such a strike. In *United States v. Stafford*, 136 F.3d 1109 (7th Cir. 1998), the court summarized the law as it stands even today: "It is necessary to distinguish among religious affiliation, a religion's general tenets, and a specific religious belief. It would be improper and perhaps unconstitutional to strike a juror on the basis of his being a Catholic, a Jew, a Muslim, etc. It would be proper to strike him on the basis of a belief that would prevent him from basing his decision on the evidence and instructions, even if the belief had a religious backing; suppose, for example, that his religion taught that crimes should be left entirely to the justice of God. In between and most difficult to evaluate from the standpoint of *Batson* is a religious outlook that might make the prospective juror unusually reluctant, or unusually eager, to convict a criminal defendant. That appears to be this case." Accord: *United States v. DeJesus*, 347 F.3d 500 (3d Cir. 2003) Compare *State v. Davis*, 50 N.W.2d 767 (Minn. 1993), *cert. denied*, 511 U.S. 1115 (1994) and *People v. Wheeler*, 22 Cal. 3d 258, 583 P.2d 748 (1978).

In dissenting from the denial of certiorari in *Davis*, Justices Thomas and Scalia argued that "It is at least not obvious . . . why peremptory strikes based on religious affiliation would survive equal protection analysis." See, generally, Annot. 63 ALR 5th 375 (1998). Religion is not an immutable characteristic, so that approach would not help the defense; on the other hand, religious affiliation is surely a "cognizable" group and would fall under the Sixth Amendment, were a statute to preclude religious persons from being placed on the wheel. Whether it violates the equal protection clause remains to be seen. Three dissenters in *J.E.B. v. Alabama ex rel. T.B.*, 511 U.S. 127 (1994), opined that *Batson* would inevitably declare such strikes unconstitutional, but the rest of the Court has not yet taken that step.

C. The Passive Jury—And Jury Reform

Imagine taking a law school course and being forbidden to ask any questions or take any notes throughout the entire semester, and having to review for the exam without any materials relating to the course. Until recently jurors were in this situation—most jurisdictions forbade them to take notes, or to ask questions, throughout the process. Allowing jurors to ask questions, even through the trial judge, would, it is thought, override the strategy of the attorneys and possibly conflict with the rules of evidence (a juror might ask for example, about hearsay, and be unhappy when told that the law does not allow that question to be asked).[54]

That, however, has changed dramatically in the past 20 years: virtually all federal circuits, and the vast majority of states, now permit jurors to provide questions to the judge, who will decide whether to ask them at all, or in an edited form. *State v. Doleszny*, 844 A.2d 773 (Vt. 2004) (collecting cases, statutes, and articles on the subject). On the other hand, a few states have concluded the process would be unconstitutional under state statutes. *State v. Costello*, 646 N.W.2d 204 (Minn. 2002); see also, *State v. Glidden*, 144 Ohio App. 3d 69, 759 N.E.2d 468 (Ohio App. 2001).[55] A growing number of states permit jurors to take notes as well. *State v. Rose*, 748 A.2d 1283 (R.I. 2000). The concern is that taking notes would distract jurors from listening (do you find that a problem as a student in class?) and that disputes would erupt in the jury room over whose notes are more accurate. (Of course, with 12 sets of notes, there is *likely* to be some form of consensus.) Moreover, in many jurisdictions, jurors in the past received no written set of jury instructions, and no copy of the indictment.

D. The Jury—Alternate Jurors

Because jurors can become sick, or otherwise unable to proceed, virtually all states provide for the selection, at the time of voir dire, of alternate jurors. In some instances, the alternates are identified as alternates at the time, in other jurisdictions, the "real" jury is determined only after the case has been heard. As a general matter, whether a juror should be replaced by

---

54. See Tiersma, Jury Questions: An Update to Kalven and Zeisel, 39 Crim. L. Bull. 10 (2003); West, "The Blindfold Is Not a Gag": The Case for Allowing Controlled Question of Witnesses by Jurors, 38 Tulsa L. Rev. 529 (2003).

55. Jurors in Spain and Russia are currently allowed to ask questions.

an alternate prior to deliberations is within the full discretion of the trial judge. *United States v. Fajardo*, 787 F.2d 1253 (11th Cir. 1986). In most jurisdictions, alternates may replace regular jurors only before the jury begins deliberating. There is a dramatic split as to the procedure to be followed if an alternate is needed once deliberations begin. In some jurisdictions, the alternates are sent to the jury room, but instructed not to participate in deliberations. In others, the (potential) substitutes are held in abeyance during deliberations; if events necessitate replacing a juror, deliberations are to begin again. The former procedure, which is obviously more efficient, has nevertheless been criticized on the basis that it invades the secrecy of jury deliberations. Some jurisdictions now allow for deliberations by the remaining 11 jurors, assuming that both parties agree.

E. Jury Behavior—Reviewing Jury Verdicts

1. Evidentiary Transgressions— Jury Experimentation and Resort to Outside Evidence

Jurors swear to decide the case based upon the evidence presented in the courtroom. But what if they violate that oath, and rely on other evidence? In "Twelve Angry Men" (and if you haven't seen this classic film, immediately stop reading this book and rent the video), the prosecutor has claimed that the murder weapon, which he said was unique, means that the defendant, who admits having owned a knife like it, is guilty. Suddenly, the protagonist juror throws onto the table an identical knife. That melodramatic action persuades several of the reluctant jurors to alter their views about the case.[56] But courts are clear that jurors should not use outside information. Where, for example, a juror who, in an effort to determine the duration of the drive which defendant might have taken to commit the crime, traced the route and timed the drive, the court found possible reversible error and remanded for a hearing. *State v. Hartley*, 656 A.2d 954 (R.I. 1995)[57] (Using a standard that

---

56. But see *People v. Holmes*, 69 Ill. 2d 507, 372 N.E.2d 656 (1978), where jurors went to a local shoe store and found two heel designs exactly like the one which the police called "unique" at the scene of the crime, and which belonged to defendant. Truth really is stranger. . . .

57. Jurors seem to love to do this. See *Russell v. State*, 99 Nev. 265, 661 P.2d 1293 (1983).

the conviction will be reversed only if the information would probably affect a reasonable, average, juror.)

Whether a juror may rely upon information, or life experience, extrinsic to the trial is raised in two separate settings: (1) May a juror be challenged for cause on the basis of his extra-court knowledge; (2) if a juror relies on such knowledge, and communicates it to other jurors during deliberations, may the verdict be impugned? Most courts embrace a broad view of the life experience information upon which a juror may rely, and hence do not view that information as either a basis of a cause challenge or of a challenge to the verdict. See, e.g., *State v. Mann*, 131 N. Mex. 59, 39 P.3d 124 (N. Mex. 2002). Some courts, however, attempt to prescribe such information. *People v. Maragh*, 94 N.Y.2d 569, 729 N.E.2d 701 (2000). The difficulty, of course, lies in seeking to define, in advance, the kind of "tainted" information, and the degree to which a juror may not use it. While most people have a rudimentary knowledge of the dangers of skidding on ice, a professional race driver, such as Al Unser, may understand them better. At what point would his "extra" knowledge become sufficiently tainted? And how would an attorney (or judge) on voir dire, frame a question to uncover not only Al Unser, but Paul Newman (an amateur race driver)?

In contrast to reliance upon life experiences, if a juror went home and obtained, from the Internet, specific information about a disputed piece of evidence, the result may well be different. For example in *Meyer v. State*, 80 P.3d 447 (Nev. 2003), one juror, who worked in a dermatologist's office, had consulted the Physician's Desk Reference to determine the possibility, raised by defendant, that the victim's bruises could have occurred accidentally. The Court there held that the use of the reference tainted the verdict.

At first blush, the ban on resort to experimentation, or even juror expertise, seems plausible, even exemplary. After all, it is not certain that the conditions under which the jury conducts its experiments are the same conditions of that obtained during the incident in the crime (in the *Hartley* case, for example, on the day the juror drove, traffic might have been unusually heavy or light). But there are difficulties, both theoretical and practical. Jurors are chosen, after all, because they reflect "common sense" in a way that neither a single judge nor lawyer could.[58] If that "common sense" includes knowledge of the way the world works, why should that knowledge be excluded from the jury room? Suppose, for example, that in the *Hartley* case, the juror, rather than driving the road *after* hearing the testimony, simply said to her fellow

---

58. E.g., *State v Arnold*, 96 N.Y.3d 358, 753 N.E.2d 846 (2001): "While the goal is utter impartiality, each juror inevitably brings to the jury room a lifetime of experience that will necessarily inform her assessments of the witnesses and the evidence. Nor would we want a jury devoid of life experience, even if that were possible, because it is precisely such experience that enables a jury to evaluate the credibility of witnesses and the strength of arguments."

jurors, "I drive that same route every day, and it does (not) take the time testified to." That is unlikely to be reversible error. While, in the case of an "expert" juror the possible violation is evident, it is usually extremely difficult to separate "common sense" from specific knowledge. If the putatively injured party's counsel was aware of the juror's knowledge, as often happens, the failure to strike the juror peremptorily may be viewed as a waiver. And if counsel were unaware of the characteristic, this might be attributable to an inadequate voir dire.[59] Furthermore, conscientious jurors experiment, or resort to outside knowledge, because they seek the truth. If their actions supplement inadequate lawyering by a party to the case, why should the attorney's failures restrict the jury in that search, particularly if it is at least plausible that the (mis)conduct is not subject to claims of changed conditions?[60] While it is true that our rules of evidence have been developed over centuries, and reflect considerable weighing of significant policy issues, it is not clear that a jury that carefully fills in the lacunae in a case is contradicting the final goal of all trials, to find the "right" answer in that specific case.

2. Juror Competence—Revealed "Cause" and Intransigence

Jurors sometimes realize during the trial, during deliberations, or after verdict, that they failed to reveal some piece of information that might have been ground for a "cause" or a least a peremptory challenge. In *People v. Kelly*, 185 Cal. App. 3d 118, 229 Cal. Rptr. 584 (1986), for example, where the defendant was tried for sexual assault, a juror belatedly recalled an incident in her early childhood which was similar to the alleged act. Should the judge excuse her and (a) proceed with 11 jurors; (b) replace her with an alternate and begin deliberations again; or (c) ignore the problem? A few states allow a trial to proceed with less than 12 jurors if a juror becomes "incapacitated," but it is not clear that this information constitutes "incapacitation."[61] Such rules often (though not always) require the acquiescence of both counsel—suppose one side objects? If the discovery is made posttrial, most courts will require the defendant to show that a correct answer to the voir dire question would have

---

59. Whether inadequate voir dire would constitute inadequate representation is another issue. See Chapter 10.

60. A good example might be the Twelve Angry Men incident related above. Even there, however, a good prosecutor would argue that the duplicate knives became available only after the defendant committed the crime; it would then behoove both the defense counsel to investigate that claim.

61. A rule permitting a trial judge to remove a juror afer deliberations have begun and to install an alternate juror "because of . . . other inability to continue" should be construed narrowly, and a juror's emotional distress over the case was not grounds for removal. *State v. Jenkins*, 365 N.J. Super. 18, 837 A.2d 1125 (2003).

resulted in a removal of the juror for cause. *McDonough Power Equipment v. Greenwood*, 464 U.S. 548 (1984).

As noted above the criminal jury's power (if not right) to "nullify" the law is historically a strong protection for the defendant. If a prospective juror reveals on voir dire, however, that she "will not" convict the defendant because she disagrees with the law under which he is prosecuted, she may be stricken for cause, and recent court decisions hold that the nonrecalcitrant juror may be removed, either during the trial or even during deliberations (and possibly even held in contempt). This is consistent with cases allowing the prosecution to "death qualify" a jury in a death penalty case, assuring the government of a fair chance at conviction and punishment although both of these lines of cases are inconsistent with the general power of nullification, which, as Justice Marshall once put it, is the "irrationality" to which every defendant is entitled. *Johnson v. Louisiana*, 406 U.S. 356 (1972) (MARSHALL, J., dissenting).

3. *Juror Competence and Pressure — Herein of Threats, Drugs, and Attention Spans*

We assume that jurors decide impartially and without coercion. If a juror receives a threat to himself or his family, unless he convicts (or acquits), the assumption is shattered, and a court may take drastic action, either to protect the juror (or the jury generally) or to protect the defendant and state's right to a fair assessment of the evidence. In a similar vein, suggestions from others that the defendant is guilty may be prejudicial. E.g., *Turner v. Louisiana*, 379 U.S. 466 (1965) (two sheriff's deputies talked to jurors during deliberations); *Parker v. Gladden*, 385 U.S. 363 (1966) (bailiff tells juror defendant "is guilty"). On the other hand, the law does not wish jury deliberations, or jury verdicts, to be subject to second guessing every time a verdict is questionable. Jury deliberations may become heated, and jurors often utter intemperate sentiments with which even they do not necessarily agree, or which may not drive them in reaching a verdict.

The difference between internal dissension and external pressure was explosively demonstrated in the infamous "Tyco" trial, where two former executives of the Tyco corporation were charged with taking $600 million through theft and stock manipulation. After six months of trial, and 10 days of deliberations, the jury sent a note to the trial judge informing him that the atmosphere was "poisonous" and that one juror was refusing to deliberate. The judge met with the jury, declaring that, "It's not surprising that things can get difficult. Try to relax as much as you can this evening." The next day, at the request of the jury, he sent them home early for the weekend. At the same time, however, several media reported that one of the jurors had been seen giving an "OK" sign to the defense attorneys (which she later vigorously denied), and she was named in several newspapers (virtually no media will print the names of jurors until after a verdict is reached). That weekend, the juror received a phone call, and an e-mail message, which she interpreted as threatening her if she continued to hold out. She described herself as "severely distressed" and "terrified." Having refused to grant a mistrial when the jury's acrimony was at high dudgeon, the trial judge nevertheless granted a mistrial based upon the juror's fears.

No person at a trial, even a defendant, can remain vigilant every second. But what happens if a juror, or jurors, become inattentive or worse? And suppose the origin of that stupor is alcohol or drugs? In *Tanner v. United States*, 483 U.S. 107 (1987) defendant alleged, on the basis of information conveyed to his attorney after conviction by two of the 12 jurors who convicted defendant, that several of the jurors drank, causing them to sleep through the afternoon sessions of the trial. One affidavit alleged that the "jury was on one big party" — seven of the jurors drank alcohol during lunch; four drank from one to three pitchers of beer; other jurors consumed mixed drinks, four smoked marijuana regularly during the trial; one juror ingested coke five times, and another juror did so one or two times; and one juror sold one-quarter pound of marijuana to another during the trial and brought drug paraphernalia into the courthouse. This would be grounds for judicial action if the report had come before verdict. But, as we will see below, timing is everything.

F. Uncovering Jury Misbehavior — External and Internal Information

We can only learn of jury misconduct if jury secrecy is breached. A great deal depends on *when and how* that breach occurs. If the court becomes aware of the problem before verdict, she has several options. The first step is to inquire about the matter, either with one or more jurors, separately or together, to determine the accuracy of the information she has received, and whether the action has tainted any possible verdict. If it has, then she must declare a mistrial. On the other hand, if she determines that an admonition to the jury will suffice, she may take that road. Or, if the matter involves only one juror, she may dismiss that juror and either continue the deliberations with 11 or replace the juror with an alternate and instruct them to begin again (if permitted by the law of the jurisdiction).

If the jury has returned a verdict, the issue becomes much more complex. Now jury secrecy must be breached in order to find a remedy. Jury secrecy, however, is a cardinal virtue; it:

- protects the finality of jury verdicts;
- guards the frankness and candor of discussion in the jury room; and
- prevents postverdict harassment of jurors.

As one court put it: "We are compelled to err in favor of the lesser of two evils—protecting the secrecy of jury deliberations at the expense of possibly allowing juror activity." *United States v. Thomas*, 116 F.3d 606, 623 (2d Cir. 1997). The courts attempt to capture the difference between the kind of evidence which *may* be heard to overturn a verdict and that which *may never* be used to do so. Virtually all states, and the federal government as well, prohibit jurors from testifying, post-trial, to any evidence of misconduct which is said to stem from an "*internal*" source; only "*external*" influences, such as a threat on the jury's safety, or a bribe, may be used to overturn a verdict.

In addition to the *kind* of evidence that may be considered, the *source* is also relevant. For well over 200 years, the general rule has been that jurors themselves may not testify as to what occurred in their deliberations Thus, in *Tanner, supra*, a majority of the Court held that, under Federal Rule of Evidence 606, the trial court was precluded from receiving this evidence. The Court reasoned that reassessing jury verdicts on the basis of jurors' deliberations would violate the sanctity of the jury room, as well as leave jurors open to post-trial pressures brought by defense counsel, media, or even fellow jurors.[62] On the other hand, if defense counsel had testimony (or even better, videotape) from the elevator operator who escorted the jurors to and from the jury room, it is possible that the trial court would have been able to listen to that evidence. (Whether it would suffice to overturn the verdict, however, is a different question.) To the defendant, of course, any such differentiation seems gossamer at best, yet the Court's concern about subjecting many jury verdicts to Monday-morning quarterbacks does not seem unreasonable. For the same reason, in many jurisdictions, post-trial contact with jurors by attorneys is prohibited by ethics rules. The ABA standards agree, but allow contact for purposes of discerning improper pressures, if no relevant statute or rule prohibits such course or conduct. ABA Standards Relating to the Prosecution and Defense Function, §§3-5.4; 4-7.3(c); ABA Code of Professional Responsibility Disciplinary Rule 7-108. The issue has become exacerbated in recent years, however, by post-verdict press interviews[63] (or even press conferences or books by jurors), in which some information is released.

If there is some permissible source of information concerning juror misconduct, the court will hold a hearing. If a hearing is held, however, the

---

62. In one case, jurors were interviewed by ABC Television after their verdict, and provided some reason to challenge their deliberations. Nevertheless, the court held, the videotapes were inadmissible hearsay evidence that cannot support a claim of juror misconduct. *People v. Fletcher*, 679 N.W.2d 127 (Mich. App. 2004).

63. "To the media, the jury appears to be just another institution about which the public has a 'right to know.'" Goldstein, Jury Secrecy and the Media: The Problem of Postverdict Interviews, 1993 U. Ill. L. Rev. 295, 297.

courts are not clear on who carries the burden of proof. In *Remmer v. United States*, 347 U.S. 227 (1954), the Court said that prejudice is "presumed" if a juror has been bribed, but left open the question of whether that presumption was rebuttable, and if so, how. Lower courts have suggested that in such instances the government must eliminate all "reasonable possibility" of prejudice. See. e.g., *Wilding v. State*, 674 So. 2d 114 (Fla. 1996). In *Smith v. Phillips*, 455 U.S. 2109 (1982), where a juror had applied for a job with the prosecutor's office, the Court indicated that the defendant had to prove actual bias by the juror, but a number of courts hold that the defendant carries only the burden of production of some "likelihood of prejudice" before the government must prove harmlessness. See *State v. Anderson*, 252 Neb. 675, 564 N.W. 2d 581 (1997).

Moreover, it is not clear what the standard for ordering a new trial should be. There are at least three possibilities:

- automatic reversal, e.g., *United States v. Keating*, 147 F.3d 895 (9th Cir. 1998);
- reversal only if the Court is convinced that the jury in this case *was* influenced by the activity;
- reversal if the Court concludes that a *reasonable jury* would have been influenced by the activity, e.g., *State v. Hartley*, supra.

Neither the first *per se* rule, nor the third, objective, approach requires probing into the actual deliberations of the jury. Once it is determined that there was an experiment, bribe, threat, etc., the judge needs no more information. These approaches, then, are more consistent with jury secrecy, and are usually employed for that reason. See *Meyer v. State*, 80 P.3d 447 (Nev. 2003).

EXAMPLES

1. Your client, Michael Milkcan, has been convicted on 47 counts of fraud. Several months after the verdict, you visit the bar in which the jurors had dinner every night. The bartender, recognizing you, says: "Boy, was your jury soused. I'm surprised they could count to 47 after the way they drank. And they really didn't have clue about the judge's fraud instruction. Before I became a bartender, I went to law school, and passed the bar, and I know — they were really in the dark about that." You've read *Tanner*. Do you have another drink? Or do you call the judge?

2. At the outset of Domingo's trial for stock fraud, the judge provides the jurors with the names of witnesses, and asks them whether they know any of the witnesses. No one responds. In the middle of the trial, defense counsel calls Emilio, a newly discovered witness; the trial judge permits this, giving the prosecution time to investigate Emilio. During

deliberations, juror Crooner points to Emilio's testimony as exculpating Domingo. At that point Lucille Sphere, another juror, declares: "Emilio's a liar. He wouldn't know the truth in a crowded phone booth. I ought to know — I dated the jerk for three years. If he says Domingo's innocent, I say he's guilty." Domingo learns of this (don't ask how) only after the jury convicts. What chance has Domingo of obtaining a new trial?

3. In a prosecution for smuggling drugs by sea, the defendants testify that they left Port Angeles on June 1, and entered Miami on June 8. There is undisputed testimony that there were no drugs on board when the ship left Port Angeles. After they are convicted, one juror writes a book in which he describes the deliberations. The jury was ready to acquit, he says, until a doctor spoke to them about the course from Port Angeles to Miami. An amateur sailor, he told his colleagues that he had traveled those waters many times, and that the trip would take no more than three days, even in bad weather, and the weather was good. The ship "must have" stopped somewhere, he argued, and that is where they loaded the drugs. You are the defense attorney. What do you do?

EXPLANATIONS

1. Put down that Chivas and get to the phone. Although the law is always cautious about investigating what occurred during deliberations, *Tanner* was based on Rule 606, which precludes a *juror* from providing evidence about jury competence. If you can find enough witnesses (the bartender alone will probably not suffice) to testify about enough occasions (particularly during the deliberative process itself) on which a substantial part of the jury appeared incompetent, you might at least get a hearing. And that's a start. But recognize that such testimony is incredibly subjective, and you've got to show that the verdict was truly influenced by the drunken stupor (if that's what it was). As for the evidence that they misunderstood the instruction, you are even less likely to win — can you *prove* that the misunderstanding continued in the jury room *and* that it prejudiced Milkcan?

2. Not very good. Clearly, Lucille should have informed the judge of her relationship with Emilio as soon as he was called to the stand. The judge almost certainly would have conducted an *in camera* hearing with Lucille. Had he found her incapable of deciding the case fairly, he might have declared a mistrial (assuming the parties could not, or would not, agree to a trial by the remaining 11), or replaced Lucille with an alternate juror. The same might have occurred if the relationship had been revealed during deliberations. Once the verdict is in, however, the burden may shift to the defendant to show prejudice (remember — the courts are divided on this issue). Moreover, he cannot bring on evidence

about what occurred in the jury room itself, nor can other jurors testify to Lucille's comments. The goal of finality outweighs the goal of assuring Domingo of a fair trial. Domingo will be spending many domingos as a guest of the state. Can the court take action against Lucille? It is *possible* that she is guilty of contempt of court. But she will claim surprise about Emilio's appearance. Most courts tend to find such mistakes, even glaring ones like this, not sufficient to warrant a sanction of contempt unless intentional and spiteful. If, of course, Lucille had known at the start of the trial that Emilio would testify, that might be a different matter. See, e.g., Ark. Stat. Ann. §16-31-107.

3. Cry. In most states, a juror's testimony about what happened in the jury room is still prohibited by Federal Rule 606 and most state equivalents. In those states that would hear such evidence, however, such as New York, it is possible that you can obtain a hearing and persuade the court that this is similar to *Maragh*. Perhaps you should have anticipated that issue, and checked out the sailing time. On the other hand, it would appear that the prosecutor also failed to pursue that avenue (or sea lane). If the jury had acquitted, the prosecutor would be wearing egg. But you've got the omelet.

9

Double Jeopardy

"... the State with all its resources and power should not be allowed to make repeated attempts to convict an individual for an alleged offense, thereby subjecting him to embarrassment, expense and ordeal and compelling him to live in a continuing state of anxiety and insecurity as well as enhancing the possibility that even though innocent he may be found guilty."

Green v. United States, 355 U.S. 184 (1957)[1]

"(T)he double jeopardy clause has produced some of the most confusing and seemingly contradictory decisions in recent Supreme Court history."

Allen, Stuntz, Hoffmann, Livingston,
Comprehensive Criminal Procedure 1354 (2001).

A. The General Issue

1. The Purpose of Double Jeopardy

The Double Jeopardy Clause of the Fifth Amendment declares that:

no person shall be subject for the same offense to be twice put in jeopardy of life or limb

It protects against (1) a second prosecution for the same offense after acquittal (autrefois acquit); (2) a second prosecution for the same offense after conviction (autrefois convict); (3) multiple punishments for the same offense. *North Carolina v. Pearce*, 395 U.S. 711 (1969).

---

1. The Court was more expansive on this last point in *Burks v. United States*, 437 U.S. 1 (1978), protesting against a "test run" in which the state had an "opportunity to supply evidence which it failed to use in the first proceeding."

The first part of this protection assures that a defendant who has been acquitted can never again be tried for that offense, even if there is later absolute proof (a video, or even defendant's postverdict confession to the crime) of his guilt. See *United States v. Ball*, 163 U.S. 662 (1896). The state has one opportunity to convict; it cannot continuously subject the defendant to the pressures outlined in *Green*. The fundamental idea is to prevent the state from "wearing down" the defendant through multiple successive litigations. The concern is that the defendant will either lose hope (and resources) and simply concede (see *Alford* pleas, Chapter 7), or that the state will use a first trial to learn both of the weaknesses in its own case and the strengths in defendant's case and adjust accordingly in a second, third, or fourth trial. In effect, without the double jeopardy protection, the motto for the State could be "If at first you don't succeed, try, try, try, try, try, again."[2] The autrefois acquit rule also assures the nullifying power of juries[3] (see Chapter 8), as well as providing against premature prosecutions. Although the question has rarely been litigated, it has been assumed by writers and courts (at least in passing) that the ban against double jeopardy applies even if the defendant's acquittal is the result of bribery. See Rudstein, Double Jeopardy and the Fraudulently-Obtained Acquittal, 60 Mo. L. Rev. 607 (1995).[4]

Similarly, a defendant who has been convicted for a crime may not be later (re)tried and punished again for that offense ("autrefois convict"). Here, the explanation is not so obvious. If the defendant has been found guilty, why not allow the state to prosecute him twice, or even 20 times? The concern must be simply the exhaustion point; there is no worry that we are convicting, in a second trial, a person already "found" to be innocent.

The third part of the *Pearce* triumvirate — protection against multiple punishments — would seem to encompass some notion of proportionality. It has been severely weakened in the last two decades. It may actually be a relatively unimportant protection as the twenty-first century begins.

Although the words of the Amendment restrict the protection to cases of "life and limb," today, when few felonies are capital, these words, if taken literally, would turn the clause into a dead letter. Instead, the courts have applied it to any crime, even those not involving prison terms.

---

2. Even in the absence of a double jeopardy clause, there might be a due process limitation on how many successive prosecutions the state could bring, but courts are usually unreceptive to such an argument. See, e.g., *Kyles v. Whitley*, 514 U.S. 419, 514 U.S. 419 (1995); the defendant who successfully appealed these convictions, was tried four times before being acquitted.

3. See Westen, The Three Faces of Double Jeopardy: Reflections on Government Appeals of Criminal Sentences, 78 Mich. L. Rev. 1011 (1980). (Arguing that the finality of acquittals is tied to the right to nullify.)

4. One court appears to have decided differently, holding that a defendant who has bribed a juror is never "really" in jeopardy. *People v. Aleman*, 281 Ill. App. 3d 991, 667 N.E.2d 615 (1996). See also Poulin, Double Jeopardy and Judicial Accountability: When Is an Acquittal Not an Acquittal, 27 Ariz. St. L.J. 953 (1995).

2. *When Does Jeopardy Begin?*

By definition, the *double* jeopardy clause only applies if the defendant has been "in jeopardy." Many of the reasons articulated in *Green* for the clause are activated almost immediately when the defendant is indicted: He may lose his job, and (if the offense is bailless, or he cannot make bail) freedom; he will certainly suffer ignominy; and begin to suffer financial loss, not the least from hiring an attorney. His psychological resources will also be at risk after a true bill is returned. One might, then, say that his jeopardy begins at that point.

Nevertheless, the case law is clear that the defendant is not considered to have been placed *in jeopardy* until after a jury has been sworn and impaneled.[5] Thus, *Downum v. United States*, 372 U.S. 734 (1963), the jury was selected at the very end of the day, but was not actually sworn. The next day, the prosecution's key witness was unavailable, and the trial court declared a mistrial. When defendant was later prosecuted, he argued double jeopardy, but the Court found that jeopardy had never "attached." Whether the swearing in of the jury should actually carry such magical powers, the rule at least establishes a bright line, which neither side is likely to seek to manipulate (in contrast, for example, to a rule that would set the bar when the indictment is signed, which would be in the control of the prosecution).

In a plea of guilty or nolo contendere, jeopardy does not attach until the plea is accepted. In a bench trial, jeopardy attaches when the trial judge begins to hear evidence. If the first Court did not have jurisdiction to try the defendant for the crime charged in the second proceeding, double jeopardy does not apply. *State v. Perkins*, 276 Va. 621, 580 S.E.2d 523 (2003).

Finally, as we will discuss in more detail in Chapter 11, the clause provides only against successive *prosecutions*—used to enhance in a current sentencing, the prior conduct of a defendant—including a charge of which he was—acquitted, does not violate double jeopardy. *Witte v. United States*, 515 U.S. 389 (1995), *United States v. Watts*, 519 U.S. 554 (1997).[6]

3. *When Is a Defendant "Acquitted"?*

The "autrefois acquit" doctrine precludes reprosecution of a defendant for a crime for which he has been acquitted. Usually determining whether the defendant has been acquitted is straightforward. But not always. In *Green v. United States*, 355 U.S. 184 (1957), defendant was tried for first

---

5. Intriguingly enough, the rule in the nineteenth century appears to have been exactly the opposite—jeopardy did not attach until the case was complete and sent to the jury.

6. *United States v. Wells*, 347 F.3d 280 (8th Cir. 2003) *United States v. Shreffler*, 47 Fed. Apx. 140, 2002 WL 31116766 (3d Cir.). See also *Nichols v. United States*, 511 U.S. 738 (1994).

182 9. Double Jeopardy

degree murder; the jury returned a verdict of second degree. After Green successfully appealed that conviction, the prosecutor sought to reprosecute for first degree, but the Court held that the jury's verdict had "impliedly acquitted" Green of first degree murder, and the double jeopardy clause precluded a second prosecution for that offense.

A judicial statement of acquittal, however, must be very clear. In *Price v. Vincent*, 538 U.S. 634 (2003), the defendant moved for a directed verdict on first degree murder, and the trial judge declared: "My impression is that there has not been shown premeditation or planning . . . what we have at the very best is second degree murder." The next day, after hearing argument from the prosecution, the judge decided to send the first degree charge to the jury, which returned that verdict. The State Supreme Court affirmed the conviction. On a habeas corpus challenge by the defendant that the trial judge had effectively granted its motion for a directed verdict as to first degree murder, the Supreme Court held that the State Supreme Court's decision was not "contrary to" and did not involve an "unreasonable application" of clearly established Federal law, as is required by the habeas statute (see Chapter 12). Indeed, in *United States v. Alvarez*, 351 F.3d 126 (4th Cir. 2003), the district court entered a "Judgment of Acquittal" after the jury deadlocked. Even that, said the court, could not preclude a reprosecution unless it were shown that the trial judge had considered the sufficiency of the evidence. Accord: *United States v. Merlino*, 310 F.3d 187 (3d Cir. 2002) (Where the first jury returned a verdict of "not proven" as to some counts, a subsequent prosecution was not barred, because there was no certainty that the verdict was an acquittal of that count). On the other hand, when a conviction is overturned on the grounds of insufficient evidence of guilt, the double jeopardy clause precludes a second trial. *Burks v. United States*, 437 U.S. 1 (1978).

There is great dispute as to whether the clause applies in sentencing at all. The Court has held that a failure of proof in a sentencing proceeding simply does not have the "qualities of constitutional finality that attend an acquittal," *Monge v California*, 524 U.S. 721 (1998), except where the first proceeding was the sentencing phase of a capital case. *Bullington v. Missouri*, 451 U.S. 430 (1981.) In *Sattazahn v. Pennsylvania*, 537 U.S. 101 (2002), the jury had "hung" on the death penalty issue, and state law had required the imposition of a life imprisonment sentence. After defendant successfully appealed his conviction, the state sought, and obtained, the death penalty in a second trial. The Supreme Court held that this did not violate the double jeopardy clause because the entry of the life imprisonment sentence in the first trial had not been an "acquittal" of the death penalty.

B. The "Same Offense" Doctrine

Almost 25 years ago, the Court declared that its double jeopardy decisions were "a veritable Sargasso Sea which could not fail to challenge the most intrepid judicial navigator." *Albernaz v. United States*, 450 U.S. 333, 343 (1981). That statement continues to apply today. In two separate recent instances, the Court in double jeopardy cases has overruled three-year-old precedents,[7] and in one more instance, overruled an eight-year-old year precedent.[8] So get ready for a rousing adventure at sea. The first shoal — the "same offense" language of the clause.

The double jeopardy clause protects against two jeopardies for the "same offense." Sounds fairly clear, right? Robbery is robbery, mail fraud is mail fraud. Not so quick. Put on your life vests; we're about to start taking on water. The question of whether two offenses are "the same" is so complex that the Supreme Court overruled itself in a three-year period; the most recent decision in this area had so many opinions, with so many concurrences and dissents, that it is difficult (perhaps impossible) to figure out who stands where, much less what "the law" of the twenty-first century is. Of course that may be comforting — whatever you answer on a law exam can't be "all" wrong. (But then again, maybe it can't be "all right" either.)

If Mortimer is prosecuted for robbing the First National Bank at 3:00 on Monday, it would seem from the words of the clause that whether he is acquitted or convicted he cannot be reprosecuted for robbing the First National Bank at 3:00 on Monday. But suppose the second indictment alleges that the robbery was done with a rifle, and seeks a conviction for *armed* robbery. Does the first verdict preclude reprosecution? The courts have used several different tests to answer that question:

- the "same elements" test;
- the "same conduct" (or "same transaction" or "same event" test);
- the "same evidence" test.

1. The "Same Elements" Test — Blockburger v. United States

In *Blockburger v. United States*, 284 U.S. 299 (1932), the Court adopted the "same elements" test to determine whether the defendant has been convicted twice of the "same offense":

> Where the same act or transaction constitutes a violation of two distinct statutory provisions, the test to be applied . . . is whether each provision requires proof of an additional fact which the other does not.

---

7. *United States v. Scott*, 437 U.S. 82 (1978) overruling *United States v. Jenkins*, 420 U.S. 348 (1975); *United States v. Dixon*, 509 U.S. 688 (1993), overruling *Grady v. Corbin*, 495 U.S. 508 (1990).

8. See *Hudson v. United States*, 522 U.S. 93 (1997), effectively overturning *United States v. Halper*, 490 U.S. 435 (1989).

This formula looks solely to the words of the statutes involved. It precludes successive prosecution (and probably, successive punishment, but see below) for offense A, and then for offense B, which is a "lesser included offense" of offense A (or vice versa). To prove armed robbery, after all, the prosecutor must prove everything she proved in the robbery case *plus* that Mortimer was armed. If only one of the crimes has an element different from the other, they are "the same offense" under *Blockburger.*

In *Harris v. Oklahoma*, 433 U.S. 682 (1977), the defendant, in the first trial, was prosecuted for murder, based solely on the theory that the death was a felony murder, occurring during a robbery. After the murder trial, the state sought to prosecute on the robbery itself. The statutes were clearly different; there are many different "elements." But the Court appeared to take a major step away from *Blockburger,* and held the second prosecution barred, although the felony murder statute did not restrict itself to homicides occurring during robbery. This view meant that the statutory words were not always the magic test — in some circumstances, the Court was willing to look at the way in which the crimes had been committed, rather than solely at the statutes involved. As the Court said in *United States v. Whalen*, 445 U.S. 684 (1980), if the legislature had separately proscribed the different specifics of felony murder under separate statutory provisions, the double jeopardy preclusion would be apparent. But there is one wrinkle in that observation — Congress did *not* act in that manner, and might have done so intentionally, with the double jeopardy issue in mind.

In *Grady v. Corbin*, 495 U.S. 508 (1990), the Court appeared to take this view to heart. In *Grady,* the Court held that the double jeopardy clause would be violated if the state prosecuted, for homicide, a driver of a car who had already pled guilty to traffic offenses which were based upon the poor driving which had caused the accident from which the victim died. Clearly the two offenses (a traffic offense; homicide) each contained unique elements, and therefore were not the "same offense" under *Blockburger.* Nevertheless, the Court focused not on the statutory elements, but on both the *conduct* which was proved in the traffic offense, and the *evidence* which the prosecutor had used in the first proceeding, and would use in the second proceeding. The Court noted that the "time, place, and circumstances" for the two offenses were virtually identical, although they obviously were composed of different elements. Even if the statutes were substantially differently worded, said the Court, and a second prosecution therefore not barred by *Blockburger,* a more expansive reading of the double jeopardy clause should prevail. The precise test laid out by *Grady* was ambiguous. But it seemed clear that the Court was abandoning, or at least supplementing, *Blockburger.*

Three years later, however, the Court, badly divided about both its rationale and about the application of its rationale, overruled *Grady.* In

United States v. Dixon, 509 U.S. 688 (1993), the Court declared that the *Grady* test had proved (in three years???) to be "unworkable," as well as not grounded in historical double jeopardy concerns. It (re)embraced *Blockburger* as the "one and only" test of a "same offense" within the double jeopardy clause.

Before *Grady*, and obviously since *Dixon*, there were still exceptions to the *Blockburger* rule. Consistent with the purpose of the clause to prevent a prosecutor from "sandbagging" a first proceeding, successive prosecutions would be allowed if there were facts that either had not yet occurred, or could not have reasonably been discovered to have occurred, at the time of the first prosecution. For example, in *Grady*, the victim of the traffic accident died almost instantly at the crash. But if the traffic prosecution had occurred prior to his death, such that the prosecution could not have "joined" that crime (see below), neither *Blockburger* (nor, hypothetically *Grady*), would bar a successive prosecution for homicide.

2. The "Same Conduct" and the "Same Evidence" Tests

Many commentators, and a number of state courts, see *Blockburger* as too narrow. After all, if Mortimer (our bank robber) took the money from three tellers and two customers, are there *five* crimes (one for each individual victim) or *three* (the two customers, and the bank)? In either instance, it means that a prosecutor could essentially turn Mortimer's "one robbery" into a multitude of offenses, for which he could be separately prosecuted, ostensibly wearing down the defendant and eviscerating the double jeopardy protection [9].

These concerns led a number of state courts to adopt different approaches. The terms ("same transaction," "same episode," "single impulse," "same evidence," "same conduct"), and therefore the results, are somewhat diverse, but the thrust is the same — to look beyond the *Blockburger,* statutory elements of offense in the abstract approach, and to the actual "event."[10] There are, of course, many difficulties in deciding when an "event" began, and when it ended. Suppose that Mortimer kidnaps one

---

9. For a case allowing multiple prosecution in just such an instance, see *People v. Borghesi*, 66 p.3d 93 (Colo. 2003). If there were any limitation on that notion at all, it would appear to lie not in the double jeopardy clause, but in the Cruel and Unusual Punishment Clause — and for those who have studied the law of proportionality, you know that there is only limited help there. See *Harmelin v. Michigan*, 501 U.S. 957 (1991); *Ewing v. California*, 538 U.S. 11(2003).

10. See, e.g, *People v. White*, 390 Mich. 245, 212 N.W.2d 222 (1973); *Comm. v. Campana*, 455 Pa. 622, 314 A.2d 854 (1974); Hawaii R. Pen. P. 8; N.R.R.Ct. 3:15-1.

of the customers, to use as a hostage, and releases the customer unhurt several miles away. Obviously, kidnaping has very different statutory "elements" than bank robbery. Just as obviously, the two crimes are intimately connected in this specific course of conduct. But many states require, or encourage, joinder of the claims in order to avoid the need of multiple prosecutions heavy drain on the defendant's resources, and the strong likelihood of prosecutorial advantage gained during the first trial.

Under the "same evidence" test, the defendant must demonstrate a reasonable possibility that the evidentiary facts used by the fact finder to establish the essential elements of one offense may also be (or have been) used to establish the essential elements of a second challenged offense. In *Lamagna v. State*, 776 N.E.2d 955 (Ind. App. 2002), for example, the court precluded convictions for both possession and conspiracy to possess cocaine: "It is apparent that the evidence relied on by the jury to find defendant guilty of dealing in cocaine was the evidence that *D* delivered to *X* a bag containing a white powder. The overt act in the conspiracy was the possession of cocaine."

The "same conduct (transaction, event)" test may clash with the "same evidence" approach. In *Taylor v. Comm.*, 995 S.W.2d 355 (Ky. 1999), the defendant was indicted for assaulting the victim with a .38 pistol, but robbing him with a rifle. At trial, however, the evidence indicted that both crimes were committed with the rifle. A court looking at the indictment might well decide that the two crimes were different, while a court looking at the evidence at trial might conclude, at least under a "conduct" approach, the two were the same.

C. "Multiplicity"

Another problem, often termed the *unit of prosecution* issue, concerns prosecutorial discretion (in criminal procedure, this is a pervasive issue). Suppose the state punishes the sale of 20 grams of cocaine with 10 years in prison. A separate statute punishes the sale of 100 grams of cocaine with 25 years in prison. If Guido sells Maximilian one block of cocaine weighing 100 grams, he is facing 25 years in prison. But suppose Guido uses 10 bags of 10 grams each. Now the prosecutor may have a choice between a single 25-year penalty or 100 years (10 bags of 10 grams each). Yet the "transaction" is the same.

It seems unduly harsh to send Guido away for life depending on how the prosecutor chooses to charge the "crime." Yet, if we hold the prosecutor to the "single event," does that mean that Mortimer's three robberies of the three customers must be boiled down to one robbery, thus making the other two robberies "freebies"? The problem may be one of sentencing—whether sentences in this situation should be concurrent or consecutive; but it can also be seen as a double jeopardy problem, particularly if the prosecutor attempts seriatim trials.[11]

In *United States v. Universal C.I.T. Credit Corp.*, 344 U.S. 218 (1952), the Court appeared to be moving away from *Blockburger*. There, it held that 32 violations of the Fair Labor Standards Act stated only three offenses, treating as one offense "all violations that arise from that singleness of thought, purpose, or action, which may be deemed a single 'impulse.'" And the Court later declared that: "The double jeopardy clause is not such a fragile guarantee that prosecutors can avoid its limitations by the simple expedient of dividing a single crime into a series of temporal or spatial units." *Brown v. Ohio*, 432 U.S. 1621 (1977).

A conclusion that two acts are (or, are not) the "same offense" has obvious implications for successive trials and, as discussed below, for multiple punishments. But the impact may go beyond that. For example, aliens may be deported if convicted of *two* (but not one) drug charges. See 8 U.S.C. § 1227(a)(2)(B)(I). And "three-strike" laws (discussed in Chapter 11) usually require two prior separate offenses. Because of these and other severe effects of multiple convictions, decisions allowing states (or individual prosecutors) effortlessly to establish multiple offenses seem to jar with the general import of the rule of lenity.

One area in which the "same offense" doctrine seems particularly unhelpful is that of the relatively new "compound crimes," where a defendant is subjected to a greater exposure once convicted of several predicate offenses. For example, in the Racketeer Influenced and Corrupt Organizations Act (RICO), a defendant who commits two predicate crimes may be sentenced for them *and* for the fact that those crimes were committed as a part of an eligible "enterprise." The Court has upheld the use of the predicates against challenges that these "second" prosecutions violated the double jeopardy clause. *Allen et. al.*, conclude that "the Supreme Court has . . . thrown up its hands and admitted that current double jeopardy doctrine is inadequate to deal with (such) complex crimes." *Id*. at 1385.

1. *Collateral Estoppel (Issue Preclusion)*

Even if the offense is not "the same," there is the possibility that a subsequent prosecution will be barred by "collateral estoppel." Students

---

11. *Blockburger* itself involved multiple punishments, and could have been so limited. However, in *Brown v. Ohio*, 432 U.S. 161(1977), the Court relied on the *Blockburger* rule in deciding when separate prosecutions for related offenses are permissible. The problem of multiplicity is hardly new. In *Crepps v. Durden*, 2 Cowp. 640 (K.B. 1777), the court held that four sales of bread on Sunday, in violation of a "blue law", should nevertheless be construed as a single offense; otherwise, said the court, "if a tailor sews on the Lord's day, every stitch he takes is a separate offense." But see, *State v. Broeder*, 90 Mo. App. 169 (1901), holding that a defendant who sells 1,800 bottles of beer without a license can be prosecuted for 1,800 separate offenses.

who have wrestled with the civil concept of collateral estoppel will be over-joyed to learn that that concept has also made its way to criminal prosecution. In *Ashe v. Swenson*, 397 U.S. 436 (1970), the defendant was prosecuted and acquitted for robbery of one of six victims. The trial record reflected that the defendant's prime claim was that he was not present and hence not the perpetrator. The prosecutor then sought to try the defendant for robbing victim number two. The Supreme Court held that the second proceeding was barred, even though the victim was different: the first acquittal, said the Court, clearly rested upon the jury's determination that the defendant was not the perpetrator. That factual determination would preclude a finding of guilt in the second prosecution, which was therefore barred by the double jeopardy clause. Similarly, where in an earlier proceeding, the defendant had been found not guilty by reason of insanity, the verdict established his insanity for all arson-related acts within the pertinent time frame and the prosecution was collaterally estopped from pursuing a second arson claim against the defendant. *United States v. Carbullido*, 307 F.3d 957 (9th Cir. 2002).

Ashe supplements *Blockburger* as a means for determining whether successive prosecutions are permissible under the double jeopardy clause. But that may be little help—applying collateral estoppel in criminal cases is no easier than in civil cases. If, for example, the defendant's only argument in *Ashe* had been that no one robbed victim number one, and the jury had acquitted, that would not have precluded a prosecution for another victim. And if the defense had raised *both* claims (victim number one had not been robbed at all, and if he had, it was not by the defendant) the Court would have to determine (if possible) which of those two predicates had been the basis of the first acquittal. The dilemma is reflected in *Standefer v. United States*, 447 U.S. 10 (1980), where the Court held that defendant *A*'s acquittal on a bribery charge did not preclude a later prosecution of defendant *B* for aiding and abetting the same bribery. Given the antipathy toward special verdicts in criminal cases, however, such an investigation is even less likely than in civil cases to provide a satisfactory resolution.

D. Multiple Punishments

Although *Pearce* declares that the double jeopardy clause protects against multiple punishments for the same crime, more recent decisions seem virtually to eliminate that protection. In *Missouri v. Hunter*, 459 U.S. 359 (1983), the defendant was tried—in a single proceeding—for two offenses which although proscribed by two separate statutes, everyone agreed, *were* the "same offense." (Thus, successive *prosecutions* for those two offenses would be barred by current reading of the double jeopardy clause.) The defendant argued that he could not be punished twice for the "same offense." But the Missouri legislature had provided for two different punishments for the two different provisions. The trial court sentenced Hunter to *consecutive* terms for the two statutory offenses. The Supreme Court affirmed, declaring that the prohibition against multiple punishments was essentially subject to legislative overruling, so long as the legislature made clear that it wished to impose multiple punishments.[12]

Several courts have concluded that *Hunter* says that the sentences are not "multiple" but "cumulative" (even if the defendant receives consecutive sentences). Justice Marshall, dissenting in *Hunter*, viewed the opinion as saying that these were not "same offense"—that the term "same offense" should be interpreted the same way for both multiple prosecutions and multiple punishments.

Whether *Hunter* applies to more than multiple punishments is unclear. In *Brown v. Ohio*, 432 U.S. 1621 (1977), predating *Hunter*, the Court declared that "Where the judge is forbidden to impose cumulative punishment for two crimes at the end of a single proceeding, the prosecutor is forbidden to strive for the same result in successive proceedings." This language might suggest that, after *Hunter*, successive prosecutions *could* be entertained where multiple (or cumulative) sentences could be imposed in one trial. Indeed, this analysis might draw some support from Justice Scalia's opinion in *Dixon*, which argued that the successive *prosecution* strand of the double jeopardy clause cannot have a meaning different from the multiple *punishment* strand because it would be "embarrassing to assert that the single term 'same offense' has two different meanings." Justice Scalia has directly challenged the orthodoxy, arguing that the clause "prohibits not multiple punishment, but only multiple prosecutions."

Hunter makes the legislature the ultimate determiner of constitutional rights.[13] If *Hunter* holds the legislature can authorize cumulative punishments for the "same offense," could it also specifically authorize, even mandate, successive prosecutions on lesser included offenses? Could the state mandate nonjoinder of claims? Finally could the state mandate that any acquitted defendant be tried again for the same offense? Ostensibly such legislation would be invalid; but that would mean that *Hunter* allows the legislature to decide what a "same offense" *is*, but not how that same offense may be prosecuted.

Some have argued that the assessment here should be the Eighth Amendment's proportionality test, however weak that standard might be at

---

12. In some—perhaps most—instances where there is no clear legislative intent to allow the imposition of both punishments, the courts will apply the more specific, or the most recent, statute. They may also apply the less harsh punishment. This, however, is a matter of state law, and of statutory interpretation.

13. "(D)ouble jeopardy analysis turns on whether Congress has authorized the result at issue. If Congress has enacted statutes that separately punish the same conduct, there is no double jeopardy violation." *United States v. Smith*, 354 F.3d 390 (5th Cir. 2003) (citing *Hunter*). See also *State v. Marlowe*, 277 Ga. 383, 589 S.E.2d 69 (2003).

the present moment. After all, if the legislature can constitutionally provide a 20-year sentence for crime Z, it would seem to be relatively insignificant if the sentence is imposed for one offense (with 20 years) or two offenses (each with 10 years). The real concern of the double jeopardy clause, oppressive and continuous litigation, seems less involved here. King, Portioning Punishment: Constitutional Limits on Successive and Excessive Penalties, 144 U. Pa. L. Rev. 103 (1995).[14]

E. Joinder and Severance — The "Kissing Cousins" of Double Jeopardy

Some of the issues generated by the doctrines just discussed might be addressed, if not fully resolved, by rules relating to joinder. Joinder of claims, or defendants, has some obvious benefits — it is more economical, reduces inconvenience to witnesses, jurors, and attorneys and lowers the possibility of conflicting verdicts. A majority of jurisdictions emulate the federal criminal rules, which provide that:

> The indictment or information *may* charge a defendant in separate counts if . . . the offenses charged are . . . based on the same act or transaction or are connected with, or constitute parts of, a common scheme or plan.
>
> *Fed. Rule Crim. Pro. 8 (a) (emphasis added)*

Clearly, these words *permit, but do not require*, joinder of related claims, and go beyond the *Blockburger* "same elements" test, thus allowing the prosecutor to decide whether to charge more than the double jeopardy clause would require. A handful of jurisdictions, however, *require* mandatory joinder of all claims arising from the "same transaction." E.g., W. Va. R. Crim. P. 8(a):

> Two or more offenses may be charged in the same indictment or information. . . . All offenses based on the same act or transaction or on two or more acts or transactions connected together or constituting parts of a common scheme or plan *shall be charged in the same indictment or information.* . . .

In those jurisdictions, the joinder rules supplant the Blockburger test — while the double jeopardy clause would allow a second trial on a separate

---

14. See also Ross, Damned Under Many Headings: The Problem of Multiple Punishment, 29 Amer. J. Crim. Law 245 (2002), a powerful argument that the issue is one of sentencing, particularly under structured sentencing schemes such as the Federal Sentencing Guidelines (see Chapter 11).

act, the joinder rules do not. Contrarily, to the extent that the separate crimes were parts of a "common plan," the efficiencies may dissipate if the charged offense were committed at different times, and places.

The rule thus places the initial decision as to joinder in the hands of the prosecution — if Hana wishes to try Dan on eight related "counts," but is worried about her proofs, she can ask the grand jury to return eight separate indictments each of one count. She may then try the first case on one count. Unless *Ashe* collateral estoppel would apply to subsequent proceedings, an acquittal on one count would not be devastating. Since Rule 8 does not *require* joinder, the defendant must carry the burden of persuading the Court to consolidate the claims (as Rule 13 of the federal rules provides). Thus, permissive joinder seems to be in tension with the double jeopardy protection against multiple trials.

On the other hand, Hana may ask the grand jury to hand down one indictment, with eight counts, fearing that while the petit jury may see each of the eight counts as separately weak, it may well conclude that Dan is a criminal at heart ("where there's enough smoke, there must be some fire"). Thus, the multiple counts may support each other. Moreover, evidence which would be inadmissible on one count, but admissible on another, may be allowed in a joint trial; the question then will be whether the instruction to the jury to use the evidence as to only one count will suffice to prevent prejudice. *Drew v. United States*, 331 F.2d 85 (D.C. Cir. 1964). See Best, Evidence: Examples and Explanations (5th ed. 2004). Here, too, the prosecutor has the choice.[15] Dan may be willing to testify as to one count, but be concerned when there are counts which are clearly distinct in time, place, and evidence. He then may move to sever the charges under Rule 14 (which is again emulated by many jurisdictions):

> If the joinder of offenses or defendants . . . appears to prejudice a defendant or the government, the court *may* order separate trials of counts, sever the defendants' trial, or provide any other relief that justice requires. (Emphasis added.)

Notice that a motion for severance is different from a motion based upon misjoinder. The latter argues that the counts (or defendants) *cannot* be properly joined in the same proceeding. Since the joinder is by definition illegal, the defendant need not show prejudice. On the other hand, even a misjoinder may not result in defendant's victory; it is subject to harmless error analysis. *United States v. Lane*, 474 U.S. 438 (1986) (see Chapter 12 for a discussion of harmless error). A motion for severance, on the contrary,

---

15. "(T)he empirical data show that a defendant faces a greater likelihood of conviction if he faces a single trial with joined offenses than if he is tried separately on all offenses, although the studies do not agree on exactly why this is so." Farrin, Rethinking Criminal Joinder: An Analysis of the Empirical Research and Its Implications for Justice, 52 Law and Contemp. Probs. 325 (1989).

agrees that the counts *may* be joined, but that prejudice to the defendant should persuade the judge to sever the counts. *Zafiro v. United States*, 506 U.S. 5343 (1993).

Generally, trial judges who are, after all, not familiar with the case, are loathe to overrule the prosecutorial decision, and to order joinder, or severance, once the indictments have been filed. And since the standard of review on either severance or joinder is "abuse of discretion" (*Johnson v. United States*, 356 F. 2d 680 (8th Cir. 1966)), a defendant is unlikely to prevail on either motion. In some states, however, joinder is allowed only if the defendant agrees.

Prosecutors may also seek to join *defendants* as well as counts. In addition to all the other benefits (economy, single use of witnesses, etc.) inherent in the joinder of claims, the prosecution is almost sure to benefit from the "birds of a feather" pastiche when several (up to 25?) defendants appear together in the courtroom, as well as from the possibility of conflicting defenses.

Other provisions of the constitution may limit joinder — or at least what evidence can be used in a joint trial. *Bruton v. United States*, 391 U.S. 123 (1968), held that in a joint trial of *A* and *B*, the admission of *A*'s confession, particularly where it mentioned *B*, violated *B*'s confrontation rights when *A* did not testify. Merely substituting a "blank" or the word "deleted" whenever *B* was mentioned in *A*'s confession is an insufficient remedy, *Gary v. Maryland*, 523 U.S. 185 (1998), although a more careful redaction, which does not lead to the inference that the "blank" refers to *B*, may be adequate. *Richardson v. Marsh*, 481 U.S. 200 (1987).

EXAMPLES

1. Indicted for six counts of mail fraud, in a case which would stretch the limits of that statute, Adolph is informed that the case has been assigned to Judge Sabatino, who is generally antithetical to such charges. Adolph elects to waive a jury and be tried by the Judge. Two days before the trial, Judge Sabatino is taken ill; the prognosis is that he will recover in three weeks. Thereupon the assignment judge assigns the case to Judge Coombs, who has always favored expansion of the mail fraud statute. After his motion for a continuance of the trial, until Judge Sabatino is better, is denied, Adolph moves to bar Judge Coombs from hearing the case, arguing double jeopardy. What result?

2. Pablo, an ardent art lover, visits the Museum of Modern Art when it has a touring exhibition of van Gogh, and removes "Starry Night." He is charged with breach of the peace, and convicted. Thereafter, he is charged with grand larceny. Double jeopardy?

3. Sigmund believes (erroneously, as it later turns out) that his wife has been cheating on him. He drives to her office, where he throws her

against the wall. When a co-worker intervenes, he throws the co-worker against the wall, and threatens her with a scissors which he picks up off his wife's desk. He then drags his wife, at scissors point, to her Jeep, which he drives to a remote location, at speeds well over the limit. At one point, he makes her exit the Jeep, which he then ignites. Ultimately, he and his wife reconcile. But the police are not so readily forgiving. Sigmund is charged with (1) assault on his wife; (2) assault on the co-worker; (3) terroristic threats; (4) family abuse; (5) unlawful imprisonment; (6) kidnaping; (7) destruction of property; and (8) arson. At a family court proceeding, he pleads guilty to the abuse charge; the prosecutor details all of the above facts. Thereafter, a different prosecutor, but from the same office, indicts Sigmund in a criminal trial court for the remaining counts. If Sigmund pleads double jeopardy, what result?

4. Paris, a basketball icon, was charged with the forcible rape of Helen Troy, a fifteen-year-old part-time worker at a spa where Paris was relaxing. At the trial, Ms. Troy indicated that she did not want to have sex, but she was unsure whether she made that clear to Paris; Paris argued that he was not the person involved; that he was shooting baskets in the hotel's gym. The jury acquitted. The prosecutor then filed charges of statutory rape (the age in the jurisdiction is 18). Paris' counsel moved to bar the second prosecution, because of double jeopardy. What result?

5. Rolanda robs a bank, and kills a teller. She is first prosecuted and convicted for the homicide. Thereafter the prosecution seeks to prosecute her for the robbery. She pleads double jeopardy. How will things go, Rolanda?

6. Harriet is convicted in her first trial of Armed Criminal Action defined as "commission of a felony with a firearm," and sentenced to the maximum permissible punishment (20 years). She is thereafter prosecuted for first degree robbery, defined as "taking of property from the presence of another by use of a firearm," and sentenced to 40 years. Is one of these prosecutions barred? If so, which one? Is one of the punishments barred? If so, which one?

7. Police seize Scott's computer, and find 46 pornographic images of children in sexually explicit conduct. Scott is charged with 46 counts of possession of pornography. Scott moves to have the counts consolidated, arguing multiplicitous pleading by the prosecution. What result?

8. Dale was acquitted of manslaughter while intoxicated; the evidence was that he had been high on marijuana. The prosecution then reindicted, charging the intoxicant was alcohol. What should the court do when the defendant moves, on double jeopardy grounds, to bar the second prosecution?

9. The police arrested Josh as he was emerging from the Ungerliter's house, carrying a DVD, a set of golf clubs, and $5,000 in pearls. The

modus operandi was similar to that used in five other burglaries in the same area over a period of six months. Further investigation strongly supports the inference that Josh is the perpetrator of all six. A search of Josh's house also turned up 50 grams of cocaine. (a) Which of these offenses may be joined in a single indictment? (b) Would your answer be different in a mandatory joinder jurisdiction? (c) If the prosecutor elects to have Josh tried, seriatim, on each of the burglaries and the cocaine charge, would there be a double jeopardy problem? (d) Assuming the prosecutor seeks to join all the burglaries, is Josh likely to succeed on a motion to sever?

EXPLANATIONS

1. This example draws the distinction between when jeopardy attaches in a *jury* trial and a *bench* trial. In the former, once the trier of fact has been determined and sworn, jeopardy attaches; any change in that trier, thereafter, may raise double jeopardy issues. As noted in the text, the courts have vigorously protected the defendant's right to be tried in one sitting, by the originally selected trier. In a bench trial, however, there is no jeopardy until the first witness is sworn. Adolph's motion to bar the prosecution is bound to lose. But Adolph might argue that the reason for the reassignment is suspect; borrowing a test from other double jeopardy situations, he might argue that there was no "manifest necessity" to reassign the case; the court could simply have waited until Judge Sabatino had recovered. If there is any indication that the reassignment was "vindictive," an attempt to convict Adolph under a broad view of the statute, it is possible that there would be a due process violation. Since there was no jury here, there was no question of whether the jurors could return at the relevant time (indeed, as we saw earlier, if a single juror becomes ill, there is always the possibility of replacing him with an alternate). The example here could also be distinguished from one where the first judge died, or retired, since his return would be impossible, and the necessity to find a different judge "manifest." But, as a matter of doctrine, the "manifest necessity" test applies only after a finding that the defendant was in jeopardy, and the Courts have not generally brought the language from one area of double jeopardy into another. Adolph is unlikely to get Coombs out of his hair (or vice versa).

2. Although every theft breaches somebody's peace of mind (at least), the two crimes have different elements. Under *Blockburger*, there is no double jeopardy. Under the "same conduct," "same transaction," or "single impulse," however, the second prosecution appears banned. If, on the other hand, Pablo made a great deal of noise after the theft was noticed, and while he was trying to escape, maybe. . . . Modern art is so confusing.

By the way, in a New Jersey case on which this example is based, the Court, employing a "same conduct" test, barred the theft prosecution.

3. These are basically the facts (with a little poetic license) in *State v. Lessary*, 865 P.2d 150 (Haw. 1994). First things first — the unlawful imprisonment and the kidnaping charges might be the "same offense" under *Blockburger*, although it is possible to unlawfully imprison someone without taking them anywhere, and kidnaping generally requires the use of force. Intriguingly, the state conceded that the imprisonment charge was barred by the abuse conviction. Similarly, if the charge of assault on his wife is based on the scissors, it might be precluded by the family abuse charge. Beyond that, however, each of these offenses seems clearly not to be the "same offense" as the one pled to in family court. In *Lessary*, the defendant sought to have the Court adopt a "same episode" approach, and argued that this entire series of events was one "episode." Whether the events in the office would be separable from the events in the Jeep thus constituting two "episodes" is unclear, but the court did not dwell on that. Instead, it adopted the "same conduct" approach adopted by the United States Supreme Court in *Grady v. Corbin*, and abandoned three years later in *Dixon*. The Court said that the test was met when "The conduct was so closely related in time, place, and circumstances that a complete account of one charge cannot be related without referring to details of the other charge." On that basis, the scissors threats were separate from the rest of the events, said the Court; even if they were the same episode, they were not the same conduct. This is simply a good instance of where the various tests might well lead to different results.

Remember that this case arose in a "successive prosecution" context. But had the charges all been joined, multiple punishments would most likely not have been permissible under *Hunter* because there was no indication that the Hawaii state legislature so intended. Thus, those crimes that "merged" could only be punished with the more severe of the penalties. Caveat: Do not confuse this with consecutive-concurrent sentences, which will be discussed in Chapter 11.

4. *Quel dommage*, Paris, you lose. Even though the charges stem from the same conduct, the two crimes are *not* the "same offense" under *Blockburger* — rape requires sex by force, whereas statutory rape can occur by consent, but only if the victim is under a specific age. Collateral estoppel might apply, but it is possible that the first jury believed that Ms. Troy still consented (or at least that Paris could reasonably believe she did). Her consent, of course, is irrelevant in statutory rape. If the jury acquitted because they believed Paris was indeed more interested in free throws, and in the gym, there would be collateral estoppel, but we can't be sure — that's one of the reasons that *Ashe v. Swenson* is not as important as it might otherwise be. Paris is simply going to have to go into overtime.

5. Clearly, under a straight *Blockburger* approach, there would be no problem with a second prosecution — robbery and homicide are not even minimally the "same offense," and have numerous diverse elements. Nevertheless, in *Harris v. Oklahoma*, 433 U.S. 682 (1977) the Court held that, because the homicide case had been premised on a felony-murder theory, which required proof (and effectively conviction) of the robbery, the autrefois conviction doctrine precluded the robbery prosecution. However, if the first prosecution was not based upon the robbery, but upon premeditation, deliberation, and willfulness, then there will be no bar to the robbery proceeding.

6. This tests the applicability of *Blockburger* after *Missouri v. Hunter*. These two offenses are obviously "the same offense" — the armed action statute is a lesser offense of armed robbery. But *Hunter* said that a clear legislative intent would allow multiple punishments. Could it be possible that the *prosecution* can rely on collateral estoppel, and then have Harriet punished for armed robbery under *Hunter*? Or will *Blockburger*'s rule preclude the prosecution? Remember — *Blockburger* was itself a multiple punishment, rather than a multiple prosecution, case. *Allen. et. al*, conclude that "the Court has apparently used different tests for determining the same offense in the successive-prosecution and multiple-punishment contexts." This "test case" would decide whether the double jeopardy clause allows legislatures to define offense and punishments, even if they were tried in separate trials.

7. Scott will lose. We employ a two-prong test when analyzing a multiplicity challenge: (1) whether the charged offenses are identical in law and fact; and (2) whether the legislature intended multiple offenses to be charged as a single count. *State v. Schaeffer*, 266 Wis. 2d 719, 668 N.W.2d 760 (2003). In the *Schaeffer* case, upon which this example is based, the Court held that even though all the pornographic photos were on a single computer Zip disk, each file was identified by a different name, and could be prosecuted as a different count. The court noted that there was no evidence as to how the photos had been downloaded (one by one, or in a group). Absent such evidence, and given the guilty plea, the court said a "reasonable inference could be that they were downloaded separately."

8. Ask the prosecutor what he's been smoking. The kind of intoxicant was clearly not an "element" of the crime; the jury's acquittal concludes that the defendant was not intoxicated — on anything. See *Ex parte Taylor*, 101 S.W.3d 434 (Tex. Crim. App. 2002).

9. Preface — the cocaine charge is so different from the burglary charges that they cannot be joined. So we deal here only with the burglaries. (a) Given the words of federal rule 8(a), the burglaries are "of the same or similar character" and *may be* joined. But the prosecutor need not join all of them; she may join some, and leave others for separate indictment.

(b) Even in most mandatory joinder jurisdictions, it is unlikely that the burglaries will meet the test; the burglaries are not "based on the same act or transaction" nor, so far as we know from these facts, are they "parts of a common scheme or plan." (c) Since *Blockburger* would only bar successive prosecutions of the "same act," the failure to join any or all of these counts would not present a *Blockburger* problem. (d) To avoid joinder, Josh will have to prove that the consolidation results in prejudice. Since the burglaries happened in different places, etc., the efficiencies often associated with joinder would seem to be minimal. Nevertheless, Josh's main argument for prejudice will turn on the premise that a jury seeing so many charges may well think that at least some of them must be accurate. A trial court is unlikely to consider that a sufficient "prejudice." And if Josh appeals the denial of his severance motion, he's almost certain to lose; it would not be an abuse of discretion to join the burglary counts.

F. Hung Juries, Mistrials, and Manifest Necessity

1. Mistrials

No trial ever runs as smoothly as either side anticipates. There are always glitches, some of which may turn into insurmountable impediments for one of the parties. A major witness (or attorney, or even a juror) may become sick, disappear, or die. New evidence may suddenly disrupt a trial plan. Inadmissible evidence (e.g., the defendant's criminal record) may inadvertently be seen by the jury or referred to in testimony. In instances like these, the adversely affected party may seek some remedy, including a judicial declaration that the problem is so severe that the trial should be stopped, and a "*mistrial*" declared. A mistrial occurs when the court, during the trial, decides to abort the procedure. The decision may be made (1) upon request of either party, or (2) *sua sponte* by the judge. A mistrial undermines what the Supreme Court has called the defendant's "valued right to have his trial completed by a particular tribunal," *Wade v. Hunter*, 336 U.S. 684 (1949). It is not quite clear whether the major concern here is the defendant's psychological well-being, or his economical resources. In *Downum v. United States*, 372 U.S. 734 (1963), the Court spoke of the possible "harassment of an accused by successive prosecution," and in *Arizona v. Washington*, 434 U.S. 497 (1978) focused on the "increased financial and emotional burden" which the accused would bear. When, however, a mistrial is called, and the state seeks to prosecute again, the defendant will raise the double jeopardy clause as a bar. Unless there was a *manifest necessity* for calling the mistrial, the double jeopardy clause will, in fact, preclude the second prosecution.

(a) Hung Juries

The classic "manifest necessity" is when a jury is "hung"—unable to reach a verdict, even after a judge has given them a "dynamite" charge urging them to reconsider their differences.[16] One might think, since the prosecution has not proved its case beyond a reasonable doubt, that a hung jury should be treated like an acquittal, but the Supreme Court has held otherwise, saying that the rule "accords recognition to society's interest in giving the prosecution one complete opportunity to convict. . . ." *Richardson v. United States*, 468 U.S. 317 (1984). More realistically, "If retrial . . . were barred whenever an appellate court viewed the 'necessity' for a mistrial differently from the trial judge, there would be a danger that the latter, cognizant of the serious societal consequences of an erroneous ruling, would employ coercive means to break the apparent deadlock." *Arizona v. Washington*, 434 U.S. 497 (1978).

(b) Trial Errors

There are four factors in considering whether a mistrial will bar a retrial declared because of a trial error:

1. who asked for the mistrial;
2. whether the requesting party had an improper motivation;
3. whether the defendant suffered special prejudice;
4. whether meaningful alternatives existed, and were considered.

When something does go wrong at trial, often a mere admonition to counsel, or continuance of the trial while both sides readjust, may be sufficient to avoid any undue prejudice to either side. Granting a mistrial is obviously more sweeping; it requires starting over again from scratch. Courts are therefore wary of endorsing such an action. In *United States v. Jorn*, 400 U.S. 470 (1971), the trial judge, over the protest of the prosecutor, declared a mistrial after concluding that prosecution witnesses had not been sufficiently warned of their Fifth Amendment rights. The Supreme Court concluded that the trial court should have considered a less drastic alternative. A nonexhaustive list might include:

1. permitting a continuance;[17]
2. ordering a severance of defendants when the prosecutor inadvertently disclosed that the co-defendant had threatened a complaining witness;

---

16. Hung juries are an American invention; in earlier times the jury was to be kept, without food and drink, until they reached a verdict.

17. Where, during a 13-day delay in the trial, two jurors lost a parent and the prosecutor was unable to appear (because, as she told the judge, she had an irreversible vacation planned for that time) and the trial judge sua sponte declared a mistrial, there was no manifest necessity. *State v. Georges*, 345 N.J. Super. 538, 786 A.2d 107 (2001).

3. permitting defense counsel to examine a witness about a conversation he had had with the counsel;
4. determining whether the defense objected to the mistrial as well;
5. issuing curative instructions;[18]
6. removing obstreperous counsel from the case;[19]
7. continuing with eleven jurors.[20]

If the mistrial has been granted against defendant's objection, and upon the prosecutor's request, or if the trial judge acted on her own, a reprosecution will be allowed only if there was a *manifest necessity* to declare the mistrial. *Oregon v. Kennedy*, 456 U.S. 667 (1982). Where there appears to be a reasonable alternative to a mistrial, a trial judge's discretionary actions will be scrutinized more carefully. As one court put it:

> The doctrine . . . stands as a *command* to trial judges not to declare a mistrial without the defendant's consent until a scrupulous exercise of judicial discretion leads to the conclusion that a termination of the trial is manifestly necessary."

Comm. v. Balog, 395 Pa. Super. 158, 576 A.2d 1092 (Pa. Super. 1990) (emphasis added).

In *Arizona v. Washington*, 434 U.S. 497 (1978), the Court declared that

> "it is manifest that the key word 'necessity' cannot be interpreted literally; instead, contrary to the teaching of Webster, we assume that there are degrees of necessity and we require a 'high degree' before concluding that the mistrial is appropriate . . . the prosecutor must shoulder the burden of justifying the mistrial. . . . His burden is a heavy one."

For example, where a trial judge, personally frustrated with the manner in which the case was being tried by the state, declared a mistrial because he feared that his anger over the "bombastic" style of the prosecutor would affect the jury and skew the result, there was no manifest necessity, and a second prosecution was barred by double jeopardy. *Comm. v. Kelly*, 797 A.2d 325 (Pa. Super. 2002). In part, the court was concerned that the trial

---

18. But see *Arizona v. Washington*, where the Court indicated that in determining whether such instructions would be helpful, greater deference should be left to the discretion of the trial judge.

19. *Rubenfeld ex. rel. Walters v. Appelman*, 230 A.D.2d 911, 646 N.Y.S.2d 79 (1996).

20. In those states where a jury may proceed with 11 jurors, declaring a mistrial when one jurors become disabled is not manifestly necessary, and a subsequent prosecution will be barred. *Hill v. State*, 90 S.W.3d 308 (Tex. Crim. App. 2002). On the other hand, if both parties must agree to 11 jurors, the prosecutor's refusal to agree requires a mistrial, and a second prosecution is not barred. *Zanone v. Comm.*, 579 S.E.2d 634 (Va. Ct. App. 2003).

court, unconsciously, was concerned that the state would lose the case not because of the merits, but because of the prosecutor's style.

Where there is no readily apparent alternative, however, the judge's decision may be given more weight. Thus, in *Illinois v. Somerville*, 410 U.S. 458 (1973), when the prosecutor noted that the indictment did not meet state law requirements, the trial court declared a mistrial. Agreeing that this was a "manifest necessity," the Supreme Court emphasized that, had the case gone through to verdict, the defense would have easily won an appeal. There was no alternative, said the Court, to the mistrial declaration. *Somerville* also seems to demonstrate the Court will not be overly concerned with who is "at fault" for the necessity. Clearly, the prosecutor was negligent for not obtaining a proper indictment, but the Court did not use that negligence to damage the state's chance at a conviction.[21]

One factor which courts weigh heavily in assessing the "manifestness" of the necessity is the degree to which the trial judge consulted with the adversely affected counsel, and often with the other counsel as well, before declaring a mistrial. Indeed, there were so many hastily declared mistrials that Federal Rule 26.3 was amended in 1993 to require the judge to discuss the issue with both counsel before declaring a mistrial and consider alternatives.

Where the defendant asks for a mistrial (for example, after the prosecution has introduced highly prejudicial inadmissible evidence), and then seeks to bar reprosecution, the Courts almost invariably reject the motion to bar a second prosecution. The common theory is that the defendant has waived his double jeopardy protection to avoid an (almost inevitable) conviction, *United States v. Dinitz*, 424 U.S. 600 (1976). There is one exception to this general rule: If the defendant can show that the prosecutor has intentionally *"goaded"* the defendant into making such a motion, retrial may be barred. This standard may be impossible for the defendant to meet; as Justice Stevens, concurring in *Oregon v. Kennedy*, 456 U.S. 667 (1982) observed: "It is almost inconceivable that a defendant could prove that the prosecutor's deliberate misconduct was motivated by an intent to provoke a mistrial instead of an intent simply to prejudice the defendant." He advocated a more flexible approach, based on overreaching and egregious prosecutorial misconduct. A substantial number of state courts find the *Kennedy* standard far too restrictive, and have used Justice Stevens', approach. See *State v. Kennedy*, 295 Ore. 260, 666 P.2d 1316 (1983) (on remand from *Oregon v.*

---

21. It is also possible that defense counsel was attempting to "sandbag." By not challenging the indictment, defense counsel might have been hoping that, if defendant was convicted, there would be a successfully appealable issue. Had he raised that issue directly, particularly prior to the swearing of the jury, the prosecutor might have obtained a new indictment, or filed a new information. Moreover, the prosecutor's motion came before the start of trial, so there was no possibility that he was attempting to "salvage" a case that was going badly. Had *he* waited until late in the trial, it is possible that *he* might have been accused of sandbagging.

Kennedy, supra);[22] *Comm. v. Simons*, 514 Pa. 10, 522 A.2d 537 (1987). On the other hand, the court in *Dinitz* argued that a rule that focused on impact, and not on prosecutorial intent, might ultimately redound to defendants' detriment saying that such a rule would:

> "give rise to much reluctance in granting mistrials because (t)he trial courts will understand that society will be better served by completing a trial, even after clear error has arisen and the defendant seeks the mistrial, than the alternative of a mistrial and the possible bar of double jeopardy based on the error."

Another way to think of this is as follows:

Did Defendant Consent to the Mistrial?

Yes—then no bar to retrial.

Unless Prosecutor *intentionally* "goaded" the motion or acquiescence.

No—

Did Trial Court consider options (continuance, preclusion of witnesses,) and discuss them with counsel?

Yes—Then standard is abuse of discretion.

No—Then subject to rigorous scrutiny.

----

22. Where the prosecutors in two earlier trials engaged in "extreme misconduct" that was a "grossly improper and highly prejudicial, both as to the defendant and to integrity of the system," a third trial was barred by double jeopardy, even if the prosecutor did not intentionally seek a mistrial. "Intentional and pervasive misconduct . . . to the extent that the trial is structurally impaired, if the prosecutor knows the conduct to be improper and which he pursues for *any* improper purpose." *State v. Minnitt*, 55 P.3d 774 (Ariz. 2002). Drawing a distinction between "simple prosecutorial error, such as an isolated misstatement or loss of temper, and misconduct that is so egregious that it raises concerns over the integrity and fundamental fairness of the trial itself." The same applied if the prosecutor has acted in a patently unfair way and obtained a conviction. *State v. Jorgenson*, 198 Ariz. 390, 10 P.3d 1177 (2000). See also *State v. Breit*, 930 P.2d 792 (N. Mex. 1996); *Ex Parte Peterson*, 117 S.W.3d 804 (2003); *Bauder v. State*, 921 S.W.2d 696 (Tex. Crim. App. 1996), *People v. Dawson*, 154 Mich. App. 260, 397 N.W.2d 277, 282 (1986), aff'd 431 Mich. 234, 427 N.W.2d 886 (1988); *State v. White*, 85 N.C. App. 81, 354 S.E.2d 324 (1987), aff'd 322 N.C. 506, 369 S.E.2d 813 (1988); *Comm. v. Smith*, 532 Pa. 177, 615 A.2d 321 (Pa. 1992). *State v. Colton*, 663 A.2d 339 (Conn. 1995); *Pool v. Superior Court*, 677 P.2d 2161 (Ariz. 1984). In *Pool*, the court formulated a three-part test, holding that a second prosecution is barred by double jeopardy if

"1. Mistrial is granted because of improper conduct or actions by the prosecution; and

2. Such conduct is not merely the result of legal error, negligence, mistake, or insignificant impropriety, but, taken as a whole, amounts to intentional conduct which the prosecutor knows to be improper and prejudice, and which he pursues for any improper purpose with indifference to a significant resulting danger of mistrial or reversal; and

3. The conduct causes prejudice to the defendant which cannot be cured by means short of a mistrial." See generally, Person, Note, Prosecutorial Misconduct and Double Jeopardy: Should States Broaden Double Jeopardy Protection in Light of *Oregon v. Kennedy?*, 37 Wayne L. Rev. 1699 (1991).

Of course, these factors may well be in tension in any given case. But they do establish at least a road map for assessing the cases.

Finally, if the judge *dismisses* the case, rather than waiting for a verdict or declaring a mistrial, the courts seem to treat this is as a mistrial, rather than as an acquittal. While most dismissals are entered before a jury is sworn and thus raise no double jeopardy problems because no jeopardy has yet attached, the result is the same where the dismissal occurs after that point. See, e.g., *Lee v. United States*, 432 U.S. 23 (1977). The issue has created one of the "flip-flops" in double jeopardy law. In *United States v. Jenkins*, 420 U.S. 358 (1975), the Court applied the double jeopardy bar in such a setting, but a scant three years later, it overruled *Jenkins*. *United States v. Scott*, 437 U.S. 81 (1978). *Scott* may be restricted to cases where the defendant seeks and obtains a dismissal on grounds *not* relating to the sufficiency of the government's case. The Court in *Scott* said that the critical question was whether the trial court's ruling was based on a failure of proof in establishing the "factual elements of the offense."

Thus, where the dismissal is on the merits, the Court views it as an acquittal which bars retrial. Where the dismissal is not on the merits, the Court appears to now treat the situation as it would a mistrial — the prosecution may appeal such a ruling, and may, if successful, reprosecute.

G. Successful Appeals: Double Jeopardy and Vindictiveness

It has long been settled that the double jeopardy clause does not bar reprosecution if the defendant successfully appeals his conviction. But the explanation for this rule has altered several times over the years: (1) defendant has waived his right to the protection of double jeopardy; (2) the jeopardy "continues" until there is a "legitimate" final verdict;[23] (3) without such a rule, courts would be reluctant to find errors and overturn convictions.[24/25]

---

23. *United States v. Ball*, 163 U.S. 662 (1896). As Justice Holmes, dissenting in *Kepner v. United States*, 195 U.S. 100 (1904) explained: "Logically and rationally, a man cannot be said to be more than once in jeopardy on the same cause, however often he may be tried, the jeopardy is one continuing jeopardy from its beginning to the end of the cause."

24. As Justice Harlan noted: "It is at least doubtful that appellate courts would be as zealous as they are now in protecting against the effects of improprieties at the trial or pre-trial state if they knew that reversal of a conviction would put the accused irrevocably beyond the reach of further prosecution." *United States v. Tateo*, 377 U.S. 463 (1964).

25. England had a rule against re-prosecution after successful appeals, but allowed its appellate courts to substitute a "fairer" verdict (usually a lower level of conviction) if it found error, but was still convinced that the defendant was guilty. A well-known

There are two exceptions to the "right to retry " rule. First, if the reversal is based on the appellate court's judgment that the evidence at trial was legally insufficient to sustain the conviction, the state has had its one fair chance at conviction, and a new prosecution is prohibited. *Burks v. United States*, 437 U.S. 1 (1978). Where the reversal is based on the *weight* of the evidence, rather than its sufficiency, however, retrial is not barred. *Tibbs v. Florida*, 457 U.S. 31 (1982).

Second, if the second prosecution appears "vindictive," it will be barred, not by double jeopardy, but by due process. In the past three decades, the Supreme Court, in a series of decisions, has prevented "vindictive" reprosecution of a defendant who successfully appeals a conviction. The Court has declared that a prosecutor who increases the charges on a second prosecution must demonstrate that the increase is based on the merits, and not cemented in vindictiveness because of the successful appeal. *North Carolina v. Pearce, supra. Blackledge v. Perry*, 417 U.S. 21 (1974).

H. The Dual Sovereignty Doctrine

Remember Mortimer, who was tried in state court for bank robbery (p. 183)? If he were later tried in a federal court for robbing a *federally insured* bank, that element would be a "new" element. Since every offense carries with it an implicit element "against sovereign *A*," it is plausible to argue that an offense in state *B*, even premised on exactly the same transaction, is nevertheless a different offense. Thus under *Blockburger*, he may be retried by a second sovereign because there is a new element in the second crime — the new victim. In this sense, the dual sovereignty doctrine can be seen as simply an application of the *Blockburger* "same offense" rule, depending, again, on how the "offense" is defined. The difficulty with this explanation is that it stretches *Blockburger* to its breaking point. Surely if nothing is different except the name of the prosecuting sovereign, the rule seems to outstrip the reason for double jeopardy protection.

A more defensible explanation is that each sovereign has a different interest in prosecuting the offense. If the state's interest was in protecting banks against robbery, the federal government's interest was in avoiding insurable losses. This explanation, however, ultimately explains little, for

---

example is *R. v. Morgan*, 2 All Eng. Rep. 347 (1975) in which the House of Lords held erroneous the jury instruction allowing a rape conviction if the defendants honestly (but unreasonably) believed the victim had consented, but then concluded that the error was harmless because "no reasonable jury" could possibly have decided that the defendants did in fact believe the victim was consenting. How an appellate court could make such a determination of credibility based on a paper record was unclear, but it demonstrates the tension a "no-reprosecution rule" might exert. England today allows some reprosecutions.

under that view, the town fathers in which the bank was located have yet a different interest than the state; yet these political entities are viewed as the "same" sovereign, and double jeopardy applies.

Still another explanation is that each sovereign fears that the other sovereign will prosecute the first case incompetently (possibly even purposefully); if a first prosecution, no matter how incompetent or sham, precluded a second prosecution by another sovereign, there would be a "race to the courthouse."[26] *Bartkus v. Illinois,* 359 U.S. 121 (1959). But this possible exception has been virtually read out of existence by subsequent decisions. See *United States v. Figueroa-Soto,* 938 F.2d 1015 (9th Cir. 1991). One concern is that it is "unseemly" to have the court of the second sovereign determine whether there was incompetence or collusion in the first prosecution. The dual sovereignty doctrine avoids that investigation.[27]

It was not until the 1920s that the dual sovereign doctrine was applied to allow a successive prosecution by a second sovereign. In *United States v. Lanza,* 260 U.S. 377, 385 (1922) the Court allowed the federal government to prosecute a group of defendants under the National Prohibition Act even though these defendants had been previously convicted, based on the same conduct, of violating state liquor laws.

Nearly all of the controversial aspects of the dual sovereign doctrine were activated by the so-called Rodney King case. After a long and dangerous car chase, King, a black man, was finally stopped by a large contingent of Los Angeles police (virtually all of whom were white), who thereupon subdued him, using batons, fists, feet, and other such weapons (many had their guns drawn throughout the arrest). A passing motorist happened to catch the entire arrest and subsequent events on videotape. That tape appeared to show a massive use of excessive force; it was played and replayed on both national and international television literally thousands of times. In

---

26. In *Bartkus,* Justice Frankfurter cited to the infamous case of *Screws v. United States,* 325 U.S. 91 (1945), where a white sheriff had fatally and brutally beaten a handcuffed black prisoner. The sheriff had never been prosecuted by the state; indeed, he was later elected to the state legislature. Were there no "dual sovereignty" doctrine, declared Frankfurter, the "trivial" one- and two-year sentences that sheriff Screws actually received could result in a "shocking and untoward deprivation of the historic right and obligation of the State" to prosecute Screws. Of course, the Court was well aware of the irony — if there were no dual sovereignty doctrine, a sham prosecution by the state in *Screws* would have prevented even the minimal sentences he received in the federal prosecution.

27. See *United States v. Angleton,* 314 F.3d 767 (5th Cir. 2002). But this is a very high hurdle to overcome — even extensive involvement by the first sovereign in a second sovereign's prosecution will not, by itself, turn the second sovereign's prosecution into a second prosecution by the first sovereign. *Bartkus v. Illinois,* 359 U.S. 121(1959). Moreover, not even the cross designation of a state agent as a federal official to assist in, or even to conduct, a federal prosecution does not bring the case within the *Bartkus* exception.

the state trial of the police officers indicted for beating King, the jury acquitted the defendants of virtually all counts. Outraged by the verdict, blacks in Los Angeles rioted, causing hundreds of millions of dollars of damage. Thereupon the federal government prosecuted four of those same officers, in federal court, for violating King's civil rights; they were convicted of many of the charges.

The "King" prosecutions exemplified more than the theoretical debate over the dual sovereignty doctrine. The federal prosecution demonstrated exactly how a second prosecution could learn from an unsuccessful prosecution and obtain a conviction — precisely one of the concerns of the double jeopardy rule. During the first trial, the state, not surprisingly, had relied extensively on the videotape which appeared to demonstrate totally unwarranted use of force. The defense, however, slowed the film down and attempted to show the jury how, frame by frame, cell by cell, the police had been justified in using the force they used. The prosecution seemed stunned by the trial tactic. While no one believed that the state prosecutors had purposely lost the case, a number of critics of the acquittal argued that the state had relied too heavily on the videotape, had not fought the change of venue with sufficient vigor, and, if not incompetent, had not put the strongest case forward, overconfident that the jury would reflect the same outrage that had greeted the nationally televised tape. The federal prosecutors were ready for that approach, and were (apparently) able to neutralize it.[28] The dual sovereign doctrine permitted the federal prosecution without requiring such a finding.

The doctrine is very controversial. It is obviously contrary to the interests the clause is designed to protect: (1) the second prosecuting sovereign can learn from the first's presentation (whether successful or not); (2) the defendant's resources (and resilience) may be worn down by the second prosecution.[29] The Executive Board of the American Civil Liberties Union, for example, divided almost exactly down the middle as to whether to oppose the second "king" prosecution; a significant number of members of that Board resigned over the decision to oppose the federal intervention. A majority of states, by statute or even by constitution, preclude prosecution

---

28. The King event highlighted one more aspect of American justice. The first trial, initially set for Los Angeles, in which the jury would likely have been heavily minority, was transferred to "Simi Valley," a substantially white suburb of Los Angeles. Many argued that the white jurors of Simi Valley identified more with the police than with the black victim. The second (federal) trial occurred inside Los Angeles, and the jury was much more interracial.

29. In England, a foreign government's prosecution of a defendant would bar reprosecution in an English court. Professor Amar, Reconstructing Double Jeopardy: Some Thoughts on the Rodney King Case, 26 Cumb. L. Rev. 1, 5 (1995), observes England would give more respect to the adjudication of a sister state than the dual sovereign doctrine requires in this country.

once another sovereign has tried the defendant.[30] Even here, however, state courts disagree. If the statute or constitutional provision precludes prosecution for an "act" which has already been the subject of prosecution, some courts will apply *Blockburger*, and conclude that the second prosecution is for a different "act", while others will note that *Blockburger* applies only to the same "offense" and not the same "act."[31]

Although the United States Supreme Court has constantly adhered to the doctrine, allowing subsequent prosecutions, the Department of Justice has, for nearly 50 years, voluntarily applied the so-called *Petite policy*, named after the case in which it was first noted — *Petite v. United States*, 361 U.S. 529 (1960).[32] That policy establishes a presumption against federal prosecution subsequent to a state trial; only in rare cases will such a prosecution be

---

30. Statutes restricting the application of the doctrine are in place in 24 states. Ala. Code §15-3-8 (1995); Alaska Stat. §12.20.010 (1995); Ark. Code Ann. §5-1-114 (Michie 1993); Cal. Penal Code §793 (West 1985); Del. Code Ann. tit. 11, §209 (1995); Ga. Code Ann. §16-1-8 (Harrison 1994); Haw. Rev. Stat. §701-112 (1993); Idaho Code §19-315 (1987); Ill. Ann. Stat. ch. 720, para. 5/3-4 (Smith-Hurd 1993); Ind. Code Ann. §35-41-4-5 (Burns 1994); Ky. Rev. Stat. Ann. §505.050 (Michie/Bobbs-Merrill 1990); Minn. Stat. Ann. §609.045 (West 1987); Miss. Code Ann. §99-11-27 (1994); Mont. Code Ann. §46-11-504 (1995); Nev. Rev. Stat. Ann. §171.070 (Michie 1992); N.J. Stat. Ann. §2C:1-11 (West 1995); N.Y. Crim. Proc. Law §40.20 (McKinney 1992); N.D. Cent. Code §29-03-13 (1991); Okla. Stat. Ann. tit. 22, §130 (West 1992); 18 Pa. Cons. Stat. Ann. §111 (1983); Utah Code Ann. §76-1-404 (1995); Va. Code Ann. §19.2-294 (1995); Wash. Rev. Code Ann. §10.43.040 (West 1990); Wis. Stat. Ann. §939.71 (West 1996). These statutes fall generally into two groups: (a) statutes which bar successive prosecution based on the same "offense" (Arkansas, Delaware, Hawaii, Minnesota, Mississippi, New Jersey, Pennsylvania, and Wisconsin); and (b) the rest bar successive prosecution based on the same "act." Sec. 21 of the Uniform Narcotic Drug Act applies the doctrine to drug offenses: "If a violation of this article is a violation of a federal law or the law of another state, a conviction or acquittal under federal law or the law of another state for the same act is a bar to prosecution in this state." A number of states have adopted this provision, in addition to a general bar on subsequent prosecutions. E.g., Ohio Rev. Code §2925.50. Accord: *State v. Hansen*, 243 Wis. 2d 328, 627 N.W.2d 195 (2001). But see *People v. Zubke*, 496 Mich. 80, 664 N.W.2d 751 (2003) where the Court found that an act giving rise to a federal drug conspiracy conviction was not the "same act" underlying a charge of possession with intent to deliver. So far as appears from the opinion, the same drugs were involved in both prosecutions. This is a good example of how a general statutory prohibition against successive prosecutions can be narrowly interpreted. The majority looked at the words of the statute which related to the "same act," while the dissent focused on the conduct which "gave rise to" the federal conviction. Accord: *United States v. Shreffler*, 47 Fed. Appx. 140, 2002 WL 31116766 (3d Cir.). See Woods, The Dual Sovereignty Exception To Double Jeopardy: An Unnecessary Loophole, 24 U. Balt. L. Rev. 177 (1994).

31. See, e.g., *State v. Hansen*, 243 Wis. 2d 328, 627 N.W.2d 195 (2001) "Our initial inclination is to conclude that Hansen's interpretation of 'same act' as meaning 'same conduct' is more consistent with the plain and ordinary meaning of the term."

32. The policy was announced one week after the *Bartkus* decision.

authorized, and then only if the Attorney General herself signs the authorization documents. Thus, while such a finding may exacerbate state relations with the executive, it avoids the scenario where a federal *court* would be determining whether the state prosecution was "weak," arguably even a greater strain on federal-state relations. Supporters of this policy argue that there is a need to avoid sham or incompetent state prosecutions; critics of the policy argue that the "King" prosecution demonstrates that the policy is subject to unprincipled political pressures. Critics also point out that the many states that preclude second prosecutions do not appear to be concerned with sham or incompetent proceedings by the same states that ostensibly worry the federal government.

Even if most states will not prosecute after another sovereign has sought to convict the defendant, so long as the federal government is restrained only by the *Petite* policy, the dialogue will continue. Indeed, given the rapid expansion of federal criminal law over the past three decades, it is likely that virtually every state offense will soon have its federal counterpart, thereby potentially testing the application of the doctrine in numerous settings.

EXAMPLES

1. Mary's husband, having embezzled her sizable trust fund, fakes his murder and frames her for it. She is convicted in Washington. When she escapes, she tracks him down to New Orleans and kills him there. Can she plead double jeopardy if she is prosecuted in the Big Easy?

2. Malcolm, an African American, is charged with beating a white female. The jury venire is 85 percent African American, although the general population is only 36 percent African American. During voir dire, the prosecutor strikes every African American, male or female. After four strikes, the trial court warns the prosecutor that he is facing a *Batson* violation (see Chapter 8). The prosecutor ignores the court, and strikes three more. The court warns him again. The prosecutor continues to use peremptoriness in this fashion. Finally, the judge declares a mistrial. When Malcolm's attorney receives notice of a retrial, he moves to bar the trial on double jeopardy grounds. He also shows that the new venire, from which any jury for the new trial would be chosen, is only 27 percent African American. What result?

3. At Bob's trial for fraud, the prosecutor asks a witness about other arguably fraudulent transactions, for which Bob has not been indicted. Upon objection from defense counsel, the judge admonishes the prosecutor. The prosecutor continues, and obtains another warning. The prosecutor continues. The defendant then moves for a mistrial, which is granted. Thereafter, Bob moves to bar reprosecution on the grounds of double jeopardy. What result? Would it make any difference if the trial judge had acted on her own, without waiting for defense counsel to move for a mistrial?

4. At the first day of Rodney's jury trial for driving while intoxicated, Ahmad, the prosecutor, appears with a videotape of defendant's arrest, which should have been disclosed prior to trial. The prosecutor explains that the arresting officer had locked the tape in his filing cabinet, and that the police department evidence technician had reported that the tape was not in the evidence room. Ahmad was unaware of the tape's location until the officer arrived in court to testify during the trial. Defense counsel, Esmerelda, moves to exclude the evidence, or for a continuance of several days has moved for all information. The court immediately declares a mistrial. When Ahmad seeks a second trial, Rodney raises a double jeopardy bar. What result?

5. During Zeke's trial for aggravated incest, Henry, the lead investigator in the case, was being vigorously cross-examined by defense counsel. Suddenly, Henry, who knew that there was a pre-trial order precluding any reference to a polygraph which Zeke had taken, blurted out a reference to the test. The Court declared a mistrial. (a) Can Zeke be retried? (b) Suppose the outburst had occurred during the victim's testimony?

EXPLANATIONS

1. Movie buffs will recognize this as the plot in Double Jeopardy. In the film, Mary was advised, by a fellow prisoner, that, having been (unjustly) convicted of killing her husband, Mary could actually kill him with impunity "in Times Square at noon." As you well know, that is *dead wrong*. Under the dual sovereignty doctrine, New York could easily prosecute Mary for a crime (killing her husband in New York) because it offended a different sovereign. (Don't worry, in the movie, Mary does not follow the legal advice she got; she actually kills her husband in self-defense). Perhaps someone should have killed the legal consultants to the movie. Some observers have suggested that even if both killings occurred in the same state, such that dual sovereignty could not apply, the proper way to deal with this hypothetical is to vacate the first murder conviction, give Mary credit for time served and convict her of the actual murder.

2. Sorry. There's no double jeopardy issue here, because jeopardy never attached—the general rule is that the jury must be sworn. Does that mean that the prosecutor (or defense counsel, in a different situation) can simply abuse the peremptory system? Not necessarily. First, there are possible disciplinary sanctions to be used against an attorney who either misuses peremptory challenges, or who baits the opponent (or the court). Moreover, in the scenario here, the court could find the prosecutor in contempt of court. But those remedies do nothing for Malcolm. Is he helpless here? Not necessarily. The Supreme Court has intimated, in several double jeopardy settings, that even if the specific

case does not violate double jeopardy protections, other protections might be available. Thus, even if multiple punishments do not violate double jeopardy, they might violate the Eighth Amendment. Here, using an analog to the mistrial cases, the second court might find that the first mistrial was not "manifestly necessary." Aside from the remedies already suggested, the trial court might have started out with a new venire, or even reinstated the removed jurors (as the discussion in Chapter 8 suggests, remedies for *Batson* violations are flexible, if nothing else). On the other hand, *if* we assume that black jurors would be favorable to Malcolm, then the prosecutor has gained "something" by the mistrial; the new venire is (stereotypically) less friendly to Malcolm than the first one was assumed to be. But the venire's percentages are insufficiently disparate from the population to raise a jury-selection-process challenge. And certainly Malcolm has been unduly put upon. On the other hand, the mistrial was declared so early in the process that it may be hard to argue that he has suffered "that much more" than he would have had the trial gone forward. (Does that suggest why the Court has drawn the jeopardy line where it has?)

3. Since the defendant asked for the retrial, the normal rule would allow the reprosecution. But if the judge hearing the motion determines that Bob's counsel was "goaded into" asking for a mistrial, double jeopardy may obtain. In most instances, however, a defendant is required to show not merely that he reacted to improper behavior by the prosecutor, but that the prosecutor *intentionally* misbehaved in order to obtain a defense motion for a mistrial. It will be the rare situation in which a trial judge will make such a finding with regard to either counsel, preferring to think that the outburst was simply done in the "heat of the moment." If the judge had acted independently, defense could argue that there was no "manifest necessity" for the mistrial. The trial judge could have recognized that the defense counsel was acting impetuously, and should not have granted the mistrial. Perhaps she should have considered other alternatives, such as curative instruction (or shooting the prosecutor). Nevertheless, Bob, unhappily, is likely to have to go through a second trial.

4. This is a close call. In *People v. Bagley*, 338 Ill. App. 3d 978, 789 N.E.2d 860 (2003), the court held that the prosecutor's failure to disclose was merely negligent, and not done in bad faith. Therefore, the exclusion of the tape would have been an excessive sanction. Given that the defendant wanted a long continuance, the appellate court concluded that the granting of a mistrial was manifestly necessary. Hence, there was no double jeopardy bar. However, the trial court appeared not to have conversed with both counsel over what might be done, a *sine qua non* before actually imposing a mistrial. Moreover, even if Ahmad sincerely did not know where the tape was, he should have—that he called the officer to testify suggests that he prepared him for testimony

beforehand, at which time he should have pursued the matter of the videotape. If he had not called that officer, perhaps Ahmad's surprise when the officer appeared with the tape would be more justified.

5.   (a) Probably. *State v. Wittsell*, 66 P.3d 831 (Kan. 2003). Although the prosecutor is not responsible for the conduct of all the state's witnesses, a court hearing in this case led the trial court to conclude that Henry had deliberately torpedoed the trial because he thought it was going poorly. An appellate court thought this sufficient to hold the prosecutor responsible to the outburst, and applied the double jeopardy clause. The Kansas Supreme Court, however, disagreed, holding that once the prosecutor informed the witnesses of the ban on the testimony, he had discharged his responsibilities, and the defendant might have a claim only if it were clear that the prosecutor had elicited the reference to the polygraph. The court explicitly rejected an analogy to the discovery cases (see *Brady* and *Kyles*, Chapter 6) and held that the *bad faith* of the detective could not be imputed to the prosecutor. This is a dubious result. After all, Henry is a professional and an agent of the state. Holding the "state" (if not "the prosecutor") responsible here avoids investigating whether the prosecutor's warnings to Henry were sufficient. Moreover, had the prosecutor asked the witness whether Zeke had taken a polygraph, at least some state courts would ask whether the prosecutor had overreached. The *Kennedy* test focuses solely on the prosecutor, and not on the effect which a second trial has upon the defendant (or upon his chances of being convicted).

(b) Retrial is more likely. If there was no double jeopardy bar in the actual *Wittsell* case, there would certainly seem to be no bar here. But even if *Wittsell* is problematic, or just plain wrong, here the witness is not an officer of the state. It is more plausible that the conduct, while clearly grounds for a mistrial, was an emotional reaction to the trial, rather than an attempt to have the trial start again.

10

Assistance of Counsel

"A lawyer in a criminal trial is a necessity, not a luxury."

Gideon v. Wainwright, 372 U.S. 335 (1963)

"No constitutional right is celebrated so much in the abstract and observed so little in reality as the right to counsel."

Bright, Gideon's Reality: After Four Decades, Where Are We,
Crim. Just. (Summer 2003), p.5

A. The Right to Counsel

At his initial appearance, if not before, Dan will be informed of his right to counsel. It was not always so. In fact, in England, until the beginning of the nineteenth century, lawyers—even those retained by the defendant—were prohibited from appearing in court in a felony case, unless the charge was treason. In part, this may be due to the fact that criminal prosecutions were often brought by the injured party (or survivors), rather than "the Crown," except in cases of treason. On the other hand, counsel was allowed in misdemeanor trials.

In early colonial times, lawyers were similarly eschewed. An article in the Fundamental Constitution of the Carolinas declared that "it shall be a base and vile thing to plead for money and reward"; a similar document for East

Jersey (1683) provided that "In all courts persons of all perswasions may freely appear in their own way . . . and there personally plead their own causes themselves, or if unable, by their friends, no person being allowed to take money for pleading or advice in such cases."[1] This animosity rapidly dissolved. The Declaration of Independence expressly complained about the denial of counsel, and 12 of the original 13 states guaranteed a right to counsel for felony cases in their constitutions. As a result, the right to have counsel present was embodied in the Sixth Amendment, which provides:

> In all criminal prosecutions the accused shall enjoy the right to a speedy and public trial . . . and to have the Assistance of Counsel for his defense.

Today, counsel are *allowed* in virtually every process in which the government pits itself against an individual.[2] The question today, as we will see below, is whether the state must *appoint* counsel in a given proceeding. Here, the first four words of the Sixth Amendment — "In all criminal prosecutions" — are critical. Not every proceeding in which a citizen can be incarcerated, or deported, or suffer serious harm at the behest of the government, is a *criminal* prosecution nor is every part of the criminal *process* necessarily a criminal *prosecution*. Remember, however, that when we speak of a "right to counsel," we are speaking of a right to have appointed counsel; at none of the proceedings discussed below would the state prohibit an attorney from appearing.

There may be a *Fifth Amendment* right to have counsel present even in noncriminal proceedings. In *Hamdi v. Rumsfeld*, 2004 WL 1431951, the Supreme Court held that citizens held by the United States military had a right to a rudimentary hearing to challenge the government's conclusion that they were "enemy combatants." The Court noted that Hamdi had recently obtained counsel, and declared that "He unquestionably has the right to access to counsel in connection with the proceedings on remand."

---

1. F. Heller, The Sixth Amendment to the Constitution of the United States, 17-19 (1951).

2. But see *United States v. Ash*, 413 U.S. 300 (1973) (no right to have defense counsel present at a pretrial photographic display to a witness). Several states preclude counsel even at a post-presentment search warrant application to obtain DNA. *State v. Blye*, 130 S.W.3d 776 (Tenn. 2004) (citing several other states with the same rule).

B. The Right to Appointed Counsel

1. The Right to Appointed Counsel—To What Does It Apply?

a. What Is a "Criminal Prosecution"?

The government may take many actions against a person which will have dramatic and possibly lifelong effects upon that person, and in which the assistance of an attorney might therefore be helpful if not crucial. But under the words of the Sixth Amendment, unless these proceedings can be characterized as "criminal prosecutions," there is no right to appointed counsel. Among those proceedings held not to be a "criminal prosecution" are:

- civil proceedings;
- forfeiture proceedings;
- deportation proceedings; or
- civil commitment proceedings.

b. What Constitutes Part of a "Criminal Prosecution"?

Even when the criminal process machinery is underway, the Sixth Amendment protections apply only to *critical stages* of a criminal case. The following *do not* constitute part of the criminal prosecution; hence there is no Sixth Amendment right to appointed counsel for these proceedings:

- probable cause (Gerstein) hearing (see Chapter 2);
- bail hearing (see Chapter 2);
- pre-indictment lineup;
- grand jury (see Chapter 4);
- forfeiture;
- probation or parole revocation;
- post-conviction proceedings, including:
  - motions for a new trial based on new evidence;
  - appeal from conviction, whether discretionary or mandatory (see Chapter 12);
  - collateral relief (see Chapter 12);
  - federal habeas corpus (see Chapter 12)[3]

---

3. Congress has provided for the appointment of counsel to assist indigents seeking collateral relief in federal court. Those challenging capital sentences or conviction in

- • interview with probation officer in preparation for presentence report;
- • discretionary reviews, including certiorari to the United States Supreme Court.

On the other hand, the Sixth Amendment *does* apply in the following:

- • preliminary hearing (see Chapter 5);
- • postindictment lineup;
- • plea bargaining discussions;
- • sentencing;
- • on a motion for a new trial immediately after conviction;
- • probation revocation which also includes sentencing;
- • presentence discussions with prosecutor over cooperation;
- • post-indictment psychiatric interview to determine competency to stand trial.[4]

As these lists may suggest, usually the official initiation of proceedings, (commonly deemed to occur when there is an indictment, preliminary hearing or information) activates the Sixth Amendment. Whether an initial appearance (see Chapter 2 for a discussion of the frequent misuse of this term) is a critical stage may depend upon the state's treatment of the defendant at that proceeding. Thus, for example, if state law deems waived defenses not raised at this proceeding, there is a right to counsel. *Hamilton v. Alabama*, 3689 U.S. 52 (1961). Similarly, because normally a plea of guilty at the first appearance could be later withdrawn, this would not be a critical stage—but if the state can use the plea against a defendant at trial, the hearing is transformed into a critical stage where a lawyer must be present. *White v. Maryland*, 373 U.S. 59 (1963); *Vitoratos v. Maxwell*, 351 F.2d 217 (6th Cir. 1965).

The "criminal prosecution" ceases once the defendant has been convicted and sentenced. Although appeal is not constitutionally required (see Chapter 12) , once the state has created such a procedure, it may not, *consistent with due process*, structure that procedure so that it is basically a

---

federal court, and those who are granted evidentiary hearings in habeas corpus, are entitled to counsel. Other petitioners may be appointed counsel when "the interests of justice so require." These latter statutes, however, have had only limited effect; after the first appeal, most prisoner petitions, particularly on habeas corpus, are prepared without outside legal assistance. In 1996, however, Congress provided expedited federal habeas review of petitions filed by capital defendants if the state of conviction provided a mechanism for the "appointment, compensation, and payment of reasonable litigation expenses" in post-conviction proceedings.

4. *Estelle v. Smith*, 451 U.S. 454 (1981). The actual holding in *Estelle* was that the defendant had a Sixth Amendment right to consult with counsel about whether to submit to the examination; the question of whether there was a right to have counsel present during the interview was not before the Court.

"meaningless ritual."[5] Thus, even if the Sixth Amendment does not apply, other constitutional protections may. The Supreme Court has held that *equal protection* required that the state provide counsel if the appeal was a matter of right. *Douglas v. California*, 372 U.S. 353 (1963). But, *Ross v. Moffitt*, 417 U.S. 600 (1974) held that there was neither an equal protection nor a due process right to counsel on discretionary appeal. Similarly, while there is no Sixth Amendment right to counsel in a probation revocation proceeding, the Sixth does apply if the defendant will be sentenced at that hearing. *Mempa v. Rhay*, 389 U.S. 128 (1967).

That there is no federal constitutional right to assistance of counsel does not, of course, preclude the state from providing such counsel, either as a state constitutional or statutory matter, or even by court rule. Thus, while many states do not provide counsel to indigent inmates seeking collateral review, all but five states provide counsel to inmates on death row for that purpose. *Murray v. Giarratano*, 491 U.S. 1, 12 (1989) (Justice Stevens, dissenting from decision that the federal constitution did not require such counsel). Several states and the federal system provide counsel for bail hearings, and virtually all states actually provide appointed counsel in parole revocation hearings, and discretionary appeals. On the other end of the spectrum, several states provide counsel "as soon as feasible" after the defendant is in custody, even if there has been no "criminal prosecution." See, e.g., Wis. Stat. Ann. Sec. 967.06; Alabama Criminal Rule of Procedure 6.1(a). ("As soon as feasible after a defendant is taken into custody"; with radios and phones in cars, how soon is "feasible?")

A critical corollary of a decision that counsel is not required at a given proceeding is that the right to *adequate* counsel does not apply either. Thus, while an attorney who slept through a *trial* would render inadequate assistance under the Sixth Amendment (see discussion below), he could sleep with impunity through a probation or parole revocation.

2. The Right to Appointed Counsel — Gideon and Argersinger

Until 1963, the Sixth Amendment was not held applicable to the states; defendants seeking the appointment of counsel had to rely upon the due process clause of the Fifth (and Fourteenth) Amendments. In *Powell v. Alabama*, 287 U.S. 45 (1932) the Supreme Court held, for the first time, that Fifth Amendment due process — not the Sixth Amendment — required the "guiding hand of counsel" at a capital criminal proceeding. This meant

---

5. See *United States v. Gouveia*, 467 U.S. 180 (1984). Courts, are divided on whether psychiatric examinations are a critical stage, with the majority of courts saying no, and explaining that an examination is a fact finding, rather than an adversarial, process. If the issues are complex enough, there may be a Fifth Amendment due process or equal protection right to the assistance of counsel.

that if the defendant could not afford counsel, the due process clause required the state to provide one.

Powell involved the infamous "Scottsboro" trial, in which nine young black men were charged with raping a white woman. The trial judge appointed "the entire bar" of Scottsboro to represent the defendants. But only one local attorney, and one out-of-state attorney, even appeared for the defendants.[6] The Supreme Court held that appointing *all* attorneys was the equivalent of appointing *no* attorney.

Powell was a capital case in which the defendants were essentially unable to help themselves. Soon thereafter, although it had required appointment of counsel in all felonies tried in *federal* court, the Court rejected an attempt to apply *Powell* to other felonies in *state* courts. *Betts v. Brady*, 316 U.S. 455 (1942). After *Betts*, only if the case demonstrated "special circumstances" — illiteracy, mental incapacity, possible bias in the courtroom — would the noncapital state defendant be entitled to an appointed attorney.

For nearly 30 years after *Powell*, the Supreme Court rendered a series of opinions attempting to define "special circumstances." The effort was frustrating. Finally, in 1963, in *Gideon v. Wainwright*, 372 U.S. 335 (1963) the Court cut the Gordian knot, holding that the due process clause required appointment of counsel for all indigent[7] persons charged with any felony.[8]

Almost a decade later, the Court expanded that requirement to all misdemeanors in which incarceration *was actually imposed. Argersinger v.*

---

6. The Tennessee lawyer announced he was retained to assist the Defendants, but, as one chronicler put it, his "modest legal abilities were further limited by his inability to remain sober." Uelman, A Train Ride: A Guided Tour of the Sixth Amendment Right to Counsel, 58 (WTR) Law & Contemp. Probs. 13, 15 (1995) citing D. Carter, Scottsboro: A Tragedy of American South 19 (1969).

7. Although the Court did not define "indigency," statutes, administrative regulations and Court rules have filled that gap. See, e.g., 18 U.S.C.A. §3006(A); Ky. Rev. Stat. §31.120; Me. R. Crim. p.44.

8. Clarence Gideon, a poor drifter with a record of minor offenses (including several burglaries) was charged with burglarizing a pool hall for approximately $25 and some alcohol. His request for appointed counsel was denied, and he was convicted and sentenced to five years. His *in forma pauperis* petition for certiorari was granted by the Supreme Court, which appointed Abe Fortas, a prominent Washington attorney, to represent him. The Court held, 9-0, that Gideon had been denied due process. On retrial, Gideon was represented by a local attorney appointed by the court, and was acquitted. Abe Fortas went on to become a member of the United States Supreme Court. Gideon's performance at his first trial, however, was quite respectable. One commentator has opined that "If a lawyer had done what Gideon did, it is doubtful that Gideon could later have successfully demonstrated that but for what the lawyer did not do there was a reasonable probability that the outcome would have been different." Geimer, A Decade of Strickland's Tin Horn: Doctrinal and Practical Undermining of the Right to Counsel, 4 Wm. & Mary Bill. Rts. J. 91, 108 (1995).

Hamlin, 407 U.S. 25 (1972). *Argersinger* refused to follow the rule for counsel, already in place for juries, that the Sixth Amendment only required a jury trial where the defendant *could* be imprisoned for more than six months (see Chapter 8). The *Argersinger* rule requires a judge to determine, prior to trial, whether the defendant might be sentenced to incarceration; if so, counsel must be appointed. If no counsel is appointed, the defendant cannot be sentenced to jail, whatever the facts may show about him, or his crime. Justice Brennan, in *Argersinger*, said that between 33-40 states used a more lenient standard than "actual imprisonment"; 23 in all cases where any length of imprisonment is authorized; an additional group where the authorized appointed counsel punishment exceeds 3-6 months, and others were uncertain, with only five adopting a "likelihood of imprisonment standard" and several others simply requiring appointment where constitutionally mandated. It is possible that, since *Argersinger*, states have cut back on the instances where counsel will be appointed.

Argersinger ended the debate over *whether* counsel must be appointed. Today, the major issue is whether the promise of *Gideon* and *Argersinger*— that every defendant would receive proper representation before being incarcerated (or executed)—has been met. There is much bleak evidence that in many parts of this country many defendants are not adequately represented at trials, including capital trials. Federal Circuit Judge Richard Posner, formerly a law professor, has announced: "I can confirm from my own experience as a judge that criminal defendants are generally poorly represented," and Justice Ruth Bader Ginsburg, also a former law professor, has declared: "I have yet to see a death case, among the dozens coming to the Supreme Court, even on the eve of execution petitions, in which the defendant was well represented at trial."[9]

3. *The Right to Appointed Counsel — Systems of Providing Counsel*

In one sense the aspirations of *Gideon*, 40 years after the decision, have been realized. Nearly three-quarters of criminal defendants, nationally, are represented by appointed counsel. These attorneys are generally provided in one of three methods. The most well known (handling about 80 percent of the cases) is a *public defender's* office—a salaried staff of full or part-time attorneys that render service through a public or private nonprofit organization, or as direct government paid employees. The second method is *contract services*, by

---

9. Ginsburg, In Pursuit of the Public Good: Lawyers Who Care, a lecture delivered on April 9, 2001. At *http://www.supremecourtus.gov/publicinfo/speeches/sp_04-09-01a.ht.*

which the responsible government unit (usually the county) contracts with a *private* group of attorneys to handle all cases arising in that area for a period of time (usually one year, but sometimes longer). These contracts may provide for a lump sum payment for the year, without regard to the caseload, or for payment per case.[10] Over the past few years, the number of jurisdictions providing some portion of their indigent defense through a contract system has increased dramatically. Finally, an *assigned counsel plan* appoints private attorneys on a *case-by-case basis*. Where either of the first two systems operates, and there is a conflict (for example, when co-defendants each need an appointed attorney) the assigned-counsel method will normally be used.

Most systems are mixed. For example, each of New York state's 62 counties pays for and manages its own public defense. New York City used a "mixed delivery system;" the legal aid society represents 85 percent; the rest are private attorneys through an assigned counsel plan. NYC's assigned counsel plans have full time administrators; and attorneys must meet certain qualifications. A screening committee reviews applications, adjudicates complaints, and has undertaken extensive recertification drives. The 1970 federal Criminal Justice Act allowed two different types of defender organizations: (1) the public defender; (2) the community defender, which allows for payment of initial and sustaining grants to nonprofit defense counsel programs operated under community control.

No institution ever believes it has sufficient funding. But virtually all agree that, however measured, most defender programs are drastically underpaid and overworked. In 1979, state and local governments spent approximately $300 million on public defender services; by 1990 this had quadrupled to $1.3 billion. By 1999, 81 surveyed counties alone spent an estimated $1.1 billion on indigent criminal defense. Compared to this last figure is the approximately $1.9 billion spent by state prosecutor. But that latter figure does not include law enforcement resources or forensic laboratory work or expert witnesses. In the recent economic downturn, states have struggled to fund these programs. In Minnesota, public defenders were no longer furnished free; the state attempted to require defendants to pay $50, or more, for their services. The State Supreme Court, on expedited review, held that experiment unconstitutional. *State v. Tennin*, 674 N.W.2d 403 (Minn. 2004).[11] On the other hand,

---

10. There are six kinds of contracts used across the nation: (1) fixed fee, all cases; (2) fixed fee, specific type of case; (3) flat fee, specific number of cases; (4) flat fee per case; (5) hourly fee with caps; (6) hourly fee without caps. U.S. Dept. of Justice, Contracting for Indigent Defense Services: A Special Report 4 (2000).

11. The purpose of counsel is to assure that the innocent defendant is not improperly acquitted. But once the defendant has been found guilty, many states allow the state to recoup the cost of appointed counsel. Of course, if the defendant was really indigent *before* trial, she's unlikely to earn millions while in prison; but if the lottery comes through, the state will be there. Such provisions have been upheld as constitutional. *Fuller v. Oregon*, 417 U.S. 40 (1974).

"In Oregon, where the Courts say they've run out of money to appoint lawyers, the prosecutors . . . brought suit to guarantee every criminal defendant the right to appointed counsel . . . In three Oregon counties, the elected district attorneys have filed writs of mandamus in state court and a federal sec. 1983 action to ensure court-appointed lawyers . . . In Oregon it is common for indigent capital defendants to spend tens of thousands of dollars on expert witnesses when the prosecutor has half that amount of his entire year's budget for such expenses . . . In Wisconsin, 25 elected district attorneys just offered to cut their own wages because the state is going to force layoffs of state-paid assistant prosecutors".

Joshua Marquis, Astoria, Oregon District Attorney, letter to the New Jersey Law Journal, June 23, 2003

Assessing the "adequacy" of resources is incredibly complicated. Caseload limits are often employed as one standard, but one major murder case may take more time than 500 misdemeanor or even minor felony cases. In 2003, the President of the National Association of Criminal Defense Lawyers contended that "part-time public defenders in Lake Charles, La. have 600 felony cases and, on average, do not meet clients until nine months after their arrest." Letter to the New Jersey Law Journal, June 23, 2003. In *Colson v. Smith*, 315 F. Supp. 179 (N.D. Ga. 1970), the court found that one defense attorney was handling some 5,000 cases a year (including capital cases). Other criticisms have been raised. In *Miranda v. Clark County, Nevada*, 391 F.3d 465 (9th Cir. 2003), a civil case, plaintiffs alleged that the county public defender (a) gave limited resources to clients who either refused to take, or "failed" a polygraph; and (b) assigned the least-experienced attorneys to capital cases without providing any training.[12] Obviously, the public defender was attempting to "triage" a heavy caseload by removing resources from those defendants least likely to be acquitted. The court held that, if proved, these allegations could establish an unconstitutional deprivation of counsel.

In most assigned-counsel systems, either by statute or other regulation, the amount to be paid per case, or per hour, is "capped" at a figure well below that which most attorneys would consider minimal, much less adequate. Not surprisingly, both defendants, and the attorneys representing them, having been unsuccessful in obtaining relief by negotiation or legislative lobbying, have sought creative litigation methods to force increased funding. In *State v. Smith*, 140 Az. 355, 681 P.2d 374 (1984), the Arizona Supreme Court struck down Mohave

---

12. As the dissent pointed out, the public defender argued that it provided experienced "back up" for the new lawyers. Incredibly, the County responded that "as a matter of law, attorneys who have graduated from law school and passed the bar should be considered adequately trained to handle capital murder cases."

County's contract defense system, which assigned contracts to the low bidder. The California Supreme Court, in *People v. Barboza*, 29 Cal. 3d 375, 627 P.2d 188 (1981) found that a contract for provision of defense services was invalid because it created financial disincentives for the attorney to state a conflict of interest, and the Oklahoma Supreme Court found that inadequate compensation for court-appointed counsel constituted an illegal taking of the lawyer's property. *State v. Lynch*, 796 P.2d 1150 (Okla. 1990). In 1992, the South Carolina Supreme Court declared rates as low as $10 per hour unconstitutional. *Bailey v. State of South Carolina*, 309 S.C. 455, 424 S.E.2d 503 (1992). And in New York, the organization responsible for public funding challenged the statutes imposing caps on amounts payable to such attorneys. Granting relief, the court decreed "The pusillanimous posturing and procrastination of the executive and legislative branches have created the assigned counsel crisis impairing the judiciary's ability to function . . . Equal access to justice should not be a ceremonial platitude, but a perpetual pledge vigilantly guarded." *New York County Lawyers' Association v. State of New York*, 763 N.Y.S.2d 397 (Sup. Ct. N.Y. Cty. 2003). The New York Legislature thereupon raised the per hour figure to $75.00.[13]

Publicly financed counsel are often demeaned as providing ineffective service; a commonly repeated comment, allegedly made by convicted defendants who, when asked whether they had a lawyer is: "No, I had a public defender." Statistics belie this widespread libel; public defenders perform the same functions every bit as well as the typical private attorney. In 1998, 92 percent of defendants with public counsel and 91 percent with private counsel either pleaded guilty or were found guilty at trial.[14] However, of those found guilty, 88 percent with public counsel, and 77 percent of private counsel received jail or prison sentences, and the difference was greater in "large state courts" (71 percent v. 54 percent).

Much of the data here is out of date. In 2003, the Constitution Project and the National Legal Aid and Defender Association created a new initiative to review the status of indigent systems throughout the nation and consider what types of improvement may be necessary.

---

13. For other litigation involving the validity of compensation to counsel, see In re Order on Prosecution of Criminal Appeals by the Tenth Judicial Circuit Public Defender, 561 So. 2d 1130 (Fla. 1990); *State v. Robinson*, 123 N.H. 665; 465 A.2d 1214 (1983); *Arnold v. Kemp*, 306 Ark. 294, 813 S.W.2d 770 (1991); *State ex rel. Stephan v. Smith*, 242 Kan 336, 747 P.2d 816 (1987). See, generally, Klein, The Eleventh Commandment: Thou Shalt Not be Compelled to Render the Ineffective Assistance of Counsel, 68 Ind. L.J. 363 (1993), arguing that many such suits have been unsuccessful or that public defendant officers are intimidated by threats of local governments. See, more generally, Brown, Rationing Criminal Defense Entitlements: An Argument from Institutional Design, 104 Colum L. Rev. 801 (2004).

14. U.S. Dept. of Justice, Bureau of Justice Statistics, Defense Counsel in Criminal Cases, NCJ 179023 (2000).

C. The Right to Effective Counsel

The right to be represented assumes that the representation must be "effective."[15] But effectiveness cannot be assessed on the basis of result—guilty criminal defendants who complain about the level of their representation know (or should know) that not even Clarence Darrow won every case. How, then, can an appellate court, looking at a cold record, determine whether the defendant received "adequately effective" help from her attorney?

The landmark Supreme Court decision on this question is only 20 years old. The law on this issue, therefore, is still in quite a state of flux, and has been subjected to scathing critiques, particularly in light of recent revelations about the numbers of defendants, both on and off death row, who have been exonerated because of "newly discovered" evidence—sometimes DNA testing. Indeed, as we shall see below, what appeared to be relatively fixed and understood doctrine prior to 2002, may have been dramatically altered by a recent Supreme Court case.

1. The "Three Prongs" of Ineffectiveness

Courts and commentators alike have divided analysis of the effectiveness of counsel into three "types" of claims:

1. instances of so-called "state interference" — *Powell*
2. claims that counsel had a conflict of interest and should not have handled the case
3. claims that counsel failed to conduct a defense in any meaningful manner. — *Strickland*

a. State Interference

The most obvious instance where the state has "interfered" with defendant's right to representation occurs when the state refuses to appoint an attorney at all. In essence, this is what the Supreme Court found to be the case in *Powell*—that although there were warm bodies with law degrees present in the courtroom, the circumstances of their appointment and the way in which the case was tried essentially prevented them from acting as knowledgeable counsel. Even if the state appoints counsel, there may be barriers to making that representation effective. Thus, for example, courts have found violations of either the Fifth or Sixth Amendments when states:

---

15. Bazelon, The Realities of Gideon and Argersinger, 64 Geo. L.J. 811, 819 (1976), "The Sixth Amendment demands more than placing a warm body with a legal pedigree next to an indigent defendant."

(1) banned an attorney-client consultation overnight, *Geders v. United States*, 425 U.S. 80 (1976); (2) forbade defense counsel from giving a summation at a bench trial, *Herring v. New York*, 422 U.S. 53, 57 (1975); (3) required the defendant to testify first, or not at all, *Brooks v. Tennessee*, 406 U.S. 60 (1972); or (4) precluded the defendant from testifying under oath, allowing him only to give an unsworn statement to the jury. *Ferguson v. Georgia*, 365 U.S. 570 (1961).[16]

Where the court concludes that the state *has* actively interfered with counsel's ability to represent the defendant, as in *Powell*, *reversal is automatic*; the defendant need not show how the state's rule undermined the specific presentation in the specific case. This stands in stark contrast to the *Strickland* rule, discussed below, where the defendant must show not only that counsel was ineffective, but that the ineffectiveness prejudiced his case.

Given the difference between *Strickland* and the "*per se* prejudice" rule, it is not surprising that a defendant will try to argue that his case is "like" *Powell*—where counsel is assigned, but is either unfamiliar with criminal proceedings, or with the facts of the case. In *Cronic v. United States*, 466 U.S. 648 (1984), the trial court appointed a relatively young and inexperienced real estate attorney, who did no criminal work, to represent a defendant charged with 13 counts of mail fraud. The appointment was made 25 days before trial; the government had taken almost five years to prepare its case. Defendant, convicted and sentenced to 25 years, argued that these factors combined to make the case "like" *Powell*—although there was a lawyer present, he could not possibly deal with the intricacies of a complex, criminal case. The Supreme Court rejected the parallel to *Powell*, concluding that a good attorney could become acquainted with the materials of the case. The defendant, therefore, would have to demonstrate specific prejudice (which was defined in *Strickland v. Washington*, decided the same day and discussed in detail below).

b. Conflict of Interest

Attorneys owe their clients undiluted loyalty. If Henry, a lawyer who is on retainer from the First National Bank in civil matters, is appointed to represent Amy, charged with robbing that very bank, there is real concern whether Henry can ardently represent her. Because Henry may wish (even subconsciously) to assure that future bank robbers are deterred, he may not be able to give Amy the 100 percent zealous advocacy she deserves, and to which she is constitutionally entitled. The general rule is that counsel should

---

16. This is not quite as anomalous as it may now seem in the twenty-first century. Well into the late nineteenth century, it was thought that defendants should not be tempted to risk eternal damnation by providing perjurious testimony in an attempt to avoid the gallows. But they were allowed to make *unsworn* statements to the jury.

be Caesar's spouse — there should not be even the slightest possibility of conflict. The standard applies equally to retained and appointed counsel.

Since many defendants become disenchanted with their lawyers (particularly appointed ones) when they learn that they were not born on Krypton, courts often take these allegations skeptically. But substantial disagreements do occur. In some instances, those disagreements may become so severe that the defendant demands to represent himself. See below for a discussion of that issue.

Conflicts may arise between or among lawyers if those lawyers representing conflicting interests belong to the same law firm. While "fire walls" may alleviate the problem, the fear that the wall will be breached moves most courts (and most attorneys) to avoid even the possibility by finding counsel outside the firm to represent "conflicted" defendants. The concern may become acute, of course, when "the firm" is a public defender's office, particularly if that office handles most (if not all) criminal defense work in the vicinity.

The first problem is determining whether there is a conflict, either actual or potential. Various state and nationally promulgated ethical standards, including but certainly not limited to, the Code of Professional Responsibility, will assist courts, and lawyers, in determining whether there is a potential conflict. Some potential conflicts are evident; when one lawyer represents multiple co-defendants, there is always a danger that loyalty to one will undercut loyalty to the other(s). If zealous representation of Hermine requires that counsel suggest that Dianne really committed the crime, counsel who represents both is in an impossible dilemma. See *Holloway v. Arkansas*, 435 U.S. 475 (1978), *McFarland v. Yukins*, 356 F.3d 688 (6th Cir. 2003).

Beyond that, however, the waters are murkier. If the representation is successive, not simultaneous, or of a witness, and not a co-defendant, the problems are compounded. For example, in *Eisemann v. Herbert*, 274 F. Supp. 2d 283 (E.D.N.Y. 2003), counsel represented two defendants, who were not actually co-defendants in a single trial, but who were subjects of parallel investigations, arrests, interrogation, and indictments. Even though an associate had handled most of the actual trial of one defendant, the court found that the conflict still existed. At the very least, said the court, the trial court should have made the defendant aware of the danger that he might face as a result of these conflicting interests: "The question is not whether or not the attorney did, in fact, pursue a sound trial strategy. Rather, it is whether or not the attorney was forced to forego a reasonable (though not necessarily better) strategy because of the conflict." *Eisemann* at 303.

i. Inquiring about Conflict. Courts distinguish between an "actual" conflict, and a "potential' one. If, for example, Joshua, the defense attorney for Sigourney, has previously represented Melinda, a listed prosecution witness, and had learned from Melinda evidence that will be used in cross-examining her, a conflict exists only if Melinda actually testifies; until that time it is nascent. Thus, courts grappled with whether to require Joshua to step aside, against Sigourney's wishes, even if it was not clear at the beginning of trial whether Melinda will testify.[17]

One major question is whether a court should "inquire" into a potential conflict, and what occurs if there is no such inquiry. In *Holloway v. Arkansas*, 435 U.S. 475 (1978), a public defender appointed to represent three co-defendants asked to have separate counsel appointed, expressly informing the trial judge that he would feel inhibited in cross-examining any defendant who testified. The Supreme Court held that the trial judge's refusal to order separate representation violated the rights of all three co-defendants, adopting a *per se* rule that such refusal violated the Sixth Amendment. In such a setting, where counsel *asked for* separate representation, there was no need for a judge to inquire whether there was real conflict that could not be avoided or waived. Instead, said the Court, such an inquiry "would require, unlike most cases, unguided speculation." Two years later in *Cuyler v. Sullivan*, 446 U.S. 35 (1980), however, where counsel had not made a request to be relieved of multiple representation, the Court appeared to hold that a trial court was not under an obligation to inquire about the defendant's waiver when he was tried separately from two other co-defendants.

Where there was a potential conflict present, and the judge either knew, or should have known, of the possible conflict, the rule appeared to be that the court was under a *duty to inquire* as to whether the defendant realized that there might be a conflict of interest, and to at least apprise the defendant of the difficulties involved in such representation. *Wood v. Georgia*, 370 U.S. 375 (1962). This investigation was to be quite aggressive. The judge should impress upon the defendant the difficulties that might occur because of the (perceived) conflict. If during this hearing (or afterwards) a conflict appeared possible, each defendant must be appointed (or retain) separate counsel,[18] or unequivocally waive the conflict (but see, below—some waivers are not valid). Failure to conduct the inquiry was said to result in a presumption of prejudice, and require automatic reversal. In *Clark v. United States*, 59 F.3d 296 (2d Cir. 1995), for example, an important government witness had been a recent client of defendant's trial counsel in a substantially related matter. Because the trial court was aware of this fact, but conducted no inquiry, the court applied an automatic reversal rule. Even beyond the constitutional question, many states follow the lead of Federal Rule 44(c) and require an inquiry whenever co-defendants are being jointly represented. See also *Hall v. United States*, 371 F.3d 969 (7th Cir. 2004).

---

17. See *People v. Morales*, 209 Ill. 2d 340, 808 N.E.2d 510 (2004). It is also not impossible that the prosecution does not actually intend to call Melinda, but placed her on the witness list in an attempt to remove Joshua. The court must consider that as well.

18. Subject, of course, to possible waiver. See below.

A defendant who shows a conflict is not required to demonstrate actual *prejudice*, as required by *Strickland*, but merely that the conflict had *adversely affected* his counsel's performance. The standards may seem the same, but they are not. Suppose, for example, Ezekial represents Joseph in a criminal matter. Marietta is a possible witness for the defense, but because he has previously represented Marietta in noncriminal matters, and is concerned that the stress might be too great for her, Ezekial does not call Marietta in Joseph's trial. Even if the court concludes that Marietta's testimony would not have altered the outcome of (*prejudiced*) the trial (see below), it may well determine that Ezekial's performance was "adversely affected" by his conflict.

In *Mickens v. Taylor*, 535 U.S. 162 (2002), the Court, 5-4, appeared to retreat from a "*per se* reversal" rule, when the trial judge knew, or should have known, of a potential conflict, but did not conduct an inquiry. The trial court in *Mickens* had appointed Bryan Saunders as counsel to represent Timothy Hall. Ten days later, after Hall was killed, the same judge appointed Saunders to represent Walter Mickens, who was accused of murdering Hall.[19] In speaking for the five-person majority, Justice Scalia, starting from the assumption that the potential conflict did not affect counsel's performance, declared that "automatic reversal (is not) an appropriate means of enforcing (a) mandate of inquiry." The Court then concluded that, even if the trial judge should have conducted such an inquiry, petitioner still had to show an "adverse effect" upon counsel's performance, which he had not done.[20] The requirement of active inquiry (and the possibility of a *per se* reversal if there is no such inquiry) where a trial judge does not, but "should" know of a possible conflict, now appears to be limited to instances of "multiple representation" settings.[21] All other cases are to be assessed under *Strickland* standards, set out below. After

---

19. *Mickens* was a federal habeas case in which the scope of review is much narrower than on direct appeal (see Chapter 12). The district court conducted a hearing and issued what Justice Kennedy characterized as a "thorough" opinion concluding that counsel's brief representation of Hall had no effect upon his later representation of *Mickens*.

20. For example, the panel of the Fourth Circuit had noted that Saunders was ethically prevented from using information he had gained in his representation of Hall to impugn Hall's character for Mickens' benefit, and that Saunders was precluded from investigating, and bringing to court, evidence of Hall's relationship with his mother. *Mickens v. Taylor*, 227 F.3d 203 (4th. Cir. 2000), opinion vacated, 240 F.3d 348 (4th. Cir. 2001). See Note, 13 Cap. Def. J. 393 (2001); Levin, An Open Question? The Effect of *Cuyler v. Sullivan* on Successive Representation after *Mickens v. Taylor*, 39 Crim. L. Bull. 55 (2003).

21. For example, the court noted that the Federal Rules of Criminal Procedure treat concurrent and successive representation differently. That, of course, was irrelevant in *Mickens* itself, since it was a state, not a federal prosecution. But the attempt to distinguish the two situations may indicate that the *Cuyler* rule that failure to inquire *in a multirepresentation setting* results in *per se* reversal still obtains. Professor Allen et. al., *supra*, suggest that there should be no *per se* rule even in multirepresentation cases,

Mickens, it is not clear whether, even in a multiple representation conflict case, defendants will now have to demonstrate prejudice, and not mere "adverse effect." See *Lombardo v. United States,* 222 F. Supp. 2d 1367 (S.D. Fla. 2002), *aff'd,* 2003 WL 21204960 (11th Cir.), *cert. denied,* 124 S. Ct. 351 (2003). Some state courts, however, do not agree with *Mickens,* and continue to follow a *"per se"* rule of reversal. In *People v. Daly,* 341 Ill. App. 3d 372, 792 N.E.2d 446 (2003), for example, the key witness against the defendant was a confidential informant whom defense counsel had represented only weeks before the defendant's trial. Finding that the prior representation might have affected counsel's performance "in ways difficult to detect and demonstrate," the court reversed the conviction.

ii. Waiving Conflict. The right to conflict-free counsel may be waived, at least generally; standards governing waiver vary with the timing and nature of the proceeding. A defendant seeking to waive such conflict immediately before the trial must ordinarily demonstrate more awareness of the potential harm than one seeking to waive during the course of police investigatory procedures. *Von Moltke v. Gillies,* 332 U.S. 708 (1948) ("a judge must investigate (a request to waive a conflict) as long and as thoroughly as the circumstances of the case before him demand").[22] As a general matter, because we wish to protect each defendant's autonomy, the Court will allow the waiver of a conflict. But because nonlawyers may not fully appreciate the nuances of potential conflict, a trial court may determine, in

---

because that approach may persuade the defendant (and defense counsel) to "sandbag" the trial court—if the defendant is acquitted, the defendant wins, and if the defendant is convicted, the trial court's failure to inquire—even though not actually notified by counsel of the multirepresentation problem—will result in a new trial. Obviously, such behavior by defense counsel may be unethical, and, if unearthed, subject him to disciplinary sanctions. Is it likely that defense counsel would risk such discipline? See *United States v. Fish,* 34 F.3d 488, 493 (7th Cir. 1994) ("Given defense counsel's's duty to avoid conflicts of interest and to advise the court promptly upon discovery of a conflict, the trial court's reliance on defense counsel's own assessment regarding the potential for conflict was entirely reasonable . . . the attorney confronted with a potential conflict . . . in the best position professionally and ethically to determine when a conflict of interest exists or will probably develop in the course of a trial.")

22. In *Von Moltke,* Justice Black provided a long list of inquiries a trial court should make before accepting a waiver of conflict. Because it was only a plurality opinion, however, *Von Moltke* has been modified by lower courts. See, e.g., *Hsu v. United States,* 392 A.2d 972 (D.C. App. 1978); *United States v. Harris,* 683 F.2d 322 (9th Cir. 1982) (The real inquiry is "what the defendant understood—not what the court said.") It is clear that the defendant must understand the charges, and possible defenses to the charges. Various lower courts have characterized a defendant's awareness of possible defenses as a basic element of an acceptable waiver. However, various other courts have virtually discarded that portion of the *Von Moltke* opinion. They focus on the charges and the range of punishment. Indeed, some courts have said that it is not clear that defendant need understand the specific elements of the crime for waiver of counsel, though it is obviously needed for a guilty plea.

extreme circumstances, that no such waiver can be allowed, and override the waiver. *Wheat v. United States*, 486 U.S. 153 (1988).[23] See *Gonzalez v. State*, 117 S.W.3d 831 (Tex. Crim. App 2003). Ultimately, the decision rests in the discretion of the trial court, who is to be "allowed substantial latitude in refusing waivers."

c. Adequacy of Representation — *Strickland v. Washington*

The third, and by far the most litigated, prong of adequate representation goes to the actual performance of trial counsel during the representation period. The law here is confused and confusing, and is so fact-specific as to make virtually any articulation of standards suspect. The rule in the abstract is, however, very clear; as usual, the devil is in the details. As articulated by the Supreme Court in *Strickland v. Washington*, 466 U.S. 668 (1984) the adequacy inquiry has two parts:

1. Did counsel perform adequately? (The performance issue.)
2. If not, did that inadequate performance actually injure the defendant? (The prejudice issue.)

i. The Standard of Performance. You may not believe this, but lawyers (like judges and other human beings) make mistakes. But not every mistake means that a defendant was inadequately represented. As observers have noted, a defendant is entitled to a "fair" trial, but not a "perfect" one. *Delaware v. Van Arsdall*, 475 U.S. 673, 681 (1986).

Until 50 years ago, most of the lower courts, both federal and state, had held that counsel was inadequate only if the representation was so poor as to make the trial a "farce and mockery." After *Gideon*, however, the courts increasingly rejected this basement-level norm and took one of two approaches in assessing performance: (1) use of ethical and nationally promulgated standards, such as those of the American Bar Association, which had promulgated its first set of standards relating to the defense function; (2) a "reasonableness" test.[24] The latter approach sometimes echoed the malpractice test in torts—whether the attorney had acted with the level of performance in

---

23. A notorious case holding that a conflict could not be waived, even after an intense pretrial court inquiry establishing defendant's clear awareness of many permutations of the conflict, is *United States v. Schwarz*, 283 F.3d 76 (2d Cir. 2002), involving the prosecution of several police officers for a brutal attack, inside a police station, upon Abner Louima. The court required each officer to be represented by a different attorney.

24. Among the various standards to which a court now could look to would be: the ABA's Model Code of Professional Responsibility, the ABA's Model Rules of

his local community; the former used national standards, sometimes enhanced by local practice.

In one of the more outstanding pre-*Strickland* opinions, *United States v. DeCoster*, 487 F.2d 11194 (D.C. Cir. 1973), Judge Bazelon had enunciated a checklist of actions which a competent defense counsel should take. Among these were:

1. Counsel should meet with his client without delay and as often as necessary to elicit matters of defense. Counsel should discuss fully, potential strategies and tactical choices with his client.
2. Counsel should promptly advise his client of his rights and take all actions necessary to preserve them.
3. Counsel must conduct appropriate investigations, both factual and legal, to determine what matters of defense can be developed, in most cases a defense attorney or his agent should interview not only his own witnesses but also those that the government intends to call . . . the investigation should always include efforts to secure information in the possession of the prosecution and law enforcement authorities.

None of these guidelines seems onerous, or excessively detailed. Yet only three years after *DeCoster*, the D.C. Circuit, finding this list both too restrictive and too broad, adopted the "reasonableness" approach. The stage was set for *Strickland*.

The procedural posture of *Strickland* is important. Defendant did not claim that his attorney's performance at trial was inadequate; the complaint concerned the capital sentencing hearing. Thus, *Strickland* appears to (1) establish a rule for all "critical stages" of a criminal prosecution; (2) allow assessment of the performance of counsel at each critical stage, rather than combining all such stages and the overall performance. The habeas corpus petition alleged that his attorney had failed to:

1. move for a continuance to prepare for sentencing;
2. request a psychiatric report;
3. investigate and present character witnesses;
4. seek a pre-sentence report;
5. present meaningful arguments to the sentencing judge;
6. investigate the medical examiner's report.

The Eleventh Circuit, like the court in *DeCoster*, had formulated some specific guidelines to define counsel's duty to investigate. The court had also ruled that if a defendant shows that counsel's failing worked to his actual and substantial disadvantage, the writ must be granted unless the state proved counsel's effectiveness was harmless beyond a reasonable doubt. The

---

Professional Conduct, the American Lawyer's Code of Conduct, or the National Association of Criminal Defense Lawyers.

Supreme Court, in an opinion by Justice O'Connor, reversed, rejecting each of those approaches.[25]

The opinion began by emphatically rejecting any attempt to employ national standards as more than guides. While not adopting the "farce" standard, and also implicitly rejecting the "malpractice" approach, the Court explicitly declared that "More specific guidelines (than reasonableness) are not appropriate," that "the basic duties" do not "form a checklist"; and that "Prevailing norms of practice as reflected in (ABA standards) are guides . . . but they are only guides." Indeed, "Any such set of rules would interfere with the constitutionally protected independence of Counsel and . . . could distract counsel from the overriding mission of vigorous advocacy of the defendant's cause."[26]

The Court then turned to what would constitute deficient performance. The critical inquiry, said the court, was *"whether counsel's assistance was reasonable considering all the circumstances."* The "variety of circumstances faced by defense counsel . . ." were so varied, said the Court, that only a broad standard such as reasonableness could be employed. The Court observed that "it is all too tempting for a defendant to second-guess counsel's assistance . . . every effort (must) be made to eliminate the distorting effects of hindsight." To reduce this possibility:

1. courts should indulge a *"strong presumption"* that counsel's conduct falls within the wide range of reasonable professional assistance;[27]
2. *defendant would carry the burden* of demonstrating that the assistance was deficient, although that burden would be less than the typical "preponderance" standard.

Strickland's approach is certainly understandable, particularly as it applies to decisions regarding trial strategy, and even more acutely to those decisions made during trial itself. Two attorneys faced with the same problem might well decide on two wholly different approaches, each of which is, at least, plausible. One counsel might choose to cross-examine an

---

25. In the same year she wrote *Strickland*, Justice O'Connor had remarked that "ineffective assistance of counsel claims are becoming as much a part of state and federal habeas corpus proceedings as the bailiff's call to order in these courts." *McKasle v. Vela*, 464 U.S. 1053 (1984) (O'Connor, J., dissenting from denial of certiorari.)

26. On the same day as its decision in *Strickland*, the Court decided *United States v. Cronic*, 466 U.S. 648 (1984). There, also, the lower court had used five factors in assessing the adequacy of performance of a real estate attorney appointed 25 days before a major mail fraud prosecution. The *Cronic* opinion rejected the use of any such factors as "determinative" of the issue.

27. Some have questioned the notion of a "presumption" here, pointing out that even in tort cases, other professions—including lawyers—are not given such a benefit. See Klein, The Emperor Gideon Has No Clothes: The Empty Promise of the Constitutional Right to Effective Assistance of Counsel, 13 Hastings. Const. L.Q. 625 (1986).

adverse witness at length, hoping to demonstrate bias. A second attorney, perceiving that the witness has not done major damage to the defendant's case, might decide not to cross-examine at all, or to tread lightly, lest the witness do more damage, or win the jury's empathy. That the defendant was convicted does not itself demonstrate that the strategy was "wrong," or that a different strategy was either "better" or "might have worked." Leaving aside the truth that either judgment might actually be correct, appellate courts will find it difficult to assess the atmosphere of the court room.

Strickland's language that tactical decisions are "virtually unchallengeable" must be read in tandem with the language which requires a "complete investigation;" an incomplete investigation may well mean that the "tactical decision" was uninformed, and hence not "unchallengeable." Thus, counsel have been held ineffective, for example, where he failed to investigate evidence of the defendant's *D*'s brain impairment, *Frazier v. Huffman*, 343 F.3d 780 (6th Cir. 2003), or failed to interview and call witnesses who would have helped impeaching the government's two key witness, *Cargle v. Mullin*, 317 F.3d 1196 (10th Cir. 2003), or failed to to investigate "a wealth of significant mitigating evidence" about defendant's background medical history in connection with the penalty phase of a death penalty case." *Laird v. Horn*, 159 F. Supp.2d 58 (E.D. Pa. 2001).

Moreover, even if trial judgments made in the heat of the moment are difficult to assess, strategic judgments made outside the courtroom, with more time for reflection, are more subject to analysis. Given five possible courses of defense, or 10 possible witnesses to interview only slightly, an attorney is forced to decide among them, and allocate time accordingly.

Strickland itself reflects this dilemma. Justice O'Connor concluded, on the basis of the record developed in the habeas proceeding, that each of the defendant's allegations of inadequate performance could be explained as a reasonable strategic decision. Defense counsel, said the Court, had

> "made a strategic choice to argue for the extreme emotional distress mitigating circumstance and to rely as fully as possible on respondent's acceptance of responsibility for his own crimes. . . . Trial Counsel could reasonably surmise from his conversation that character and psychological evidence would be of little help . . . Restricting testimony on respondent's character to what had come in at the plea colloquy ensured that contrary character and psychological evidence and respondent's criminal history . . . would not come in. *On these facts, there can be little question . . . that trial counsel's defense, though unsuccessful, was the result of reasonable professional judgment.*"

> *Strickland, emphasis added.*

Justice Marshall, dissenting, argued that the performance standard "is so malleable that, in practice, it will either have no grip at all or will yield excessive variation in the manner in which the Sixth Amendment is interpreted. . . . To tell lawyers and the lower courts that counsel for a criminal defendant must behave 'reasonably' . . . is to tell them almost nothing." To Justice Marshall, the standard established in *Strickland* echoed the "totality of circumstances" test of *Betts v. Brady* which some had thought had been interred by *Gideon.* The ad hoc inconsistency of *Betts,* which had been one of the prime reasons for a bright line adopted in *Gideon,* seemed resurrected.[28]

The debate has not subsided over the years since *Strickland.* For example, any nonlawyer would be stunned to learn that a series of cases have debated whether *Strickland* is violated when the defense counsel appears intoxicated,[29] or distracted, or even sleeping during trial testimony. But to a lawyer, particularly to an attorney whose conduct is called into question, and who fears disciplinary sanctions, there may be many explanations for the apparent conduct. First, there is the challenge that the counsel may not have been intoxicated or sleeping; he may have simply had his eyes shut. Only counsel knows with certainty, and he is likely to say he was not asleep. Additionally, a counsel who closes his eyes may be entertaining a strategy to demonstrate how unimportant the testimony was.[30] Finally, even a few seconds napping in a long trial, some judges have concluded, is not sufficient in itself to demonstrate unequivocally inadequate representation.[31] Recently,

---

28. Murphy, The Constitutional Failure of the Strickland Standard in Capital Cases Under the Eighth Amendment, 63 Law and Contemp. Probs. 179 (2000): (*Strickland* "made unmistakably clear that bright line rules for representation were not part of the Sixth Amendment"). As the Court said in *Strickland*: "Representation is an art. . . . And an act or omission that is unprofessional in one case may be sound or even brilliant in another." 466 U.S. 668, 693 (1984).

29. E.g., *Gardner v. Dixon*, No. 92-4013, 1992 U.S. App. LEXIS 28147 (4th Cir. 1992) (counsel's use of cocaine during trial did not result in inadequate representation.

30. Although Clarence Darrow was never accused of sleeping at trial, he was known to use various techniques to distract the jury—or to suggest to them that he found the (possibly devastating) testimony boring. A classic "distraction" was to light up a massive cigar during prosecution testimony and have the jury watch to see when the ashes from the cigar would fall into the ashtray. Darrow, however, had placed wires in the cigar before trial, making it difficult, if not impossible, for the ashes to actually fall.

31. E.g., *McFarland v. Texas*, 928 S.W.2d 481 (Tex. Crim App. 1996), *cert. denied*, 519 U.S. 1119 (1997). See also *United States v. Katz*, 425 F.2d 928 (2d Cir. 1970) ("the testimony during the period of counsel's somnolence was not central to the accused's case and . . . if it had been (the trial judge) would have awakened him rather than waiting for the luncheon recess to warn him." As those who may have catnapped during a class may attest, a few somnolent seconds may not affect one's ability to understand the process, and power naps do not necessarily affect ultimate performance. The problem, however, is that the critical questions—Was he asleep? Did it affect performance?—can only be fairly answered by the attorney. The witnesses in a hearing involving such a matter—jurors, or possibly court personnel—are unlikely to be keeping minute details of the duration, or precise occurrence, of counsel's

however, the Fifth Circuit established a "presumption" that counsel who were perceived as sleeping had not performed adequately. *Burdine v. Johnson*, 262 F.3d 336, *cert. denied, subnom., Cockrell v. Burdine*, 535 U.S. 1120 (2002) (mem).[32]

(Allegedly) sleeping counsel are merely the tip of the iceberg. A plethora of complaints have been lodged against counsel both before and after *Strickland*. Among the multitude of complaints, some upheld, most not, have been counsel's failure to:

- put forth a valid, viable defense;
- request an appropriate charge to the jury which was favorable to the defense;
- properly investigate contradictory statements made by prosecution witnesses and to call witnesses who could have raised doubts regarding the occurrence of the crime;
- file necessary motion to suppress illegally seized evidence;
- effectively participate in the selection of a jury;
- adequately cross-examine witnesses;
- avoid eliciting information on cross that was damaging, even after having been cautioned by the trial judge;
- be sufficiently involved in the trial proceedings;
- fully explain the consequences of a guilty plea;
- inform his client of the facts before allowing a guilty plea;
- investigate and utilize an exculpatory government record;
- let defendant testify;
- deny, but rather concede, in opening statement, that defendant had committed the murder;
- investigate and present evidence of defendant's brain impairment;
- pursue an appeal, after expressly being informed by the Court of Appeals that he was responsible for doing so;
- interview or call witnesses, and failure to impeach key state witness;
- object to motion to strike defendant's entire testimony;

---

siestas. Indeed, if the jurors were watching the defense counsel rather than the witness, we would have other concerns. The judge, similarly, may be concerned with the testimony, or other matters, and paying little attention to defense counsel. The person most likely to be sufficiently interested to keep notes is the defendant—who will perhaps nudge his attorney, but who will hesitate before "waking" him, or before complaining to the judge.

32. Some two decades earlier, the Ninth Circuit had created an identical presumption in another sleeping counsel case. *Javor v. United States*, 724 F.2d 831 (9th Cir.1984). Plus que sa change. . . . Unhappily, the presumption came too late in one instance. The same lawyer who slept during Burdine's trial, slept during the trial of Carl Johnson, but both the Texas court of Criminal Appeals and the Fifth Circuit upheld the conviction and sentence. Neither court published its opinion. Dow, The State, the Death Penalty and Carl Johnson, 37 B.C. L. Rev. 691, 711 (1996).

- request a diminished capacity instruction where the sole issue was premeditation;
- read all discovery materials, not conduct an independent investigation;
- misunderstand the statute governing evidence;
- call, or even consult, a competing expert;
- assert favorable interpretation of ambiguous sentencing statute;
- file a brief on behalf of defendant before withdrawing;
- seek mitigation of the immigration consequences of a guilty plea;
- failed to request an instruction on the voluntary safe release of a kidnaping victim, even though that was a specific mitigating element of the crime.

Each decision is fact-specific; in one case a specific failing may, on balance, not outweigh the general good level of representation, while in another, superficially similar case, a court may reach a different conclusion. Any attempt to summarize these, and the myriad other reported cases, both state and federal, decisions is on very unstable ground. Still it is probably not inaccurate to say that any instance of lack of judgment is likely to be met with the claim that every move is strategic. Counsel unfamiliar with the law[33] or one inattentive, however, may be more likely to be proclaimed inadequate. In earlier cases, the failure to investigate, and particularly to interview witnesses, was least likely to succeed, but in recent years, particularly in death cases, and particularly after *Wiggins* (discussed below), that may be changing.

Justice O'Connor's view that the test of due process was whether the result was fair, whether the error "undermined confidence in the outcome of the proceeding," effectively adopted the *Brady-Kyles* approach (discussed in Chapter 6) that requires that a reviewing court to assess each possible error of defense counsel both singly and cumulatively. Thus, *Strickland* requires a detailed, retrospective fact-specific investigation into the entire record, into defense counsel's mental state at the time of the trial, and the ways in which a "competent" attorney might have handled the trial, absent the error. As we saw in *Kyles*, any attorney, much less those on appellate courts both state and federal, are liable to disagree vehemently about the effect that a "good"

---

33. Lower court cases have found ineffective performance appears to be caused by an attorney's legal error. Thus, attorney error has been found when counsel:
- did not challenge the legality of a search because he was unaware of the rule that allowed him to do so;
- failed to object to illegally seized evidence because he misread the leading case on the issue;
- advised a plea of guilty to the charge of forgery, unaware that there was a statute which carried a lighter penalty, and which applied more directly;
- "induced" the defendant to plead guilty on the "patently erroneous advice that he may be subject to a sentence six times more severe than that which the law would really allow."

lawyer might have had in a hypothetically errorless trial. At the very least, this test leads to unfettered speculation, well after the fact.

As Justice Marshall said, dissenting in *Strickland*, "Seemingly impregnable cases can sometimes be dismantled by a good defense counsel. On the basis of a cold record, it may be impossible for a reviewing court confidently to ascertain how the government's evidence and argument would have stood up against rebuttal and cross examination by a shrewd, well-prepared lawyer."[34] In most cases, a single mistake, even a significant one, by counsel will not meet *Strickland* standards. Instead, defendant will normally attempt to show a series of errors, which should be considered cumulatively. See *Miller v. Senkowski*, 268 F. Supp. 2d 296 (E.D.N.Y. 2003). This general rule, of course, has its exceptions. When there were only two eyewitnesses to the crime, failure to interview one of them was inadequate performance. *Anderson v. Johnson*, 338 F.3d 382 (5th Cir. 2003). See also *Schnelle v. State*, 103 S.W.3d 165 (Mo. App. 2003), where counsel failed to object to a motion to strike the defendant's *entire* testimony was ineffective assistance of counsel.

Strickland also endorsed the general view that many apparently inadequate counsel may be simply using a different trial strategy. In *Clozza v. Murray*, 913 F.2d 1092 (4th Cir. 1990), for example, defendant's counsel proclaimed to the capital sentencing jury: "If the victim were my son, I'd execute my client." The court found, however, that this was an acceptable strategy to maintain credibility with the jury.

Recent Supreme Court decisions continue to reflect tension and uncertainty in assessing performance. In *Bell v. Cone*, 535 U.S. 685 (2002), counsel, after presenting medical evidence regarding insanity during the guilt phase of a capital murder trial, did not introduce additional evidence at the punishment phase, and waived closing argument. The Court found this within the bounds of reasonable representation. A year later, however, in *Wiggins v. Smith*, 539 U.S. 510 (2003), the inadequacies which defendant alleged occurred in his capital sentencing hearing paralleled uncannily those involved in *Strickland*. The Court divided 7-2, primarily on whether counsel's decisions not to investigate further certain evidence or present it to the jury, was reasonable trial strategy or inadequate representation. Intriguingly, *Wiggins* was also written by Justice O'Connor. Whether *Wiggins* portends a more liberal examination of counsel errors is unclear; whether it might point to that path in death cases will be discussed below.

Beyond the question of whether standards can be enunciated, much less adopted, is the question of the burden and standard of proof. One could after all, require the defendant to allege specific errors in representation, and

---

34. Certainly many would attribute to masterful defense lawyering, the acquittals in the O.J. Simpson murder trial and the state prosecution of the police officers involved in beating Rodney King, two cases which, on their face, appeared to be "slam dunks" for the state.

to meet a burden of production, but require the state to demonstrate that the representation was adequate. Instead, *Strickland* both put the burden of proof on the defendant, and then added the "strong presumption" that the representation was effective. Although Justice O'Connor clearly announced that the standard only required the defendant to prove ineffectiveness by a "reasonable probability," and explicitly rejected higher standards of proof, as the Court observed in *Kimmelman v. Morris,* 477 U.S. 3655 (1986), the placement of the burden of proof, and the strong presumption of competence makes the defendant's task "though . . . not insurmountable . . . a heavy one."

ii. Demonstrating prejudice.

ii. Demonstrating prejudice. Given the hurdles which the defendant must overcome to demonstrate inadequate performance, one might think that at the very least a circumstantial inference might arise that this performance hurt the defendant in some way. Not so, according to *Strickland*. Even if the defendant overcomes the presumption that trial counsel's apparent inadequacy was actually trial strategy and proves inadequate representation, the reviewing court should not grant relief unless, as well, the defendant demonstrates that the result would have been different. The purpose of counsel, said Justice O'Connor, was "to ensure a fair trial . . . a trial whose result is reliable. . . (one which did not show) a breakdown in the adversary process that renders the result unreliable."[35] In this one paragraph were the seeds of discord: whether the primary purpose of the representation was (1) to assure a *fair trial*, as the first sentence suggested, or (2) as the last clause suggested, to obtain a reliable *result*.

Justice Marshall, dissenting in *Strickland*, argued that focus on the *result* vitiated the purpose of both counsel and other Sixth Amendment guarantees. Even the guiltiest defendant, argued Marshall, was entitled to a fair trial; concern with a "reliable result" would mean that an obviously guilty defendant could never obtain relief even after a "sham and a mockery."[36]

Strickland made prejudice relevant. Justice O'Connor placed upon the defendant the burden of proving that there was a "reasonable probability" that he had been prejudiced. While, as Justice O'Connor indicated, this was not the most difficult hurdle the Court could have erected, it was more stringent than some. Earlier, lower court decisions (and the Eleventh Circuit in *Strickland*) had placed upon the prosecution the burden of demonstrating

---

35. This test, of course, was identical to the one employed in assessing the effect of a prosecutorial violation of *Brady*. See Chapter 6, *supra*.

36. Some states, such as New York, have taken Marshall's approach, focusing not on the outcome, but "on the fairness of the process as a whole, rather than any particular impact on the outcome of the case." *People v. Henry*, 95 N.Y.2d 563, 144 N.E.2d 112 (2000).

that the (proven) ineffective assistance had not harmed the defendant.[37] The chart below suggests the span of positions one might take in this regard.

Table 10.1

Lowest Burden on Defendant			*Highest Burden on Defendant*	
Automatic	Presume	*D* must show	*D* carries by	*D* carries BRD
Reversal	Prejudice	Reason prob	Preponderance	("Farce")
NonRebuttable)	(Gov't. may rebut)	*Strickland*		

The prejudice standard must also be read in tandem with the performance standard. Justice O'Connor's opinion made clear that a reviewing court need not assess counsel's performance if the defendant did not carry the proof on prejudice. This holding provided courts a method by which they could avoid the unpleasant task of "grading" performance at all.[38]

2. *Making Trial Counsel More Effective*

Long before *Strickland*, commentators and judges were bemoaning the level of representation from lawyers, both appointed and retained. Thus, Chief Justice Warren Burger opined that one-third to one-half of the courtroom counsel are "not really qualified" and that "only the tip of the iceberg" of this dilemma has been addressed.[39] Although few studies appear to have been conducted recently, in the mid 1980s, one study found that appointed defense counsel interviewed witnesses in only *twenty-one percent* of homicide cases, and *four* percent of other felony cases. *McConville and Mirsky*, Criminal Defense of the Poor in New York City, 15 N.Y.U. Rev., L. & Soc. Change 581 (1986-1987). This has surely been improved over the past two decades, given the increase in public defender offices. But there also can be no doubt, that in part because of inadequate funding, such inadequate interviewing continues far beyond any acceptable level.

---

37. See the discussion in Chapter 12 of the *Chapman* "harmless error" rule that "Proof of a constitutional error . . . casts on someone other than the person prejudiced by it, a burden to show that it was harmless . . . the original common law harmless error rule put the burden on the beneficiary of the error either to prove that there was no injury or to suffer a reversal of his erroneously obtained judgment." *Chapman v. California*, 386 U.S. 18, 24 (1967).

38. Cf. *White v. Singletary*, 972 F.2d 1218 (11th Cir. 1992): "We are not interested in grading lawyers' performance; we are interested in whether the adversarial process at trial, in fact, worked adequately."

39. Quoted in Berger, The Supreme Court and Defense Counsel: Old Road, New Paths—A Dead End?, 86 Colum. L. Rev. 9 (1986). See also, Burger, Some Further Reflections on the Problem of Adequacy of Trial Counsel, 49 Fordham 1, 19; Burger, The Special Skills of Advocacy, 3 J. Contemp. Probs. L. 163, 170 (1977).

Strickland has been subjected to much criticism, either as hopelessly fact-specific or aggressively protective of the reputations of lawyers. Perhaps the most vitriolic comment is that of Professor Geimer:[40] "Had *Strickland* been already decided, the appellants in *Powell* probably would have lost."[41]

But what alternatives are there? One might suggest that trial judges become more active in the trial, but as Judge Bazelon, no friend of incompetent counsel, recognized:

> "While no conscientious judge wants to sit by silent while an attorney butchers his case, the judge cannot take over the defense's case altogether. Moreover, the steps he can take are stopgaps; they are inefficient and open to abuse. Clearly, it would be unreasonable to rely on the trial judge alone to deal with the problem of ineffective counsel."

> Bazelon, *The Defective Assistance of Counsel*,
> 42 U. Cin. L. Rev. 1,16 (1973)

Adoption of national standards at least as significant guidelines, or the elimination of the prejudice requirement, are also frequently suggested, but the national standards, even those in ethical codes (as opposed to the aspirational standards of the ABA, for example) are not much more specific than the "reasonableness" standard of *Strickland*, and abolishing the prejudice requirement might result in even fewer attorney actions being deemed inadequate.

The solution may be not post hoc, but ante hoc. Several writers have suggested that the state should be required to certify and regularly recertify any attorney, retained or appointed, who seeks to represent a criminal defendant. Such a program would reduce, if not eliminate, those instances in which young, often inexperienced attorneys are willing to be assigned to criminal cases, both for the income and the experience. But the basic truth — one which the Strickland Court recognized and to which, perhaps, it paid too much obeisance — is that even competent, well-trained, certified criminal attorneys may, in a given case, make mistakes which may have drastic impact on their clients' freedom, or even lives.

Of course, disciplinary action against attorneys whose inadequacy has not resulted in a reversal because of lack of prejudice to the defendant, is yet another route to pursue. But according to Geimer, *supra*, n.40, a computer

---

40. Geimer, A Decade of Strickland's Tin Horn: Doctrinal and Practical Undermining of the Right to Counsel, 4 Wm. & Mary Bill Rts. J. 91, 97 (1995). Prof. Geimer is also Director of the Virginia Capital Case Clearinghouse.

41. Geimer correctly notes that, so far as *Powell* is seen as a "late appointment" case, it is overruled by *Chambers v. Maroney*, 399 U.S. 42, 54 (1970), where counsel's appointment on the day of the trial was held not to violate automatically either the Fifth or Sixth Amendments. See also *United States v. Cronic*, 466 U.S. 648 (1984), in which the defense counsel, a real estate attorney, was appointed 25 days before the trial of a nine-million dollar mail fraud case which the government had taken four years to investigate.

search in 1995 showed no reported case of an attorney being disciplined for failures related to criminal defense. There may be other sanctions. In one recent civil case, the trial judge was so appalled at the attorney's misuse of process that, rather than dock the lawyer for fees filing a frivolous suit, he ordered him back to law school, to take courses in federal practice and procedure, professionalism, and legal ethics. *Balthazar v. Atlantic City Medical Center*, 179 F. Supp. 2d 574 (D.N.J. 2003).

3. *Death and Inadequate Counsel*

Although this book does not discuss the death penalty, it is impossible to discuss assistance of counsel without at least recognizing the recent revelations, particularly relating to death penalty cases, in which DNA testing, as well as other methods, have disclosed that truly innocent defendants have been sentenced to death (and sometime executed). Professor Bright found that one-third of the lawyers who represented people sentenced to death in Illinois have been disbarred or suspended. One of the lawyers, a convicted felon and the only lawyer in Illinois history to be disbarred twice, represented four men who were sentenced to death.[42]

Strickland itself involved counsel's failure to investigate and find information relevant not to *Strickland's* guilt, but to the capital sentencing process. Putting aside the above criticisms of *Strickland* as it applies to typical felony prosecutions, many have found it troubling that these flexible guidelines apply to capital cases. Professor Lance Liebman, author of a major study of death penalty cases, has been quoted as saying that: "There has been this broad set of courts . . . that has reached the conclusion under *Strickland* that if the trial attorney gave a strategic or tactical explanation for failing to do something, that was essentially impenetrable." Coyle, New Standard in Death Penalty Cases Predicted, New Jersey Law Journal, July 28, 2003, p.6. A substantial number of the reported cases deal with allegations of inadequate representation either at trial or sentencing in capital cases. Several of the "sleeping counsel" cases noted above involved the death penalty.

The American Bar Association has declared that "inadequacy and inadequate compensation of counsel at trial" is one of the "principal failings of the capital punishment systems in the states today." Toward a More Just and Effective System of Review in State Death Penalty cases, 40 Am. U. L. Rev. 1, 16 (1990). Death cases, said the ABA, require "a significantly greater degree of skill and experience on the part of defense counsel is required than in a noncapital case. . . . (and) extraordinary efforts on behalf of the

---

42. See Bright, Gideon's Reality, Crm. Just. (Summer 2003) p.5. See also Bright, Counsel for the Poor: The Death Sentence Not for the Worst Crime, But for the Worst Lawyer, 103 Yale L.J. 1835 (1994).

accused," and it has adopted a highly detailed set of guidelines, expressly for death cases, separate from its general standards relating to the defense function. See Standards For the Appointment and Performance of Defense Counsel in Death Penalty Cases (2d ed. 2003), reprinted in 31 Hofstra L. Rev. 913 (2003). It is now commonplace, as it was not even 15 years ago to have two lawyers in death penalty cases, one to focus on the guilt phrase, the other to concentrate on the matter of penalty.

The current situation in the Supreme Court is unclear. After failing to find ineffective assistance in any case since *Strickland*, the Court, badly divided in two very complex death cases, *Williams (Terry) v. Taylor*, 529 U.S. 362 (2000) and *Williams (Michael) v. Taylor*, 529 U.S. 420 (2000), found incompetent assistance in the sentencing phase of each case, primarily from lack of investigation of witnesses. Similarly, in *Wiggins v. Smith, supra*, the Court examined in detail counsel's failure in the sentencing phase of a capital case to investigate possible sources of mitigating evidence, and declared the representation inadequate. The *Terry Williams* decision, written by Justice O'Connor (the author of *Strickland*) for a 7-2 majority, purported to apply the *Strickland* standards, but the case may suggest a new and more intense scrutiny of the standards to be applied in an adequacy case generally, or at least in capital cases. In what some interpret as a move toward adopting more specific standards for representation generally, the Court cited the general ABA standards. One veteran capital litigator said: "It's a huge development in our part of the world". . . *Coyle, supra* p. 238. Another commentator opines: "*Wiggins* will have a profound effect on the way capital sentences are reviewed. It will no longer be possible for courts to dismiss claims of ineffectiveness lightly by characterizing the failure to present mitigation as a 'strategy.' "[43][44]

4. The Right to Effective Assistance — Expert Witnesses

Lawyers, even the best of lawyers, are only lawyers; they are not experts on psychiatry, medical technology, or firearms. It is sometimes argued that for counsel to be "effective" and for a trial to be "fair," the state must appoint not merely an attorney, but an expert witness. In *Ake v. Oklahoma*,

---

43. Mickenberg, Criminal Cases, Ineffective Counsel, The National Law Journal (Aug. 4, 2003).

44. On the other hand, even since the *Williams* cases, the Court has also rejected claims of ineffective assistance (see e.g., *Bell v. Cone*, 535 U.S. 685 (2002) (8-1, per Rehnquist, J.) and denied certiorari in other cases.

470 U.S. 68 (1985), the trial court had, *sua sponte*, ordered the defendant, charged with a capital offense, to be examined for competency to stand trial. When the trial actually occurred, appointed defense counsel asked for funding sought to hire a psychiatrist to support a claim of insanity. The Supreme Court held that, in these circumstances, the state was obligated, as a mater of due process (not the Sixth Amendment) to provide the assistance of one competent psychiatrist, which was a "basic tool" in this case. The Court noted that most states would provide such assistance in similar circumstances, so long as the defendant points to "substantive supporting facts" that could make such a plea feasible.

Federal and state courts are divided on whether *Ake* applies outside the psychiatric realm. Courts have concluded that, depending on the precise factual setting, due process may require providing a forensic expert, a hypnotist, and an investigator to find critical evidence.[45] But see *Conklin v. Schofield*, 366 F.3d 1191 (11th Cir. 2004) (Refusal by trial court to provide funds for an independent medical expert in capital case did not render counsel ineffective.)

As might be expected, because the state is paying for this assistance, the defendant must make a compelling showing that the expert is necessary. While nonindigent defendants may hire (and present) as many experts as they wish (subject to problems of multiplicity, etc.), indigent defendants must show that the issue in the case is "pivotal" and of "critical importance." Even then, as *Ake* itself declared, the indigent defendant is limited to one expert per issue, and that expert *may* be designated by the court.

Since 1964, a federal statute has provided for paid expert witnesses for indigent defendants; that statute has been interpreted rather beneficently. A sizable number of states, through decision, statutes, or court rules, provide such assistance, but they may be limited to specific issues, or specific charges (e.g. Ariz. Rev. State. Sec. 13-4013(B) (capital cases).

5. *Raising the Right to Effective Counsel*

In most instances, the same counsel who handled the trial will represent the defendant on appeal. It is therefore unlikely that any claim of ineffective assistance will be raised on direct appeal. Moreover, even if it were raised, the record of the trial would be unlikely to reflect even trial errors (such as inadvertence, sleeping, etc.), and would certainly be devoid of any reference to out-of-court events. On rare occasions, the appellate court might be able to

---

45. Ironically, at least one court has relied on the "presumption" of sanity to distinguish *Ake* from other areas in which experts are requested, saying that the defendant needs an expert to rebut this legal presumption, but not to rebut evidence going to other elements of the crime. See *Davis v. State*, 863 S.W.2d 259 (Ark. 1993).

decide at least some parts of the claim, but in most cases, some extra-record evidence will be necessary. This leaves the appellate court (even assuming the issue is raised) with two options: (1) to remand for a hearing at that time; or (2) to ignore the claim, rule on the other issues, and suggest to the defendant that he try another procedural route to have his claim heard. As a result, virtually all claims of inadequate representation are raised on collateral attack, and usually generate a hearing, at which the trial counsel is examined by defendant (or defendant's new counsel in those states that provide counsel in these proceedings). If the appellate process is lengthy, however, these hearings may occur several years after the trial, when memories have dimmed, witnesses have died, and a paper trail has grown cold (not to mention that defendant has been imprisoned for this time). Each of these factors, combined with the fact that trial counsel is seeking to protect his reputation, make more difficult the process of a true assessment of counsel's representation.

6. *Frivolous Appeals*

Counsel at trial (or during plea bargaining) are enjoined by ethical standards to be "fierce advocates." This may allow, or even require, that defense counsel proffer even the most extreme of claims. Once there is a conviction, however, the lawyer has an ethical obligation not to assert frivolous claims. In *Anders v. California*, 386 U.S. 738 (1967), the Supreme Court agreed that a defense counsel could withdraw from representing the defendant on appeal if he thought the appeal frivolous, so long as the defense counsel provided a brief referring to anything in the record that might support the appeal. In *McCoy v. Court of Appeals of Wisconsin*, 486 U.S. 429 (1988), the Court upheld a procedure which required the defense counsel to explain why the lawyer thought the contentions were frivolous. The Court reasoned that this would ensure that counsel had researched the relevant issues. Several states require counsel to follow through on appeal, even if the lawyer thinks the appeal is frivolous.

In *Jones v. Barnes*, 463 U.S. 745 (1983), the Court held that appellate counsel did not have to present a nonfrivolous claim that his client wished to press if the attorney believed that the better strategy was to limit his argument. *Jones*, however, did not resolve whether a strategic decision not to raise a claim urged by defendant would bar consideration of that claim on collateral attack, but many other cases have strongly suggested that review would be barred.

D. The Right to Self-Representation

It is often said that "the lawyer who represents himself has a fool for a client." Perhaps. But the Constitution protects the right to be a fool, even in capital cases. Our concern for the defendant's autonomy and dignity is so strong that we allow such a choice. The right of self-representation was specifically noted in various colonial and state constitutions and statutory provisions that established a right to counsel. In *Faretta v. California*, 422 U.S. 806 (1975), the Supreme Court, in holding that the trial court had improperly denied Faretta the right to represent himself, made clear that the Constitution protected this right (which has been declared by one commentator the "right to shoot oneself in the foot").[46] Justice Stewart, speaking for the Court in *Faretta*, relied heavily on the "structure of the Sixth Amendment," in particular, pointing out that the Amendment refers to the defendant's right to the "assistance" of counsel. This, said Stewart, indicated a desire to make counsel "like the other defense tools guaranteed . . . in aid to a willing defendant, not an organ of the State interposed between an unwilling defendant and his right to defend himself personally." At least seven times in the opinion, Justice Stewart spoke of protecting defendants from having counsel "forced" upon them.[47]

The waiver of the right to counsel, however, like all other waivers of constitutional rights, must be "voluntary and knowing." The courts have employed the general competency standard — whether the defendant has "sufficient present ability to consult with his lawyer with a reasonable degree of rational understanding." *Dusky v. United States*, 362 U.S. 402 (1960); *Godinez v. Moran*, 509 U.S. 389 (1993).

In *Iowa v. Tovar*, 124 S. Ct. 1379 (2004), the Supreme Court addressed the question of what a trial court should do when a defendant indicated he wishes to waive counsel and plead guilty. Tovar had appeared at several hearings in connection with a driving while intoxicated charge. On each occasion, the trial court explained that if Tovar pleaded not guilty, he would be entitled to be represented by an appointed attorney who could "help him select a jury, question and cross-examine the State's witnesses, present evidence, if any, on his behalf, and make arguments to the judge and jury on his behalf." Tovar chose to represent himself.

The Iowa Supreme Court found these admonitions insufficient to make Tovar's self-representation knowing, and instead required that every trial judge explicitly advise the defendant (a) that there are defenses to criminal charges that may not be known by laypersons and that the danger in waiving

---

46. Decker, The Sixth Amendment Right to Shoot Oneself in the Foot: An Assessment of the Guarantee of Self-Representation Twenty Years After Faretta, 6 Seton Hall Const. L.J 483 (1996); Sabelli and Leyton, Train Wrecks and Freeway Crashes: An Argument for Fairness and Against Self-Representation in the Criminal Justice System, 91 J. Crim. L. & Criminology 161 (2001). Chief Justice Burger, dissenting in *Faretta*, decried the result: "The system of criminal justice should not be available as an instrument of self-destruction." 422 U.S. 806, 840.

47. 422 U.S. 806, 815, 817, 820, 825, 833, 834.

the assistance of counsel in deciding whether to plead guilty is the risk that a viable defense will be overlooked; (b) that by waiving his right to an attorney he will lose the opportunity to obtain an independent opinion on whether, "under the facts and applicable law, it is wise to plead guilty." The Supreme Court unanimously held that those two, specific, "rigid," admonitions were not required by the Sixth Amendment. The Court distinguished earlier cases concerned with self-representation at trial, on the ground that "the full dangers and disadvantages of self-representation . . . are less substantial and more obvious to an accused than they are at trial." (Quoting *Patterson v. Illinois*, 487 U.S. 285, 299 (1988)).

The precise reach of *Tovar* is not yet clear. The opinion was short, and the unanimity suggests that its holding really should be construed merely as rejecting the explicit and "rigid" guidelines set out by the Iowa Supreme Court.

Even if there are no "Miranda warnings" which a judge must expressly and rigidly provide during either a guilty plea decision or before a defendant represents herself at trial, good policy at least requires that a trial court should:[48]

- ascertain that defendant is aware of the various matters noted in the *Von Moltke* case;[49]
- take special care to advise the defendant as to the pitfalls of self-representation;
- inform defendant that "presenting a defense is not a simple matter of telling one's story," but requires adherence to various "technical rules";
- be sure defendant understands that a lawyer has substantial experience and training in trial procedure and that the prosecution will be represented by an experienced attorney, and that a person unfamiliar with legal procedures may allow the prosecutor an advantage by failing to make objections to inadmissible evidence;
- be sure that defendant understands that there may be possible defense of which counsel would be aware;
- emphasize that a defendant proceeding *pro se* will not be allowed to complain on appeal about the competency of his representation;
- inform the defendant that the dual role of attorney and accused may undercut his defenses.

The trial court should "individualize" to determine the extent to which defendant really understands the issues. This record will assist the appellate court once an appeal is taken (which of course is almost sure to follow a

---

48. For a list of specific, suggested questions, as well as an analysis of pre-*Tovar* law, see Moskovitz, Advising the *Pro Se* Defendant: The Trial Court's Duties under *Faretta*, 42 Brandeis L.J. 329, esp. 344-345, n.52 (2003-2004).

49. *Von Moltke v. Gillies*, 332 U.S. 708 (1948), discussed *supra*, nn.23, 25.

conviction). These procedures, however, have not yet been held to be constitutionally required; they are the consensus of appellate court decisions, court
rules, or statutes seeking to provide guidance for the trial court confronting
this dilemma.

There are three possible grounds for denying the request for self-representation:

1. *Timing.* The request in *Faretta* was made "well before the date of trial";
   a late request might be so disruptive of orderly proceedings that it
   would be disallowed.
2. *Defendant's behavior.* If the defendant has been, or becomes, obstreperous and obstructionist, counsel, or standby counsel, may be appointed
   to return civility to the trial process.
3. *Lack of intelligence.* If the trial judge finds that the defendant truly is
   not able to make a knowing waiver. But in such a case, there might be
   question as to his competence to assist in his own defense.[50]

Even if a trial judge feels compelled to recognize the *Faretta* right, she is
not totally powerless to leave the arrogant, but clearly capable, defendant totally
in the lurch. She may appoint a "standby counsel" to assist the self-representing
defendant. Although these counsel are to be "advisors" only, and may not
"direct" the defendant. They may provide legal, or even tactical, advice if
requested to do so by the defendant[51]. A variation of the "standby counsel" is
"hybrid representation," with defendant or the attorney speaking for the
defense during different phases of the trial. Courts have been leery of allowing
this kind of procedure, in part because it becomes unclear whether the defendant is in fact representing herself, or being represented by counsel. See
Colquitt, Hybrid Representation: Standing the Two-Sided Coin on Its Edge,
38 Wake Forest L. Rev. 55 (2003). This reticence is not unreasonable, but it
does seem inconsistent with the fairly persuasive semantic argument that the
Sixth Amendment protects the defendant's right to "assistance" of counsel.

---

50. Colin Ferguson, accused of shooting 19 individuals on the Long Island Railroad
(killing six), insisted on self-representation, in large part because he did not accept his
appointed counsel's strategy of relying on an insanity defense. During his (nationally
televised) trial, Ferguson, at one point, argued that the original counsel was part of a
conspiracy to prevent him from identifying the real murderer, whom, he said, must
have stolen his gun while he was asleep and did the shooting. See *Sabelli* and *Leyton*,
supra n.46.

51. Poulin, The Role of Standby Counsel in Criminal Cases: In the Twilight Zone of
the Criminal Justice System, 75 N.Y.U. L. Rev. 676 (2000). There is no right to
standby counsel, although better practice is to appoint one. See, e.g., Minn. R. Crim
P. 5.02. There is, indeed, no right to standby counsel even in death penalty cases,
although some courts have found failure to appoint such counsel to be an abuse of
discretion. See *People v. Bigelow*, 691 P.2d 994 (Cal. 1984); *People v. Gibson*, 556
N.E.2d 226 (Ill. 1990).

According to statistics of the Department of Justice, virtually no felony defendants availed themselves of the *Faretta* right in 1998, but 38 percent of federal misdemeanants did.[52]

Faretta calls into some question a long line of decisions that had held that the attorney, and not the client, can make various defense decisions on his or her own initiative, sometimes without even consulting the defendant. Other decisions, however, were in the exclusive control of the defendant (whether to plead guilty, whether to waive a jury, whether to testify). The Supreme Court has stated, in dictum or holding, that it is for the defendant to decide each of the following steps, sometimes referring to these as "fundamental" rights, without further explanation:

- plead guilty;
- waive jury;
- waive right to be present at trial;
- testify on his own behalf;
- forego an appeal.

Lower courts have added:

- right to attend important pre-trial proceeding (deposition, speedy trial hearing);
- right to a speedy trial;
- refusal to enter an insanity plea;
- decision to withhold a defense until the sentencing phase of a capital case;
- whether to waive a grand jury.

The overriding concern here is to protect the defendant's control over his own destiny; after all, as the Supreme Court stressed several times in *Faretta*, "It is (the defendant) who suffers the consequences if the defense fails," 422 U.S. 806, 819, 834.

On the other hand, the Supreme Court has indicated, in dictum or holding, that counsel has the ultimate authority in a host of decisions, most of them dealing with trial tactics. These include:

- obtaining dismissal of an indictment on ground of racial discrimination;
- striking an instruction;
- foregoing cross-examination;
- providing discovery to the prosecution.

Lower courts have added to this list as well:

- whether to exercise a peremptory challenge;

---

52. Department of Justice, Bureau of Justice Statistics, Defense Counsel in Criminal Cases 1 (N.C.J. 17903, 2000).

- whether to request a mistrial;
- whether to seek a change of venue;
- whether to seek a competency determination;
- choosing among different lines of defense;
- which witnesses to call (or not).

Of course, no list can be complete, because of the myriad of events which can occur at trial. (See the discussion of *Strickland*, supra.) And lower courts have often divided on specific "decisions" depending on occasion on the specific facts of the case. *Strickland* itself hinted at the division of labor, declaring that counsel has a duty "to consult with the defendant on *important decisions and to keep the defendant informed in the course of the prosecution.*" (Emphasis added). The terms above in italics strongly suggest (though they do not "hold") that counsel does not have to consult about *every* decision, and may make decisions during the course of the case about which he will inform his client at a later point.

There is some suggestion that the Court's imprimatur on the right to self-representation may have recently waned. In *Martinez v. Court of Appeals of California*, 528 U.S. 152 (2000), the Court held unanimously that the *Faretta* right does not extend to appeals. In the course of so doing, the Court seemed to be unenthusiastic about its decision in *Faretta*.

EXAMPLES

1. After a jury trial, in which the defendant's background and child abuse was highlighted, defense counsel presents no evidence at the capital sentencing stage; his only summation is as follows:

   "Ladies and Gentlemen. I appreciate the time you took deliberating; the thought you put into this. I'm going to be extremely brief. I have a reputation for not being brief. Jesse, stand up.
   The Defendant: Sir?
   Counsel: Stand up. You are an extremely intelligent jury. You've got that man's life in your hand. You can take it or not. That's all I have to say."
   Is this ineffective counsel?

2. Gerry, charged with grand larceny, hires Dudley to represent him. He gives Dudley a $10,000 "up front" retainer, with a promise of $30,000 more. By the middle of the trial, and at the start of what promised to be a two-week defense presentation of witnesses, Dudley has asked Gerry on three separate occasions to pay his bill. Gerry keeps postponing the due date. Dudley asks the judge to allow him to withdraw, but is denied. Thereafter, Dudley calls three witnesses, who testify in one day. Gerry ultimately brings a claim of ineffective assistance of counsel during collateral attack. What standard should be used by the collateral attack court?

3. Lileth has been convicted of three counts of bank robbery. Before her trial began, she noticed that very few of the potential jurors were women. She mentioned this to her counsel, Helen Brown, but Helen told her "not to worry; let's just get on with this." As it turned out, only one of the actual jurors was a woman. After her conviction and appeal, Lileth learned that the process for establishing a jury wheel in the county had been declared invalid because it failed to secure sufficient women in the wheel. Does Lileth have a viable claim of inadequate representation by counsel?

4. Glenn Near was convicted of killing a bunny rabbit belonging to her lover's child. Her appointed counsel, Mike Kirk, remained silent as the prosecutor removed all nonparents off the jury with eight peremptory challenges. Can Glenn win a claim of inadequate assistance?

5. Johann is charged with burglary, punishable by 0-10 years, in an unstructured sentencing system. After his arrest, the police searched his car, which was in his driveway, without a warrant, and found a gun. That the search was warrantless, however, is nowhere recorded in the official police reports. Roberta, Johann's defense counsel, knows that the judge assigned to the case is particularly harsh in sentencing defendants who carry guns. She negotiates with the prosecutor so that there will be no reference to the gun in any official document. The gun is not mentioned, and Johann is sentenced to four years. Later, Johann's newly appointed counsel, Debbie, finds dead-on precedent that clearly leads to the conclusion that the gun would surely have been suppressed had Roberta made such a motion. Has Debbie demonstrated inadequate assistance of counsel?

6. Martha, a vice president in a stock brokerage firm, has been involved in a conspiracy with other executives to artificially inflate the price of certain stocks. At a cocktail party, a junior associate warns her that "the feds have been sniffing around." The next day, Martha contacts Ramin, the U.S. Attorney, who offers to indict her for one count, carrying a five-year maximum, on the condition that Martha cooperates fully. Ramin assures her that this is a good deal, but urges her to consult counsel. Martha does so. The lawyer, Jonathan Periwinkle III , fails to call Ramin, or investigate in any way the facts of the charges. He advises Martha not to accept the offer. Later, Martha is charged with 35 counts of securities fraud, and receives a twenty-year sentence. Ineffective assistance of counsel?

7. Georgia has been indicted on 10 counts of drug possession. When she was arrested, her retained counsel, Burger Kemp, was in her office, and accompanied her to the police station, where she was booked. The police officers at the station were not authorized to set bail, and because the courts were closed, Georgia spent the evening as the guest of the

state. The next morning she arrived at her initial appearance. But Burger was nowhere to be seen. She asked the judge to delay her case until Burger arrived. She even tried, twice, to reach Burger on her cell phone. She was told he was "on his way." "Time, tide, and this court wait for no one," bellowed the judge, who proceeded to set bail at $5,000,000, noting that Georgia had her own private jet, and was facing a possible 50 years imprisonment. Rather than arguing that she was not an escape risk, Georgia merely protested her innocence of the charges, believing that that was the issue before the court. She didn't make the $5,000,000, and spent the next week in jail, before Burger was able to move (successfully) for a lower bail, which she made. Was Georgia inadequately represented at the bail hearing, such that she could raise such a claim if she's convicted?

8. Alejandro has been charged with several drug offenses. He offers to cooperate with the U.S. Attorney's offer, and is told that if he cooperates fully, he may be given a "cooperation letter" under the Sentencing Guidelines, which would allow the sentencing judge to "depart" from the guideline sentence to which he would otherwise be exposed. (See Chapter 11). Alejandro meets with the U.S. Attorney several times but his attorney is never there. Alejandro provides some information, and even wears a wire to one meeting with a drug supplier, which leads to that supplier's arrest. At sentencing, the government indicates that while Alejandro did cooperate, they do not believe the cooperation was substantial enough to warrant a "departure motion." May Alejandro complain of ineffective assistance of counsel?

9. Kafir has pled guilty to several drug offenses. He is contacted by the probation officer, Meredith Wilson, for an interview to establish facts which will be communicated in Wilson's "pre-sentence report" to the judge (see Chapter 11). Kafir asks his lawyer, Jackie Moran, to accompany him, but Jackie does not show up. Is this inadequate assistance of counsel?

10. (a) Remo, a first time home buyer, goes to Fabian, an attorney, for some legal advice on how to finance the transaction. He follows Fabian's advice, which turns out not only to be wrong, but results in charges of fraud. Nevertheless, not understanding the connection between the advice and the criminal charges, Remo hires Fabian to represent him. The case law provides for a defense to fraud charges of "reliance on advice of counsel." Fabian urges Remo to plead guilty. Nothing is said at the allocution about Fabian's advice. If Fabian is aware of this defense, but does not tell Remo, can Remo successfully claim inadequate representation if convicted?

(b) Same facts, but Fabian is unaware of the possible defense.

11. Ludwig discovers, after he has been convicted of burglary in a jury trial presided over by Judge Marvin Atwater, that his appointed counsel had,

several months previously, testified against Judge Atwater in an ethics investigation, and that a preliminary report sustaining the charges against the judge had issued only a week prior to Ludwig's trial. Ineffective assistance?

12. Harlow is charged with shoplifting, a misdemeanor that carries a maximum penalty of one year. The judge tells him that, even if convicted, as a first offender he will not be sentenced to jail. Nevertheless, concerned that, if convicted, he could lose his job and benefits, he hires Moishe. After he is convicted, Harlow discovers that there was a video recording of him at his workstation, at the exact time the shoplifting occurred. Harlow told Moishe that he was at work, and that several people saw him there. May he successfully claim ineffective assistance? [Harlow was sentenced to probation.]

13. On the day of trial defendant, Miller Azinger, complains that he cannot communicate with his counsel, and asks you, the judge, to appoint a new attorney. Otherwise, he says, he will defend himself. What do you do?

EXPLANATIONS

1. Not in the Fifth Circuit. In *Romero v. Lynaugh*, 884 F.2d 871 (5th Cir. 1989), the appellate court reversed a district court conclusion that "the decision not to present any argument at the sentencing phase" was so "patently unreasonable" as to "constitute a deficiency. . ." The court considered the summation a "dramatic ploy" which did not "fall off the constitutional range." Perhaps. But perhaps before such a "dramatic ploy," counsel should have reminded the jury, if not through argument, then through witnesses, of the possible mitigating factors.

2. This would seem like the prototypical case where an attorney has a conflict of interest. He wishes to be paid, his client hasn't paid, and he thereafter "walks through" the case. It might appear that this should apply the *Cuyler* standard on the presumption of prejudice, and that the *state* will have to demonstrate no "adverse effect." But a number of courts have held that some personal interests of counsel should be judged not by the "automatic" prejudice approach of *Cuyler*, but by the looser standards of *Strickland*. See, e.g., *United States v. O'Neil*, 118 F.3d 65 (2d Cir. 1997). In that event, Dudley is entitled to a "strong presumption" that he acted not from a conflict, but from Gerry's best interest. Gerry will have to carry the burden of proof on both poor performance and on prejudice. If Dudley can explain his change of trial strategy, perhaps by arguing that he thought the prosecution case so weak that he did not wish to give the prosecution more opportunities than necessary, Gerry will be hard-pressed to win his claim.

3. First things first. As we saw in Chapter 8, there is no right to a cross-section of the community on the actual petit jury, so Helen was correct in not challenging the jury that tried Lileth. But there is a need for cross-section on the wheel, and the state did not provide that here. The law on the issue was very clear when Lileth was tried. If Helen simply didn't know the law, there may be a challenge on ineffectiveness grounds. But if Helen knew the law, and simply thought it wasn't worth delaying the trial while the state revamped its jury selection process, the court may be more than willing to assume that this was a strategic decision, rather than an incompetent one. At least that's what the Supreme Court did in *Tollett v. Henderson*, 411 U.S. 258 (1973).

4. This is a toughie. In cases where the error has resulted in a "structural" effect upon the trial, such as a wrongful denial of a change of venue, or a rejection of a challenge to jury composition, appellate courts, somewhat along the lines of the harmless error doctrine (see Chapter 12), have imposed a "*per se*" automatic reversal rule, because it is simply impossible to know what would have happened in a different (proper) venue or a properly representative jury. But those cases involved wrong decisions by trial courts, not by defense counsel. Moreover, while the prosecutor's tactic is obvious, it is not even clear that parents are a "cognizable group" under the Sixth Amendment, much less a "suspect class" under the Fourteenth. (See Chapter 8.) If, by some chance, all the parents had been males, Kirk might have had a *Batson* claim. In short, if there was no legal basis to protest the prosecution's actions, then there was no inadequate assistance. And, even if there was ineffective assistance, some courts would apply an automatic reversal requirement, while others would demand that the defendant show prejudice.

5. Unlikely. First, it is not clear that Roberta's decision not to pursue the suppression motion was not trial strategy, to which courts almost always defer. If Roberta was simply unaware of the case (rather than misread it, or thought it still unlikely that the gun would be suppressed), Johann may have a better chance. Courts are less indulgent of mistaken errors as to the law, than they are as to mistaken trial tactics. On the other hand, in *Strickland* itself, the trial counsel had taken the tack he did because of what he believed were the judge's individual sentencing idiosyncrasies. While many lawyers consider precisely such facts, the *Strickland* court abjured assessing reasonableness on the basis of such individual traits; the test would be whether a defense counsel, scheduled to appear before an unknown judge, would have done what Roberta did. So there may be an argument of inadequacy here, but that's only the first step. Even if the collateral review court would conclude that Roberta's performance was inadequate, Johann must still show prejudice. In a widely discretionary system, this will be difficult at best. He

was, after all, guilty of the burglary. And the court could have sentenced him to the same four-year term even if the gun had been suppressed (indeed, the best evidence of this is that the court DID sentence him to four years without knowledge that there was a gun). Moreover, the gun was not even an element of the crime; it was purely an "independent" fact. Debbie will have to argue that, had the gun been suppressed, Roberta might have been able to achieve a better plea; perhaps reducing the charge to "unlawful entry," which carries a maximum of two years. But this is, of course, highly speculative, and courts don't like to speculate this much in seeking prejudice.

6. The right to effective assistance of counsel begins only when the right to counsel begins, when there is a formal initiation of judicial proceedings. This is a bright line test. Thus, no matter how ineffective Jonathan was, his ineffectiveness is irrelevant under the Sixth Amendment. He may be the subject of disciplinary proceedings, and possibly even a legal malpractice suit but Martha is going to spend many long years decorating her jail cell.

7. As in example 6, Georgia has no claim. First, while this is a "no counsel" case which appears to fall under *Powell*, a bail hearing is not, as a federal constitutional matter, a *"critical stage"* at which there is a right to counsel. And only eight states have expressly provided, as a matter of statute or decisional law, that there is such a state-granted right. Where there is no right to counsel, there can be no constitutionally ineffective counsel. And the lack of counsel at a first bail hearing does not violate due process, which obtains primarily at trial. But even if we assume that there was inadequate counsel, Georgia must show prejudice to her case. Although, as we saw in Chapter 2, persons who are not released on bail fare worse, both in terms of acquittals and lower sentences, than those who are released, and although that *may* be due to their inability to vigorously pursue their own defense, a one-week hiatus in such a pursuit is unlikely to be found to have prejudiced Georgia in her case (unless a key witness—whom Georgia believes would have fully exonerated her —died in the interim, and even here she could have instructed Burger to interview that witness first). Burger may well have been ineffective, and he may well be fired. But his performance, however harmful, did not prejudice Georgia's trial and while the judge's refusal to hold off on setting Georgia's bail until Burger arrived was crude, and perhaps contemptible, there was no violation of Georgia's constitutional rights. But she's had the experience of being in jail for a week. Maybe she can write a book.

8. Yes. The right to competent counsel applied to the postconviction, presentence period as well, *United States v. Leonti*, 323 F.3d 1111 (9th Cir. 2003), particularly where defendant might obtain a government motion suggesting that the court depart downward because of defendant's

cooperation with the government. A critical stage is a trial-like confrontation, "in which potential substantial prejudice to the defendant's rights inheres and in which counsel may help avoid that prejudice." *Beaty v. Stewart*, 303 F.3d 975, 991-992 (9th Cir. 2002). The essence of a "critical stage" is not its formal resemblance to a trial, but the adversary nature of the proceeding, combined with the possibility that a defendant will be prejudiced in some significant way. The profound effect a substantial assistance motion can have on a defendant's sentence qualifies the cooperation period as a "critical stage" of the criminal process. In *Leonti*, the court remanded for a hearing: "Should the hearing provide evidence that a drug deal could have been arranged with the competent assistance (of defendant's attorney), there is ample reason to think that the government would have recommended a downward departure, given its demonstrated interest in Leonti's information." There is another aspect to this case as well. As noted in Chapter 7, most plea arrangements are now in writing; certainly an arrangement for cooperation should be spelled out in as much detail as possible, so that each side, and the judge, may determine whether the terms for "cooperation" were met. An attorney is essential to spelling out those details in a written agreement.

9. No. Most courts hold that an interview such as this is not a "critical stage" of the criminal process, in large part because the proceeding is not seen as adversarial. If it is not a critical stage, there is no right to effective assistance; Meredith's absence may be unethical, but it does not render her assistance ineffective. See *United States v. Gordon*, 4 F.3d 1567 (10th Cir. 1993), see also *United States v. Tisdale*, 952 F.2d 934 at 939-940 (6th Cir. 1992) (holding that because the probation officer "does not act on behalf of the prosecution," a presentence interview is not a critical stage); *United States v. Jackson*, 886 F.2d at 844 ("A federal probation officer is an extension of the court and not an agent of the government."); *Brown v. Butler*, 811 F.2d 938, 941 (5th Cir. 1987) and *United States v. Washington*, 11 F.3d 1510, 1517 (10th Cir. 1993); *United States v. Bounds*, 985 F.2d 188, 194 (5th Cir. 1993); *United States v. Johnson*, 935 F.2d 47, 50 (4th Cir.1991).

10. (a) This is clearly a case of conflict of interest. Aside from possibly ending up in a malpractice law suit, or a disciplinary hearing, Fabian is simply not likely to want anyone to know of the (mis)advice he has given the client. And since there are few instances where advice of counsel is a relevant claim (see Singer and Lafond, Criminal Law Examples and Explanations, Chapter 5 (3d ed. 2004)) for a more detailed analysis), it might never occur to the court, at allocution, that this would be a possible avenue to pursue. Twenty years ago, this case would have been assessed under *Cronic*, perhaps resulting in an automatic

reversal, or at least a hearing. See *United States v. Taylor*, 139 F.3d 924 (D.C. Cir. 1998). But after *Mickens*, it is possible that the court will apply *Strickland*. Even if Fabian's failure is ill-motivated and is poor practice, the Court might decide that Fabian's overall performance did not sink below the *Strickland* norm. This leaves aside entirely whether, after *Mickens*, the new standard for "harm" is still whether the conflict "adversely affected' the presentation of the case (which it almost surely did) or whether defendant must now show that it reached the level of prejudice.

(b) Extraordinarily enough, Remo may have a better case here than in the first example. Courts have generally treated lack of knowledge of the law as much more serious than most other errors. And many have shown a greater willingness to find prejudice where a possible legal argument was not made because counsel was unaware of the law.

11. Apparently not — at least in New York. In *Frase v. McCary*, 2003 WL 57919 (N.D.N.Y. 2003), the court held that defendant had not articulated any plausible alternative defense strategy that his counsel might have pursued. There is nothing in the opinion that considers the possibility that the "alternative strategy" might have been asking the judge to recuse himself, or have the case reassigned.

12. Not successfully. Since there was no possibility of jail, there was no right to be represented by counsel. And if there was no right to counsel, there was no right to effective assistance of counsel. And any Fifth Amendment right to effective counsel argument that, even though there was no *RIGHT* to counsel, he sufficiently relied upon counsel, who was empowered by the state to represent him, that the state should not gain by Moishe's reliance, will fall on deaf ears. If, on the other hand, the trial judge had observed clearly incompetent conduct by Moishe, perhaps the complaint *now* would be that the trial judge should have interceded. But that is not this case. Too bad Harlow. Hope you find a good job.

13. Pray. Defendants in high profile trials often want to represent themselves. In the case of the Unabomber, Ted Kaczynski, the trial court found that at least six weeks in advance of the trial, Kaczynzki had known that he had an irreconcilable conflict with his attorneys about whether to claim mental instability. Since Kaczynski waited until the first day of trial to move for their removal, and to represent himself, the trial court concluded the only reason for the request was to delay the proceedings. *United States v. Kaczynski*, 239 F.3d 1108 (2000), rehearing denied, 262 F.3d 1034 (9th Cir. 2001), *cert denied*, 535 U.S. 933 (2002). Kaczynski ultimately pled guilty. But as the trial judge here, you may not get that luxury. You will have to assess whether Miller is competent to defend himself. And if you find that he is, you must allow him to do so.

Although there is no magic list of questions you should ask, you should try some suggested in the text, or in the Moskovitz article, cited in footnote 48. Remember that *Tovar* may not apply here at all, because this is a trial, not a guilty plea. Miller may be running into a hornet's nest, but assuming your inquiry is sufficiently probing, you must, under *Faretta*, recognize his right to eschew lawyers. You should, however, also appoint a standby counsel. This may create headaches for you, but it's better than having a conviction reversed at a later time.

11

Sentencing

FIRST WARNING. No field of criminal procedure is more in flux today than sentencing. In June 2004, the United States Supreme Court decided *Blakely v. Washington*, 2004 U.S. LEXIS 4573, which held unconstitutional, as implemented, a state structured sentencing scheme virtually identical to the federal sentencing guidelines. The decision threw into doubt all the structured schemes which had been embraced by at least ten states, as well as that of the federal system, each of which is discussed in section E, below. Within three weeks of *Blakely*, the Court granted expedited certiorari in two cases, collectively known as *United States v. Booker*, to determine whether *Blakely* applied to the federal system. Argument in those cases was heard on the first Monday in October, on an accelerated schedule. The publication of this book was delayed for several months, awaiting a decision by the United States Supreme Court in *Booker*, but when, by mid-December 2004 the Court had not issued an opinion, the decision was made to publish this book without that opinion BUT to comment at length on the possible outcome of that case, and the potential impacts it will have in sentencing across the country. It is *possible*, but only barely, that the Court will not invalidate at least the way in which the federal (and similar state) guidelines are implemented; a major issue will be the "severability" of the federal provisions. If, as expected, *Booker* does invalidate the guidelines, in whole or in part, that decision could throw constitutional doubts on much of the material discussed in this chapter. Section G will explore the possible reactions which courts or legislatures, including Congress, may take to totally revamp their sentencing processes. Whether this rethinking will occur quickly, or be prolonged, every reader should be alert to the possibility that massive changes are underway in sentencing. We will try to suggest some paths the legislatures may take, but those are mere hunches; obviously you will have to read the daily advance sheets to update some of these materials.

Moreover, even if *Booker* does not invalidate the federal system on constitutional grounds, there was great unease about current sentencing in the United States—the American Bar Association had proposed drastic revisions of sentencing schemes, and the American Law Institute (promulgator of the Model Penal Code) seemed headed in the same direction. It is possible that some legislatures may seize these proposals and enact them in toto.

In the midst of this maelstrom, every student of sentencing must understand, in depth, the historical background against which current sentencing change is occurring, as well as the policy choices that are generally available to legislative bodies. In litigation, for example, one major issue is the extent to which earlier precedents, written when substantially different systems and sentencing philosophies were in place, are now binding, or even persuasive.

A. The Importance of Sentencing Law — An Introduction

Few things are more important to the defendant, even before conviction, than the possible length of incarceration she faces if convicted. But, far less obviously, the sentencing structure of a jurisdiction is also crucial in ascertaining the real impact of substantive criminal law.[1]

Although we commonly refer to a judge as "sentencing" a defendant, at least five separate institutions may be involved in making actual determinations of sentence duration: (1) the legislature; (2) the prosecutor; (3) the fact finder; (4) the sentence imposer (usually but not always a judge); (5) corrections officials. Depending on the particular sentencing structure established by the legislature, each of the last four, sequentially, may have the right, or the power, or both, to affect the "sentence" imposed on a given defendant—and each earlier actor, aware of this subsequent power, acts with that knowledge. Any sentencing scheme, therefore, may be one of "multiple discretions." Zimring, Making the Punishment Fit the Crime: A Consumer's Guide to Sentencing Reform, 12 Occasional Papers of the University of Chicago Law School (1977).

The legislature controls the formal articulation of both the definitions of crimes, and the punishment structure as well. The prosecutor chooses among the possible crimes and thereby affects (or may affect) the potential sentence, depending on the sentencing structure. Fact finders may refuse to find aggravating (or mitigating) circumstances, thus convicting the defendant of a lesser (or greater) crime. Corrections officials may affect "good

---

1. For example, if the sentences for murder and manslaughter are exactly the same, the careful parsing of homicide doctrines becomes suspect, if not irrelevant, in the real world.

time," and parole boards will determine whether the offender will be released prior to the expiration of his sentence.

Prosecutorial charging discretion can set the outer limits of punishment. If, for example, the prosecution charges assault, and only assault, in what appears to be a first degree murder, the defendant's exposure is limited to the potential sentence for assault. This, of course, is the grist of the plea bargaining mill. (See Chapter 7). Since, as we have seen in Chapter 3, the charging decision is essentially unreviewable by a Court in the common law, not even the most "determinate" system of sentencing restricts this discretion.

We often ignore the sentencing power of fact finders (we will often use the term jury to refer to this function, but keep in mind that almost half of "trials" are bench trials). In any system, the fact finder may, and often does, structure its verdict to accord with what it thinks the sentencing scheme will implement. Even if the prosecutor charges aggravated assault, the fact finder can either agree or, perhaps, find assault, or no crime; in many instances, it will be try to manipulate the facts in accord with what it anticipates will be the sentence it thinks "right."[2] After the fact finder has resolved this question, the sentence must be imposed.

1. Determinate Systems

On the surface, there is little discretion in a determinate system—the term of imprisonment is legislatively set. In a *totally determinate system*, the legislature sets the exact sentence, based upon the crime. For example: "Robbery shall be punished by six years in prison." Once the defendant is convicted, no other institution may affect the sentence; the judge must impose a six-year sentence, and that is what the defendant will serve; there is no parole, and no "good time." In a *totally determinate* sentencing scheme, therefore, the prosecutor sets the sentence, by establishing the (only) charge available, subject only to the jury's power of fact finding.

2. Indeterminate Systems

At the other end of the sentencing structure spectrum lies the *totally indeterminate* system. This structure establishes legislative punishments (1-5 years for larceny and 6-10 for robbery); the judge has no power to affect either the minimum nor maximum sentence; the minimum is mandatory, and the release date is determined solely by a releasing authority (parole board). Here again, however, there may be more (or less) than meets the

---

2. Except in capital sentencing, juries are not entitled to be informed, and usually are not informed, of any of the sentencing consequences of a particular conviction. That often does not prevent them from speculating on what the sentences might be not only for the charged crime, but also for various lesser included offenses.

eye. If the sentences for burglary and robbery overlap substantially, there will be significant discretionary points within the process. Indeed, if the sentences for larceny and robbery are the same (1-10 for each), the substantive criminal law differences between the two crimes become meaningless. This virtually occurred in some states during the middle twentieth century, when the governing philosophy was "individualization" and "rehabilitation." Even assuming that robbery was "generally" worse than larceny, the philosophy went, it might take more time to rehabilitate some thieves than some robbers. A *totally* indeterminate system (0-life for all crimes, however defined) would, on its face, remove all prosecutorial and judicial discretion on the sentence imposed.

Beyond this point, there is still much variation. In some so-called "indeterminate" systems, the sentence imposer has discretion to decide on either a *determinate* point within the range (e.g., three years for larceny in the above system), or to establish a shorter *range* (2-4) with the larger legislative range; in others there is no such discretion. Once the initial sentence has been established, however, it becomes subject to the indeterminacy possibilities outlined in the section above.

In an indeterminate system, someone must decide when to release the prisoner. But even in many determinate systems, there is some further sentencing power. Suppose, in a totally determinate scheme, Edwina is charged with burglary, and the statute declares, "Burglars shall be punished with 10 years in prison." If the jury convicts of burglary, Edwina's going to serve 10 years, the whole 10 years, and nothing but the 10 years, right? Wrong. Very wrong. Possibly very, very, very wrong. Once that determinate sentence has been imposed, the game, far from being over, may have just begun. Even if the *judge* has no discretion to sentence Edwina to less than 10 years, there may still be a wide range of indeterminancy remaining. Most obvious is the decision, made by a "parole board," whether to release the defendant before her maximum sentence had been served, on condition of good behavior in the community. Moreover, a correctional authority may also affect the actual eligibility date for parole or, at least, inform the parole board whether it believes the prisoner has in fact behaved well.

The mathematics here, while apparently simple, can be incredibly complex. Thus, a state legislature might provide for parole eligibility at one-half the defendant's sentence. For a 10 year sentence, that would appear to be five years. If so, then the defendant's "determinate" 10-year sentence becomes an "indeterminate" 5-10, depending on the parole board's decision. But legislatures also frequently provided for various "good time credits," to discourage particularly bad behavior during incarceration. If Edwina receives 20 months off her sentence for "good behavior," then Edwina's effective maximum sentence would be reduced to eight years, four months (assuming she receives the maximum good time), and her "real sentence" would appear to be reduced to five (earliest parole eligiblity) — 8 1/3 years (maximum sentence less good time, even if she is not paroled).

But now a further wrinkle — in many states, either legislatively or administratively, the "sentence" is immediately reduced by the full amount of good time (even though, of course, it had not been yet "earned" by actual good behavior). *Now* if the "one-half sentence" applies to parole eligibility, Edwina's sentence is four years, two months (half of the eight years, four months she will serve assuming good time) — 10 years (the maximum sentence if she receives no good time, and no parole). Let's go further. Assume that (as in many states) any maximum may be reduced by X months for good behavior, X months for extraordinary good time, and X months for extraordinary cooperation. If each of the good time periods is 20 months, Edwina can earn a total of 60 months good time. The 120-month (10 year) maximum has now shrunk to an *effective* 60 months (assuming no good time is "revoked" — if the prisoner loses good time, the 10 year maximum sentence still remains intact). But since, by statute, the defendant is eligible for parole release at one-half of her maximum sentence, her sentence now becomes 2 ½ (half the five year sentence she will serve if she receives all the good time credit) — 10 years, depending on whether (a) any of her good time is revoked; (b) whether and when the parole board decides to release. To complicate matters even further, some jurisdictions provided for "presumptive" parole release at a defendant's first eligibility.

To many observers this sounded like a shell game; in the past 20 years or so, under a title something like the "Truth in Sentencing Act," 12 states (and the federal system) have either abolished parole, or severely limited parole eligibility (particularly for violent offenders). But no state has eliminated entirely correctional good time — the argument has been that corrections officials need some incentive to discourage bad behavior within the prisons.

In short, while in theory determinate and indeterminate sentence systems are polar opposites, most systems have aspects of the other. The critical question is who has discretion, and the degree to which that discretion is subject to alteration by some institution later in the chain. As we examine the sweeping changes that appear to have occurred in the past two decades in this country, keep looking for that hidden needle of discretion; it may actually be a pitchfork.

B. Theories of Punishment and Sentencing

If you don't know what you're trying to achieve, you can't determine whether you're succeeding. Assessing sentencing schemes, therefore, requires at least a quick review of the purposes of punishment.[3] The utilitarian goals of

---

3. For a longer discussion, see Singer and LaFond, Criminal Law; Examples and Explanations, Chapter 2 (3d ed. 2004).

incapacitation and rehabilitation are only achievable if the criminal is held until the goal has been achieved. Thus, a full-blown system of either of these would have a truly indeterminate sentence — to life — for virtually every crime. Some method of assessing the prisoner's progress would be required.

Deterrence theory would be a bit different. That theory focuses not on the individual prisoner, but upon other possible criminals. As one reported colloquy put it:

> "(It) is very hard, my lord, said a convicted felon at the bar to the late excellent Judge Burnet, to hang a poor man for stealing a horse. You are not to be hanged, sir, answered my ever honoured and beloved friend, for stealing a horse, but you are to be hanged that horses may not be stolen."[4]

The punishment (discounted by the possibility of capture) threatened must be sufficiently severe to deter the *future* criminal. In theory at least, this cost-benefit analysis could be resolved mathematically, and there would be no need for anyone, judge or other official, to vary from a legislatively preset sentence.

Retribution focuses on the harm, and the mental culpability with which that harm was inflicted. The punishment inflicted must be proportionate to those factors. Assuming an ability to properly define the requisite harm and culpability levels, retributive sentencing schemes, like deterrent systems, could also be totally determinate.

Although neither incapacitation nor rehabilitation require proportionality as a restriction on sentencing, both deterrent and retributivist approaches to sentencing require that the punishment imposed be "proportionate" to the crime, though for different reasons. Proportionality is required for a deterrence theorist only insofar as we wish to deter criminals from committing greater crimes to avoid capture (punishing theft of a sheep with death might encourage thieves to kill their pursuers). A retributivist by definition may impose no more harm than the offender's act caused society; while this may be difficult to assess, it sets a limit on punishment which the other three do not. After several attempts, a majority of the Supreme Court appears now to have concluded that this requirement is included in the Eighth Amendment. *Harmelin v. Michigan*, 501 U.S. 957 (1991). The devil, however, is in the details — even the seven Justices in *Harmelin* who agreed there was such a principle disagreed both about the methodology to be employed in determining the proportionality of the sentence, and about how to apply the principle to a statute that established a life sentence without parole for a first-time possessor of 650 grams of cocaine (the sentence was upheld, because a plurality of this group, which held that the sentence was not disproportionate, was joined by two other Justices who found

---

4. As quoted in L. Radzinowicz, A History of English Criminal Law 411, n.40 (1957).

Table 11-1   Reflects these different purposes and possible sentencing structures:

PURPOSE	TYPICAL SENTENCE	SENTENCE DETERMINER
Rehabilitation	Highly indeterminate. 0-Life would be best, but some cap or minimum sentence might be tolerable.	Experts in human behavior; parole board.
Incapacitation	Same as Rehabilitation.	Same as Rehabilitation.
Deterrence	Proportionate sentences, but limited and channeled by scientific understanding of how much threat is needed to deter from this specific crime. Determinate.	Legislature, as aided by experts on deterrence.
Retribution	Proportionate sentences based on harm and mental state. Determinate	Legislature or other body reflecting community standards.

no such principle in the Amendment).[5] In its most recent decision on this point[6], dealing with recidivist legislation, the Court held that a sentence of 25 years to life was not unconstitutionally disproportionate for a person whose third offense was shoplifting several videotapes worth less than $300. *Ewing v. California*, 538 U.S. 11 (2003).

C. A Short History of Sentencing in the United States

Few sentencing schemes in history, and certainly none in the United States, has been a "pure" system of any of these theories. Each of these theories has been dominant at different times in our history. But even in the height of rehabilitation, for example, legislatures placed maximum caps upon the duration of punishment — recidivist jaywalkers, or even burglars, would rarely be subjected to a possible life (or death) sentence. Similarly, when retribution was the dominant theory, there were still possible methods by which a defendant could avoid the determinate sentence (e.g., probation).

---

5. Immediately after *Harmelin*, the Michigan Supreme Court declared the statutory sentence violated the *state* provision against cruel and unusual punishment. *People v. Bullock*, 440 Mich. 15,485 N.W.2d 866 (1992).

6. Another case, *not* involving aspects of federalism, held a forfeiture of $357,144 for failing to report that the defendant was carrying that amount of money outside the country *was* disproportionate to the offense. *United States v. Bajakajian*, 524 U.S. 321 (1998).

Prior to the American Revolution, incapacitation seemed to be the primary goal of punishment for felonies; the death penalty, the common sanction for any felony, assured that the defendant would not offend again. The only discretion lay in the jury's fact finding ability. While there is scant evidence of that power being exercised in this country, it is clear that English juries early in the nineteenth century commonly engaged in "pious perjury" so as to avoid imposing the death penalty upon many defendants. Thus, many juries determined the value of objects stolen to be 39 pence — because the distinction between grand (capital) larceny and petit (noncapital) larceny was 40 pence.

Almost immediately after the American Revolution, Quakers in Pennsylvania created a new form of punishment, incarceration. Not only did this limit the death penalty (to which the Quakers were opposed), but it provided the defendant with an opportunity to become penitent (hence the name penitentiary). Legislatures began enacting statutes with wide sentence ranges, so that the penitentiary could have time to work its magic. Within those ranges, in a substantial number of enthusiastically democratic states, juries, and not judges, set the sentence.[7]

By the end of the nineteenth century, jury sentencing declined, as criminal jurisprudence embraced a modified rehabilitative model of sentencing. If pure rehabilitative and individualized sentencing had been embraced, judges would simply have imposed an established legislative indeterminate range, allowing experts in the corrections system to determine when to release the prisoner. In practice, however, judges were usually empowered to establish the "first cut", first (for many offenses) by deciding whether to place a defendant on probation, and second by setting, within the indeterminate range, either a determinate term, or a shorter indeterminate range. Although this approach would be compatible with jury sentencing it was also believed that judges were (or could become after much experience with sentencing) more professional in determining what the "proper" range or specific sentence would be. Juries, who saw only one defendant, and were unfamiliar with most of the information upon which judges might rely, were seen as "nonprofessional" sentencers.

A system which allows at least some discretion to some institutional authority to consider variations in how crimes are actually committed is very

---

7. This is a slight overgeneralization. The prospect of a revival of jury sentencing (discussed in the text below) has generated significant revision of the story of jury sentencing in America. The most detailed examination thus far is Lillquist, The Puzzling Return of Jury Sentencing: Misgivings About Apprendi, 82 N.C.L. Rev. 621 (2004). Other outstanding works are: Iontcheva, Jury Sentencing As Democratic Practice, 89 Va. L. Rev. 311, 317 (2003); Wright, Book Review, 108 Yale L.J. 1355 (1999); Bowman, Fear of Law, 44 St. Louis L.J. 299, 311 (2000); Lanni, Jury Sentencing in Noncapital Cases: An Idea Whose Time Has Come (Again), 108 Yale L.J. 1875 (1999); Hoffman, The Case for Jury Sentencing, 52 Duke L.J. 951 (2003).

appealing; other systems may be attacked as "mechanical" or "rigid." As Aristotle noted more than two millennia ago, legislatures must, by definition, speak in terms of universals; they cannot (because language cannot) describe every detail which might be relevant in determining the "precisely right" punishment for a specific crime. As many critics argued, the thug who threatens a victim with a crow bar and the playground bully who obtains lunch money from a cowering third grader have both committed "robbery," but the circumstances of the two crimes seem relevant to assessing punishment. Only those who deal with the individual instance of the defined crime will see those nuances. This, at heart, was the engine behind the individualization movement.

A system of rehabilitation,[8] which seeks to "punish the criminal and not the crime," and which is essentially predictive, is based on a minute and complex assessment of the character of the defendant—whether he "needs" treatment, and if so what kind, and how long that treatment is "likely" to take. No information (not even the rankest hearsay) is necessarily irrelevant; the defendant's criminal record, charges against him which have not been pursued (or of which he has been acquitted), his employment record, and even whether he kicks cats, are all grist for the individualization mill. This information is provided by a "presentence report," prepared by a probation officer, trained in obtaining such information.

The high water mark of the individualization movement, and hence of judicial sentencing authority, was reached in *Williams v. New York*, 337 U.S. 241 (1949). A jury convicted Williams of first degree murder during a burglary, but recommended a life sentence. The judge, rejecting that recommendation, relied upon information in the presentence report, which asserted "many material facts concerning appellant's background which . . . could not properly have been brought to the attention of the jury," including 30 other burglaries which the police attributed to the defendant (although the defendant had not been convicted of any of these). The report also indicated that the appellant possessed "a morbid sexuality." The United States Supreme Court upheld the death sentence, and the process, declaring:

> A sentencing judge . . . is not confined to the narrow issue of guilty. His task . . . is to determine the type and extent of punishment after the issue of guilt has been determined. Highly relevant—if not essential—to his selection of an appropriate sentence is the possession of the fullest information possible concerning the defendant's life and characteristics. . . . (he should not be) denied an opportunity to obtain pertinent information by a requirement of rigid adherence to restrictive rules of evidence properly applicable to the trial. . . . To deprive sentencing judges of this kind of information would undermine modern penological polices that have been cautiously adopted throughout the nation after careful consideration and experimentation.

---

8. These observations also pertain to an incapacitative system—but the growth of the rehabilitative ideal really spurred this activity.

Williams reflects the general assumption, both for incapacitation and rehabilitation theories, that a defendant's past criminal record, including bad conduct even not resulting in conviction, is relevant in determining the sentence. Even if the defendant had been acquitted of an earlier alleged crime, sentencers were still allowed to consider such conduct. The rationale here is that the standard of proof in a criminal case, beyond a reasonable doubt, does not apply in sentencing procedures, and hence the conduct, if proved by a preponderance of the evidence, may still be considered by the sentencing judge. This facially outrageous result may be a bit more palatable when it is considered that a criminal trial may suppress much truth in search of other goals. The exclusionary rule, for example, in order to deter improper police behavior, prohibits the jury from knowing that the defendant has confessed in a totally believable manner to the crime charged, and has given details (for example, where the body is buried) that only the perpetrator would know. Under an individualizing sentence scheme such as that in *Williams*, however, the sentencing court may consider such evidence.

D. Procedures at Sentencing[9]

As *Williams* clearly held, throughout the reign of individualization and rehabilitation, the rules of evidence did not apply, lest the judge, seeking to impose the "right" sentence for the specific individual before her, not have sufficient information. Indeed, until the 1970s, this notion went further—because some of the information relied upon could only be obtained upon promises of confidentiality, defendants were not entitled to see that information. *United States v. Dockery*, 447 F.2d 1178 (D.C. Cir. 1971)[10] Moreover, since this information was collected over a period of time, the jury could not be asked to return, and the judge, rather than the jury, was to decide the proper sentence. And since this was not a criminal proceeding the criminal standard of proof (beyond a reasonable doubt) did not apply; the judge, using her fully informed judgment, would have to find any fact only by a preponderance of evidence. (Even this last statement is an exaggeration; since, as noted before, the sentences were not reviewable,

---

9. For a tour de force examining all these questions in detail, see Michaels, Trial Rights at Sentencing, 81 N.C. L. Rev. 1771 (2003).

10. In *State v. Pohlabel*, 61 N.J. Super. 242, 160 A.2d 647 (App. Div. 1960), defendant, convicted of stealing a checkbook and passing checks totaling approximately $1500, was given seven consecutive 3-5 year sentences. After eight years in prison, he learned that the probation officer had described him in the presentence report as a "master of deception" who had "spent the greater part of his life in penal institutions." In fact, the defendant had previously been convicted only once, as a juvenile. His case was remanded for resentencing. But there were many who never learned the contents of their presentence reports.

there was no official standard of proof; indeed, there was no requirement in most jurisdictions that there be any "findings of fact";[11] additionally, since the rules of evidence do not apply, it is somewhat misleading to use the term preponderance of the "evidence.")[12]

In recent years courts, in both their rule-making and adjudicatory functions, have begun to change these views. Thus, in *Gardner v. Florida*, 430 U.S. 349 (1977), the Court, effectively overruling the narrow holding of *Williams*, held that a defendant in the sentencing phase of a capital case was constitutionally entitled to see the prosecution's evidence. Although the Court explicitly restricted *Gardner* to capital cases, it has, in its supervisory function, provided in Rule 32(e)(2) and 32 (I) (A) for virtually full discovery of the presentence report in all cases, not merely capital. Recently, in *Burns v. United States*, 501 U.S. 129 (1991), the Court hinted that this right might be grounded in the due process clause, but because of Rule 32, did not have to reach this issue. And in *Mitchell v. United States*, 526 U.S. 314 (1999), the Court affirmed that the defendant retained the right to remain silent at sentencing, and that no adverse implications could be drawn from her silence. Virtually all states now provide that the defendant may see the report, although some portions maybe restricted as "confidential."

More important than specific holdings has been the change in attitude toward the process of sentencing. In *Mempa v. Rhay*, 389 U.SD. 128 (1967), the Court determined that, *for purposes of the Sixth Amendment right to counsel*, sentencing was a "critical stage" of a criminal proceeding. This was reaffirmed recently by the Court's declaration in *Mitchell, supra*, that "To maintain that sentencing procedures are not part of "any criminal case" is contrary to law and to common sense." Whether this may suggest that there is a right to a jury trial, (but see the discussion, below, of *Blakely*), or to direct confrontation of all those who submit information to the trial court, is unclear; the likelihood is that the courts will continue to hold that these rights do not obtain at sentencing.[13]

---

11. The common explanation for this was that it was impossible to articulate reasons for a specific sentence. See, e.g., *State v. Douglas*, 87 Ariz. 182 (1960). If sentencing was indeed "individualized" and "subjective," this explanation has some plausibility . Also, if the judge DID give reasons, the defendant might attempt (almost always unsuccessfully) to appeal on the grounds of irrationality. Judges learned never to give reasons, even from the bench.

12. A casebook on sentencing and prisoners' rights written by the present author included a cartoon in which the sentencing judge assesses the defendant's sentence by adding the wheelbase (98 inches) and length (175 inches) of the car he stole, multiplied by the number of wheels (4) to a sentence of 1092 days in the county jail.

13. This is not unusual: the Court has established different standards for triggering the right to jury and the right to appointed counsel, both guaranteed by the Sixth Amendment. See Chapters 8 and 10.

The move toward structured sentencing may require a new assessment of sentencing processes. As the cloud of mysticism created by the theory of individualization has been removed from sentencing by the embrace of rationally declared sentencing factors, the idea that sentencing is totally a subjective activity has diminished. Thus, for those states which continue to use largely indeterminate sentencing with wide discretion, the structured sentencing movement raises possible due process issues. So long as rehabilitation, or even incapacitation, were the dominant goals of sentencing, the contention that it was not possible, either at sentencing nor at parole release, to articulate the relevant factors was plausible. The ability of nearly 20 jurisdictions to articulate such factors, however, undercuts that argument and urges that there is no policy need to allow sentences to be imposed without a statement of reasons which could then be reviewed, for conformity with whatever goals the legislature has articulated. It is more difficult to contend that this is required by substantive or procedural due process, although at least some of the procedures which are now considered not constitutionally required at sentencing (for example, the right to see the presentence report and to present rebutting witnesses) might fall within those rubrics.

On the other hand, the Court has recently reaffirmed that, at least in the "run of the mill" sentencing process, the judge may use the "preponderance" standard in assessing facts which might increase a defendant's sentence. *Harris v. United States*, 536 U.S. 545 (2002). The Court had earlier declared itself agnostic as to whether a higher standard should be applied when the sentence was dramatically increased on the basis of specific evidence, *Jones v. United States* 526 U.S. 227 (1999), and the circuit courts are also split on this issue, several using the "clear and convincing evidence" standard where a sentence is doubled or more. Compare *United States v. Hopper*, 2177 F.3d 1999); *United States v. Kikumura*, 918 F.2d 1084 (3d Cir. 1990) (both using the higher standard) with *United States v. Mayle*, 334 F.3d 552 (6th Cir. 2003); *United States v. Cordoba-Murgas*, 233 F.3d 704 (2d Cir. 2000) (both using preponderance).

Sentencing is not unreasonably seen as an "administrative" process rather than as a criminal trial. It is not, therefore, unreasonable to allow the sentencer, as with other "administrative agencies," to consider hearsay, or suppressed evidence, so long as these are subject to vigorous challenge and cross-examination of the source. Consideration of conduct for which the defendant has not been charged, or for which she has been acquitted, is relevant if the purpose is to "individualize" sentences within the narrow ranges of structured sentencing (what Professor Huigens calls "interstitial" facts). But if sentencing is seen as retributivist, then the sentence must be based upon the crime, and not upon the defendant, and this evidence would seem irrelevant, and prejudicial.

Time will tell.

In summary, while there are few definitive holdings, the following abbreviated list of "trial rights at sentencing" reflects the likely situation today:

Table 11-2 Constitutional Rights and Sentencing

Clearly Applicable	Likely to Apply	Clearly Inapplicable or unlikely to Apply
Right to counsel and appointed counsel	Discovery	Right to jury trial*
Right to present evidence	Speedy hearing	Right to confrontation
Right to remain silent	Right to see relevant evidence	Rules of evidence (the Court may consider suppressed evidence,[14] hearsay,[15] acquitted conduct[16] and conduct which has not been charged)
Right to public resolution		Standard of beyond a reasonable doubt*
Right to allocution		Double jeopardy clause[17]

*But see *Apprendi* and *Blakely, infra.*

E. A Revolution in Sentencing— Structured Sentencing

The perceived problem with such a widely discretionary system was that the ranges were so broad that individual judges were implementing their own view of what was important in sentencing, and why sentences were imposed. One judge could use deterrence as a determining philosophy, while another might use rehabilitation. Moreover, one judge might see in a 20-year-old ghetto dweller with a long juvenile history a threat of a long and increasingly violent future, and sentence him to 20 years, whereas another might see the defendant as much as victim as perpetrator, and provide probation, or a "relatively short" period of incarceration.

Individualization and rehabilitation were discarded by a wide number of legislatures as operative philosophies during the 1970s and 1980s. Studies of

---

14. *United States v. Tejada*, 956 F.2d 1256 (2d Cir. 1992); *United States v. Tauil-Hernandez*, 88 F.3d 576 (8th Cir. 1996). The theory here is that whatever deterrent effect the exclusionary rule may have has already operated at trial. If, of course, the police have seized the evidence for the purpose of using it in sentencing, the result may be different. See *United States v. Kim*, 25 F.3d 1426 (9th Cir. 1994).

15. *Williams v. New York, supra.*

16. *United States v. Watts*, 519 U.S. 148 (1997).

17. *United States v. Witte*, 515 U.S. 389 (1995).

rehabilitation programs were, accurately or not, interpreted to say "nothing works." Philosophically, the notion of rehabilitation as a determining factor in the length of imprisonment was attacked by the Quakers (the original creators of the idea) who also argued that "unfettered discretion" in the hands of sentencing judges had led to blatant racial and economic[18] discrimination. American Friends Service Committee: Struggle for Justice (1972). The Quakers recommended that equality of sentencing could best be found by a determinate sentencing scheme, in which the crime, and not the defendant, was the focus. Four years after the Quakers, a call for a return to retribution as the key purpose of sentencing was well received. A. Von Hirsch: Doing Justice (1976). At the same time, many who thought that individualized sentencing had been too lenient, resulting in the premature release of convicts who thereafter recidivated, called for longer, incapacitative sentences, which could not be shortened by correctional officials. Finally, the entire notion of unreviewable discretion, was eloquently attacked by Judge Marvin Frankel, in a book entitled "Criminal Sentences":[19]

> The almost wholly unchecked and sweeping powers we give to judges in the fashioning of sentences are terrifying and intolerable for a society that professes devotion to the rule of law.

Today, although the majority of states retain indeterminacy to at least some degree, no state is entirely indeterminate. Moreover, a substantial movement, now supported by the American Bar Association and by at least a preliminary report of the American Law Institute,[20] has resulted in sweeping changes in almost half the states and in the federal government. This movement, though diverse in actual operation, has one primary objective — to reduce the perceived disparity in sentences by restricting the discretion of judges (and parole boards) in sentencing.

This dramatic alteration in theory and practice has undercut at least one premise of the traditional, indeterminate system — that it is not possible within some limits and accepting some variations — to articulate the relevant factors that most actors in the system (legislators, judges, experts, etc.) believe relevant, and to avoid the kind of disparity which wide indeterminacy allowed. Most systems now articulate the factors which most persons would concede are potentially relevant in determining punishment. Among these are: (1) whether a weapon was used (brandished, possessed); (2) the degree of involvement; (3) the amount of harm inflicted measured by loss of money or amount of drugs; (4) the degree of trust betrayed; (5) factors reducing,

---

18. Allegedly, white-collar workers were only rarely sentenced to prison; they did not need rehabilitation, and any necessary incapacitation usually occurred because they lost the positions which allowed them to commit their crimes.

19. M. Frankel , Criminal Sentences, p.5 (1973).

20. American Law Institute, Report, Model Penal Code: Sentencing (Apr. 11, 2003).

but not removing, moral culpability such as age, influence by a superior, etc., (6) perhaps 10 other factors. Whether these factors seem relevant, the structured sentencing movement has brought the debate into the open. Once these factors, and their impact upon sentence, have been agreed upon by a legislative body, the actual sentencer can fill in interstices within narrowly drawn ranges. For example, a legislature might declare that an assault carries a punishment of *X* plus or minus two months, leaving for the jury or judge the precise sentence, depending on whether there are variations on the facts which have not been clearly eliminated by the legislature.

A SECOND WARNING—As noted at the outset of this chapter, the *Blakely* and *Booker* decisions, discussed in detail in section G, may make the following discussion totally academic, in the pejorative use of that term. It is possible that *Blakely* makes any structured sentencing system unconstitutional, or that it may be read that way by legislatures and courts. On the other hand, as suggested in section G, it is at least plausible that the decision may also invalidate totally unstructured sentencing processes. Whatever the ultimate effects of *Blakely-Booker*, at this stage it is important to understand the structured sentencing movement and the different structures adopted in different jurisdictions.

1. *Mandatory Minimum Sentences*

There are many ways to remove, or reduce, discretion in sentencing. A full ban on plea bargaining (see Chapter 7), coupled with a fully determinate sentencing structure, and no parole or good time, would fully remove all discretion. But no state has yet adopted anything approaching such a sweeping rejection of discretion throughout the process. Virtually all states, however, have adopted at least one restriction on sentencing discretion—mandatory minimum sentences.[21]

Although some statutes simply establish a minimum sentence based upon the crime simpliciter (burglary carries a 3-10 sentence), many mandatory statutes depend upon the fact finder concluding that a certain fact is present. Thus, a defendant who commits burglary may face a maximum sentence of 10 years, which allows the sentencer to impose any sentence

---

21. By 1983, 49 states had passed some mandatory minimum provision; in 1984, and every two years thereafter, Congress enacted an array of mandatory minimum penalties specifically targeted at drugs and violent crimes. There are now over 60 federal criminal statutes that contain mandatory minimum penalties. U.S. Sentencing Commission, Mandatory Minimum Penalties in the Federal Criminal Justice System (1991). The Government Accounting Office in Oct. 2003 found that of 68,000 federal drug sentences imposed during 1999-2001, 41,000 carried a mandatory minimum term of imprisonment.

between 0-10 years; but if the fact finder concludes that the burglary was committed with a weapon, the sentence may be 5-10. The sentence imposer thus loses discretion to sentence to any term less than five years.

Most commentators (not to mention judges) oppose these statutes not only because they severely reduce the power of judges to individualize sentences but because (opponents argue) these statutes provide the prosecutor with greater bargaining power, by indicating a willingness to "ignore" the fact which triggers the minimum penalty in exchange for a plea. Proponents of these statutes contend that individualization must yield to a need for deterrence, and that persons contemplating crime who think they can otherwise obtain a light sentence (or probation) will rethink their possible crime if they know they face a definite term of imprisonment. Retributivists can also support these statutes, assuming the length of sentence is proportionate, by suggesting that the critical fact may reflect greater moral blameworthiness.

If mandatory minimum laws are primarily incapacitative, even more obviously aimed at incapacitation are statutes which provide a minimum sentence, usually quite long, for "recidivists." Recidivist (or "habitual offender") laws have existed since 1928, but today a sizable number of states have enacted so-called "three-strike" laws, which usually provide that a defendant who is now being convicted of a third predicate felony[22] will serve a specified minimum amount of incarcerative time (frequently 25 years) before being considered for parole.[23]

2. *The Disappearance of Parole Release*

The reaction to parole release, and good time, which often resulted in an offender serving less than 1/5 of his sentence in incarceration generated a move to abolish, or restrict, parole. This movement, dubbed "Truth in Sentencing," reflects the perceived public animosity toward a "bark and bite" system of criminal justice. Today, seven states have abolished parole entirely, while a much larger number effectively restrict it to nonviolent offenders The impact of good time, including in those states retaining parole, has also been dramatically transfigured. Virtually all states have adopted statutes providing that violent offenders (variously defined) must serve 85 percent of their sentence before being released even conditionally.

---

22. The statutes differ significantly. In California, for example, at least one of the two prior felonies must be of violence, but the third may be nonviolent, as in *Ewing v. California*, 538 U.S. 11 (2003), discussed above. In other states, the current felony must be violent, but the earlier ones need not be. Of course, there is also widespread difference in the definition of which crimes qualify as "violent" in those states where that is necessary to activate the three strikes legislation.

23. The defendant may be eligible for parole after serving the relevant minimum sentence, even though the statute declares that he shall be imprisoned "for life"; another statute may then define "for life" as a minimum of (X) years.

On the other hand, a number of states which have abolished "early parole release" still provide for "postincarceration community supervision," which is thought to assist prisoners in acclimating upon their return to society. Thus, while "parole release" has been abandoned, "parole supervision" remains; the major difference is that the defendant has served most or all of her sentence before being supervised in the community.

3. *Presumptive Sentences*

A major criticism of indeterminate sentencing was that the ranges were so wide (e.g., 2 - 20 years) that individual judges, using their individual punishment philosophies, could settle on any possible sentence. Judge shopping, as well as sentence bargaining, was the order of the day. In response, several states have adopted a "presumptive" sentence scheme, in which the judge is given a range within which to sentence, but told explicitly to begin at a "presumed" sentence (usually in the middle), which may be varied only if the judge finds specific aggravating or mitigating facts. For example, in New Jersey, first degree felonies are punishable by a sentence between 10 and 20 years imprisonment, but the "presumed" sentence is 15 years. The legislative list of 26 factors (13 aggravating and 13 mitigating), while not exclusive, closely resembles those factors which judges, in traditional discretionary sentencing states, would consider, including:

- the nature and circumstances of the offense, and the role of the actor therein, including whether or not it was committed in an especially heinous, cruel, or depraved manner;
- The gravity and seriousness of harm inflicted on the victim, including whether or not the defendant knew or reasonably should have known that the victim of the offense was particularly vulnerable or incapable of resistance due to advanced age, ill-health, or extreme youth, or was for any other reason substantially incapable of exercising normal physical or mental power of resistance;
- The risk that the defendant will commit another offense;
- A lesser sentence will depreciate the seriousness of the defendant's offense because it involved a breach of the public, or the defendant took advantage of a position of trust or confidence to commit the offense;
- There is a substantial likelihood that the defendant is involved in organized criminal activity;
- The extent of the defendant's prior criminal record and the seriousness of the offenses of which he has been convicted;
- The defendant's conduct neither caused nor threatened serious harm;
- The defendant did not contemplate that his conduct would cause or threaten serious harm;
- The defendant acted under a strong provocation;

- There were substantial grounds tending to excuse or justify the defendant's conduct, though failing to establish a defense;
- The defendant has no history of prior delinquency or criminal activity or has led a law-abiding life for a substantial period of time before the commission of the present offense;
- The defendant's conduct was the result of circumstances unlikely to recur.

The statute does not specify the amount of increase (or decrease) from the presumptive sentence that any one factor might afford; thus, one mitigating factor might reduce the sentence to 10 years, while three aggravating factors might result in a one-year increase to 16.

4. *Sentencing Commissions*

Each of these responses to criticisms of indeterminate sentencing reduce, or remove entirely, judicial sentencing discretion. These statutes constitute one very important part of the structured sentencing movement. But the most important part of that movement is the creation of "sentencing commissions," which were first proposed by Judge Marvin Frankel in "Criminal Sentences," supra, as an ingenious solution to unlimited judicial sentencing discretion. Judge Frankel suggested that the legislature place the basic decision about what factors would be relevant in sentencing not in the hands of individual judges, but in an administrative agency which would create "guidelines" which would be used by judges in imposing individual sentences. The extent to which these guidelines would "bind" the judge, or merely "assist" her, was left to later development.

A growing number of states have adopted this approach, which is now endorsed by the ABA (and in all likelihood the ALI, when its final proposals are promulgated, unless the *Booker* decision, discussed below, alters its view). In most such states the Commission establishes presumptive sentences, using a combination of the crime of conviction and the offender's past criminal record. Although the rough outline of state and federal commissions are similar, in many details they are extraordinarily different. We will, therefore, discuss state commissions separately from the federal system.

a. State Guideline Systems

As of 1996, 16 states had adopted guideline systems; nine were determinate while seven adhered to the indeterminate mode. While these varied in some significant ways, the heart of the process is to establish guidelines, like those proposed by Judge Frankel, which will curtail judicial discretion. Few of these systems abolish such discretion entirely, and six make compliance with their guidelines only "voluntary." Nevertheless, these systems share some salient characteristics:

- an administrative agency sets and reviews the guidelines;
- the guidelines set "presumptive" sentences or sentence ranges, within which a judge may sentence; most list "aggravating and mitigating" circumstances which may increase or decrease that range, to a specified degree;
- a judge who wishes to "depart" from the guidelines entirely (as opposed to varying within the guidelines) must give written reason for so doing;
- either side may appeal on the grounds that the guidelines were ignored or improperly applied;
- the guidelines consider many of the factors which "individualizing" judges would have considered in earlier systems, but create narrow sentencing "ranges" in which the judge may act;
- all the guideline systems, to some extent, consider past criminal record, even if the defendant is not eligible for the recidivist statute of the jurisdiction;
- seven states require the commission to consider "resources" (i.e., prison capacity) in setting guidelines;
- many systems abolish, or severely restrict, early release upon parole.

i. The "Commission." Guidelines systems generally establish a commission, which has a permanent staff, but whose members are only part-time. While the number of commissioners and the length of their terms varies widely, the ideal is to have representatives from every side of the criminal justice system (e.g., judges, prosecutors, defense counsel, victims, and prisoners) as well as "citizen members." The concern here is that the guidelines reflect the experiences, and interests, of all sides in the system, so that the guidelines will be acceptable to most (institutional) actors in the process. The commission staff also collects and analyzes actual sentences, to determine whether the gridlines are being followed by sentencing judges and to assess whether reasons given for departing from the presumptive sentence should be incorporated into later versions of the guidelines. The record on revision is mixed: Some Commissions have been quite active in revising the guidelines, while other Commissions have been relatively quiescent.

ii. "Presumptive" Sentencing. Most guideline systems establish a "*heartland*" of sentences, in which the vast majority of sentencing decisions should presumptively fall. If the judge finds certain legislatively specified facts, she may increase or decrease the sentence, but again usually by a specified amount or within a specific range. If the judge wishes to "*depart*" from the guidelines entirely, essentially ignoring the guidelines, she must provide a written reason; there may be a presumption that such a departure is unwarranted. Minnesota, for example, requires that the judge demonstrate through "clear and convincing evidence" that a departure is warranted.

Commissions have employed several methods of determining the "heartland." Minnesota, which created the first Commission, developed its guidelines only after heated debate about the purposes of sentencing. Its initial guidelines therefore adopted a normative framework based primarily on retribution, but reflecting as well a significant impact of the defendant's criminal history. This "prescriptive" approach, which has been adopted by a majority of state commissions, can be contrasted to the "descriptive" approach in which the guidelines seek to reflect current sentencing practices, to the degree they can be ascertained. The descriptive approach has one obvious strength and one obvious weakness. Because these guidelines will emulate current judicial practice, there is likely to be less judicial resistance. On the other hand, to the extent that the guidelines capture, as a "fly in amber," the precise problems with existing judicial practice they were designed to remedy, they will fail to achieve that objective. On the other hand, the "prescriptive" approach may jar with the hierarchy of seriousness levels established by the legislature; if so, to the extent that there is no legislative participation in the process, the guidelines might be attacked as antidemocratic.

iii. Offense-Based Sentencing; Criminal Record. In contrast to the federal commission, discussed below, every state which has adopted a determinate sentencing scheme has opted for "offense-based" sentencing. The offense seriousness, as reflected by the offense of conviction, is the primary factor.[24] Of secondary, but still substantial, importance, is the defendant's past criminal record. Although variously defined (some states include all offenses, including misdemeanors; some states provide "sunset" clauses, while others do not) this reflects the view that past conduct is relevant in assessing current sentence. Most states restrict the use of uncharged or acquitted conduct.

Most states adopt a "grid" approach which incorporates these two factors as the two axes of the grid. The complexity of the grid varies; the number of "offense gravity score levels" range between nine and 15. Within each "box," the ranges in which the judge may choose a sentence may be broad, or narrow, but in virtually all cases they are much narrower than those embraced in the preguidelines era. Thus, a single grid cell may provide the judge a choice of, e.g., 15-28 months; in virtually no case would a guideline read "24-240 months," which was often the situation in preguideline statutes. The Minnesota grid is typical:

---

24. A few states, such as Florida, have separate guidelines for different categories of offenses (e.g., drugs). Most states, however, rank all offenses on a single scale of seriousness.

Table 11.3 Minnesota Sentencing Grid

Seriousness Levels of Conviction Offense	Criminal History Score						
	0	1	2	3	4	5	6 or more
1. Unauthorized use of motor vehicle Possession of marijuana	N	N	N	N	N	N	19 18-20
2. Theft-related crimes	N	N	N	N	N	N	21 20-22
3. Theft crimes	N	N	N	N	19 18-20	22 21-23	25 24-26
4. Nonresidential burglary Theft crimes (over $2500)	N	N	N	N	25 24-26	32 30-34	41 37-45
5. Residential burglary Simple robbery	N	N	N	30 29-31	38 36-40	46 43-49	54 50-58
6. Criminal sexual conduct, 2d degree	N	N	N	34 33-35	44 42-46	54 50-58	65 60-70
7. Aggravated robbery	24 23-25	32 30-34	41 38-44	49 45-53	65 60-70	81 75-87	97 90-104
8. Criminal sexual conduct, 1st degree assault, 1st degree	43 41-45	54 50-58	65 60-70	76 71-81	95 89-101	113 106-120	132 124-140
9. Murder, 3d degree murder, 2d degree (felony murder)	105 102-108	119 116-122	127 124-130	149 143-155	176 168-184	205 195-215	230 218-242
10. Murder, 2d degree (with intent)	120 116-124	140 133-147	162 153-171	203 192-214	243 231-255	284 270-298	324 309-339

Notes: "N" denotes a presumption of a nonimprisonment sentence.

This grid allows us to distinguish three important terms. Using residential burglary (offense level five) as an example:

1. The statutory maximum sentence, which is not reflected on the grid itself, is 10 years. The longest sentence that a Court, *using the grid*, could impose for a residential burglary upon an offender with a criminal history score of six or more is 50-58 months.
2. The range for residential burglary is probation to 58 months, depending on the defendant's past criminal history.
3. If the judge wishes to depart from whichever grid box the defendant's criminal history requires, she must provide reasons. That departure can be at any level up to, but not exceeding, the 10-year statutory maximum.

iv. Institutional Resources. A number of states, following Minnesota's lead, caution the commission to adjust its guidelines to take into consideration "correctional resources," assuring that prisons do not fill beyond their capacity. The requirement has had some effect in some jurisdictions (although as a nation the United States continues to have the highest per capita rate of incarceration in the world). In those commissions taking this exhortation seriously, legislatively-prescribed mandatory terms for some offenses must mean lower terms for other crimes. Some commission guidelines also incorporate noncustodial and intermediary sanctions.

v. Appellate Review. Prior to the advent of presumptive sentences and guidelines, there was no meaningful review of trial Court sentences; the only restriction was that the sentence fall somewhere within the statutory minimum and maximum. *Stanford v. State*, 110 So.2d 1 (Fla. 1959). On some, rare occasions, a sentence could be assessed for an "abuse of discretion," *United States v. Wiley*, 267 F.2d 453 (7th Cir. 1959), but reversal was rarer than a Cubs' World Series pennant. This may well have been defensible when judges had "unfettered" discretion, did not have to give reasons or find facts, and could rely on any factor to warrant "individualization." But in the new guidelines systems which articulate factors that should be considered in sentencing, and sometimes mandate findings on those factors, legislatures, spurred by the apparent disparity in such sentences, have allowed either side to appeal sentences which vary from the guideline sentence, either on the basis of alleged mistake in factual finding (the defendant carried, but did not brandish, a firearm) or in law. In some systems (e.g., North Carolina), if the judge moves into a different range, he must provide a written (appealable) reason selected from a long list.

Proponents of appellate review anticipate that the effect will be to create a "common law" of sentencing which will supplement the legislature's initial attempt to rationalize sentencing. Although the experiment has been extant for two decades, it is not clear whether that goal has been achieved; one can read the opinions of the Supreme Court of Minnesota (the state with the oldest guidelines system) as either clarifying or muddying the guidelines.

Even if appellate review does not result in clearer reasons for sentencing, it may have one other unseen benefit. Some commentators argue that before appellate review was allowed, courts who were upset with the sentence imposed, but had no power to alter it, might stretch the substantive rules of criminal law, or the rules of criminal procedure (search and seizure, interrogation) to overturn the conviction. As Holmes said, "hard cases make bad law." Now at least where an appellate court believes the conviction valid, but questions the sentence, it can do so directly.

b. The Federal Guidelines

The federal guidelines (which often form the bulk of materials in casebooks) appear, on their face, to be similar in structure to the state guidelines.

Closer inspection, however, shows that they are starkly different in many aspects from the state processes. Although they affect only 5 per cent of criminal defendants, the federal guidelines have been the target of unrelenting criticism since their adoption, unlike the state processes which, to varying degrees, have been hailed by commentators and judges alike as at least partially successful. We will briefly examine below some of the main differences, and criticisms, of the federal guidelines.

i. The Commission. Unlike almost all of the state analogs, the federal Commission is housed in the judicial branch of government. A United States Supreme Court decision upheld this placement against a challenge that it breached the separation of powers. *Mistretta v. United States*, 488 U.S. 361 (1989). In contrast to state commissions, which are often quite large, the federal commission consists of seven members. The initial statute required that at least three of these must be federal judges; the statute has now been amended so that no more than three may be on the federal judiciary. There is no statutory requirement that any of the remaining members have any experience in the actual criminal justice practice.

ii. The Basis of the Grid. In addition to having a smaller (and less diverse) membership, the Commission (again in contrast to many state commissions), opted to follow a "descriptive" approach in establishing the initial guidelines. Perhaps because of its empowering legislation,[25] the Commission explicitly refused to choose among sentencing goals. Instead, it drew upon an empirical assessment of over 10,000 federal sentences which had been handed down by federal judges in the year preceding the guidelines.[26] In explaining this decision, the Commission declared:

> Such a choice (among purposes of sentencing) would be profoundly difficult. The relevant literature is vast, the arguments deep, and each point of view has much to be said in its favor. A clear-cut Commission decision in favor of one of these approaches would diminish the chance that the guidelines would find the widespread acceptance they need for effective implementation.

Federal Sentencing Guidelines Manual, ch. 1, pt. A, introductory cmt. reprinted in 52 Fed. Reg.18,046-138 (1987).

---

25. The Senate Report creating the Commission specifically declared that it "has not shown a preference for one purpose of sentencing over another in the belief that different purposes may play greater or lesser roles in sentencing for different types of offenses committed by different types of defendants." Senate Judiciary Committee's Report on the Sentencing Reform Act, S. Rep. No 98-225, p.77 (1983).

26. Parker and Block, The Limits of Federal Criminal Sentencing Policy; or, Confessions of Two Reformed Reformers, 9 Geo. Mason L. Rev. 1001, 1010 (2001) (Prof. Block was an original member of the federal sentencing commission).

Critics have argued that this leads to no sturdy foundation on which to sentence. See Osler, Must Have Got Lost: Traditional Sentencing Goals, the False Trail of Uniformity and Process, and the Way Back Home, 54 S.C.L. Rev. 649 (2003): "By simply replicating past patterns, the Commission passed on this opportunity . . . no underlying principle other than uniformity was the functional basis for the Guidelines as written." *Id* at 657.

iii. Real Offense Sentencing. The federal guidelines, unlike any of the state systems, adopt a "real offense" sentencing scheme. This allows the judge to sentence the offender based not solely on the offense of which the defendant has been convicted (or pled), but upon his "relevant conduct" so long as the sentence is within the maximum permissible penalty for the offense of conviction. For example, if Herbert, a first offender,[27] has committed mail fraud, an offense that carries a five-year maximum sentence, he may be eligible under the guidelines for a sentence of 14 - 18 months. If, however, the court determines that Herbert abused a position of trust in committing the fraud, the guidelines may require an increase in "offense level" which will then trigger a higher range of sentencing (e.g., 26-34 months). Similarly, the amount of money involved may well affect the range in which the offender is ultimately placed before the sentence is actually imposed. This reliance on "extra crime" factors was endemic to individualized sentencing. *Williams* itself is the quintessential "real offense" case — Williams's life was ended because the trial judge there considered both alleged past offenses (see below) *and* Williams's "attitude."

Because in establishing the grid, the Commission relied on past sentencing practices which were based on a vast array of factors which federal judges, unguided by anything but their individual predilections, had found relevant, the guidelines embraced large numbers of possible "sentencing factors" by which a "presumptive sentence" level could be changed. Chapter 2 of the Guidelines, which provide "relevant conduct" sentencing factors for literally hundreds of federal offenses, is extraordinarily detailed (some would characterize this as "nuanced"). Thus, the guidelines on robbery list six different ways in which a weapon might be employed, and prescribe a different level of sentence enhancement for each one of the six. This complexity, reflected by 258 boxes within the sentencing grid (in contrast to most states, which have significantly fewer boxes) has caused many to criticize the guidelines as arcane and unduly byzantine. See Reitz, The Federal Role in Sentencing Law and Policy, 543 The Annals 116,121 (1996); Huigens, *Harris, Ring* and the Future of Relevant Conduct Sentencing, 15 Fed. Sent. Rept. 88 (2003).

Proponents of "real offense" sentencing argue that the "crime of conviction" approach, which bases its sentences exclusively on the charges to which the defendant pleads, places the dominant power in the hands of

---

27. See the discussion below of the role of criminal history.

the prosecutor during plea bargaining — whatever charge is settled upon will dictate the sentence to be imposed. Under a "real offense" approach, these supporters argue, the judge will be empowered to consider the real facts, thereby lessening the power of the prosecutor. As one commentator has put it:[28]

> The Commission created the relevant conduct provisions primarily to ensure that the discretion withdrawn from judges was not merely transferred to prosecutors.

Critics, however, argue that plea bargaining continues, Nagel and Schulhofer, A Tale of Three Cities: An Empirical Study of Charge and Bargaining Practices Under the Federal Sentencing Guidelines, 66 S. Cal. L. Rev. 501 (1992), and that bargaining now concerns not merely the charges, but the various sentencing factors which permeate the federal guidelines (fact bargaining). As one court recently put it, "(T)he phenomenon known as 'fact bargaining' has come to flourish as never before in the federal Courts." *United States v. Green*, 2004 WL 1381101 *4 (D. Mass).

Again in contrast to state systems, federal judges may consider both uncharged criminal conduct and conduct for which the defendant has been acquitted in setting the "real offense" offense level. The Supreme Court has upheld this process against both due process and double jeopardy challenges. *United States v. Watts*, 519 U.S. 148 (1997); *Witte v. United States*, 515 U.S. 389 (1995).

iv. Past Criminal Conduct. Like the state systems, the federal commission gives criminal history (including misdemeanors) a substantial role in ascertaining the presumptive sentence. As in state systems, the guidelines assign various "points" for different "levels" of past convictions, and provide for sunset timelines for some past crimes.

v. Departures. Few aspects of guideline systems in general, and the federal system, in particular, have been as contentious as the ability of judges to "depart" from the guidelines. This power must be distinguished from the right, within the guidelines, to move within the grid, based upon particular findings of fact. "Departures" occur when the judge simply ignores the guideline structure, and sentences the defendant within the statutory range, based upon whatever factors the judge feels relevant.

On the one hand, the precise purpose of the structured sentencing movement was to preclude judges from indulging their idiosyncrasies upon the sentencing process, and thereby impose sentences drastically different from those imposed by other judges upon defendants who, at least superficially, seemed similar or identical. On the other, the federal legislation, and

---

28. Bowman, Fear of Law, 44 St. Louis L.J. 299, 339 (2000).

the Commission, argued that no set of standards, however detailed, could fully capture the intricacies of sentencing, at least if sentences were to be individualized at all.

Prior to 2003, the federal guidelines permitted judges to depart in two instances: (a) where the government moves for a "substantial assistance" departure; (b) where the departure is based upon "an aggravating or mitigating circumstance of a kind, to a degree, not adequately taken into consideration" by the Sentencing Commission.

The obvious intent of the substantial assistance provision is to encourage defendants to "turn state's evidence" on higher defendants.[29] Substantial assistance departures are, under section 5K1 of the guidelines themselves, allowed only "upon motion of the government." *Wade v. United States*, 504 U.S. 181 (1992) held that this provision precluded a judge, *sua sponte*, from recognizing such assistance. Thus, the discretion as to whether even to consider the defendant's cooperation is placed solely in the prosecutor's hands. There is only one exception; if the defendant can demonstrate that the prosecutor's refusal to move for such a reduction is based upon constitutionally infirm grounds (race, political activism, etc.), the Court may grant relief. As of 2000, 18 percent of all sentences reflected 5K1 departures.[30]

The second ground for departure has been hotly contested. In *Koon v. United States*, 518 U.S.81 (1996), the police officers who were convicted for beating Rodney King (see Chapter 9) were exposed to 70-97 months, but received sentences of 30-37 months. The trial judge gave several reasons for each "level" of departure:

- the victim's misconduct, which contributed significantly to provoking the offense;
- petitioners were unusually susceptible to abuse in prison;
- petitioners would lose their jobs and be precluded from employment in law enforcement;
- petitioners had been subject to successive state and federal prosecutions;
- petitioners posed a low risk of recidivism.

---

29. Some states also expressly recognize this factor. See, e.g, *Brugman v. State*, 339 S.E.2d 244 (Ga. 1986), interpreting O.C.G.A. 16-13-31(e) (2).

30. A study in 2003 by the General Accounting Office found that three-quarters of the downward departures in drug cases were (1) substantial assistance departures; (2) pursuant to a plea agreement; or (3) "fast track" departures. GAO, Federal Drug Offenses; Departures from Sentencing Guidelines and Mandatory Minimum Sentences, Fiscal Years 1999-2001 (GAO-04-105). Moreover, there was wide difference among the circuits. Offenders sentenced in the Third Circuit were over three times more likely to receive a substantial assistance departure than offenders sentenced in the First Circuit. And offenders in the Ninth Circuit were over 18 times more likely to have received a nonsubstantial-assistance departure as those sentenced in the Fourth Circuit.

The Ninth Circuit, in reviewing these departures, had applied a standard of *de novo* review. That standard, said the Supreme Court, was inadequate; more deference had to be afforded the discretion of the trial judge. Indeed, the Court declared:

> Before the Guidelines system, a federal criminal sentence within statutory limits was, for all practical purposes, not reviewable on appeal . . . we are . . . convinced that Congress did not intend, by establishing limited appellate review, to vest in appellate Courts wide-ranging authority over district Court sentencing decisions. Indeed, the text of §3742 manifests an intent that district Courts retain much of their traditional sentencing discretion. "Although the Act established a limited appellate review of sentencing decisions, it did not alter a Court of Appeals' traditional deference to a district Court's exercise of its sentencing discretion. . . . The development of the guideline sentencing regime has not changed our view that, except to the extent specifically directed by statute, it is not the role of an appellate Court to substitute its judgment for that of the sentencing Court as to the appropriateness of a particular sentence."

Koon was extremely hard to interpret. Some commentators saw it as "liberating" the federal judiciary from the "shackles" of the guidelines, and returning to judges most, if not all, the individualizing power they had held before the guidelines were adopted. Others noted the Court's willingness to review each factor given by the trial judge, and suggested that this indicated antipathy toward widespread departures. Empirical research five years after *Koon* strongly suggested that trial courts (and their appellate superiors) which had departed frequently pre-*Koon* continued to do so; those which had overturned departures pre-*Koon* continued to do so as well.

In 2003, Congress enacted the "Feeney Amendment," which establishes a "de novo" standard for appellate review and which precludes departures in all but "substantial assistance" cases, and a few other "extraordinary" cases. The statute requires the Sentencing Commission to keep data on the rate of departures.[31] Within weeks of the passage of the statute, Attorney General John Ashcroft announced that the Department of Justice would also keep data on departures, and expressly instructed all federal attorneys not to "stand silently by" while a defendant moved for a downward departure. This was also part of the Attorney General's broader declaration severely restricting the ability of individual prosecutors to

---

31. Representative Feeney explained these provisions as follows: "The Sentencing Commission must, upon request, provide any data . . . This disclosed information includes the name of the sentencing judge. *Such information helps ensure that federal judges are properly accountable for their sentencing decisions comporting with the law* . . . America is not going to return to the days of unfettered power resting in the hands of a single district judge." Feeney, Reaffirming the Rule of Law in Federal Sentencing, Crim. Just. Ethics 2, 72-73 (Wint./Spr. 2003). (emphasis added).

Table 11-4   Federal Sentencing Guidelines Table in months of imprisonment

	Offense Level	*Criminal History Category (Criminal History Points)*					
		I (0 or 1)	II (2 or 3)	III (4, 5, 6)	IV (7, 8, 9)	V (10, 11, 12)	VI (13 or more)
Zone A	1	0-6	0-6	0-6	0-6	0-6	0-6
	2	0-6	0-6	0-6	0-6	0-6	1-7
	3	0-6	0-6	0-6	0-6	2-8	3-9
	4	0-6	0-6	0-6	2-8	4-10	6-12
	5	0-6	0-6	1-7	4-10	6-12	9-15
	6	0-6	1-7	2-8	6-12	9-15	12-18
	7	0-6	2-8	4-10	8-14	12-18	15-21
	8	0-6	4-10	6-12	10-16	15-21	18-24
Zone B	9	4-10	6-12	8-14	12-18	18-24	21-27
	10	6-12	8-14	10-16	15-21	21-27	24-30
Zone C	11	8-14	10-16	12-18	18-24	24-30	27-33
	12	10-16	12-18	15-21	21-27	27-33	30-37
	13	12-18	15-21	18-24	24-30	30-37	33-41
	14	15-21	18-24	21-27	27-33	33-41	37-46
	15	18-24	21-27	24-30	30-37	37-46	41-51
	16	21-27	24-30	27-33	33-41	41-51	46-57
	17	24-30	27-33	30-37	37-46	46-57	51-63
	18	27-33	30-37	33-41	41-51	51-63	57-71
	19	30-37	33-41	37-46	46-57	57-71	63-78
	20	33-41	37-46	41-51	51-63	63-78	70-87
	21	37-46	41-51	46-57	57-71	70-87	77-96
	22	41-51	46-57	51-63	63-78	77-96	84-105
	23	46-57	51-63	57-71	70-87	84-105	92-115
	24	51-63	57-71	63-78	77-96	92-115	100-125
	25	57-71	63-78	70-87	84-105	100-125	110-137
	26	63-78	70-87	78-97	92-115	110-137	120-150
	27	70-87	78-97	87-108	100-125	120-150	130-162
Zone D	28	78-97	87-108	97-121	110-137	130-162	140-175
	29	87-108	97-121	108-135	121-151	140-175	151-188
	30	97-121	108-135	121-151	135-168	151-188	168-210
	31	108-135	121-151	135-168	151-188	168-210	188235
	32	121-151	135-168	151-188	168-210	188-235	210-262
	33	135-168	151-188	168-210	188-235	210-262	235-293
	34	151-188	168-210	188-235	210-262	235-293	262-327
	35	168-210	188-235	210-262	235-293	262-327	292-365
	36	188-235	210-262	235-293	262-327	292-365	324-405
	37	210-262	235-293	262-327	292-365	324-405	360-life
	38	235-293	262-327	292-365	324-405	360-life	360-life
	39	262-327	292-365	324-405	360-life	360-life	360-life
	40	292-365	324-405	360-life	360-life	360-life	360-life
	41	324-405	360-life	360-life	360-life	360-life	360-life
	42	360-life	360-life	360-life	360-life	360-life	360-life
	43	life	life	life	life	life	life

engage in plea bargaining. The statute resulted in a firestorm of criticism, and in late Sept. 2003 the Judicial Conference of the United States, headed by the Chief Justice, voted unanimously to ask Congress to repeal the law. As of the writing of this chapter, the Feeney Amendment was still law, but be sure to check the newspapers (as well as legal databases) to determine whether it has survived, and if so whether it has been modified in important respects.

The difference between a "real offense" system, such as the federal government's, and an "offense of conviction" systems such as Minnesota's (and all other guideline states) can be seen in the following example. Suppose Ronald, who has previously been convicted of three felonies, none of them involving violence, has robbed a federally insured bank at gun point.

1. He points the gun at three different customers;
2. His take is $75,000;
3. Ronald is a recovering alcoholic;
4. Ronald has a fourth grade education.

If Ronald is prosecuted in Minnesota state Court, his "offense level" is 7 ("aggravated robbery"). Let us assume his three priors were severity level IV; the guidelines make his criminal history score a 3. Thus, he will be facing a possible 45-53-month sentence. The judge may consider the amount stolen as a reason for going toward 53, as opposed to 45-months, but if the judge wishes to go beyond 53 months on the basis of this information, she must "depart" and give a written set of reasons for doing so. On the other hand, she may consider Ronald's low level of education or his attempt to rehabilitate himself as moving him toward the 45-month sentence. (The Minnesota guidelines expressly forbid "departing" based upon social factors or educational attainment, but allow a judge to consider these items *within* the sentencing range).

In the federal system, Ronald's "base offense" level (the Y axis) is 20. With three prior felonies, his crimnal history score (the X axis) is likely to be IV; his "base sentence' would be 51-63 months. By specific guidelines language, the "pointing" of the gun, which is equivalent of "brandishing," raises that by five levels (if a dangerous weapon other than a gun was brandished, there is a increase of four levels). The guidelines also distinguish offense level by the amount of money involved; a loss of $75,000 raises the level by two levels; a loss of $800,000 by four levels. Thus, Ronald now has an offense level of 27 (20 + 7). He is now facing a sentence of 100-125 months (more than double the initial sentence). Now the judge has discretion *within this range*, and may consider Ronald's alcoholism or his education level as mitigating factors. (Again, the judge may not consider such factors in "departing" from the guideline range on the basis of these factors.)

The critical point here is that while the Minnesota judge "may" consider the gun, or the amount taken, the federal judge "must"—each of these

Table 11-5

	Federal Guidelines	State Guidelines	Traditional Sentencing
Commission Composition	Seven members; not more than three federal judges*	{Sixteen states} Wide range; many require "roles" of criminal justice system (prosecutor, defense counsel)	Judges appointed or elected
Basis of original "guidelines"	Past practice; now often altered by normative decisions or Congress	Past practice or re-examination of normative purposes	Not applicable
"Base" of sentencing decision	Relevant conduct; real offense	Charge of conviction	Charge of conviction
How Guidelines may be altered	New guidelines effective 180 days after promulgation unless Congress affirmatively negates	SAME as federal or need affirmative legislative approval	Not applicable
Binding or voluntary??	Binding	Ten binding, six voluntary	Binding
Range of sentences	Narrow within each grid box. But many grid boxes	Narrow within grid boxes, many fewer than federal grid	Usually wide range
Movement from box to box?	Controlled by highly detailed set of "relevant conduct" factors; given quantified impact on sentence	Aggravated and mitigating circumstances listed, but generally no specific quantitative effect for specific favor	Not applicable
Departures	Downward departures for cooperation, only on motion of government; otherwise, now severely limited by Feeney Amendment	Allowed in "extraordinary cases"	Court typically considers factors which would be allowed under guidelines systems, but many others as well
Personal Facts? (Age, employ-ment, family, health, etc.)	Typically discouraged or explicitly forbidden	Often allowed, if not encouraged	Always considered
Criminal history	Forms one axis of grid; specific restriction on what may be considered; quantifiable impact on "offense level"	Typically same as federal, but impact may vary from federal, as may past offenses which may be considered	In nonrecidivist setting, always considered. No specific quantitative effect; no limits on what past offense may or may not be considered
Appellate Review	Yes, for both sides	Yes, for both sides	No
Incarceration Constraints?	In statute, but Commission has not implemented	Varies, but many states have such restrictions, and follow them	No

* Originally; "at least three" had to be federal judges.

factors has a specific increase in base offense level that removes much of the discretionary judgment of the judge and which substantially increase the defendant's potential incarceration.

F. Structured Sentencing — An Assessment

Notwithstanding all the diverse state and federal provisions, and all the criticism of the guidelines (particularly the federal system), the structured sentencing movement has demonstrated several important facts:

- it is possible, even if difficult, to prioritize purposes of sentencing, and to establish a system which reflects those purposes;
- it is possible, within limits, to articulate the specific factors which judges (or other sentencers) consider relevant, and then to assess those factors in light of the purposes discovered above;
- while actors in the system will seek ways to avoid what they perceive as overregulation of their power, they also will often recognize the need for some uniformity and regularization of the results of their actions, particularly if their representatives are included in the process of initial establishment of this regularization.

G. Undoing the Revolution? Or Reframing it? *Blakely, Booker* and the Future of Sentencing in the United States

As indicated in the two "warnings" earlier in this chapter, structured sentencing schemes are now under constitutional scrutiny. Although the story has many ancestors,[32] for current purposes it begins with *Apprendi v. New Jersey,* 530 U.S. 466 (2000). Charles Apprendi pled guilty to illegal possession of a

---

32. In *McMillan v. Pennsylvania,* 477 U.S. 79 (1986), the Court introduced the concept of a "sentencing factor," which was not an "element of the crime," and could be decided by a judge after trial, by a preponderance of the evidence. The difficulty, of course, is that *every* phrase in a statute clearly affects the sentence; the line between elements and sentencing factors seemed semantic at best. Justice Rehnquist, who wrote the majority opinion, agreed that if it were clear that the legislature was manipulating the factor in an attempt to avoid *In Re Winship,* 379 U.S. 358 (1970), and the new fact so dramatically increased the sentence that it could be said that the "tail was wagging the dog," the Court would step in — otherwise, both federalism and separation of powers concepts left these declarations to the legislature.

firearm. After hearing evidence, the trial court held that the state had proved by a preponderance of the evidence that the defendant had acted with racial bias. Invoking a state statute which increased the maximum possible sentence to twenty years upon such a finding, the court sentenced the defendant to twelve years — two years above the maximum ten year sentence he could have received for the basic crime. The Supreme Court, 5-4, reversed the sentence, holding that any factor which "increased the maximum sentence" must, under the Sixth Amendment, be submitted to a jury, and must, under the Fifth Amendment, be resolved beyond a reasonable doubt. Although the Court might have relied on the notion that racial animus was not a "motive," but closer to a "mens rea," it took a much broader approach:

> any fact that increases the penalty for a crime beyond the prescribed statutory maximum must be submitted to a jury and proved beyond a reasonable doubt. . . . (W)e endorse the statement of the rule set forth in the concurring opinions in (*Jones v. United States*): "it is unconstitutional for a legislature to remove from the jury the assessment of facts that increase the prescribed range of penalties to which a criminal defendant is exposed. . . . " (T)he relevant inquiry is one not of form, but of effect — does the required finding expose the defendant to a greater punishment than that authorized by the jury's guilty verdict? . . . In terms of absolute years behind bars, and because of the more severe stigma attached, the differential here is unquestionably of constitutional significance. When a judge's finding . . . authorizes an increase in the maximum punishment, it is appropriately characterized as a "tail which wags the dog of the substantive offence."

Four years later in *Blakely v. Washington*, 2004 U.S. LEXIS 4573, the trial judge had departed from the sentencing range in a structured sentencing scheme, based on a finding that the crime had been committed with "deliberate cruelty" and imposed a 90 month sentence, rather than the 49 month sentence established in the range (though still less than the 120 month statutory maximum). The state argued that since the 90 month sentence did not exceed the statutory maximum, *Apprendi* did not apply. But Justice Scalia, speaking for the Court, disagreed:

> The "statutory maximum" for *Apprendi* purposes is the maximum sentence a judge may impose *solely on the basis of the facts reflected in the jury verdict* or admitted by the defendant. . . . (T)he relevant statutory maximum is not the maximum sentence a judge may impose after finding additional facts, but the maximum he may impose *without* any additional findings. When a judge inflicts punishment that the jury's verdict alone does not allow, the jury has not found all the facts "which the law makes essential to the punishment" and the judge exceeds his proper authority. (First emphasis added; second in original.)

The heart of *Apprendi* and *Blakely* was *not* antipathy toward sentencing guidelines, but a desire to assure that the jury would play a critical role in the criminal process.[33] The Court in *Jones v. United States*, 526 U.S. 227 (1999), hypothesizing a system in which the legislature would require a jury finding only as to the lowest rung of the sentencing ladder (e.g., whether the defendant injured the victim) and then allowing the judge to increase sentences based upon a myriad of "sentencing factors" (e.g., whether the injury was serious, whether the crime was done with a weapon, whether it was intentional, etc.), had feared that juries could be turned into "mere gatekeepers." As Justice Scalia declared in *Blakely*, the focus was on the function which the jury had played and should play in American criminal jurisprudence:

> "This case is not about whether determinate sentencing is constitutional, only about how it can be implemented in a way that respects the Sixth Amendment."

Four dissenters nevertheless argued *Blakely* meant the death of structured sentencing: Justice O'Connor lamented that "Congress and States, faced with the burdens imposed ... will either trim or eliminate altogether their sentencing guidelines schemes and, with them, 20 years of sentencing reform ... the practical consequences of today's decision may be disastrous ... What I have feared most has now come to pass: over 20 years of sentencing reform are all but lost. . . ."

Justice Breyer, an original member of the United States Sentencing Commission, also read *Blakely* as invalidating all structured sentencing schemes: "Whatever the faults of guidelines systems — and there are many — they are more likely to find their cure in legislation emerging from the experience of, and discussion among, all elements of the criminal justice community, than in a virtually unchangeable constitutional decision of this Court." He further argued that other proposed replacement systems would enhance plea bargaining, and hence increase reliance on a system "in which punishment is set not by judges or juries but by advocates acting under bargaining constraints ... I am unaware of any variation that does not involve the shift of power to the prosecutor ... inherent in any charge offense system. . . ."

After *Blakely*, the prospect that the federal sentencing guidelines were totally invalid was so ominous that the Court expedited the appeals involved in *United States v. Booker*, and held argument on the very first day of the Court's new, 2004-2005, term. Virtually all commentators believe that the *Booker* Court will find *Blakely* to invalidate the provisions of the federal

---

33. *Blakely* is the most important, but scarcely the only, recent decision enhancing the function of the jury. In *United States v. Gaudin*, 515 U.S. 506 (1995), the Court (also per Justice Scalia) held that the jury, not the judge, should determine whether a statement was "material" under federal fraud statutes.

statute that require factfinding to be made by the judge, rather than a jury.[34] The crucial question, on which much of the oral argument focused, may well be "severability"—whether the statute can be saved by construing the rest of the provisions to allow jury factfinding, or whether the entire statute must be jettisoned. Of course, since this book is being written before *Booker* is decided, it is possible that the Court might, at least in dictum, suggest (or even adopt, pursuant to its supervisory power) an interim remedy were it to make such a finding. A number of alternatives have been suggested by commentators and adopted by some courts commentators:[35]

1. Use the guidelines as informational and suggestive, rather than mandatory. This option retains the concept of guidelines to assist judges, without requiring that they follow the guidelines in a given case. It is possible that there could be appellate review of the sentence, if the Court, or Congress, were to make the guidelines "presumptively" correct, and allow either side to argue that there had been an abuse of discretion. This solution, however, ignores the critical role of the jury, which was at least one of the lynchpins in the *Blakely* opinion.[36]

2. "Decap" the Guidelines. This proposal, known as the "Bowman fix", after Professor Bowman, of Indiana University Law School, who first

---

34. Less than one week after *Blakely*, the dissenters' worst fears occurred—a district court in Utah, on the basis of *Blakely*, declared the federal sentencing guidelines unconstitutional. *United States v. Croxford*, 2004 WL 1462111 (D. Utah). The lower courts are now severely split over a plethora of issues involving *Blakely's* reach. The United States Sentencing Commission has established a database to track all *Blakely* opinions, which will almost surely be continued after *Booker* is decided. It can be found at *www. ussc.gov/blakely/11_30_04.pdf.*

35. After *Blakely*, Congress and the Sentencing Commission held hearings on the effects of *Blakely*. The American Bar Association, in response to a speech by Justice Kennedy at the Association, established the Justice Kennedy Commission, which reported to the Association in August 2004. That report succinctly and objectively outlines most of the major alternatives available to legislatures in the aftermath of *Booker*. The ABA Criminal Justice Section established a "*Blakely* Committee" to analyze that opinion (and *Booker*). The interim report of that committee can be found at *aba_blakely_consensus_memo_ii.rtf* (as obtained from Prof. Berman's blog below). The Federal Sentencing Reporter dedicated three separate issues exclusively to *Blakely* and the issues it raises; it is likely that it will do the same, if not more, after *Booker*. The best on-line source for information about these groups, as well as sentencing developments in general, is Prof. Doug Berman's blog, Sentencing Law and Policy, *http://www.sentencing.typepad.com.*

36. At least one state court has already rejected the suggestion that its system of guidelines could be made "non-mandatory" and thereby comply with *Blakely*. *Oregon v. Gornick*, No. 02C53376; A121042 (Or. Ct. App. Dec. 8, 2004). In New Jersey, which has a "presumptive" system in which additional facts may increase (or decrease) the sentence to the statutory maximum or minmum, but are not given specific weight, the appellate courts have divided over whether *Blakely* controls. Compare *State v. Natale*, 2004 WL 2599892 (N.J. App. Div.) with *State v. Abdullah*, 372 N.J. Super. 252, 280-281, 858 A.2d 19 (App. Div. 2004).

suggested it, would adopt a system with ranges whose minimum would be established by the guidelines, but whose upper limit would coincide with the statutory maximum. Under this alternative, judges would be free to exercise discretion within the entire range of sentences and assumes the continuing validity of allowing judges to find facts triggering mandatory minimum sentences. That power was upheld in *Harris v. United States*, 536 U.S. 545 (2002), notwithstanding its apparent inconsistency with *Apprendi*. *Harris* was a 5-4 decision in which Justice Breyer, who provided the swing vote, essentially agreed the logic of earlier cases meant that juries, rather than judges, had to find such facts, but asserted that he was not "yet" ready to so rule. If, as many presume, *Booker* requires jury findings with regard to virtually all other sentencing factors, that may well be enough to alter Justice Breyer's reluctance. This remedy would establish a discretionary, but determinate, sentencing policy. On this point.

3. "*Blakely-ize*" the Guidelines. This proposal, put forth by Professor Kyron "Huigens" prior to *Blakely*, in Huigens, Solving the *Apprendi* Puzzle, 90 Geo. L. J. 387 (2002)—allows the jury to decide, using the beyond a reasonable doubt standard, the FACTS relating to "relevant conduct," which would then increase the offense level as established by the guidelines, but allow the judge, within the grid, to determine the amount of increase in the sentence that each finding would carry. Thus, a jury would decide the amount of money stolen in a fraud case, or whether a defendant had acted in a "supervisory" role in a criminal conspiracy. If the legislature has allowed an increase of up to six months for each of these factors, the judge could still rely on "interstitial" facts (those "inexpressible" facts upon which individualizing judges relied) to decide what increase—between 0 and 6 months—should be imposed. Some object that this solution would flood the jury with numerous factual questions, and might prolong the trial.[37] Supporters of this proposal respond that in most instances, only a small number of factual questions would be raised, and that if juries are capable of deciding complex conspiracy cases involving multiple defendants and multiple counts, they are capable of resolving several factual disputes in this setting. Moreover, if the concern is a real one, it might require the prosecutor to select, among a wide panoply of factual charges, a smaller number, thus not increasing the sentence as much as now occurs. Others object to this solution by suggesting that at least some of the factual questions now in the guidelines, such as whether the defendant cooperated with officials or demonstrated remorse, would not be known until well after the trial.

---

37. For example, Justice Breyer, dissenting in *Blakely*, raised such factors as "(1) the nature of the institution robbed; (2) the (a) presence of (b) brandishing of, or (c) use of a firearm; (3) making a death threat; (4) presence of (a) ordinary, (b) serious, (c) permanent or life threatening, bodily injury; (5) abduction; (6) physical restraint; (7) taking of a firearm; (8) taking of drugs; (9) value of property loss, etc."

Moreover, information now obtained during a presentence investigation, conducted by the probation officer after the trial, would have to be obtained pre-trial and presented to the jury either during the trial or post-sentence.

4. Bifurcate the process. Conduct the trial as currently, and then conduct a separate "sentencing" hearing with the same (or possibly another) jury. Kansas, which has a structured sentencing guideline system very much like that of the federal system, adopted this approach when, on the basis of *Apprendi,* the Kansas Supreme Court held that judges could not make factual determinations. This approach would still allow the judge to decide, within the specific range related to a specific finding, the amount of increase in the sentence. Appellate review could be allowed of both the fact finding and of the sentence imposed. This procedure is similar to that in #2 above, but bifurcates the proceeding.

5. Adopt jury sentencing. Some observers argue that, taken to their logical conclusion, *Apprendi* and *Blakely* would require jury sentencing. Supporters of jury sentencing contend that six states retain jury sentencing in at least some instances, and that empirical studies are mixed as to whether juries or judges are more disparate in the sentences they impose. Further, they suggest that to the extent jury sentences are more random, because each one is imposed by a "newcomer" to sentencing, providing the jury with information about sentencing, particularly information reflecting how other juries have treated similarly situated defendants, would resolve some of that discrepancy.[38] Finally, proponents of jury sentencing point out that every state leaves the decision of life or death to juries (see below). If juries can be trusted with that critical decision, they urge, they can be similarly trusted with lesser determinations. Opponents argue that jury sentencing is undesirable, both because it is time consuming and because it is erratic.

6. Create a simple "charge offense" system, in which no "relevant conduct" or aggravating and mitigating factors are considered at all.

7. Repudiate the guidelines entirely and return to the totally discretionary sentencing system endorsed in *Williams,* and still in effect in most states. This view appeals to those who believe that individualizing sentences is more important than even rough equality among defendants, and that only each judge, facing each individual defendant, can assess the "right" sentence. Neither

---

38. Currently, "(N)o state provides juries with anywhere near the amount of sentence-related information that is currently provided to judges." *Iontcheva,* supra, n. 7 at 367; indeed, in Missouri, the rules of evidence preclude informing juries of sentences in similar cases, and the Kentucky Truth in Sentence statute does not give juries sentencing guidelines or statistics. See Heumann and Cassak, Not-So-Blissful Ignorance: Informing Jurors About Punishment in Mandatory Sentencing Cases, 20 Am. Crim L. Rev. 343 (1983)

Blakely (nor, in all likelihood, *Booker*) discusses this kind of scheme, and during the oral argument in *Booker,* all parties, as well as the Justices, appeared to assume that full indeterminacy was constitutional. It is possible, however, that, in the past thirty years, legislative articulation of the most important sentencing factors, and the impact they may have, has undercut, at least in part, the notion that it is not possible to discern those factors which actually affect sentences. On a doctrinal level, the very premise of *Williams,* and of individualization, was that the purpose of sentencing was rehabilitation, no longer articulated as such. It is not inconceivable that an indeterminate approach which allows the tail of judicial fact finding to wag the dog of the jury's base determination might be deemed unconstitutional, and violative of the Fifth, if not the Sixth, Amendment. As one critic has put it, "I remain at a loss to understand why unexplained, indeterminate decision-making is constitutionally permissible, but explained, reasoned decision-making is not."[39]

Finally, *Blakely/Booker* will drastically affect the procedure to be followed at "sentencing," at least in structured sentencing states. The informal administrative process which now attends a sentencing hearing will disappear, since the process will be governed by the Sixth and Fifth Amendments, and either occur during, or parallel the processes of, a criminal trial.

It is likely that neither *Blakely*, nor *Booker* when it is decided, necessitates the end of structured sentencing. The structured sentencing movement has given all systems, including those which have not adopted it, rational enunciations of most of the factors that "should" impact sentencing and, in addition, has articulated some consensus on the weight to be afforded those factors. To throw the baby of rationalized sentencing factors out with the bathwater of judicial fact finding on a lower standard would be tragic.

H. Sentencing and Death

The death penalty has always been controversial. In recent years, with the revelation of a number of defendants who, though actually innocent, were convicted of capital offenses, and an even larger number of defendants who were inadequately represented at trial or at the capital sentencing process (see Chapter 10 for details), a growing cry for a moratorium on the death penalty has emerged. There has been, as well, a growing consensus that no death penalty should be imposed unless the jury — the cross-section of the community — concludes that there are sufficient facts to impose death.

But the jury deciding death is not fully representative of that community. As noted in Chapter 8, prosecutors are able to "death qualify" a jury, to remove, for cause, any potential juror who acknowledges that he could not

---

39. Paul Rosenzweig, Testimony before the United States Sentencing Commision, 17 November 2004.

impose the death penalty under any circumstances. *Witherspoon v. Illinois*, 391 U.S. 510 (1968). This process is hotly debated for several reasons. First, one might argue that death should be imposed only if all members of the community, including those staunchly opposed to the death penalty in the abstract, believe the facts to be so gruesome as to warrant death. This argument has not been successful. Second, there is some evidence that "death qualified" jurors are more prone to convict. If so, some might argue that the guilt jury should not be death qualified, and that only if the defendant is convicted should persons opposed to the penalty be removed and replaced by others not so opposed. Again, this argument has been unsuccessful. Third, opposition to the death penalty surely lies across a spectrum of persuasion; many persons who believe themselves to be opposed to the penalty might be persuaded in a particularly heinous offense to impose the penalty. The precise wording of the voir dire question, and the precise depth of questioning about the potential juror's beliefs, are therefore critical to assuring the state and defendant that the jury as "as" representative as possible.

Prior to 1972, the decision between life and death was left almost exclusively to juries without any instructions about when the death penalty might be imposed. Most states allowed the death penalty to be inflicted on those convicted of "first degree" murder, which was commonly defined as "premeditated, deliberate and willful." Beyond that, the jury was left to its own devices. In *McGautha v. California*, 402 U.S. 183 (1971) the Supreme Court rejected a challenge, based upon the due process clause, that capital juries were "standardless" in whether to impose the penalty. Echoing the view that individualization precludes rationalization, Justice Harlan, speaking for the Court, declared:

> "To identify before the fact those characteristics of criminal homicides and their perpetrators which call for the death penalty and to express these characteristics in language which can be fairly be understood and applied by the sentencing authority (is) beyond present human ability."

Nevertheless, one year later the Court, by a vote of 5 - 4, with each of the nine Justices writing an opinion, held that the death penalty *as then implemented* violated not the due process clause, but the Eighth Amendment. While at least two of the majority Justices concluded that the death penalty would never be constitutionally acceptable, the thrust of the other three was that the penalty was arbitrarily imposed: as "freakish as being hit by lightning." *Furman v. Georgia*, 408 U.S. 238 (1972).

The states immediately rewrote their death penalty provisions. Four years after *Furman*, the Court decided that a statute seeking to avoid the "freakishness" of the death penalty by mandatorily imposing the death penalty upon all persons convicted of "capitally eligible" offenses also violated the Eighth Amendment. *Woodson v. North Carolina*, 428 U.S. 280 (1976). On the other hand, statutorily enacted aggravating and mitigating factors (most of which were copied from the Model Penal Code) gave sufficient structure to the sentencer to overcome Furman's concern of freakishness. *Gregg v. Georgia*, 428 U.S. 153 (1976) Among the common factors aggravating are:

- that the method of death was particularly heinous or cruel (this particular factor has been held constitutionally vague in some contexts);
- that the murder was done for profit, or for hire;
- that there was more than one victim, or potential victim;
- that the victim was particularly vulnerable.

Similarly, mitigating factors include:

- that there was a defensive claim, such as duress or necessity, though not rising to the level of a total defense;
- the perpetrator was particularly young, or influenced by another;
- that the victim "provoked" the killing in some way;
- the defendant's role was "relatively minor" or he did not actually kill.[40]

Twenty-five years have passed, and the jurisprudence of death is indeed complex. For our purposes, however, the decisions can be easily summarized: While the state may be limited in what evidence it presents to persuade the sentencer that death should be imposed, the defendant is entitled to present any evidence, whether or not consistent with statutorily enunciated mitigating factors. In effect, the defendant may plead for mercy based upon facts which are statutorily irrelevant; the sentencer may be freakish in granting mercy, but not in imposing death.[41] The death penalty decision, then, is to be intensely individualized, and no goal of normal sentencing is necessarily dominant.

The process of deciding the death issue is virtually uniform throughout the country. A second hearing is held at which the jury which convicted the defendant determines the penalty. The death-eligible defendant has a constitutionally protected right to see the presentence report, which, as we have already seen, is not clearly guaranteed to a nondeath defendant. See *Gardner v. Florida*, 430 U.S. 349 (1977). Moreover, the defendant has the right to present evidence (including hearsay), subject only to typical rules on cumulative evidence. Hearsay evidence is allowed, as it is in non capital sentencing.

---

40. The Virginia statute under which John Muhammad was prosecuted for the "sniper" killings in the Washington, D.C. area in 2002 allowed the death penalty only for the actual shooter. Thus, Muhammad's attorneys sought to show that, if he was guilty at all, it was only as an accomplice who drove the car, and that Lee Malvo was the actual sniper.

41. See, e.g., *Skipper v. South Carolina*, 476 U.S. 1 (1986), allowing the defendant to show good behavior in prison (which theoretically has nothing to do with deterrence or retribution for the offense); *Lockett v. Ohio*, 438 U.S. 586 (1978) and *Eddings v. Oklahoma*, 455 U.S. 104 (1982) (defendant must be allowed to offer any evidence regarding his background, character, or circumstances of the offense). Sundby, The Lockett Paradox: Reconciling Guided Discretion and Unguided Mitigation in Capital Sentencing, 38 UCLA L. Rev. 1147 (1991). See generally, Klein and Steiker, The Search for Equality in Criminal Sentencing, 2002 Sup. Ct. Rev. 223.

The decision whether facts suffice to impose death is now the sole province of the jury. Prior to *Apprendi*, the Court had upheld a system by which a judge could make that decision, either acting alone, or even after a decision by a jury. In *Ring v. Arizona*, 536 U.S. 584 (2002) the trial judge had concluded, afer a sentencing hearing, that the murder in question had been committed "in an especially heinous, cruel or depraved manner" and in pursuit of something of "pecuniary value." The United States Supreme Court overthrew the death sentence, holding that *Apprendi* applied, and required such a fact, which increased the maximum sentence from life to death, to be made by a jury.[42]

The constitutionalization of capital sentencing procedures has been called a "dismal failure."[43] It might be argued that Justice Harlan was correct—that it is not possible to both individualize death sentences while still regularizing the process. While individualizing non-capital sentences clearly does not involve as dramatic a question, the lesson *may* be important for policy determination, even if it does not constitutionally require structured sentencing.

EXAMPLES

1. (a) The following appears in the presentence report on Herbert Wooldridge, who is convicted of 20 counts of indecent exposure, mostly to prepubescent girls: "Wooldridge's former wife Delores recounts a story in which he appeared at their front door at 4 A.M. wearing a mask and screaming in some foreign language. He banged on the door until she admitted him. She said it left her hair white; she doubts whether he has all his marbles." The judge relies on this information, but does not disclose it to Herb. Has Herb a complaint?

---

42. *Ring* precludes a state from giving the judge a role in determining the facts which would support a death penalty. But three states (Alabama, Florida and Delaware) provide for a jury determination of aggravating factors, followed by a recommendation for life or death. In a footnote in *Ring*, the Court pointed out what was *not* at stake: defendants did not claim that the judge's mitigating findings fell within the scope of *Apprendi*, nor that the Sixth Amendment prohibited a judicial determination of the ultimate sentence imposed, nor that appellate Courts could not reweigh aggravating and mitigating circumstances, nor that the failure to allege the aggravating factors in Ring's indictment violated his rights. Since, in these three states, the jury still makes the factual determination (though not the determination of the life versus death),it is possible that such a scheme is constitutional. Even in a nonweighing state, the Courts are divided on whether Ring forbids a judge to impose a death penalty when the sentencing jury is deadlocked. *State v. Whitfield*, 107 S.W.3d 253 (Mo. 2003). In that case, the jury deadlocked at 11-1 in favor of life imprisonment versus death. Allowing the weighing to be by a judge: *Ex parte Waldrop*, 859 So. 2d 1181 (Ala. 2002), *Brice v. State*, 815 A.2d 314 (Del. 2003). Contra: *Woldt v. People*, 64 P.3d 256 (Colo. 2003); *Johnson v. State*, 118 Nev. 737, 59 P.3d 450 (Nev. 2002); *State v. Ring*, 104 Ariz. 534, 65 P.3d 915 (Ariz. 2003).

43. Klein and Steiker, *supra*, n.42.

(b) The judge discloses the presentence report, including this incident, to Herb, who disputes the story, and says that his ex-wife is vengeful. What can he do at the sentencing hearing: (a) require Delores to be present and cross-examine her; (b) require the probation officer to be present and cross-examine him; (c) give his own version of the story, and a recounting of her alleged animosity toward him.

2. Suppose, in the above example, the victims of Herb's exposure, or their parents, wish to say something at the sentencing hearing. (a) May they? (b) May Herb's attorney cross-examine them if they do?

3. Sally, charged with possessing 50 grams of cocaine, successfully moved to suppress 40 grams of that cocaine because the search violated the Fourth Amendment. She was still convicted of possessing the 10 grams. At her sentencing, the judge declared: "You've only been convicted of 10 grams, which carries a sentence between 3-10 years. Since you're a first offender, I'd normally impose the 3-year minimum. But you really had 50 grams, which carries a sentence of 10-30. Your sentence is 10 years. And consider yourself lucky that the cops violated your Fourth Amendment Rights." May Sally complain, successfully, that the judge considered the illegally seized coke?

4. Suppose Sally had been charged with 50 grams, and there had been no suppression, but the jury had returned a verdict of acquittal on the 40 grams. Could the judge use the 40 grams in assessing Sally's sentence?

5 (a) Lenny was convicted of 40 counts of mail fraud, each count of which carries a five-year maximum term. Lenny swore on the stand that he was totally unaware of any fraud in the thousands of brochures he mailed to particularly vulnerable victims. At the sentencing hearing, the judge, Roy Bean, told Lenny that while he would normally sentence him to only two years, "You lied on the stand, and that, sir, is perjury." He gave Lenny the full five years on each count, to run concurrently. Has Lenny been deprived of any constitutional right?

(b) Same facts, except that the judge now imposes consecutive sentences on three of the counts, the rest to run concurrently, so that Lenny might now serve 15 years.

6. Bonnie and Clyde rob the First National Bank, a federally insured institution. Each is a first offender; each have similar backgrounds. Bonnie is convicted in state court and sentenced to two years probation. Clyde is convicted in federal court. The federal guidelines call for a 10-year sentence. The trial judge, "departs" from the guidelines, announcing that, if anything, Bonnie was more blameworthy than Clyde, and "concepts of equity, as well as equal protection, forbid these wildly disparate sentences upon similarly situated accomplices." The federal prosecutor appeals the sentence. What result?

7. Section 101 of the relevant penal code provides: "It is a felony to possess a controlled dangerous substance." Section 102 provides a long list of penalties for violating section 101, depending on the kind of drug involved and the amount possessed. Constantine is indicted for "possessing a controlled dangerous substance." The evidence at the trial shows that he grew marijuana in his backyard. There is substantial dispute about how many pot plants there were. The judge instructs the jury not to consider the amount of marijuana involved. The presentence report, which both Constantine and his lawyer see, concludes that Constantine had 5,000 plants, which, by statute, requires a sentence of 10 years. Had he possessed only one plant, the statute would permit probation. Constantine argues that (a) the type of CDS and (b) the amount should have been submitted to the jury. Is he correct?

8. In a state having an indeterminate sentencing scheme, Antonin is convicted of a crime carrying a 2-30 sentence. Susan B., the judge, relies upon all the kinds of evidence laid out in examples 1-7 above (assessment of defendant's mental capacity, perjury, illegally obtained evidence, possible other crimes, victim declarations, and acquitted conduct) and gives Antonin the maximum sentence. What now?

EXPLANATIONS

1. (a) As a matter of federal constitutional law, Herb has no right to see any of the presentence report. But virtually every state and the federal courts have provided by rule or decision for disclosure of the report generally. *However*, a judge may deem some information so confidential that she may refuse to disclose it to the defendant. The purpose of the confidentiality pledge is to obtain information now and in future presentence reports. This is solely in the discretion of he judge, and will not be overturned unless the judge has abused that discretion.

    (b) Herb has no *right* to have Delores at the hearing, much less to cross-examine her. The Sixth Amendment confrontation clause only applies at a "criminal prosecution" and, for these purposes, sentencing is not such a proceeding. Nor would due process require either compulsory process or cross-examination. Nor, perhaps more surprisingly, does Herb have a right to the presence of, or to cross-examine, the probation officer who wrote the report. Although these officers are almost always present during sentencing, they are only rarely subjected to cross-examination. Herb's best path is simply to contest the report, and to persuade the judge that she shouldn't rely on that episode nor on Delores's assessment of him. He might also argue that the story, even if true, is simply irrelevant to both his crime and his possible sentence. But since "everything is relevant" in an individualizing jurisdiction, that argument is unlikely to succeed. And, biggest surprise, although virtually all Courts allow the defendant to allocate, there is at least some doubt as to whether it is constitutionally required. See *Hill v. United States*, 368 U.S. 424 (1962); *Specht v. Patterson*, 386 U.S. 605 (1967). But see *McGautha v. California*, 402 U.S. 183 (1971).

2. In most jurisdictions, whether the victims, or their surrogates, may testify is totally in the judge's discretion. Some states, however, expressly provide for victims' statements, at least in capital sentencing cases (where the practice has been highly controversial). In theory, these statements are irrelevant, since the concern at sentencing — what to do with the defendant — does not normally involve an assessment of the harm which he has caused (which was an element of the crime for which he has been convicted). Allowing victims to present their views at sentencing is a part of a larger "victims' rights" movement, which also usually provides for notification of parole hearings, or other situations where the defendant's future is being considered. If a victim testifies, a court may require that the testimony be given under oath and subjected to cross-examination; but that, too, is in the hands of the judge.

3. There's an easy answer to this one. No. Although the Supreme Court has never held unequivocally that the exclusionary rule of the Fourth Amendment does not apply at sentencing, both the lower courts and analogous decisions from the Court itself support this conclusion. E.g., *United States v. Brimah*, 214 F.3d 854 (7th Cir. 2000); *United States v. Tauil-Hernandez*, 88 F.3d 576 (8th Cir. 1996); *United States v. Montoya-Ortiz*, 7 F.3d 1171, 1181-82 (5th Cir. 1993). In *United States v. Calandra*, 414 U.S. 338 (1974), the Court held that illegally seized evidence could be admitted and relied upon in grand jury proceedings. The Court reasoned that the purpose of the exclusionary rule, to deter police misconduct, is sufficiently served by suppressing the evidence at trial, thus making defendant's conviction less likely. There will be little marginal deterrence, said the Court, if the evidence is *also* suppressed at the grand jury. If, however, it appears that the police seized the evidence *for the purpose* of influencing sentencing, courts are inclined to preclude its use. *United States v. Kim*, 25 F.3d 1426, 1435 & n.8 (9th Cir. 1994); *State v. Habbena*, 372 N.W.2d 450 (S.D. 1985). On the other hand, confessions obtained in violation of the Fifth Amendment must be suppressed even at a sentencing hearing. *Estelle v. Smith*, 451 U.S. 454 (1981).

4. Yes. Well, maybe. As noted in the text, in *United States v. Watts*, 519 U.S. 148 (1997), the Court upheld the use, in sentencing, of conduct of which the defendant had been acquitted. The Court explained this conclusion by noting that while the jury had not found the defendant guilty beyond a reasonable doubt, this did not preclude the trial judge

from concluding, by the lower standard of preponderance of the evidence, that the defendant had acted as charged. Under *Williams*, that conclusion could inform the sentence. Caveat — *Watts* was decided pre-*Blakely*. Since the later case seems to say that any fact used to increase the sentence must be proved beyond a reasonable doubt, *Watts* may no longer be good law. Indeed, even if the judge were, after *Blakely*, to say that he had found, beyond a reasonable doubt, that Sally possessed the 40 grams, he might be "collaterally estopped" from using that conclusion. If you haven't gotten the idea yet — all bets are off after *Blakely*.

5.   (a) NO. NO???!!! How can that be? The judge decided, using some unarticulated standard of proof, that Lenny had committed a crime. There was no cross-examination, no specific chance to rebut that conclusion. Yet no violation of due process, or *Winship*, has occurred because the judge did not sentence Lenny for perjury; he merely used this one conclusion (that Lenny had abused the trial process) as a factor in deciding what the penalty for mail fraud should be. This is simply another variation of *Williams*, which allows the trial judge to rely on any information, or conclusion about that information, while assessing the penalty. The Supreme Court has held this to be perfectly proper. See *United States v. Grayson*, 438 U.S. 41 (1978). Indeed, in *Grayson*, the Court noted that courts had almost without exception concluded that "a defendant's truthfulness or mendacity while testifying . . . is probative of his attitudes toward society and prospects for rehabilitation . . ." However, in footnote 11 in *Blakely*, Justice Scalia threw signfiicant doubt upon the continued viability of *Grayson*, suggesting that the proper approach was to indict and prosecute such a defendant for perjury. See, after *Blakely*, all bets *are* off.

      (b) Most states allow the judge discretion to impose either concurrent or consecutive sentences, but a majority also provide that concurrent sentences are presumed, unless the court finds a specific reason to run the sentences consecutively. A handful of states presume that sentences should be consecutive. See Goffette, Sovereignty in Sentencing: Concurrent and Consecutive Sentencing of a Defendant Subject to Simultaneous State and Federal Jurisdiction, 37 Val. U.L. Rev. 1035, 10510-51 (2003). But even then the sentences are not reviewable at all, or only for "abuse of discretion," which is highly unlikely here.

6.   Clyde should pack everything he has; he's off to prison for a long time. The federal appellate courts have consistently held that wide disparities between state sentences and federal sentences are not grounds to depart from the federal guidelines. *United State v. Vilchez*, 967 F.2d 1351 (9th Cir. 1992). In part, the courts view the necessity for *intra* jurisdictional

uniformity as more important (and more in their control) than *inter* jurisdictional uniformity. In part, as well, these decisions are driven by a respect for the prosecutorial discretion which chose to prosecute Clyde in federal court and leave Bonnie to the state. (See Chapter 3).

7. Yes. Before *Apprendi*, Constantine's argument was rejected by every federal court that confronted it. The "crime," said those courts, was possession of *any* controlled dangerous substance, of *any* amount. After *Apprendi*, however, the courts agreed that, since the maximum sentences were increased depending on the type and amount of drug, those issues would have to be submitted to the jury. Virtually all states had submitted both issues to juries long before *Apprendi*. *Blakely* reaffirms this entire approach. The larger issue focuses on how one decides what the "crime" is. To some degree, this may be a matter of comfort as well as of semantics. A charge of "assault with a deadly weapon" could be said to charge "assault" only, and that "with a deadly weapon" is not an element of the offense, but a "sentencing factor." Intuitively, we reject that analysis because we have become inured to "assault with a deadly weapon" as a single "phrase" and hence as a single "offense." It is more difficult to see "possession of 30 grams of cocaine, while acting as a supervisor of a drug trade, and "armed with a firearm" as a single "phrase" or " offense," even if each of those added factors adds years to the potential sentence. The crucial question in this area is how to determine which facts must be determined (1) beyond a reasonable doubt; (2) by the jury. As to this specific statute, the resolution is now clear — both these facts are jury facts because they increase the potential maximum.

Irrelevant caveat — and a straw in the wind? The wording in the paragraph above (and that of the Supreme Court in both *Apprendi* and *Blakely*) seeks to avoid saying that the type and weight of drug are "elements" of the crime, although that it is often the language used by the Courts. If these are elements of the crime, the next question (not for *this* course, but for substantive criminal law purposes) is whether the government must not only prove them beyond a reasonable doubt, but whether the government must also show a *mens rea* with regard to these facts — (i.e., that the defendant "knew," or was reckless with regard to, the type or amount of drug he took). Some Courts, to avoid this implication, have noted that in *Apprendi* itself, the Court sometimes used the phrase "functional equivalent of an element," in discussing "*Apprendi/Blakely* facts" rather than the phrase "element of the crime." Stay tuned. This is an issue for the second half of this decade.

8. This may be the $64 billion question. Since *Blakely*, many have contended that the states will return to a totally indeterminate sentencing scheme, in which nothing constrains a judge's discretion within

wide ranges. (That is to say, nothing requires the judge to find "deliberate cruelty" before sentencing, nor does anything require that, if she finds "deliberate cruelty," she must affect the sentence.) Both the *Blakely* majority and the dissent discounted the possibility that states would take this course. But each also appeared to assume that, if the states did so, there would be no constitutional impediment to that action, particularly if the state systems did not require a judge to articulate why she imposed the sentence in question. Yet an argument surely can be made that (a) the constitution requires articulation of the reasons for the sentence — particularly how that structured sentencing systems have demonstrated that it is possible to do so; (b) those reasons should be subject to appellate scrutiny; (c) once there are articulable grounds for increasing a sentence, they are subject to *Blakely.* As Paul Rosenzweig, a senior Legal Research Fellow at the Heritage Foundation, testified before the United States Sentencing Commission, 17 November 2004: "I remain at a loss to understand why unexplained, indeterminate decision-making is constitutionally permissible, but explained, reasoned decision-making is not." That is far in the future (10 years???), but it is something upon which to muse. Happy musing.

12

Appeals and Collateral Attack

"If at first you don't succeed, try, try again"

"Enough already!!!"

A. A General Overview of Review

Just because Dan has been convicted doesn't mean he'll go gently into that good night. Guilty or not, Dan will certainly want some institution other than the jury (or judge) to determine whether he's been treated fairly. In modern America, Dan has three[1] separate, and very distinct, routes to follow:

- (direct) appeal in the state courts;
- collateral attack in the state courts;
- federal habeas corpus.

We will discuss these seriatim. But there are some overarching questions that will apply to each of these processes:

1. Why allow review of any decision at all?
2. When should such review be allowed, or prevented (i.e., what is the timing of the review)?
3. What should the scope of review be?

---

1. If Dan has been convicted of a federal crime, the second and third processes merge.

4.   What effect should a reversal have (a) upon the party seeking review;
     (b) upon other persons?

1. *Why Allow Review at All?*

It is easy to see why Dan wants review, but what advantages does the
state see to allowing him to seek such review? Several benefits may be
suggested:

- *A perception of justice* — others assessing the system might perceive
  that some method of review, removed from the moment of the
  events, and therefore not as likely to be consumed by possible prejudice or vengeance, gives Dan (and other citizens) a surer sense of
  impartiality.
- *Uniform application of the law* — assuring that the lower courts are
  indeed enforcing the laws, both statutory and common law, that apply
  to the case.
- *A review of the facts* — particularly if fact finders are viewed warily.
- *Reconsideration of existing law* — an opportunity to assess the principles
  actually applied in the trial and determine whether those principles
  should continue to be applied.

In England, there was no review of a trial jury's verdict of guilt.
Hanging often occurred *tout suite* after the verdict. (Remember — felons
were not entitled even to retained counsel, so there was no one who could
have pursued an appeal, even if one had been provided.) In fact, for most
criminal cases, appellate processes came to England only at the end of the
nineteenth century. In large part, this was driven by ideology; if the court
(King) is always right, there is no need for appeal.

On the other hand, if government is distrusted, or thought to be falli-
ble, appeal becomes appealing. In most of the American colonies, therefore,
defendants had a statutory right to appeal their convictions to an "appellate
court," which usually meant the state's supreme court; there were few if any
intermediate appellate courts prior to the middle twentieth century. By the
middle of the nineteenth century, appeal was universally available in the
states; the federal government adopted appeals in 1879.

Even so, for over a century, the rule has been clear — *there is no federal
constitutional right to appellate review of a criminal conviction. McKane v.
Durston*, 153 U.S. 684 (1894). But every state provides statutorily for at
least one appeal "as of right," and the Supreme Court has surrounded *that*
appeal with several ancillary rights, including the right to appointed (and
competent) counsel, and the right to a transcript.

2. At What Time Should Review Be Allowed?

While any erroneous decision by a trial court may cause an erroneous conviction (or acquittal), allowing review of any such decision *when it occurs* is simply impractical; trial courts make too many decisions over the course of a criminal prosecution, both before and during trial, that the trial would never end. A few decisions, usually those which would preclude a trial entirely (such as a decision either way on a motion to bar trial on double jeopardy grounds, or a denial of pre-trial release or intervention) or those which might structurally affect a trial (such as venue), are subject in some jurisdictions to interlocutory review (before trial). Otherwise, all jurisdictions impose the "final judgment" rule, which requires both parties to wait until after defendant is convicted (an acquittal of course would make all errors moot).

But when should a conviction be reviewed? Dan may be of mixed minds about this answer, which may be intertwined with the question of remedy, discussed below. If he seeks a change in the law, but the rule in the state is that any such change in the law will not apply even to him, he will not care. But if he successfully "changes" the law and may receive either exoneration or at least a new trial, he would initially be anxious to have review immediately. On the other hand, a delayed decision might make it harder for the state to retry him. The state, on the other hand, wants a review, if it is to happen, to be instantaneous; should a new trial be required, it wants to be sure that the witnesses are available to reconvict Dan. Not surprisingly, then, states place "statutes of limitations" upon most available review processes, presumptively precluding Dan from seeking review if there is a likelihood that evidence has gone stale. Each of the processes we will discuss this problem of "finality."

3. What Is the "Scope of Review"?

Although review could be *de novo*—hearing the witnesses again and deciding the case as though no proceeding had occurred below—that virtually never[2] happens in either civil or criminal processes. As students of *civil* procedure are aware, over the centuries, courts have divided questions below into three categories: (1) purely legal questions; (2) purely factual questions; and (3) "mixed" questions. Courts are generally agreed that *purely legal* questions should be assessed *de novo*, because a decision from a higher court

---

2. In many states, a person charged with a petty misdemeanor, or a traffic offense, can opt to be tried first before a magistrate and then may seek *de novo* review in a higher level tribunal. But this is not true for felonies.

will bind all lower courts within the jurisdiction. At the other end of the spectrum, significant (but not total) deference is given to the fact finder concerning *factual* questions, in large part because the resolution often turns on credibility, which in turn depends as much upon character assessment as upon the actual testimony.

The real thorn has been "mixed questions." Here, the decisions are so "mixed" that it is almost impossible to state what "the law" is. The first problem is deciding how "mixed" a question is. In recent years, the United States Supreme Court, rather than address this question directly, has simply moved toward allowing *de novo* review of issues which previously would have been called "mixed." State supreme courts appear to have pursued the same path.

4. What Remedy? Retroactivity and Finality; Herein of Legal Realism and Other Relevant Irrelevancies

Every judicial decision is influenced by concepts of law (jurisprudence). Often, the influence is unspoken, but in assessing the question of retroactivity, philosophical questions of the nature of the law leap to the forefront. Until the twentieth century, most lawyers, including law professors, believed (or at least said) that the common law (as opposed to legislatively established law) was "natural" — that judges "found" rather than "made" law. In such a setting, courts would always apply any decision they reached to any person who had been, or could be, affected by application of the "wrong" law. After all, the earlier decisions announcing a different rule had been *"wrong"* (gasp) — the law had always been X (as we now discovered) and X should have been applied to every possible case.

In the twentieth century that view was rejected, perhaps most famously by Justice Holmes's aphorism that "The common law is not a brooding omnipresence in the sky." Judges who believe (or recognize) that they "make" law may also determine whether to make the "new" law retroactive. Note the double-edged sword aspect of each perception: Judges who feel duty bound to apply any "newly discovered" law to all past cases may be highly reluctant to "find" new law, particularly if there are many persons who could legitimately ask to have the new law applied to their already settled cases. On the other hand, judges who believe they "make" new law and are therefore not *required* to give it retroactive effect may be more willing to "craft" new rules for future application.

A court seeking to determine the impact of its "new rule" may take any one of at least the following possible paths:

1. Apply it only to defendants who are tried after the announcement of the rule; do not apply it even to the defendant who obtained the "new rule" (prospective application only);[3]
2. Apply it only to the specific defendant whose case resulted in the new rule (and those in the future);
3. Apply it to all defendants who, while tried under the "old" rule, have still not had their judgments of convictions affirmed by an appellate court (the "pipeline," or "partial retroactivity" approach);
4. Apply it to all defendants who, while tried and convicted under the old rule, are still in some way being affected by that conviction, and are in that sense, injured (full retroactive approach).

The first of these approaches implicitly asserts that the primary, perhaps the only, function of appellate review is to announce new rules, and not to assure the fairest trials for earlier defendants. So long as the trial courts accurately applied the "old" rule, the conviction stands, because that trial was "fair" as "fair" was then defined and understood. But this approach would probably discourage defendants from appealing; while their dedication to truth and justice might be very strong, the knowledge that it would not accrue to them personally might dissuade them from appealing.

The second approach provides a "finder's fee" for the defendant whose attorney was sufficiently persuasive to convince the Court to jettison an old rule and adopt a new one; it encourages defense counsel to argue for new rules. But, assuming either that judges "look" for opportunities to change rules, or that all lawyers on appeal would be equally persuasive, this approach seems too random, particularly where an appellate court has discretion to take any case, and simply "opts" to choose one of 10 cases raising the same legal question. Thus, the third approach, applying the rule to everyone in the pipeline and who "could" have been the engine of the new rule, appears more equitable.

If the third approach makes sense, then the fourth approach, seems even fairer. Suppose, for example, an appellate court (or the United States Supreme Court) decides that due process requires that prosecutors open their files (subject to confidentiality and other such concerns) to defendants. Not only prisoners who are in the pipeline, but all those languishing in prison (including those whose conviction became final one day before the announcement of the "new rule") have suffered the same deprivation. How can the right to due process depend on which day one's conviction became "final"?

---

3. Such decisions are called "Sunbursts," after Justice Cardozo's opinion in *Great Northern Railway Co. v. Sunburst Oil & Refining Co.*, 287 U.S. 358 (1932). Prospective decisions are rare in criminal cases. See Schaefer, The Control of "Sunbursts": Techniques of Prospective Overruling, 42 N.Y.U. L. Rev. 631 (1967).

Those who argue for limited (retroactivity) argue that whether anyone (including the defendant whose appeal resulted in the new rule) was deprived of a fair trial depends on how one defines the term. Dan, and all others, by hypothesis, received what, at the time of their trial, was considered due process (or equal protection, etc.). If the purpose of review is solely to assure whether lower courts were following "the law" (statute or rule, state or federal constitution), they were — and that should be the end of that. But if the purpose is to assure an "accurate" verdict, then *perhaps* review should be allowed. The resolution of that question, discussed in more detail below, might rest on the degree to which the old process might have unfairly affected a fair trial.

At this point the state's interest in finality becomes even more relevant than it was in determining the timing of review in the first instance. Applying a "new" rule to *everyone* who might be affected, including the thousands of prisoners currently incarcerated (and possibly thousands more who are suffering "collateral consequences" of their convictions), would raise the risk that the state might be inundated with new trials. And since this approach might cover persons convicted decades earlier, the state, because it has lost witnesses, or memories have faded, etc., may be unable to provide a new trial, and a defendant who may actually be guilty, and who was provided a fair trial as that term was defined at the time of the proceeding, will be unconditionally freed. Some would call this a "windfall" to such defendants; the damage to the state (and its citizenry) might be extensive. Moreover, there is simply an interest in finality in and of itself ("If I've told you once, I've told you a hundred times. Don't ask again"). The state, and its citizens, must also, at some point, enjoy the protection of repose. Moreover, beyond these issues of balance and fairness, there is the crass, but not totally irrelevant, question of administrability and costs; assuming that the new trial would come to the "right" conclusion, should economic considerations matter? Finally, if full retroactivity were embraced, "new rules" could be applied *ad infinitum*; there would never be assured finality, even decades after a conviction had been "settled."

Each of these concerns will be present in every step of any review process. Never lose sight of these overarching questions. They will appear and reappear in slightly different guises, but they will always be there.

If there was error in the court below, the typical remedy is a retrial of the defendant, as we saw in Chapter 9, that is not precluded by the double jeopardy clause. As a general rule, a reversal of the conviction does not say that the defendant was not guilty, only that there was a flaw in the process by which he was found guilty. A new trial, where that error does not occur, may well result in another conviction. This is also true if the appellate court concludes that, weighing the prosecution's case against the defendants, the conviction was "against the weight of" the evidence. If, however, the grounds upon which the conviction is reversed is that there was insufficient evidence to convict (i.e., that the government did not even make out a *prima facie* case), then retrial is barred.

B. Appeals

> "Errors are the insects in the world of law, traveling through it in swarms, often unnoticed in their endless procession. Many are plainly harmless; some appear ominously harmful. Some, for all the benign appearance of their spindly traces, mark the way for a plague of followers that deplete trials of fairness."

> Judge Roger Traynor, *The Riddle of Harmless Error*

Immediately after a defendant is convicted, he will seek to "appeal" his conviction, based upon decisions that were made before trial (such as a ruling denying a motion for discovery of specific items), at trial (rulings on evidentiary points, or on jury instructions), or after trial (motions for a hearing to impeach the verdict based upon allegations of extrinsic impact upon the jury). In each instance, appellate counsel will claim that the trial court committed "error," and that the error requires reversal of the conviction.[4]

1. Plain Error — The "Contemporaneous Objection" Rule

If an error occurs at trial, but no one notices, is it error? This is not a deep philosophical question, but an intensely practical one. After all, there is no such thing as a perfect trial. As the quotation from Judge Traynor suggests, errors, big and little, permeate trials, and pre-trial proceedings. Errors of law and errors of fact. Not because lawyers, or jurors, or witnesses are malevolent, but because they are human, and the law is often complex. Allowing appeals for every error would result in immediate inundation of

---

4. All defendants want their convictions reversed, and it is in this context that virtually all of the legal rules we have considered in earlier chapters of this book have been considered. But it is possible to have remedies for such errors that do not result in any relief for the prisoner. An attorney can be brought up on disciplinary charges for unethical conduct; trial judges can be assigned to family law parts. Any of these actors could be publicly castigated in an appellate judicial opinion. All too often appellate courts, fearful that a "truly guilty" defendant would be released (or at least retried), refuse to find error (or harmful error) in the proceedings. If recourse against the attorney-offender were more common, and relief for the defendant not always required, perhaps the courts would more rigorously monitor the behavior of "officers of the court."

the appellate courts. On the other hand, the stakes are high; often life and almost always many years of imprisonment.

Courts therefore have established several methods by which to reduce the impact of determining that an error has occurred. One method of reducing the number of errors, and therefore of the appealable issues, is to be sure that the trial court has had an opportunity to correct any mistake.[5] Thus, in earlier times, appellate courts generally required that the defendant make a "contemporaneous objection" to any purported error; failure to raise the objection, waived the right to appeal the ruling.[6]

This doctrine, however, was seen as excessively harsh. While it is lawyers, prosecutors, judges and defense counsel, who make such errors, defendants pay the ultimate price—conviction and punishment. Courts therefore adopted the concept of "plain error" to ameliorate the rigidity of the "contemporaneous objection" rule. Although different states use somewhat different verbal formulae, the heart of a "plain error" rule is that if the error was *really* significant, and affected the heart of the trial, the appellate court may reverse the conviction notwithstanding the absence of a contemporaneous objection. The federal approach, while no means universal, is typical. In *United States v. Olano*, 507 U.S. 725 (1995), the Court announced that an appellate court would have to find four criteria before reversing on the basis of an unobjected-to error:

1. There must be error;
2. The error must be plain;
3. The error must affect the substantial rights of the defendant;
4. Failure to correct the error could bring the criminal justice system (especially the courts) into disrepute.

The first criterion clearly goes to verdict accuracy. The second appears to be concerned with monitoring trial courts. But in *Olano,* the Court explained that the "plainness" of the rule is assessed not at the time of trial, but at the time of appeal. Thus, even if the trial court (and the lawyers) were following the law as it applied at the time, *Olano* allows reversal if, in the interim, a higher court has determined that the process of which the appellant complains has now been determined to be illegal. The focus here, then,

---

5. Another method is to restrict the remedy. While England applied the "Exchequer" rule—that any error, no matter how small, would require reversal (and no new trial)—American courts did not apply such a rule, both (a) finding some errors not to require reversal at all; and (b) allowing subsequent proceedings if reversal was required. (See Chapter 9 for a discussion of the double jeopardy issues.)

6. This rule also prevents "sandbagging"—when a defense lawyer, believing that an error has been made, sits silently, hoping that his client will be acquitted (in which case the error has done him no harm) but also hoping that the appellate court will reverse on the basis of the error. The degree to which courts are concerned about sandbagging is reflected by the degree of harshness in "plain error" rules.

is on the fairness and accuracy of the conviction, rather than on monitoring trial courts.

The third prong of the "plain error" rule is concerned primarily with the effect of a violation of the legal rules. The prosecutor's failure to turn over a police report may violate state discovery rules, but it is not clear that, either in the abstract or the specific case, the defendant actually suffered harm. On the other hand, failure to turn over *Brady* material, or striking of all minority venire members (even if not objected to) may so undermine the values of a fair trial that remedy is required. In most instances the inquiry will be a fact-specific one, involving this defendant and this crime.

If the defendant's substantive rights were impinged, some would argue that reversal should be automatic. But remember that we are discussing errors *to which the defense counsel did not object*. In that context, the fourth prong asks an institutional question—whether the trial court's failure to notice the error was so egregious that appellate failure to upbraid the trial court would weaken the "public reputation of judicial proceedings." In some ways this seems in tension with the third prong; one might think failing to remedy any error which affected substantial rights would adversely affect the reputation of the judicial system. And surely any such error should have been noticed by an alert trial court. But a *Brady* violation, or even introduction of hearsay evidence, may not be so obvious during the heat of trial as it is in the cool light of postconviction deliberations. Moreover, trial courts well know that defense counsel sometimes decline to object because they do not wish to call attention to a specific piece of testimony. In the end, the fourth prong usually turns on whether there is "overwhelming" evidence that the defendant is guilty—the "guilty as sin" rule. Perhaps this reflects the understanding that reversing the conviction of a person who is "obviously" guilty would taint the reputation of the courts more than failing to chastise the trial court for allowing an error which affected that defendant's "substantial rights."

Because the defendant did not object to the error at trial, and thereby helped "create" the error, appellate courts have placed upon the defendant the burden of meeting each of the four prongs of the "plain error" rule.

2. *"Harmless" Error*

a. Nonconstitutional Mistakes

Where the defendant *has* objected, and the trial court has nevertheless committed error, the equities are significantly different. Most states now place the burden upon the state, not the defendant, to show that the error did not cause substantial harm. Courts have used such terms as "miscarriage of justice," which suggests a concern with the accuracy of the verdict, rather than with the fairness of the process.[7] Some courts distinguish between "structural" and "nonstructural" nonconstitutional errors (for example, a wrong instruction to the jury), asking whether the defendant was denied a substantive right. If the non-constitutional error is characterized as a "trial error" (for example, a ruling on admissibility of evidence), the miscarriage-of-justice language was more frequently employed.

On the other hand, it is certainly tempting to ignore, or severely discount, an error, even a large one, where the "other" evidence of the defendant's guilt appears irrefutable. If the trial court admitted hearsay, but the defendant was caught on videotape committing the crime, reversing his conviction because of the violation of a rule of evidence seems "nonutilitarian," "counterintuitive," even "obsessive." Thus, some courts began articulating a "correct result" test of harmless error — if the appellate court was convinced that the "correct result" had been reached, any error was harmless. In *Kotteakos v. United States*, 328 U.S. 750 (1946), the Supreme Court rejected a "correct result" test, and adopted, at least for federal criminal cases, an assessment of whether "substantial rights" had been impaired:

> "if one cannot say, with fair assurance . . . that the judgment was not substantially swayed by the error, it is impossible to conclude that substantial rights were not affected."

In practice, the difference between the two rules, while stark in the black letter law (which side carries the burden of proof and the degree of (lack of) harm that must be demonstrated) often disappears in practice. Where the evidence of guilt is "overwhelming," the courts are likely to find the error harmless or, in the alternative, determine that failure to reverse the conviction of a "clearly guilty" defendant would not hold the judicial system up to obloquy. It is in the cases where the evidence is truly close that the difference in approaches, which turns primarily on whether defense counsel objected or not, is manifested. That should be a sobering lesson for defense counsel.

But prejudice of some sort must be shown. The Court recently applied the *Bagley-Brady* requirement of showing prejudice to a defendant's claim of a plain, non-constitutional error violation of Rule 11. *United States v. Benitez*, 124 S. Ct. 2333 (2004).

b. Constitutional Errors

The *Kotteakos* approach applies in federal cases (and in many state courts) so long as the violation is "merely" one involving a statute, rule, or common law doctrine. If the error violates the United States Constitution, the *standard* is raised significantly. Prior to 1967, the federal courts consistently held that any violation of any constitutional provision resulted in automatic, *per se*,

---

7. Cf. The discussion of *Strickland*, Chapter 10.

reversal. No constitutional error could be "harmless." But such a rule, much like the Exchequer's rule (see n.5 above) had the effect of dissuading courts from articulating new constitutional doctrines. A court, such as the Warren Supreme Court, willing (if not anxious) to establish new constitutional protections, could not ignore the pressures of the Exchequer's tension. Thus, in *Chapman v. California*, 386 U.S. 18 (1967), the court held that while a prosecutor's comment, during summation, on the defendant's failure to testify violated the defendant's Fifth Amendment right against self-incrimination, reversal was not required if the prosecutor demonstrated that the error was "harmless" *"beyond a reasonable doubt."* This sea change in assessing constitutional error has been called "the most far-reaching doctrinal change in American procedural jurisprudence since its inception." Childress and Davis, Federal Standards of Review, sec. 7.01 (2d ed. 1986).

But, as it turns out, not all constitutional errors are equal. As we saw in Chapter 10, while the courts will attempt to assess the prejudice when counsel was ineffective, if counsel was absent, or if there was an inevitable conflict of interest, the Courts will *not* inquire as to the depth of the prejudice; prejudice will be irrebuttably presumed. A similar tack is taken in the harmless error analysis: While most constitutional errors are now subject to *Chapman* analysis, some constitutional errors (such as the total absence of counsel) simply result in immediate reversal. In these cases, there was an irrebuttable presumption of harm.

How, then, does one distinguish between those constitutional errors which require reversal (per se errors, in which the prejudice is irrebuttably presumed) and those which merely allow, but do not require reversal? A footnote in *Chapman* cited three illustrative cases of *per se* reversals — (1) where a coerced confession had been admitted; (2) where the judge had not been impartial; and (3) where the defendant had been denied counsel. The Court has since added the following to this category of error:

- discrimination in the selection of the petit jury;
- denial of consultation between defendant and his counsel;
- denial of a public trial;
- erroneous reasonable doubt instructions;
- denial of the right to self-representation.[8]

On the other hand, the Court has found many constitutional errors to be subject to the harmless error analysis, including:

- admission of evidence obtained in violation of the Fourth Amendment;
- admission of evidence obtained in violation of the defendant's right to counsel;

---

8. The failure of a trial court to be sure that the defendant knows the dangers and disadvantages of self-representation has been held to be a *Faretta* error requiring automatic reversal. *Cordova. v. Baca*, 346 F.3d 924 (9th Cir. 2003).

- admission of an out-of-court statement in violation of the confrontation clause;
- a jury instruction containing an unconstitutional rebuttable presumption;
- submission of an invalid aggravating factor to a capital sentencing jury;
- a misdescription of an element of the offense.

Twenty-four years after *Chapman*, in *Arizona v. Fulminante*, 499 U.S. 279 (1991), the Court suggested that the line between these groups of errors could be seen as involving, on the one hand, *trial* errors which could, in some metaphysical sense, be "quantified"and measured against the other evidence in the case and, on the other hand, *indeterminate, structural* errors whose impact could not be easily assessed, and which was a pervasive influence on the entire trial.[9]

The distinction drawn by *Fulminante* is remarkably similar to the approach taken by state courts assessing non-constitutional trial errors. Even if, as critics of *Chapman-Fulminante* argue, it is difficult (perhaps impossible) to assess the actual damage which *any* error, no matter how "trivial" might have in actual jury deliberations, a return to the Exchequer rule is not only unrealistic but counterproductive. As unsatisfying as current law may be on where to draw the line between errors that require automatic reversal and those that allow a weighing of the facts (and law) adduced at trial, it is probably inevitable that that line will be drawn somewhere.

Nor has the Supreme Court been extremely clear in how one measures the "harmlessness" of a constitutional error. Some decisions appear to focus on the possible impact of the error on the trial, without looking at the other evidence in the trial, determining whether the error might have "contributed" to the conviction, while other opinions speak in assessing the degree of harm which the constitutional error wreaked in light of the "overwhelming" (or less than overwhelming) evidence of guilt. In 1995, Judge Harry Edwards conducted a survey of fellow judges, and concluded that, whatever the legal standard, it was "hard for a judge to discount a strong feeling that the defendant is guilty." Edwards, To Err is Human, But Not Always Harmless: When Should Legal Error Be Tolerated, 70 N.Y.U. L. Rev. 1167, 1205 (1995). The profusion of standards for assessing the degree of harm necessary in plain versus harmless error cases, and distinguishing direct appeal from collateral review, may be overnice. In *United States v. Benitez*, 124 S. Ct. 2333 (2004), Justice Scalia, concurring, observed that "By my count, this Court has adopted no fewer than four assertedly different standards of probability relating to the assessment

---

9. *Fulminante* held that even the admission of a coerced confession might be harmless in the context of a case in which there was (other) overwhelming evidence that the defendant was guilty.

of whether the outcome of trial *would* have been different *if* error had not occurred, or *if* omitted evidence had been included. . . . Such an enterprise is not fact finding, but closer to divination." (Emphasis in original.) Indeed, Justice Souter, in the same decision, noted that even the Courts of Appeal appeared to confuse the tests, and when to apply them. 124 S. Ct. 2333, 2339, n.8.

Table 12.1 summarizes these rules:

Table 12.1   Direct Appeal

	Not Objected To (Plan)	*Objected To (Harmless)*		
		Non-Constitutional	*Constitutional*	
			Structural	*Trial*
Burden of Proof	Defendant Carries	Prosecutor Carries (by Preponderance)	Prosecutor Loses, Automatic Reversal	Prosecutor Carries Burden
Standard of Proof	Miscarriage of Justice; Varied	Likely to Produce Guilt; Tendency to Produce Guilt		BRD Did Not Contribute to Verdict

EXAMPLES

1. When Curtis was indicted for unlawful possession of a weapon, he was given Miranda warnings, but nothing more. At trial, he unsuccessfully objected to the admissibility of the confession he gave immediately after those warnings. While his case was pending on appeal, the State Supreme Court in another case (*Sanchez*) determined, as a matter of state, not federal, constitutional law that any interrogation outside the presence of counsel after a defendant had been indicted was invalid. May Curtis take advantage of the intervening *Sanchez* decision to have his conviction reversed?

2. In Alan's trial for murder, he raised self-defense. The trial judge instructed the jury that Alan carried the burden of proof that the killing occurred in self-defense. He did not instruct them on what the standard of proof on that issue was. (a) Alan's counsel did not object; (b) Alan's counsel did object. State law actually requires the prosecution to carry the burden of proof once the defendant "adequately" raises the issue (meets the burden of production). What result on appeal?

3. (a) Donald is tried for possession of cocaine. Under the state statute, the possible punishment increases with the amount of cocaine possessed. At the time of the trial, the amount of drugs is considered to be a sentencing factor. Donald's counsel makes no motion to have the issue decided by the jury. Donald is convicted; the court finds the amount to be 5 kilograms and sentences Donald accordingly. While Donald's appeal is pending, the state supreme court, applying *Apprendi*, (see Chapter 11), concludes that the amount is an element of the offense. Donald wants to take advantage of the new decision. May he?

    (b) Suppose that, after the trial, Donald learns that two of the jurors were threatened, by a competing drug dealer, if they did not find Donald guilty. Now what?

EXPLANATIONS

1. Yes. First, Curtis is "in the pipeline" — if the new *Sanchez* rule is to apply to anyone beyond *Sanchez*, it should reach Curtis as well. The question, then, is whether the decision should be given any retroactive effect. Most courts now simply say yes. *Griffith v. Kentucky*, 479 U.S. 314 (1987); *State v. Waters*, 296 Mont. 101, 987 P.2d 1142 (Mont. 1999). Other state courts, applying an approach previously endorsed in *Linkletter v. Walker*, 381 U.S. 618 (1965), use various factors, but they generally include: (1) the purpose of the rule; (2) the degree of reliance placed on the old rule by those who administered it; (3) the effect a retroactive application would have on the administration of justice. Under this approach, the purpose of the *Sanchez* rule is to assure reliable confessions, but also to discourage police interrogation of indicted, unrepresented defendants. As to the second and third prongs, police policy, even before *Sanchez*, actively discouraged interrogations of an *indicted* defendant in the absence of counsel. Thus, police had not in fact relied upon a prior, more generous interrogation rule, which also meant that there would unlikely be a sea of cases currently pending that would require retrial if *Sanchez* was made retroactive. *State v. Knight*, 145 N.J. 233, 678 A.2d 642 (1996).

2. (a) In both instances, Alan is likely to prevail, although the analysis is likely to be differently articulated. Where there was no objection, the analysis will be done under the "plain error" rule, the general outlines of which are discussed in the *Olano* case, cited in the text. Here, there is no question but that there was error, and it was plain. Moreover, it obviously affected Alan's rights. Note, however, the issue is not one of federal constitutional right; the Supreme Court has decided (much to the chagrin of many, see Singer and LaFond, Criminal Law, Chapter 16 (3d ed. 2004)) that the state may put the burden on the defendant, although only one state does. The remaining question under *Olano*,

which some state courts do not undertake, is whether the failure to correct this plain error would cast the judiciary (both trial and appellate) in a poor light. Since the law (by hypothesis) was clear at the time of the trial, and dramatically shifted the burden of proof, the answer is almost surely yes.

(b) Absolutely. Since counsel objected, the court employs the "harmless error" rather than the "plain error" approach. Here, the state must prove beyond a reasonable doubt that the error had no impact on the jury. While many errors in jury instructions may not be so severe, this one surely is. Unless there was absolutely *no* evidence beyond Alan's protestation, and (as well) substantial evidence that the victim was not aggressive, etc., the likelihood that the error was manifestly harmless would be virtually infinitesimal.

3   (a) Maybe. Since Donald is still "in the pipeline," the state supreme court decision will apply to him. Then the issue is whether there was error, and if so whether it was "harmless." Since this is a constitutional error, the plain error rule does not apply, even though Donald's counsel did not object. If the error is a "structural" one, reversal is automatic; if it is seen as a "trial" constitutional error, it will be up to the prosecutor to convince the appellate court that the error did not affect the verdict. This is a fact-specific question, and you would have to know more (for example, on an exam) before you could really answer the example fully. If the evidence showed that Donald was a significant dealer over a long period of time, that the amount of cocaine for which he was responsible far exceeded the 5 kilograms, and that there was no possibility that the cocaine belonged to others, a court might well find that this constitutional error was, nevertheless, harmless.

(b) Since the evidence is of an "outside influence," the jurors may testify about it (see Chapter 8). If the court is convinced that there was a threat, it will constitute a constitutional error. And this error is "structural"—it permeates the entire deliberations and brings into question every aspect of the jury's verdict. This will result in automatic reversal of Donald's conviction.

C. Collateral Attack

Once Dan has unsuccessfully gone through the state's appellate procedure, he may still pursue "collateral" remedies. Suppose that (a) Dan learns that Gulliver, another inmate, in another state, has confessed to the crime for which Dan was convicted. Or suppose that (b) he is sitting quietly in his prison cell, reading the most recent law reviews, and learns that, shortly after he had lost his appeal in the state supreme court, that very court changed its mind about an issue on which he had lost his case (see, e.g., *Blakely*, Chapter 11).

Or (c) the prosecutor in his case now admits suppressing certain evidence from Dan's trial, some of which was arguably covered by *Brady*, other of which was required to be disclosed only by state statute or court rule. Or (d) Dan learns that his counsel (contrary to his explicit instructions) did not interview any of the witnesses Dan told him about, did not research the law, and was unaware that the search which led to the incriminating gun was palpably illegal, and should have objected to various pieces of evidence which were inadmissible under state law. Does Dan have any remedies?

1. State Collateral Review

Prior to the middle of the twentieth century, Dan would have been unable to raise almost any of these claims in most states (and in federal tribunals as well, but let's take one step at a time). Final was final was final. One bite at the apple was all that was allowed, or tolerated. In the mid 1960s, however, the Supreme Court seemed poised to consider whether the Constitution required the states to provide "collateral processes,"[10] by which a prisoner who had already lost his appeals could nevertheless attack his conviction on specified grounds. Before the Court could reach that point, however, the case was mooted; since then, fearing the handwriting on the wall, the states have responded by establishing such procedures.

As with appeals, most collateral relief statutes establish some procedural barriers, before the claim may even be considered. Typically:

1. a prisoner may not raise a claim which was already adjudicated during the appeals process;
2. the claim must be filed within a specified time period after a specific event (such as the entry of final judgment by the state's highest appellate court, or a denial of certiorari from the United States Supreme Court) has occurred[11] unless the delay is excused;
3. a claim must be "new" — which means that the claim
   (a) could not have been raised on appeal; or
   (b) could have been raised on appeal, but was not, due to an "excusable" failure.

---

10. *Case v. Nebraska*, 381 U.S. 336 (1965). Such a holding, of course, would have been stunning in light of the view that the Constitution did not require even direct appellate processes. But all states provided those processes, while many did not have collateral attack mechanisms in place even as late as 1965. See D. Wilkes, Federal and State Postconviction Remedies and Relief 216 (1983). Indeed, the Court has since declared, in dictum, that the Constitution imposes no such duty upon the states. See *United States v. MacCollum*, 426 U.S. 317 (1976). See also *Felker v. Turpin*, 518 U.S. 651 (1996).

11. E.g., Nev. Stat. §34.726 ("within one year of the decision of the state supreme court . . . unless good cause is shown for delay").

Parallel to the "contemporaneous objection" rule at trial, the failure to raise an issue on direct appeal will usually preclude a prisoner from raising that issue during collateral attack, for reasons similar to those on appeal — (1) the desire to bring all claims to the attention of a single court at one time, and the fear that prisoners would continue to raise issues seriatim simply to exhaust the process; (2) the concern that prisoners would wait until proof had dissipated in the hope that the state would face significant difficulties in retrying the case.

But some failures to raise an issue may be beyond the control of the defendant. As with the "plain error" doctrine of appeal, there is concern that a defendant should not be penalized because her attorney was negligent (or worse). Thus, some failures to raise issues on appeal may be excused. The most obvious of these is a claim of ineffective assistance of (trial) counsel. In most instances, trial counsel also handles the original appeal. Because it is unlikely that the attorney will raise her own negligence as an issue for consideration by the court of appeals, states generally allow a prisoner to raise this issue on collateral attack. Moreover, the trial record is unlikely to contain all the facts necessary to assess the efforts of trial counsel. Indeed, in a parallel case involving a federal prisoner, the court recently held that even if a defendant "could" raise a claim of ineffective assistance on direct appeal, if he did not he would not be precluded from raising the issue on collateral attack. *Massaro v. United States*, 538 U.S. 500 (2003).

Even if Dan's counsel was not so poor as to be "inadequate," in some states[12] his counsel's failure to raise a specific issue may be excused, and he may be allowed to raise that issue on collateral attack. In determining whether to allow the issue to be raised, state courts have applied several different approaches, but the most common are the *deliberate bypass* rule and the *cause and prejudice* rule. Each of these tests originated in United States Supreme Court decisions on federal habeas corpus. The deliberate bypass rule, enunciated in *Fay v. Noia*, 372 U.S. 391 (1963) held that a prisoner should not be precluded from raising a complaint which his counsel had failed to raise on appeal unless the defendant had *personally* agreed to the attorney's decision. The rule was premised on the view that attorneys often make decisions without consulting the client, but that the client pays the price if the decision is incorrect. The *Fay* Court analyzed the decision not to pursue a particular issue as a "waiver" of that issue, which had to be done personally by the defendant in a "knowing and intelligent " way. The *Fay* rule, however, was shortlived. It was overturned only 14 years later in *Wainwright v. Sykes*, 433 U.S. 72 (1977). *Sykes* declared that the *Fay* rule had proved unworkable — that it was impossible to determine whether a defendant had been informed of, and if informed of, understood, the nuances of

---

12. But not in federal habeas corpus. See *Murray v. Carrier*, 477 U.S. 478 (1986).

foregoing a particular legal challenge. The Court there adopted a new standard that the petitioner carried the burden of demonstrating a *cause* for her counsel's failure at trial, and to show an actual *prejudice*.[13] Virtually all states have now abandoned the "deliberate bypass" approach, and moved in the direction of (if not actually adopting) the much stricter *Sykes* test. See, e.g., *Younger v. State*, 580 A.2d 52 (Del. 1990). Several state statutes or rules speak of counsel's "reasonable" or "due" diligence. E.g., Colo Rev. Stat. 16-12-206(1) (c); Idaho Code §19-4901.

Measuring Dan's claims under the "cause and prejudice" standard, or even the "due diligence" approach, will be tricky. His claim of new evidence, even a confession such as Gulliver's, will face difficult times. First, a defendant's failure to discover the "newly discovered" evidence, if not due to ineffective counsel, may not be excusable. Gulliver, after all, might have been a witness known to Dan, or Dan's counsel, or discoverable through a more thorough investigation. Even if that were not true, the "new" evidence may not be subject to real testing, either because it is stale, or for some other reason. *Herrera v. Collins*, 506 U.S. 390 (1993). Even where claims of new evidence are allowed and considered, the defendant carries an extremely heavy burden of demonstrating both reasonable excuse for not discovering the evidence earlier, and a probability of "actual innocence." See, e.g., *People v. Washington*, 171 Ill. 2d 475, 665 N.E.2d 1330 (1995). Dan's complaints about the prosecutor's violation of discovery rules, whether based on state statute or *Brady*, raise similar questions. Since some jurisdictions have narrow discovery rules (see Chapter 6); it may be some time before a defendant can obtain even a hint that these rules (or others like them) were arguably violated.

Claims the law, whether statutory, court rule, or constitutional (state or federal), was violated are generally cognizable on collateral review, particularly where the evidence supporting them was not available at the time of trial or appeal. Thus, Dan's final complaint, that the law has changed since he was convicted, raises both the problem of *retroactivity* and the issue of *cause*. In our discussion of retroactivity, we noted that most states apply new interpretations to those "in the pipeline"; but that was defined as those whose convictions had not been affirmed by the state's highest court of appeal. Under that definition, Dan is out of time, and luck. The bite of those rules on retroactivity now becomes apparent. Assuming that Dan's trial was fair as "fair" was defined at the time of his trial, the need for finality appears to outweigh the concern that Dan's trial might have been "unfair" (as we *now* define unfairness). Here, more than in any of the other claims, the question comes down to the purpose of allowing collateral review. If it is to monitor erring trial (or appellate) courts, there is no

---

13. Compare this rule to that of the *Strickland* case, discussed in Chapter 10.

obvious remedy for Dan, because the trial court was not errant in its application of the then extant law. If, on the other hand, the concern is with the accuracy and fairness of the proceedings as we now understand fairness, Dan *may* have a claim. Remember that it was for that reason that even under the "plain error" rule, the "plainness" of the error was assessed by the law at the time of the appeal, rather than at the time of the trial. If that same approach were taken here, all prisoners who would benefit by the new rule would be entitled to at least raise the issue on collateral review. The crunch between fairness and efficiency, between justice and administrative feasibility, is reached.

But it's not over yet. Dan must still demonstrate that his counsel's failure to anticipate the new rule was itself not a lack of "due diligence." Here, the trial court will review the precedents upon which the appellate court announced the "new rule," and ascertain whether a diligent counsel would have anticipated the new rule. If so, the failure to raise the legal issue at the original trial will mean that Dan could not avail himself of the new rule even if it were otherwise given retroactive effect to prisoners like him.

If Dan convinces the state collateral relief court that his claims are not barred by procedural lapses, the court will assess the claims on their merits. With some claims, the already existing trial record will be sufficient for resolution. But in others, particularly an ineffective assistance of counsel claim, that record will have to be supplemented, which may, in turn, necessitate a hearing.

Of course, simply because the state collateral attack court will *listen* to Dan's complaint(s) does not mean that he will succeed. The court may also conclude that the new evidence is either unbelievable, or, even if believed, is insufficient to warrant relief. On all claims, he will carry the burden of persuasion. For example, as we saw in Chapter 10, his claim of ineffective counsel, at least under *Strickland*, will require him to prove both inadequate performance and "prejudice," and the *Brady* claim will confront the latter test as well, insufficient to warrant a new trial. In short, Dan has a very long road ahead of him.

2. *Federal Habeas Corpus*

Hope springs eternal. Even if Dan has unsuccessfully pursued his appeal through both the intermediate appellate court and the state supreme court, and tried collateral review in the state courts, he won't give up. One last opportunity remains—federal review, in the form of a writ of "habeas corpus." Here, however, the prisoner may only raise claims that the proceedings in state court violated his federal constitutional rights; decisions on state law matters are solely within the state courts' jurisdiction.

a. A (Very) Short History of the "Great Writ" of Habeas Corpus

The "Great Writ" of habeas corpus originated, at least in part, with the Magna Carta. Ever since, it has been seen as the one insuperable barrier preventing the abuse of royal authority and protecting the freedoms of subjects. In one of many famous examples, when the trial jury in the prosecution of William Penn refused to convict him, the trial judge "attainted" them and threw them in jail, threatening to hold them there until they returned the "right" verdict. Several of the jurors invoked the right of habeas corpus, plead their case, and were released, thus establishing the right of the jury to nullify. *Bushell's* case is discussed in Chapter 8. When President Thomas Jefferson tried to prevent those charged, along with Aaron Burr, for conspiracy to commit treason, from using the writ of habeas corpus, he failed. During the Civil War, President Lincoln suspended the writ, but Chief Justice Taney issued an order stating that only Congress could suspend the writ. The military ignored Taney's order, and Congress later ratified Lincoln's action. See *Ex parte Miligan*, 71 U.S. (4 Wall.) 2 (1867), thus avoiding a constitutional crisis. The most recent example of the power of the "Great Writ" has been seen in the (noncriminal) decisions involving the Guantanamo Bay detainees and the "enemy combatants," in which the Court held that the federal courts, and hence the writ of federal habeas corpus, is available for citizens and noncitizens alike to have their detention by military authority reviewed. *Hamdi v. Rumsfeld*, 124 S. Ct. 2633 (2004). ("Executive imprisonment has been considered oppressive and lawless since John, at Runnymede, pledged that no free man should be imprisoned, dispossessed, outlawed, or exiled save by the judgment of his peers or by the law of the land. The judges of England developed the writ of habeas corpus largely to preserve these immunities from executive restraint") (quoting *Shaughnessy v. United States ex rel. Mezei*, 345 U.S. 206 (1953)); *Rasul v. Bush*, 124 S. Ct. 2686 (2004) ("Habeas corpus is . . . 'a writ antecedent to statute. . . . throwing its root deep into the genius of our common law'") (quoting *Williams v. Kaiser*, 323 U.S. 471 (1945)).

During Reconstruction, federal courts began tentatively applying a federal habeas statute to provide relief for state prisoners as well. In one stirring phrase, Justice Holmes, in *Frank v. Mangum*, 273 U.S. 309 (1915) declared that the writ "cuts through all forms and goes to the very tissue of the structure." By the 1940s, the courts were entertaining habeas petitions from state prisoners who argued that they were being held in custody on the basis of convictions obtained in violation of specific federal procedural requirements. In 1948, Congress, in a new "codification" of the earlier law, provided that a petition could not be entertained unless the prisoner had "exhausted the remedies available in the state courts" or there was "an absence of available State corrective process or the existence of circumstances rendering such process ineffective to protect the rights of the prisoner." The prisoner would not be "deemed to have exhausted" remedies if he had "the right under the law of the State to raise, by any available procedure, the question presented."

In the landmark decision of *Brown v. Allen*, 344 U.S. 443 (1953), however, the Court read the statute only to codify the exhaustion doctrine that the Court itself had established in an earlier case.[14] Once prisoners gave state courts one opportunity to address federal claims, they were free to file petitions for the writ in federal court. Although *Brown* confirmed that federal courts could deny the writ if they were "satisfied by the state court record" that the "state process" had given "fair consideration" to the issues and the evidence and reached a "satisfactory conclusion," Justice Reed also said that federal courts had "discretion" to hold their own hearings. Moreover, a previous state court decision on the merits of a federal claim was not *res judicata*, but was entitled only to the weight the federal court would give to the conclusion of a court of last resort of another jurisdiction on federal constitutional issues.

As the Warren Court expanded the application of constitutional provisions to the states, and as the embryonic civil rights movement grew, the Court, in a trilogy of cases[15] expanded the writ to ensure that virtually every state prisoner could obtain one *federal* court interpretation of federal constitutional law as it applied to his state court criminal conviction. Federal district court consideration of such petitions might (again) serve two goals:

1. assuring that state courts did not misunderstand, and improperly apply decisions by federal courts interpreting the constitution; this view argues that because federal courts more frequently decide federal issues, they are more expert in resolving those questions; and
2. assuring that defendant received fair trials; this view posits that state courts understand the federal law, but simply ignore it.

For over 50 years the debate raged, primarily within the Supreme Court itself, as advocates of each view waned and waxed. During the Warren years, federal "review" was significantly broadened. New views of Federalism, however, emerged in the 1980s and 1990s, and the Supreme Court either overruled outright or significantly limited the decisions of the 1960s. In 1996, Congress, in the Antiterrorism and Effective Death Penalty Act (AEDPA) appeared to codify those changes — or enact even more severe limitations upon both state and federal prisoners. We will explore those decisions and AEDPA below. Suffice to say here that AEDPA is incredibly arcane and difficult to interpret; Justice Souter has declared: "in a world of silk purses and pigs' ears, the Act is not a silk purse of the art of statutory drafting." *Lindh v. Murphy*, 521 U.S. 320 (1997).

---

14. *Ex parte Royall*, 117 U.S. 241 (1886).
15. *Fay v. Noia*, 372 U.S. 391 (1963); *Sanders v. United States*, 371 U.S. 1 (1963); *Townsend v. Sain*, 372 U.S. 293 (1963).

b. Federal Habeas Corpus — More Procedural Barriers

Federal courts will not oversee state trials unless the prisoner has previously presented his federal claim to the state court. Thus, as with state collateral attack and appeal, before the federal court will even consider the merits of a claim, the prisoner seeking federal review of his state court conviction must show that:

- the petition is timely filed;
- he has exhausted his (available) state remedies;
- he is not precluded from relief by procedural default.

i. Timeliness. AEDPA establishes, for the first time, a deadline by which a petition must be filed; prior to AEDPA, the question of timeliness was one of reasonableness in the district court's discretion. Now, a state prisoner must file within one year after:

1. the date on which the state court judgment becomes "final" by the conclusion of direct review; or
2. the date on which an unlawful state "impediment" is removed; or
3. the date on which the constitutional right asserted is "initially recognized by the Supreme Court," *provided* that the Supreme Court has explicitly made it retroactive to cases on collateral review; or
4. the date on which the factual predicate of a claim is discoverable through the exercise of due diligence.

If the prisoner files timely, but must exhaust other state remedies, the filing "tolls" the one-year statute of limitations. Thus, there is still a requirement that the prisoner "exhaust" whatever state remedies are left. In *Duncan v. Walker*, 533 U.S. 167 (2001) the Court held that the tolling period did not apply if the state prisoner was seeking federal habeas corpus for "unexhausted" claims, which meant that if a habeas petitioner mistakenly filed a petition in which there were both exhausted and unexhausted claims, and had to return to state court, he might well find that his year had expired before he returned to federal court. Seven of the eight circuits that have confronted the issue encourage or require the district court to employ a "stay and abeyance" procedure, by which the one-year period is tolled while the state prisoner exhausts those remedies, thus retaining federal jursidiction over the claims. See *Pliler v. Ford*, 124 S. Ct. 2441 (2004), (Breyer, J., dissenting) (citing jurisdictions)[16] Although *Pliler* was thought to raise the issue, the Court there

---

16. A four Justice plurality in *Pliler* held that district judges need not give defendants the specific warnings which the Ninth Circuit had imposed; a five-person majority, however, clearly indicated that the equitable tolling doctrine was desirable, if not constitutionally required. It is virtually certain that the Court will constitutionalize the "stay and abeyance" procedure, assuming the personnel remain the same.

avoided deciding whether the "stay and abeyance" process was required by habeas corpus, but within days after that opinion, granted certiorari in another case raising the issue directly. *Rhines v. Weber*, 346 F.3d 799 (8th Cir. 2003), certiorari granted, 124 S. Ct. 2905 (2004).

The exception for state 'impediments" refers to instances where correctional officials (or others) make it difficult for the state prisoner to comply with the time periods in the statute. Thus, a state prosecutor's discovery violation "impedes" the prisoner, and thereby tolls the filing period.

The third and fourth restrictions provide extension of the one year period for "newly discovered" facts or newly decided case law.

ii. Exhaustion of Remedies. More than a century ago, in the seminal case of *Ex Parte Royall*, 117 U.S. 241 (1886) the Court articulated the notion that it should not "review" a state decision until all relevant state authorities had been afforded the opportunity to do so first. The salient notion is to provide the state court a real opportunity to assess the federal claim. As noted above, the exhaustion requirement was hotly debated in the 1940-1960s. The exhaustion requirement is not a jurisdictional prerequisite, but rests on the comity that federal courts owe to the states and state courts. When a petition fails to satisfy the exhaustion requirement, the federal court *postpones, but does not lose,* the exercise of jurisdiction. The importance of the filing deadline is primarily formal — to alert all concerned that the prisoner intends to seek federal review if state procedures prove unfruitful.

Ironically, at least one aspect of the exhaustion doctrine may exacerbate federal-state relations. Under *O'Sullivan v. Boerckle*, 526 U.S. 838 (1999), a state prisoner must ordinarily seek discretionary review in the highest state court in order to satisfy the exhaustion doctrine. But state courts may not be anxious to be inundated with petitions for discretionary review in the teeth of state procedure rules that invite only especially important or novel issues. The state highest court need not reach the merits of the case, however, nor it is enough if it has been given a fair opportunity to reach the merits. *Smith v. Digman*, 434 U.S. 332 (1978).

Using the state appellate process does not complete the exhaustion requirement. If the state provides other processes (such as state collateral relief, discussed above), the prisoner must present through those channels all claims which she wishes the federal court to consider should state processes not result in a new trial. AEDPA's language is similar — exhaustion has not occurred if the prisoner "has the right . . . to raise, *by any available procedure*, the question presented" (emphasis added).

Under case law, futile or uncertain remedies were not "effective" avenues of relief, and did not need to be exhausted. *Duckworth v. Serrano*, 454 U.S. 1 (1981). AEDPA similarly provides that the state prisoner need not exhaust a process "if circumstances exist that render such process ineffective to protect the rights of the applicant."

The exhaustion doctrine covers *all* claims raised by the prisoner; federal district courts should dismiss "mixed" petitions (raising both exhausted and nonexhausted claims) in their entirety, to encourage prisoners to litigate all their claims in state court before proceeding to federal court. A prisoner who takes premature claims out of his petition runs the risk that those claims will be foreclosed, if and when they are renewed in a subsequent habeas application. *Rose v. Lundy*, 455 U.S. 509 (1982).

Exhaustion requires that the prisoner has "fairly present(ed)" the issue to the state court; if he has not done so, the federal court may refuse to consider the habeas petition. In *Baldwin v. Reese*, 124 S. Ct. 1347 (2004), the brief in the state collateral relief proceeding merely complained that defendant's appellate counsel provided "ineffective assistance," but did not expressly cite or rely upon federal (as opposed to state) standards. The *Baldwin* Court, 8-1, held that this was not a "fair presentation" and petitioner had therefore not exhausted his state remedies.

iii. Procedural Default. As on state appeal and collateral relief, the state prisoner seeking federal review has one more procedural hurdle to overcome, and it is by far the most complicated and the most foreboding. Exhaustion, after all, simply delays federal assessment of the prisoner's trial. If, however, he has *procedurally defaulted* the claim, he has lost all hope that a federal court will consider his claim. In earlier times, at least, the doctrine was applied with excessive rigor. In *Daniels v. Allen*, 344 U.S. 443 (1953), a state rule required that an appeal on a jury composition issue had to be "filed" within 60 days of the judgment. Mailing on the 60th day would have met the deadline, but counsel decided instead to file the papers by hand on the 61st day; had he mailed the papers on the 60th day, they would not have arrived earlier than they did when he brought them to the clerk's office. Nevertheless, the state appellate court refused to hear the appeal, and the United States Supreme Court held this was a procedural default which precluded review of the jury claim.[17] Daniels was later executed.

In *Fay v. Noia*, 372 U.S. 391 (1963), as discussed earlier, the Supreme Court dramatically altered this approach. *Fay* declared that only if a state defendant had personally been involved in a decision not to raise an issue or objection would he be said to have "deliberately bypassed" the state-created remedial processes and precluded from having a federal court assess his claim. Otherwise, counsel's inadvertent (or even intentional) failure to object at trial, or to have raised the question during the appeals process, would not bar the prisoner from federal review.

---

17. As a technical matter, the Court applied the "adequate state ground" test which is applied on direct review from a state court. But the deference to state procedure is the basis of the decision.

Within two years, however, the requirement that defendant personally participate was softened, and over the next 15 years the Court gradually whittled away at *Fay*, imposing higher hurdles to review. In *Wainwright v. Sykes*, 433 U.S. 72 (1977), the Court finally jettisoned *Fay* and adopted the *cause and prejudice* standard which it has applied since.[18] Under this rule, the prisoner who has not followed state procedural rules must show both:

1. that there was a "cause" for his failure to do so; and
2. the procedural default has "prejudiced" his case.

   iv. Procedural Default under AEDPA. Although AEDPA does establish rules for when a hearing should be held to resolve factual disputes relating to a cognizable claim, it does not explicitly set out standards for assessing the effect of a procedural default. Therefore, the pre-AEDPA case law is likely to continue to apply, although the general tenor of AEDPA may influence the courts into a more restrictive mode generally with regard to each of these tests.

   The requirement that a prisoner provide the state court system with at least one opportunity to correct any possible federal or constitutional errors makes obvious sense if the purpose of federal habeas corpus is to assure that state courts are properly applying federal constitutional decisions. On the other hand, the procedural default rule ironically grants a second review to defendants who have had a claim considered (and rejected) by state courts, but no review to defendants who have not raised the issue in state court.

3. Cause

The Supreme Court has identified three circumstances that could excuse default:

1. the legal or factual basis for the claim was not reasonably apparent at the time it should have been presented to the state courts and there are now no state processes available, *Murray v. Carrier*, 477 U.S. 478 (1986);
2. the state has prevented a defendant from presenting the claim;
3. defendant's representation was inadequate.

   The last of these, of course, is essentially an independent claim. As such, it means that any failure of counsel which does not rise to the level of a

---

18. Aside from Federalism issues, the Court might have been nudged toward this result by its conclusion that federal prisoners seeking similar relief under 28 U.S.C. §2255 were required to show "cause" for procedural defaults. See *Davis v. United States*, 411 U.S. 233 (1973) (overruling, on the basis of Federal Rule 12(b), *Kaufman v. United States*, 394 U.S. 217 (1969), which had accepted the application of *Fay*).

Strickland violation (and few do, as seen in Chapter 10) may bar the prisoner from a review of his claim by both state and federal courts.[19] The second circumstance parallels the earlier inquiry into state intervention. For example, in *Amado v. Zant*, 486 U.S. 214 (1988), the prosecutor requested jury commissioners to underrepresent African Americans and women, and then (not unnaturally) did not disclose that request. The Court held that this constituted "impairment" sufficient to excuse the prisoner from having raised the jury issue in a timely fashion. In *Banks v. Dretke*, 540 U.S. 668 (2004), the Court found that a prosecutor's nearly 20-year refusal to disclose *Brady* material, despite defense counsel's reliance on the statement that "you have everything we have," constituted cause. See also *Strickler v. Greene*, 527 U.S. 263 (1999).

The first provision, that counsel did not, and could not, have anticipated a "new rule" will be discussed in detail below. Here, it is sufficient to note that if the claim is "really" so new that counsel can not be faulted for not having raised it, the claim may be barred under the "new rule" standard of *Teague*.

In *Murray v. Carrier*, 477 U.S. 478 (1986), the Court created a "narrow exception" to the rule that a procedural default will bar consideration of a constitutional claim even if the defendant cannot show cause and prejudice, where the defendant can show "actual" or "legal" innocence of the crime, or, in a capital sentencing context, of the aggravating circumstances rendering the inmate eligible for the death penalty. In *Dretke v. Haley*, 124 S. Ct. 1847 (2004), the Court avoided the question whether the last exception should be expanded to include cases where the defendant could show legal "innocence" of a crime which was used as a predicate in finding him to be an habitual offender, but several members of the Court clearly indicated a desire to so hold.

4. Prejudice

It is difficult enough for a prisoner to show cause under the *Sykes* standard. But beyond that, she must also demonstrate that the failure to raise the issue in a timely manner resulted in prejudice. As suggested above in the discussion of appeals and waivers, the decisions are unclear, but it appears that the prejudice test here is similar to, if not identical with, the *Strickland-Brady* criterion: that there is a "reasonable probability" that the outcome would have been different, which undermines confidence in the verdict.[20]

---

19. At the same time, the ineffective assistance claim is one concerning that which the prisoner must exhaust existing state remedies.

20. See *United States v. Brady*, 456 U.S. 152 (1982). See also Jeffries and Stuntz, Ineffective Assistance and Procedural Default in Federal Habeas Corpus, 57 U. Chi. L. Rev. 679 (1990).

These are not easy hurdles to overcome. But the court left the prisoner a final safety net—if a prisoner shows that the result in conviction was a "miscarriage of justice," and that he is "probably innocent" of the charge, a federal court is authorized to address the merits of a claim even in the face of an unexcused procedural default. See *Schlup v. Delo*, 513 U.S. 298 (1995). But the safety net may itself be full of holes. In *Schlup*, Justice Stevens declared that a prisoner who hopes to satisfy the "probable innocence" test must claim the presence of "new reliable" evidence (whether it be exculpatory scientific evidence, trustworthy eyewitness accounts, or critical physical evidence) that was not presented at trial. Further, the prisoner carries the burden of showing not merely that there might have been prejudice, but that "it is more likely than not that no reasonable juror would have convicted in light of the new evidence." Justice Rehnquist, dissenting in *Schlup*, would apparently have raised the standard of proof to "clear and convincing evidence."

c. The Merits of the Claim

If Dan has not procedurally defaulted on the claim, and it *was* resolved by the state courts on the merits, will the federal court consider that claim? Both before and after AEDPA, the answer is extremely complicated.

i. Issues of "Pure" Law. If Dan's claim is one of law only, for example, that some action in the state court violated a rule of constitutional law, the first question is: *Was the rule of law extant at the time of the state proceeding?*

If so, then Dan's sole claim is that the state court improperly applied a fixed rule of federal, constitutional law. Ostensibly, this was *precisely* the reason for the Warren court's expansion of the writ—to assure that states were not avoiding constitutional doctrines, particularly in an era when constitutional rights were being established in rapid order. Remember that at the point the state prisoner files a habeas corpus petition, at least two state courts have passed on the issue: the trial court and at least one state appellate court. It is possible (indeed likely) that the state supreme court has considered the issue on direct appeal and, depending on the state, one or more of those courts might have reconsidered the issue on collateral review.

In *Brown v. Allen*, 344 U.S. 443 (1953), the Court, per Justice Frankfurter, held that federal courts were to "independently apply the correct constitutional standard" "no matter how fair and completely the claim had been litigated in state courts." This reflected the view that federal courts were simply more knowledgeable about constitutional standards than state courts. In an era when few provisions of the Bill of Rights applied to the states, and few constitutional issues would therefore be argued in the state courts, that might well have been the case. By the 1980s, however, states were daily dealing with the nuances of the Fourth, Fifth, and Sixth Amendments in state criminal trials; the only claim federal courts then could make was not greater knowledge but possibly greater impartiality. But such a claim flew in the face of the notions of federalism and comity. In *Wright v. West*, 505 U.S. 277 (1992), the Court specifically asked the parties to address the question whether a federal habeas court should "give deference to the state court's application of law to the specific facts of the petitioner's case" or "review the state court's determination *de novo*". But the Court still avoided that question.

Congress resolved the question in AEDPA. That statute provides that habeas shall not be granted unless the adjudication of a claim:

> "resulted in a decision that was contrary to, or involved an unreasonable application of, clearly established Federal law, as determined by the Supreme Court of the United States."

28 U.S.C. §2254(d)(1)

The thrust of this provision is clear: if a state court reasonably, but incorrectly, interprets federal constitutional law in resolving a defendant's claim, the prisoner, who by hypothesis was deprived of a constitutional right in his state trial, obtains no relief. This established the function of habeas not as protecting state defendants' constitutional rights, but as chastising (only) "unreasonable" state courts, whose decisions are *contrary to* federal law. Moreover, the decision which is ignored by the state court must have been written by the Supreme Court[21] — the decision of a Circuit Court of Appeals concerning a constitutional right, no matter how clearly articulated, does not fit within the words of the statute. By implication, state courts can ignore those decisions with impunity. Moreover, the decision of the Supreme Court must *clearly establish* the constitutional principle which the state court has ignored. Law students can probably count on one finger the opinions which "clearly establish" a specific rule of law. Lawyers (and therefore courts) know how to narrow opinions and decisions so that they only apply to the exact facts before them. (If that were not so, there would be no need for the examples at the end of every chapter of every book in this series.)

The Court grappled with the meaning of (d)(1)'s restrictions in *(Terry) Williams v. Taylor*, 529 U.S. 362 (2000). There, a fractured Supreme Court appeared to decide that the "contrary to" clause of AEDPA meant that the state court decision had to be "opposite to," "diametrically different," or "substantially different," from the "relevant" precedent of the Court, if the set of facts of the current case were "materially indistinguishable" from those in the guiding precedent. Moreover, "clearly established federal law" refers to the holding, as opposed to the dicta, of the Supreme Court's decisions

---

21. *Tyler v. Cain*, 533 U.S. 656 (2001).

and "governing legal principle or principles set forth by the Supreme Court" at the time the state court renders its decision. *Lockyer v. Andrade*, 538 U.S. 63 (2003).

The *Williams* Court further declared that under the "unreasonable application" clause, a federal court "may grant the writ if the state court identifies the correct governing legal principle . . . but unreasonably applies that principle to the facts of the prisoner's case." Rejecting Justice Stevens argument that relief could be granted if the state court decision was simply "erroneous" or "wrong," the majority responded that the unreasonableness of the state court's decision is to be assessed "objectively" *Taylor, supra*. This means that even if a state court decision is incorrect, it may still not be "unreasonable." *Woodford v. Visciotti*, 537 U.S. 19 (2002); *Price v. Vincent*, 538 U.S. 634 (2002); *Wiggins v. Smith*, 539 U.S. 510 (2002).

Clearly, AEDPA, as interpreted by the Court, has made habeas corpus a method solely of assuring that state courts do not purposely misread and misapply federal precedent. Short of that, the state court decision and the conviction will stand, even if, now, all would agree that the decision was incorrect.

The relationship of AEDPA and a doctrine articulated by the Supreme Court only seven years before AEDPA was enacted, is unclear. In *Teague v. Lane*, 489 U.S. 288 (1989), the Court crafted the view that a federal court could not grant relief on the basis of a " new rule" of constitutional law which had not been available at the time of a relevant state court proceeding. Under *Teague*, the federal habeas court should:

1. determine when the defendant's conviction became final;
2. ascertain the "legal landscape as it then existed";
3. ask whether the earlier decisions rule *compelled* the new rule sought to be applied; if prior precedent "compelled" the rule, then it is not new, and may be applied by a habeas court. If it is new, it may not be so applied.

Both AEDPA and *Teague* are driven by the same basic notion — that the function of federal habeas "review" is to be sure that state courts aren't simply flouting federal constitutional decisions. But the interplay between the two rules is far from obvious. In *Williams v. Taylor*, the Court declared that the AEDPA language "bears only a slight connection to our *Teague* jurisprudence. . . .". The Court reiterated this view in *Horn v. Banks*, 536 U.S. 266 (2002):

> "none of our post-AEDPA cases have suggested that a writ of habeas corpus should automatically issue if a prisoner satisfies the AEDPA standard . . . If our post-AEDPA cases suggest anything about AEDPA's relationship to *Teague*, it is that AEDPA and *Teague* inquiries are distinct."

When the Third Circuit, on remand from the Court, held that *Teague* did not prohibit retroactive application of prior Supreme Court cases because the application did not involve a "new rule," *Banks v. Horn*, 316 F.3d 228 (3d Cir. 2003), the Court again reversed. *Beard v. Banks*, 124 S. Ct. 2504 (2004), finding that the cases had established a "new rule." Justice Thomas' opinion did not even cite AEDPA, perhaps because the habeas petition was filed prior to AEDPA's enactment. But *Beard* reaffirms the view that the defendant must satisfy *both* AEDPA and *Teague* to secure review.

Whether AEDPA "replaces" or merely "supplements" *Teague* does not initially seem critical. Both doctrines severely restrict the authority of the federal court to issue a writ based upon "new rules." But there is one distinction — *Teague* had two "exceptions," which are not included in the AEDPA language. While these are relatively narrow exceptions,[22] they could become important if *Teague* is not displaced entirely by AEDPA. Federal courts *could* apply a "new rule," said the Court in *Teague,* if the rule:

(a) places certain kinds of primary private individual conduct beyond the power of the criminal law-making authority;

(b) implicates "fundamental fairness" by mandating procedures "central to an accurate determination of innocence or guilt."

Both standards are extremely restrictive. The first appears to have been applied in *Penry v. Lynaugh*, 492 U.S. 302 (1989) (the same year as *Teague*), in which the Court discussed the rule barring the execution of mentally ill defendants. The courts have been equally frugal in finding rules "central to an accurate determination of innocence or guilt." This language, which sounds strikingly like that used to describe "structural" rules (see above in the discussion of the harmless error doctrine) has never been invoked by the Supreme Court; in fact, the Court has consistently rejected arguments that new rules are "fundamental" either because they were not sufficiently fundamental[23] or because they did not go to the fact finding process.[24] As the Court recently acknowledged: "We have yet to find a new rule that falls under the second *Teague* exception." *Beard v. Banks*, U.S. , 2004 WL 1402567, A.8.

In *Tyler v. Cain*, 533 U.S. 656 (2001), the Court held that no Court decision had held that a "structural error" applied retroactively, nor that all "structural errors" fell within the *Teague* exception: "The standard for determining whether an error is structural, see generally, *Arizona v. Fulminante . . .* is not

---

22. Prof. Larry Yackle, a leading authority, says that the *Teague* exceptions are so "microscopic" that it is irrelevant whether *Teague* survives AEDPA. Yackle, Federal Courts: Habeas Corpus 79 (2003).

23. E.g., *Sawyer v. Smith*, 497 U.S. 227 (1990) (new rule prohibiting prosecutorial argument which suggested that capital juries need not be overly concerned with accuracy of a guilty verdict because the case would be appealed).

24. E.g., *Teague* itself, in which the Court held that the cross-section guarantee (see Chapter 8) did not go to the accuracy of the verdict *per se*.

coextensive with the second *Teague* exception, and a holding that a particular error is structural does not logically dictate the conclusion that the second *Teague* exception has been met."[25] This declaration not only explains the relationship of *Teague's* second category with "structural errors" under *Fulminante,* but certainly implies that the *Teague* exceptions have survived AEDPA.

The AEDPA-*Teague* rule is a "gatekeeper." In *Beard,* the Court reaffirmed that a state court must conduct a *Teague* analysis before going to the merits of a prisoner's claim. While at first glance this appears to be consistent with deciding nonconstitutional issues first, *Teague* itself requires both a constitutional analysis of prior case law, and an analysis of whether the prior case law establishes a "bedrock" constitutional, "structural" principal (exception (b) above). The process does, however, possibly allow the federal court to avoid assessing the bona fides of a state court legal decision.

ii. "Issues of Fact" or "Mixed Questions of Fact and Law." Every law

student knows the adage: "If you don't have the facts, argue the law. If you don't have the law, argue the facts." If Dan can't make a good "pure law" claim (because, for example, it's "new")what about a factual dispute? Suppose he concedes that the state courts applied the correct *rule,* but that they determined the facts incorrectly, and therefore arrived at a wrong result. By the time Dan reaches federal court, having exhausted all his state remedies, and having stated all claims so as not to be procedurally barred from raising them in federal court, at least one state tribunal (and perhaps many others) has conducted a hearing, and resolved questions of fact; there are transcripts of the trial, and of the collateral proceedings, including any hearings which the state courts held. Each of those courts has made "findings of fact," in which at least some number of appellate judges have concurred (or at least not disagreed).

Some questions will involve only factual disputes. Suppose, for example, that Dan has testified that before he confessed he used the explicit words "I want to talk to a lawyer," but that the police ignored his comment and continued to interrogate him for 15 more hours. The police, on the other hand, testified at the suppression hearing that he said no such thing, and the state trial (or collateral relief) court credited that testimony. Should the federal habeas court even hold a hearing to determine the credibility of the witnesses?

Under Warren Court doctrine, acquiesced in by Congress, federal district courts were authorized (and in some instances compelled) to hold

---

25. In *Beard,* the Court emphasized that it had referred *"only"* to *Gideon v. Wainwright* as a case that would qualify as a second category decision. Thus, the category is substantially smaller than even the "structural" analysis applied on appeal. (see section B(2)(b), *supra,* p.310 et seq.)

evidentiary hearings at which Dan might challenge many, if not all, of the factual conclusion reached by the state courts. Some, but little, deference was due to those findings.

In light of earlier discussions, you shouldn't be surprised to learn that that is all changed. The Supreme Court had already substantially altered its view before AEDPA, but that statute has rewritten the framework relating to factual resolutions, and hearings to allow challenges to them. First, the statute provides that any actual factual finding by a state court "shall be presumed to be correct" and that "the applicant shall have the burden of rebutting the presumption . . . by clear and convincing evidence." On the basis of the record developed in the state courts, it is unlikely that Dan will be able meet that burden. So he will seek an evidentiary hearing at which he can "supplement" the state court record. But he has a heavy burden of persuasion before that may occur.

Dan may run directly into section (3e)(2) of AEDPA, which provided that if he has "failed to develop the factual basis" of a claim, the federal court "shall not" hold a hearing unless the applicant shows:

> "(A) the claim relies on
> (i) new rule of constitutional law, made retroactive to cases on collateral review by the Supreme Court, that was previously unavailable; *OR*
> (ii) a factual predicate that could not have been previously discovered through the exercise of due diligence; *AND*[26]
> (B) the facts underlying the claim would be sufficient to establish by clear and convincing evidence that but for constitutional error, no reasonable fact finder would have found the applicant guilty of the underlying offense."

This is an almost insuperable barrier, particularly since the prisoner must meet these standards *before* the evidentiary hearing can be held. In *(Michael) Williams v. Taylor*, 529 U.S. 420 (2000)[27] the Court seemed to interpret the AEDPA language ("could not have been previously discovered . . .") to apply primarily to evidence that truly "could not have been" discovered, such as new scientific tests, or recanting witnesses. Otherwise, said the Court, a prisoner (or his attorney) did not exercise "diligence" when he had an opportunity to pursue a claim in state court. On the other hand, the Court also suggested that the prisoner (and not his counsel) might have to be personally involved in inadequate record making. In *Williams* itself, the

---

26. Emphasis and capitalization added.

27. Incredibly, the Supreme Court decided two cases, each involving a capital habeas corpus petitioner named Williams, each from Virginia, in back-to-back decisions. When citing *"Williams" v. Taylor*, be sure that you distinguish between "Michael" and "Terry" Williams.

Court found that the prisoner had not exercised the necessary diligence in developing the factual basis for one claim, but found him diligent as to another claim, involving a juror and prosecutor who had divulged that the juror had been previously married to a prosecution witness, and that the prosecutor had previously represented that juror in the divorce proceeding.

Thus, the habeas applicant is caught in a Catch $21\frac{1}{2}$: if he has not developed the state record, he will almost never get a hearing because his failure to do so will not be excused. If, on the other hand, he *has* developed the facts at those hearings, he must show not merely improper procedure, but essentially that he is innocent of the crime.[28] At any hearing, he will carry the burden "by clear and convincing evidence" that the state court determination is incorrect.

That makes it very unlikely that Dan's going to succeed on a factual claim. What, then, about "mixed" questions of law and fact? The standard for review of "mixed" questions has always been important, and murky. And even on direct review, it is not yet clear what the standard, either constitutional or otherwise, is. But on habeas corpus under AEDPA, that distinction may literally mean the difference both between obtaining a hearing and not, and the standard (if not the burden) of proof involved in the subsequent proceeding.

The Court has always been sensitive to the "factual" or "mixed" distinction; but it has taken a wide-ranging policy approach to deciding how to characterize each issue. See *Miller v. Fenton*, 474 U.S. 104 (1985). This distinction would seem to retain its importance even under AEDPA.

If a district court dismisses the habeas petition, §2253(c)(1) requires a state petitioner to obtain a "certificate of appealability" from the relevant Circuit Court of Appeals. This process, which could be quite cumbersome if followed assiduously, was enacted to relieve circuit courts of habeas cases.

What is one to make of these developments? One objection to the narrowing of federal habeas corpus, sometimes called the "percolation" argument, is that by precluding federal district courts from announcing new constitutional rights on habeas corpus, *Teague* (and AEDPA) interferes with the ability of issues to "percolate up" to the Supreme Court. Thus, prior to *Teague* and AEDPA, both district and circuit courts were able to grapple with the constitutional issue over a period of time before the Supreme Court "had to" take a case to resolve the issue. Another aspect of this argument is that, prior to *Teague* and AEDPA, federal and state courts would engage in a

---

28. The requirement of showing "actual innocence" is echoed in the Court's decision in *Stone v. Powell*, 428 U.S. 465 (1976) that habeas applicants will not be allowed to claim Fourth Amendment violations, in part because the evidence which the defendant-petitioner wanted suppressed demonstrated his guilt, not his innocence.

"dialogue" concerning the proper scope of federal constitutional protections, but that this dialogue is now threatened (if not stopped cold) by the restrictions engendered by *Teague* and AEDPA.

d. Federal Habeas Corpus — Successive Petitions

Even after Dan has been through state appeals, state collateral relief, and federal collateral relief, and has lost every time, hope keeps springing eternal. After all, the prospect of many years in prison can concentrate the mind, and he may, indeed probably will, continue to look for ways to obtain release, or at least a new trial. If he discovers a new claim, or if new case law develops a possible new argument that had not been available before, he is still unlikely to even obtain a hearing on such a new claim. Prior to AEDPA, district courts decided whether a second habeas petition was an "abuse of the writ," using approaches similar to those of the "deliberate bypass" rules of *Fay v. Noia*, or even the "cause and prejudice" rules of *Wainwright v. Sykes*. AEDPA adopts a much more stringent approach. New claims raised in second petitions are assessed by virtually the same standards established for evidentiary hearings where the applicant had failed to develop a factual basis for the claim.[29] A hearing may be granted only if the new claim relies upon

(A):

1. A new rule;
2. Of constitutional law;
3. Explicitly made retroactively applicable to collateral review;
4. By a Supreme Court *holding*.[30]

OR (B): a "factual predicate" which

1. Could not have been discovered earlier;
2. By the exercise of *due diligence*.

Even if these latter tests are met, the applicant must show "by clear and convincing evidence" that "no reasonable fact finder" would have found the applicant guilty of the underlying offense. While there are some semantic

---

29. 28 U.S.C. §2244(b)(2).
30. In *Tyler v. Cain*, 533 U.S. 656 (2001), the Court implicitly rejected the view that merely announcing the principle of determining a question might activate this provision of AEDPA. That, in turn, would have allowed lower federal courts, after deciding that a rule of constitutional law was "new," to further decide whether the "new" rule fell within the two exceptions of *Teague*. After *Tyler*, it would appear that only the United States Supreme Court can decide that question.

differences between the two statutory provisions, the effect is likely to make second petitions, even based upon new decisions of the Supreme Court, virtually a waste of the prisoner's (and the court's) time.

Furthermore, AEDPA requires that the Circuit Court of Appeals, not the district court, decide whether the second petition falls within AEDPA's narrow rules. Leaving aside any other considerations, the difference in numbers of circuit court judges (179) versus district court judges (680) make it less likely that the circuit courts will be able to seriously consider second petitions. While many circuit courts have "habeas offices," the sheer logistics of filing and considering these complaints in circuit courts makes any happy resolution for the applicant unlikely.

Finally, a petition that raises the *same* claim that an earlier petition raised "shall be dismissed." This statutory language seems unequivocal, but there is a possibility that if the petitioner showed evidence of "actual innocence," the theory discussed in *Herrera v. Collins*, 506 U.S. 380 (1993) might allow such a claim to be considered a "new" claim (thus subject to the standard set out just above) or even in an original petition to the Supreme Court. These arguments, however, are highly speculative; at this point the law seems clear—a defendant should not actually pursue the habeas route until he (and the state courts) have carefully considered all the possible claims, at which time he should put them all in the same basket. Two bites will not be allowed at the federal apple.

EXAMPLES

1. Sheba, convicted of possessing cocaine, has lost her appeals to the State Appellate and Supreme Courts. She thinks her lawyer was incompetent, and she files a federal habeas corpus petition alleging that as the sole ground. What should the district court do?

2. Febrezio was convicted in state court of securities fraud. While his appeal was pending in state court, the United States Supreme Court decided *Batson*. The state supreme court remanded for reconsideration in light of the new decision, but the state trial found against the defendant concluding that the prosecutor's explanations were race neutral. The United States Supreme Court denied certiorari. For the next five years, Febrezio sought relief from state court collateral relief, but ultimately lost. He then files a petition for habeas corpus. The state argues that the U.S. District court should not entertain the petition because there was no constitutional violation at his trial. Should the court deny the petition?

3. Remember Curtis? (see example 1, *supra*, p.311) Suppose the *Sanchez* decision was rendered after his conviction became final. Could he still take advantage of *Sanchez* (a) on collateral review; (b) on federal habeas corpus?

4. Assume that the Fourteenth Circuit has decided that the Fourth Amendment requires that police officers must obtain a signed permission slip from the owner before searching a car or truck, under any and all circumstances. Lionel was tried in a state court where the trial judge refused to follow that rule. The state supreme court affirmed the conviction, announcing that the defendant's claim, while plausible, does not comport with its own reading of the precedent for the United States Supreme Court. What should the district court do on Lionel's habeas petition?

5. On the day she planned to call three alibi witnesses to testify for her client, Maya has discovered that those witnesses are absent from the courtroom. She asked for time to find them, but the court refused. The defendants were convicted. On appeal to state court, the government argued, for the first time, that Maya had not put her request for a continuance in writing, as required by state court rule. The appellate court therefore concluded that the claim had been defaulted. Assume that the case finally gets to federal court. Will the Federal Court hear the complaint?

6. (a) Cleopatra was convicted, in 1982, under a state statute which used the term, "especially heinous, atrocious, or cruel (HAC)." On appeal, however, her attorney focused on other concerns, and did not attack the phrase as vague. The state appellate court upheld the conviction and death penalty in 1984. Cleopatra filed her first state post-conviction petition in the state trial court on June 22, 1984, attaching the conviction and death sentence. The trial court held a hearing and denied the petition. The State Court of Criminal Appeals affirmed the denial and the State Supreme Court declined her request to appeal. Five years later, in June 1989, Cleo filed a second state post-conviction petition. In her second petition, Cleo alleged numerous constitutional violations including, for the first time, an Eighth Amendment claim that the language of the aggravator considered by the jury in the sentencing phase was unconstitutionally vague. The trial court dismissed the second petition as barred by the successive petition restrictions of the state's postconviction statute, holding that all the grounds raised in the second petition were barred because they either had been previously determined or were waived. The judgment was affirmed by the Court of Criminal Appeals and the State Supreme Court denied the application for permission to appeal. The United States Supreme Court denied Cleo's petition for a writ of certiorari. In its consideration on appeal of the denial of Cleo's second post-conviction petition, the state Court of Criminal Appeals refused to address Cleo's constitutional challenge to the HAC aggravator because, according to the court, it had been either previously determined or waived. She now seeks federal habeas corpus. The state has

moved to dismiss, on the ground that the claim is procedurally barred. What should you, as the District Court judge, do?

(b) Assume you, as the district judge, have decided that the court did decide that claim on the merits. You must now determine whether Cleo's death penalty was legal. Your research reveals the following: (1) In *Godfrey v. Georgia*, 446 U.S. 420 (1980), the Supreme Court held that a state statute which considered, as an aggravating factor in determining the death penalty, whether the homicide was "outrageously or wantonly vile, horrible or inhuman," standing alone, was unconstitutionally vague. That implied any inherent restraint on the arbitrary and capricious infliction of death sentence. (2) Later, in *Maynard v. Cartwright*, 486 U.S. 356 (1988) the Court held that the "especially heinous, atrocious, or cruel" aggravating circumstance (HAC) of another statute was unconstitutionally vague, as it did not offer sufficient guidance to the jury in deciding whether to impose the death penalty. Although Cleo's trial court did instruct the jury in terms of HAC, it also gave a limiting instruction, which defined some of the terms of the aggravating factor as follows: "Heinous" means extremely wicked or shockingly evil. "Atrocious" means outrageously wicked and vile. "Cruel" means designed to inflict a high degree of pain, utter indifference to, or enjoyment of, the suffering of others, pitiless. The state courts, through a long series of appeals and post-conviction petitions, upheld the death penalty. (3) In *Proffitt v. Florida*, 428 U.S. 242, (1976), decided eight years before Cleo's conviction became final, the Court held that Florida's HAC aggravator was not unconstitutionally vague in light of the Florida courts' narrowing construction that the term "heinous, atrocious, or cruel" means a "conscienceless, or pitiless crime which is unnecessarily torturous to the victim." *Id*. At 255-256. The narrowing language is the identical language the state Supreme Court used in narrowing the state's aggravator. (4) However, in *Shell v. Mississippi*, 498 U.S. 1 (1990) (per curiam), the Supreme Court announced that the "heinous, atrocious, or cruel" language, along with the same "limiting" definitions as were provided to the jury in Cleo's case, was unconstitutional. (5) Finally, in *Stringer v. Black*, 503 U.S. 222, (1992), the Court declared that the language [in *Maynard* ("especially heinous, atrocious or cruel")] gave no more guidance that did the statute in *Godfrey* [("outrageously or wantonly vile, horrible or inhuman")] . . . *Godfrey* and *Maynard* did indeed involve somewhat different language. But it would be a mistake to conclude that the vagueness ruling of *Godfrey* was limited to the precise language before us in the case." What do you do now?

7. Juanita is convicted in state court. Her counsel on appeal does not raise certain issues. New counsel files a claim asserting that Juanita's first

appellate counsel was inadequate, in the appropriate state court, one hundred days after the judgment affirming Juanita's conviction. State rules requires the filing to be within 90 days "unless the applicant shows good cause of filing at a later time." The state court dismisses the inadequate counsel claim, on the grounds that it was untimely filed. What should the federal habeas court do?

EXPLANATIONS

1. We start off with an easy one — don't touch the claim; instead tell Sheba to exhaust her state remedies. Whether the policy behind federal habeas corpus is to assure a fair trial, or to be sure that state courts were accurately applying federal law (in this case *Strickland*) the state courts have had no chance to act on this claim. Come back little Sheba, when the state courts have acted.

2. In *Miller-El v. Cockrel*, 537 U.S. 322 (2003), the Court held that since defendant's federal claim had never been decided by a federal court, his procedural posture was that he had a right to assert the new rule because his case was still on direct review when *Batson* was decided. *Teague* was intended to prevent federal courts from applying a "new rule" to a situation in which the state courts had never had an opportunity to apply the rule. Here, there was such an opportunity. The Court remanded for a decision on the merits of the federal claim.

3. (a) Possibly, but not likely. Many states either refuse totally or are at least reluctant to review again any issue which was, or could have been, raised on appeal. Had Curtis raised the question on appeal, the leading case might be "*State v. Curtis*" rather than "*State v. Sanchez*." The serious point here is that we want to encourage defendants to raise every possible argument on appeal, not wait to see whether the law develops in their favor and then become a free rider. Collateral attacks are frequently limited to those issues which were not, and "could not" have been raised on appeal (such as ineffective assistance of counsel) e.g., Okla. Stat. Tit. 22 §1089(c), or those on which more evidence would be necessary to resolve. Most state statutes also allow raising an issue if a "manifest injustice" would be done if the claim were not allowed to be raised. See, e.g., 42 Penn, Con. Stat. §9453(a). Even in a state allowing broader collateral review, the application of a newly announced decision may depend on whether the new decision is seen as announcing a "new rule" which the trial court could not have anticipated. This position, which is the state analog of *Teague*, focuses on supervising trial courts rather than on a retrospective view of whether the trial was "fair" as we now understand it.

    (b) No. Absolutely not. As the problem is written, the *Sanchez* case is not based on the United States Constitution. The first predicate of federal jurisdiction is a federal constitutional issue. There is none here. Case over.

4. Affirm the conviction. Even though the Circuit Court has declared its view of the Constitution, under AEDPA, so long as the state court's interpretation of the law is not "contrary" to "established *Supreme Court* precedent," the decision is to be upheld, even if the district judge thinks it is incorrect. AEDPA makes clear that in these circumstances, the petition "shall not be granted." The result would be the same even if *all* circuit courts agreed with the Fourteenth Circuit. It is true that states courts have never been "bound" by federal circuit court opinions, even from circuit courts in their own circuit. But AEDPA makes clear that the state courts may effectively ignore those courts, as well as district courts.

5. Probably not. This, after all, is a legitimate state procedural rule, and the issue was precluded. There is no "cause" for Maya's failing to put it in writing. *However,* in *Lee v. Kemna*, 534 U.S. 362 (2002), the Court found that the defense attorney's strenuous oral objections to the judge's refusal to grant the continuance, coupled with (a) the state trial court's reason for not allowing the continuance (he had a personal matter the following day), and (b) the fact that the trial court knew that the witnesses had been present throughout the trial, sufficed to show that the purpose of the state rule — to make the trial court fully aware of the dilemma — had been fulfilled. Therefore, the district court should not have precluded further inquiry into the matter. As it turned out, the three witnesses later filed affidavits that they had been told, by court officers, that they would not be called until the following day. *Kemna* seems extremely fact-specific; but it also reflects the Court's impatience with restrictive application of the procedural default rules. By the way, the *Kemna* court barely cited AEDPA, or its limiting language. On the other hand, in *Steward v. Smith*, 534 U.S. 157 (2002), the Court reaffirmed the general rule that a defendant's failure to comply with a state procedural rule bars a federal court from dealing with that question.

6. This Example reflects the complicated nature of timing in habeas cases. If this were not a death penalty case, Cleo's claim would almost surely be procedurally barred. She, or her counsel, appears not to have clearly and unequivocally put the issue to the state courts. Even on a "deliberate bypass" test, the failure to raise the claim would preclude federal review. To overcome the default under the more restrictive "cause and prejudice" test of *Sykes*, Cleo would have to show that her counsel excusably did not focus on the language of the statute. As a general rule, on habeas review, federal courts may not consider procedurally defaulted claims. *Seymour v. Walker*, 224 F.3d 542, 549-550 (6th Cir. 2000). Thus, if the prisoner has "waived" the claim, such waiver

will constitute a procedural default and will serve as an adequate and independent state ground barring habeas review in the court. On the other hand, if the state courts "previously determined" the claim, the federal court may consider the merits. You, as the district judge, must determine which one actually describes the status of Cleo's constitutional claim in the state courts. If she is not barred, you may move on to the merits (whether the state courts' determination "resulted in a decision that was contrary to, or involved an unreasonable application of, clearly established federal law, as determined by the Supreme Court of the United States"), which, of course, is still a high hurdle for her to vault. To reach your conclusion on this, you'd have to review the precise wording of state court precedents to determine whether this state court carries out "implicit review" in death penalty cases. In death penalty cases, some federal courts strive to avoid finding procedural default of important constitutional issues. Some federal courts frequently hold that a state court reviewing a death penalty appeal "implicitly" review all issues that could arguably be considered as raised within the wording of the petition or other moving papers.

(b) Your call. Under AEDPA, when a petitioner's claim has been adjudicated on the merits in a state court, a federal court may not grant a writ of habeas corpus with respect to such claim, unless the state court's determination resulted in a decision that was contrary to, or involved an unreasonable application of, clearly established federal law, as determined by the Supreme Court of the United States. A state court's decision must be evaluated against the clearly established Supreme Court precedent at the time the petitioner's conviction became final. Therefore, as a normal matter, only the *Godfrey* and *Profitt* decisions would be relevant. But in *Cone v. Bell*, 359 F.3d 785 (6th Cir. 2004), the case upon which this example is based, the Sixth Circuit found that the language of the Supreme Court in *Stringer* clearly set the "tone" for interpreting language of the kind involved in the death penalty aggravator here. Any such vague wording, whether explicitly addressed by the Supreme Court or not, was palpably unconstitutional after *Godfrey*, and before *Maynard*. Thus, at the time of Cleo's trial (1982), the use of that aggravator was contrary to "clearly established federal law." The example demonstrates how carefully a federal habeas court must parse earlier opinions, particularly Supreme Court opinions, particularly in light of AEDPA's limiting language.

7. After *Edwards v. Carpenter*, 529 U.S. 446 (2000), the federal court should dismiss the application for habeas corpus because the inadequate counsel claim has been procedurally defaulted by procedural default in raising the claim. (Does this sound like Rod Serling to you?) What happened to the argument (see Chapter 10) that recognized that it is the defendant, not the attorney, who suffers when the attorney makes a

mistake? Two mistakes? Two attorneys? Note, however, that the Court in *Carpenter* did recognize that if the defendant could demonstrate a "sufficient" probability that our failure to review his federal claim "will result in a fundamental miscarriage of justice," the federal claim could be heard, notwithstanding the default of the claim. On the other hand, as the Court in *Carpenter* noted, if there were no procedural default rule, "habeas petitioners would be able to avoid the exhaustion requirement by defaulting their federal claims in state court."

Table of Selected Cases

Index